A Modern Guide to Citizen's Basic Income

ELGAR MODERN GUIDES

Elgar Modern Guides offer a carefully curated review of a selected topic, edited or authored by a leading scholar in the field. They survey the significant trends and issues of contemporary research for both advanced students and academic researchers.

The books provide an invaluable appraisal and stimulating guide to the current research landscape, offering state-of-the-art discussions and selective overviews covering the critical matters of interest alongside recent developments. Combining incisive insight with a rigorous and thoughtful perspective on the essential issues, the books are designed to offer an inspiring introduction and unique guide to the diversity of modern debates.

Elgar Modern Guides will become an essential go-to companion for researchers and graduate students but will also prove stimulating for a wider academic audience interested in the subject matter. They will be invaluable to anyone who wants to understand as well as simply learn.

Titles in the series include:

A Modern Guide to State Intervention
Economic Policies for Growth and Sustainability
Edited by Nikolaos Karagiannis and John E. King

A Modern Guide to Citizen's Basic Income
A Multidisciplinary Approach
Malcolm Torry

A Modern Guide to Citizen's Basic Income

A Multidisciplinary Approach

Malcolm Torry

Director, Citizen's Basic Income Trust, and Senior Visiting Fellow, London School of Economics, UK

ELGAR MODERN GUIDES

Cheltenham, UK • Northampton, MA, USA

Published by
Edward Elgar Publishing Limited
The Lypiatts
15 Lansdown Road
Cheltenham
Glos GL50 2JA
UK

Edward Elgar Publishing, Inc.
William Pratt House
9 Dewey Court
Northampton
Massachusetts 01060
USA

Paperback edition 2021

A catalogue record for this book
is available from the British Library

Library of Congress Control Number: 2019956662

This book is available electronically in the **Elgar**online
Social and Political Science subject collection
DOI 10.4337/9781788117876

ISBN 978 1 78811 786 9 (cased)
ISBN 978 1 80037 602 1 (paperback)
ISBN 978 1 78811 787 6 (eBook)

Printed and bound by CPI Group (UK) Ltd, Croydon CR0 4YY

Contents

Figures

Tables

Preface

A Citizen's Basic Income is an unconditional and nonwithdrawable income paid to every individual. It is sometimes called a Basic Income, a Citizen's Income, or a Universal Basic Income. They all mean the same thing: an unconditional income for every individual. The amount that someone receives might differ in relation to their age – with working age adults receiving a standard amount, younger adults maybe less, less for each child, and perhaps more for elderly people: but age is the only conditionality permitted. Whatever someone's employment status, income, wealth, relationships, household structure, gender, or anything else: everyone of the same age would receive the same amount, every week or every month. The amount might be uprated each year, but otherwise it wouldn't change. Someone's Citizen's Basic Income could be turned on at their birth, it would adjust automatically with their age, and it would be turned off at their death. It would be the simplest possible social policy.

The idea is simple enough, and the administration of an entire country's Citizen's Basic Incomes would be simple enough, but that does not mean that things would be entirely simple, for the obvious reason that the Citizen's Basic Income would have to relate to a country's other social security benefits, to its taxation system, to its society, to its economy, to its politics, to its law, and so on. The implementation of a Citizen's Basic Income scheme – that is, a Citizen's Basic Income with the levels specified for different age groups, along with specified changes to existing benefits and existing taxes – would set up complex new interactions between benefits, taxes, wage levels, employment patterns, and much else. It isn't that a Citizen's Basic Income would ever be complicated: the complexities would be the result of the ways in which it related to the existing complexities of social security benefits, taxes, social structures, politics, economics, the legal system, and so on.

It is because there are so many aspects to the effects that a Citizen's Basic Income would have, and to the issues that the now global debate about Citizen's Basic Income raises, that a multiplicity of disciplines are needed to study them. The language of Citizen's Basic Income needs to be studied; historians need to study the history of the idea; ethicists and philosophers need to study the ethics of the proposal; economists need to study possible economic effects; and so on.

Until about ten years ago, it was fairly easy for someone to read every book published on Citizen's Basic Income. That is no longer possible. The literature on the subject is now vast: a symptom of the way in which the debate has increased in both extent and depth so rapidly during the past few years. There are now numerous introductions to the subject, plenty of books on various aspects of the debate, a new comprehensive international handbook, and thousands of journal articles. But the one book missing was a volume that approached the subject from the perspectives of a wide variety of different disciplines as an attempt to understand the complex ways in which Citizen's Basic Income would relate to social realities, the economy, politics, the law, and so on. This is that book.

Acknowledgements

Acknowledgements must always begin with my thanks to those who first introduced me to the UK's benefits system and to options for its reform: my Uncle Norman for inviting me to work in Bexleyheath's Department of Health and Social Security (DHSS) office during my university holidays, filing the cards on which employers stuck stamps to the value of their employers' and employees' National Insurance Contributions; the staff of Brixton's Supplementary Benefit office, where I worked for two years after leaving university; Sir Geoffrey Otton, the DHSS's Permanent Secretary, who invited me to a departmental summer school when I was a curate at the Elephant and Castle, where the Department's headquarters were then located; and Hermione (Mimi) Parker, whom I met at that summer school, and who invited me to join the group that became the Basic Income Research Group and which later became the Citizen's Income Trust and now the Citizen's Basic Income Trust. It has been a pleasure to have served the Trust as its honorary Director for most of its existence, and I am grateful to its trustees for making that possible, and to successive Bishops of Woolwich for permission to undertake the task.

I am grateful to those who have facilitated my subsequent work on Citizen's Basic Income: to Professor David Piachaud for supervising my London School of Economics (LSE) Master's Degree dissertation on the subject; to the LSE's Social Policy Department for appointing me a Visiting Senior Fellow; to Professor Hartley Dean for supervising much of my work at the LSE; to Professor Holly Sutherland and her colleagues at the Institute for Social and Economic Research for introducing me to the microsimulation programmes POLIMOD and then EUROMOD, and for publishing my work in EUROMOD working papers; to participants of the various meetings at which some of the ideas in this book have been tested; and to the trustees of the Citizen's Basic Income Trust for permission to quote from material previously published by the Trust.

Parts of this book have presented a particular challenge. Four of my other books on the subject – *Money for Everyone, 101 Reasons for a Citizen's Income, The Feasibility of Citizen's Income*, and *Why we need a Citizen's Basic Income* – have relied on understandings of the disciplines of economics and social policy that I have built up over a number of years. The book *Citizen's Basic Income: A Christian social policy* relied as well on an understanding of Christian theology that has evolved over an even longer period. But deciding to write a book based on a wide range of disciplines has meant attempting to understand disciplines of which I had little previous knowledge, and particularly history. I am grateful to Dr Peter Sloman for his assistance with that chapter. I am particularly grateful to Professor Hartley Dean for reading the entire book. Both of them have offered wise advice. As always, any remaining mistakes and misunderstandings are entirely my fault, and not theirs.

In relation to my attempts to understand disciplines of which I had little previous knowledge: While it must be true that nobody can have a truly comprehensive understanding of any particular academic discipline, there will be many people with far more of a grasp of each of the disciplines than I have, and they will be justified in regarding my understandings of their fields as inadequate. All I can say is that I have done my best to understand those aspects of each discipline that seem to me to have the clearest contributions to make to the Citizen's Basic Income debate; and that the inadequacies of my treatments of the disciplines might be best treated as invitations to experts in those disciplines to ask what their own understandings of them have to offer to the debate about Citizen's Basic Income.

Parts of the book summarize previously published material. The section of Chapter 10 that deals with implementation draws on a report issued by the Institute for Chartered Accountants of England and Wales, *How might we implement a Citizen's Income* (Torry, 2016c). I am grateful for permission to reuse material in the report. Chapter 2 draws on a paper presented at the 2017 BIEN Congress in Lisbon, 'What's a definition? And how should we define "Basic Income"?', and a paper, '"Unconditional" and "universal": Definitions and applications', presented at the meeting of the Foundation for International Studies on Social Security held in Sigtuna, Sweden, the same year; and the section on feasibility in Chapter 9 draws on a paper presented at the 2014 BIEN Congress in Montreal, 'A Basic Income is Feasible. But what do we mean by feasibility?' (Torry, 2014). I am grateful to those who contributed to the discussions that followed the presentations.

All royalties from the sale of this book will be donated to the Citizen's Basic Income Trust.

A note on terminology

A Citizen's Basic Income is an unconditional, regular, automatic and nonwith-drawable income for every individual. A Citizen's Basic Income is sometimes called a Basic Income, a Universal Basic Income, or a Citizen's Income.

A 'Citizen's Basic Income scheme' is a Citizen's Basic Income with levels specified for each age group, with the funding method fully specified, and in particular with any changes to existing taxes and benefits fully specified.

A 'marginal deduction rate' is the proportion of additional earned income that the worker does not receive because means-tested benefits have been withdrawn and income tax and other deductions (such as National Insurance contributions in the UK) have been charged.

A 'revenue neutral' Citizen's Basic Income scheme is defined as one that funds a Citizen's Basic Income from within the current tax and benefits system by reducing tax allowances, increasing income tax rates, altering other deductions from earned income, and reducing social security benefits. A 'strictly revenue neutral' scheme is one that funds a Citizen's Basic Income from within the current tax and benefits system by altering income tax rates, income tax *personal* allowances, and other deductions from earned income (such as National Insurance Contributions in the UK), and not such allowances as those for private pension contributions.

'Means-tested benefits' are benefits that are reduced as earned and other income rises. There is often a single payment each week or each month to each household rather than to each individual, with the amount of the payment being partly determined by the structure of the household. There might also be a work test: that is, payment might only be made to a claimant who is employed or is actively looking for paid employment.

'Contributory benefits' are paid on the basis of contribution records: that is, a record of regular payments made to a government or independent agency. The amount of benefit paid out, and the length of time for which it is paid, might or might not be affected by the number of contributions made or the amounts of those contributions.

An 'unconditional benefit' is one that is paid to an individual (and is not affected by the structure of the household), it is not means-tested (that is, the amount paid does not depend on the amount of other income or wealth), and it is not work-tested (that is, it is paid regardless of employment status, and does not depend on someone unemployed looking for or training for paid employment). The one conditionality normally permitted is that the amount paid might depend on someone's age.

A 'universal benefit' is one that is paid to every individual within a particular jurisdiction. However, the terminology is sometimes used differently to apply to a benefit that is universal within a particular age group, or to one that is potentially universal but that might be paid at different amounts, or might not be paid at all if certain conditions are not met.

An unconditional income is by definition universal. A universal benefit might be unconditional for a particular age group, but if it is a benefit that might vary then it is not unconditional. So, for instance, the UK used to provide a Child Bond for every child, with higher amounts for children in poorer families. The Child Bond was universal for all children, but it was not unconditional.

1. Introduction to a multidisciplinary study of Citizen's Basic Income

This introductory chapter introduces the book by exploring the meanings of two of the terms in the book's title and subtitle: 'Citizen's Basic Income' and 'multidisciplinary'.

'CITIZEN'S BASIC INCOME'

A Citizen's Basic Income is an unconditional income paid to every individual. It is as simple as that. It has a number of different names: Basic Income, Citizen's Income, Citizen's Basic Income, Universal Basic Income. They all mean exactly the same thing: an unconditional income paid to every individual.

The amount that an individual received would not depend on their income, wealth, household structure, employment status, or anything else. Every individual of the same age would receive exactly the same: the same amount, every week or every month, automatically.

Older people might receive more than working age adults, younger adults less, and less for children. Does adjusting the amount with someone's age compromise Citizen's Basic Income's unconditionality? No, it does not. What is unique about Citizen's Basic Income, what matters, and what makes it work, is that it can be turned on at each individual's birth, and turned off at their death, and that no active administration is required in between. Once the computer knows someone's date of birth, it never needs to ask about their age: it can seamlessly adjust the amount paid as the person's age increases. Everyone of the same age would receive exactly the same income, unconditionally.

Sometimes words are added to 'Citizen's Basic Income' or 'Basic Income' – for instance, 'universal', as in 'Universal Basic Income' – but they are not necessary. A Citizen's Basic Income would be unconditional, so within the jurisdiction in which it was paid, everybody would get it, so it would be universal by definition. There would be no need to say that it was. A Citizen's Basic Income would be unconditional, which means that it would not fall if other income rose, so it would be nonwithdrawable. There would be no need to say that it was. It would be universal, and it would be nonwithdrawable, but all we would need to say would be this: Every individual of the same age receives exactly the same income, unconditionally (Torry, 2018b).

There is no need to say more about the idea of a Citizen's Basic Income at this point. The purpose of the book is to enable a wide variety of disciplines to offer their perspectives, and to say more about the idea at this point would pre-empt that process.

'MULTIDISCIPLINARY'

The purpose of this book is to study Citizen's Basic Income from the perspectives of a wide variety of academic disciplines, or fields of study. It is 'multidisciplinary', because the different disciplines are employed separately. It attempts not to be 'interdisciplinary': that is, as far as possible it does not employ two or more disciplines at the same time.

Academic disciplines have a history. In the Medieval university, students studied first grammar, logic, and rhetoric, and then arithmetic, music, geometry, and astronomy, and some would go on to study divinity, canon law, civil law, and medicine (University of Cambridge). Then the multiplication began, and it has continued ever since.

To take examples of evolution represented by some of the disciplines on which chapters in this book are based: 'Psychology' evolved from the seventeenth century onwards from denoting the study of the soul to being the study of human behaviour and how the mind works; and since the late nineteenth century, 'social psychology' has studied how, 'given the native propensities and capacities of the human mind, all the complex mental life of societies is shaped by them and in turn reacts upon the course of their development and operation in the individual' (Oxford English Dictionary). Similarly, but in a rather more complex fashion: In the seventeenth century, 'political economy' meant the study of the financial aspects of government, before its meaning was extended in the nineteenth century to mean the study of what became known as 'the economy' as a whole, that is, 'the development and regulation of the material resources of a community or state'; and then the term 'political economy' was displaced by the term 'economics', which had previously meant study of the management of the household before it came to mean 'the branch of knowledge (now regarded as one of the social sciences) that deals with the production, distribution, consumption, and transfer of wealth' (Oxford English Dictionary). Since the 1960s, the term 'political economy' has seen something of a revival: a somewhat chaotic one that has led to it having a rather indeterminate meaning. Following a thorough survey of modern usage of both 'economics' and 'political economy', Groenewegen (1987) concludes that they might best be treated as synonyms, and that their somewhat indeterminate and shifting meanings reflect an important characteristic of the science of economics/political economy. In this book, 'economics' and 'political economy' are not treated as synonyms, as the reader will discover: but the point is well taken that to treat them differently is this author's choice from within the possibilities offered by the varying historical and current uses of 'economics' and 'political economy'.

The general point that the above two examples illustrate is that academic disciplines, or fields of study, are social constructions, they evolve over time, and their boundaries and interconnections are fluid. For the sake of the exercise tackled in this book – that is, to understand the different perspectives that different disciplines might offer in relation to the Citizen's Basic Income debate – it has been essential to fix on a working definition of each discipline, because only by doing that can anything like a coherent treatment be offered. Because each discipline has to be understood and then employed in the space of a single chapter, it has also been essential to restrict the sources from which an understanding of each discipline is extracted, so for each chapter a small number of guides to the discipline are chosen. Similarly, within each chapter it has only been possible to offer a restricted number of particular perspectives in relation to an equally restricted number of aspects of the Citizen's Basic Income debate. Because any single aspect of the debate might benefit from perspectives from more than one discipline, and because the disciplines overlap, a certain amount of repetition is inevitable: although an attempt has of course been made to reduce it to a minimum.

The reader will always need to be aware that different choices might have been made: different disciplines might have been selected; different definitions of those disciplines might have been offered; different guides to the disciplines might have been followed; different aspects of the Citizen's Basic Income debate might have been chosen, and they might have been differently allocated to the different chapters; and the perspectives offered in relation to those aspects of the debate might have been different. This, along with space constraints, means that the book cannot claim to be a comprehensive or a definitive collection of perspectives on Citizen's Basic Income. It is a single and necessarily somewhat arbitrary selection of possible perspectives, which means that it might best be seen as an invitation to the reader to undertake their own exercise, by asking what a particular discipline, understood in a particular way, might have to say about a particular aspect of the Citizen's Basic Income debate.

While the main purpose of this book is to ask how a variety of disciplines might contribute to the Citizen's Basic Income debate, a subsidiary outcome might be developments of the disciplines themselves generated by their relationships to that debate. Occasionally such possibilities might be tentatively noted in the conclusions to the chapters. Experts in the different fields of study might be able to propose additional disciplinary developments following their reading of the relevant chapters and their own reflections on the relationship between the Citizen's Basic Income debate and their own areas of expertise.

In general, readers might wish to regard the omissions and inadequacies of this book – of which there will be many – as invitations to repair them. For instance, where disciplines have not been tackled – for instance, anthropology and social anthropology – experts in those fields might wish to ask how those disciplines might contribute to the Citizen's Basic Income debate, and how that debate might contribute to the development of those disciplines. If historians find the implied definition of Citizen's Basic Income history too narrowly restricted to histories of discussion and activity in relation to genuine Citizen's Basic Incomes, then they might wish to extend the discussion to include histories of such related broader developments as the transition from communal to individual income support, and the evolution of money as a means of exchange and therefore as a means of poor relief and taxation.

This book will have served its purpose if experts from a wide variety of academic disciplines contribute their own understandings of how their disciplines might contribute to the Citizen's Basic Income debate, and of how that debate might contribute to the development of their disciplines.

CONTEXT

Although Citizen's Basic Income would have the same definition in every country, and its administration would be remarkably similar from country to country, the same cannot be said for existing tax and benefits systems, or for other elements of the contexts within which Citizen's Basic Income schemes might be implemented. Because this book envisages a global readership, most of the material will not make assumptions about existing tax and benefits systems, but will treat them in terms as general as possible. However, where it would be useful to give an example of how a real world tax and benefits system might relate to the implementation of Citizen's Basic Incomes, the UK's system will be employed. This is for two reasons: it is the system with which the author is most familiar; and it contains a large number of different elements, meaning that readers in different countries should be able to find parallels in their own countries' systems. The normal convention will be followed: where a particular kind of benefit or tax is in view, lower case will be used: so 'income tax' means any tax on income, and 'means-tested benefit' means any payment that is adjusted in relation to an individual's or household's existing financial means. However, where a particular UK tax or benefit is being discussed, upper case will be employed: so 'Income Tax' means the UK's income tax, and 'Jobseeker's Allowance' and 'Universal Credit' are two of the UK's means-tested benefits.

A few details about the UK's tax and benefits systems might be helpful: Income Tax is charged on earned and investment income and on some other kinds as well; and National Insurance Contributions are charged on earned income. Time-limited and non-means-tested National Insurance benefits are paid for sickness and unemployment on the basis of National Insurance Contributions records (although there is little relationship between the contributions paid and the levels and durations of the benefits awarded); and the amount of someone's Basic State Pension is also based on their National Insurance Contributions Record. A variety of means-tested benefits exist (Jobseeker's Allowance for those out of work, Employment Support Allowance for those who are ill, Working Tax Credits and Child Tax Credits for those in work who are not earning enough to live on, Housing Benefit to help with housing costs, and so on). These are slowly being replaced by the means-tested and work-tested Universal Credit. The one very different benefit is Child Benefit, which is paid unconditionally for every child. (There is now some confusion over this. In 2010, the UK Government said that it wished to means-test Child Benefit for higher earners. This proved to be impossible to achieve: so there is now an additional tax charged on high earning individuals living in households that receive Child Benefit. Child Benefit is still unconditional.) There are also various benefits and services for people living with disabilities; there is an unconditional Winter Fuel Allowance for pensioners; Council Tax Support is a means-tested benefit regulated and administered by Local Authorities; and so on. The system is diverse and complicated.

THE STRUCTURE OF THE BOOK

Each of the following chapters studies a variety of aspects of the Citizen's Basic Income from the perspective of a particular discipline. First of all the discipline is discussed, generally with the assistance of one or two particular guides; then a number of aspects of the Citizen's Basic Income debate will be studied from the perspective of the discipline; and conclusions will be drawn. Each chapter will end with a case study, except for Chapter 3 about histories of Citizen's Basic Income, because in that chapter the different histories discussed all function as case studies.

Because disciplinary boundaries are fluid and to some extent arbitrary, some fairly arbitrary choices have had to be made. For instance, discussions of both climate change and reciprocity could have been located in Chapter 4 on ethics, but climate change has been located in Chapter 5 on economics (because the discipline of economics might be the best lens for studying the relationship between climate change and Citizen's Basic Income), and reciprocity will be found in Chapter 7 on social psychology (again, because that appears to provide the most useful perspective from which to understand the relationship between Citizen's Basic Income and a society's reciprocity norm). Some disciplines might have been given chapters of their own – for instance, gender studies and theology – but because in the context of the Citizen's Basic Income debate the perspectives that they offer fit well within ethical perspectives and sociological perspectives respectively, it is in Chapter 4 that a theological perspective will be found, and in Chapter 8 that a gender perspective is located.

CONCLUSION

The debate about the radically simple idea of a Citizen's Basic Income is now global, widespread, and deep, and it is time for a book that enables practitioners and theorists from a wide variety of disciplines to ponder the contribution that their own and other disciplines might make to that debate. This book sets an agenda in the hope that others will contribute to it.

2. The language of Citizen's Basic Income[1]

Language: The vocabulary or phraseology of a particular sphere, discipline, profession, social group, etc.
(Oxford English Dictionary)

INTRODUCTION

In this first substantive chapter, the language – the vocabulary and phraseology – of the Citizen's Basic Income debate will be discussed, both to shed light on the current debate, and to contribute to the study of language.

My guide to the subject of language will be the philosopher Wittgenstein, who will lead us into a discussion of the meanings of language; and our method will be his method: studying how language is used. From there we shall explore a variety of understandings of how definitions are constructed, and we shall come to understand how important and complex the issue of definition is in the context of the Citizen's Basic Income debate.

Chapter 1 discusses the somewhat arbitrary nature of the way in which subject matter has been allocated to disciplines and therefore to chapters in this book. This is certainly true of this chapter. In principle, the way in which language is used in relation to the Citizen's Basic Income debate is a proper subject for every chapter in the book; and the subject matter of every chapter could have found a home in this chapter. The policy throughout the book has been to include in each chapter the subject matter that in the view of the author fits most clearly into the chapter and would fit less easily into other chapters. The matter of definitions clearly relates closely to the study of language and its use, and in relation to any other chapter it would function as prolegomena rather than subject matter: so it is entirely appropriate to make it the central focus of a chapter about language. But a chapter on definitions is by no means all that needs to be said about language in relation to the Citizen's Basic Income debate. To take just one other highly relevant area of language and its

---

[1] This chapter is partly based on papers delivered at the BIEN (Basic Income Earth Network) Congress in Lisbon, Portugal, in 2017, and at the Foundation for International Studies on Social Security conference at Sigtuna, Sweden, also in 2017 (Torry, 2017a; 2017b).

use: questions about how the Citizen's Basic Income is framed – that is, the language used by individuals and the media to discuss, recommend, or criticize Citizen's Basic Income – are explored in Chapter 6 on psychology, Chapter 7 on social psychology, and Chapter 11 on politics. Because the disciplines of psychology, social psychology, and politics are relevant to such exploration, it is in those chapters that it will be found.

THE MEANING OF LANGUAGE IS ITS USE

At the beginning of his *Investigations*, Wittgenstein envisages a shopkeeper responding to a request for 'five red apples': 'But what is the meaning of the word "five"? – No such thing was in question here, only how the word "five" is used' (Wittgenstein, [1953] 2001: §1, 2). When we use language, we undertake an activity: we play 'language games'. 'The term "language-*game*" is meant to bring into prominence the fact that the *speaking* of language is part of an activity, or of a life-form' (Wittgenstein, [1953] 2001: §23, 10). 'Life-form' or 'form of life' is a crucial idea for Wittgenstein, for it is within forms of life that language is located: and language itself is one of those forms of life – or, rather, it is many of them (Grayling, 1988: 97).

Always it is language *use* that is the criterion for the meaning of language (Grayling, 1988: 90): that is, how language is used in a particular context of actions and words – which means that the same word can have different connections with different words and different actions in different contexts, and therefore different meanings in different contexts. But that does not mean that each language game is completely isolated from other language games (Wittgenstein, [1953] 2001: §68, 28). 'Our knowledge forms an enormous system. And only within this system has a particular bit the value we give it' (Wittgenstein, 1969: § 410) – a value described and appropriated in terms of language and other forms of life. So while language games are not reducible to one another, they are not totally dissimilar from each other either, and there will often be what Wittgenstein calls *Familienähnlichkeiten*, 'family resem-blances', between them (Wittgenstein, [1953] 2001: §67, 27). Similarly, in dif-ferent contexts the same word will have different meanings (Sherry, 1977: 4), but the different meanings will not be entirely dissimilar, and each word will have '*eine Familie von Bedeutungen*', 'a family of meanings' (Wittgenstein, [1953] 2001: §77, 31). Wittgenstein takes the example of the games that people might play: board games, card games, and so on. They are all games, and one game will exhibit similarities with other games: but there is nothing identifiable that will be common to all of them. Instead, 'we see a complicated network of similarities overlapping and criss-crossing; sometimes overall similarities, sometimes similarities of detail … Now I know how to go on … *This is how these words are used*' (Wittgenstein, [1953] 2001: §66, 27; §180,

62; §179, 62). Accordingly, the only way to know 'how to go on' and 'how ... words are used' is by experiencing examples of the use of words in a wide variety of circumstances. No non-linguistic foundation will ever be discovered, we shall exhaust justifications, and in the end we can only say 'This is simply what I do ... *this language-game is played*' (Wittgenstein, [1953] 2001: §217, 72; §654, 141).

DEFINITIONS

We have concluded that it is only within the context of the vast network of interrelated, diverse and changing language games with shifting meanings in changing contexts that we can explore the meanings of words, and this means that we can only explore the meanings of words by referring to a changing diversity of other words (Bambrough, 1969: 94). So what is the meaning of 'definition': that is, what are we doing when we 'define' something? ('How should we define "define"?' Take care, reader, that you do not disappear down an infinite regress.) In this section, we shall discover a variety of ways of defining, and we shall then apply those different methods to the task in hand.

By 'definition' we generally mean a set of words that together indicate the 'meaning' of a word or group of words. As we have discovered, this immediately poses a problem. If we study a particular use of a word and then construct a set of words to express the meaning of that use, then the use of the new set of words, and of each of its component words, will be specific to a particular context: so even if we employ the same definition (in the sense of the same set of words in the same order), it will have different meanings in different contexts. However, there really will be a family *resemblance*: and it is on that that dictionaries rely when they define a word or group of words. Thus the Oxford English Dictionary not only offers a definition or definitions of each English word commonly in use, but it also lists the particular usages on which it has based its definition or definitions.

We shall take as examples two words that we shall often encounter in the course of this book: 'unconditional' and 'universal'. The words are found in such combinations as 'unconditional cash transfers', 'universal benefits', 'unconditional benefits' ... But what do these terms mean? How should they be defined? And are those two questions the same?

We shall discuss four ways in which definitions can be achieved: by identifying current usage; by listing characteristics; by comparison with a prototype; and by a legitimate authority. These methods will then be employed in order to define the terms 'unconditional' and 'universal', and, on the basis of the definitions constructed, relationships between the two terms will be discussed.

a)   Definition by Usage

Defining 'unconditional' in relation to its use
The Oxford English Dictionary defines 'unconditional' as:

> Not limited by or subject to conditions or stipulations; absolute, unlimited, complete;

the entry on 'condition' contains the following:

> ... Something demanded or required as a prerequisite to the granting or performance of something else; a provision, a stipulation;

and the entry on 'stipulation' includes:

> The action of specifying as one of the terms of a contract or agreement; a formulated term or condition of a contract or agreement.

The dictionary gives as one of its examples of the use of 'unconditional', 'The Kuwait authorities insisted that the [hijackers'] surrender was "unconditional"'; and as a use of 'condition' it offers a quotation from John Wesley: 'The word *condition* means neither more nor less than something sine quâ non, without which something else is not done.'

If usage is the key to a word's meaning, then we must seek examples of usage. Take these examples of uses of the words 'conditional', 'condition' and 'unconditional' drawn from an International Labour Organization publication:

> Improvements in schooling are not restricted to conditional cash transfer programmes. Positive effects on schooling can also be observed for unconditional transfers or workfare programmes. ... Brazil's *Bolsa Familia* provides income transfers to poor households, on condition that they regularly send their children to school and that household members attend health clinics. ... In Chile, *Programa de Pensiones Asistenciales*, a non-contributory and unconditional social pension programme, is found to have reduced poverty amongst people in old age by about 9.2 per cent. (International Labour Organization, 2010: viii, 2, 11)

This passage provides a useful case study in how the word 'unconditional' is used. In relation to its first use, 'unconditional' is employed in direct contrast to 'conditional', where the conditionality is clearly 'something demanded or required as a prerequisite': in this case, that parents send their children to school. In relation to the second use of 'unconditional', the author finds it necessary to add 'non-contributory'. This suggests that in the author's mind 'unconditional' does not necessarily mean 'recipients do not have to have paid social insurance contributions of some kind'. Also, the pension is presumably paid only to individuals above a certain age, which suggests that it is conditional on the recipient's age: but this does not appear to compromise the payment's description as 'unconditional'.

There is clearly a wide variety of meanings of the word 'unconditional' in circulation. A categorization might be helpful. There will be conditions that we cannot affect (such as one's age); there will be conditions that we have affected and that relate to events in the past (such as the payment of social insurance contributions); and there will be conditions that we can affect and that relate to future or current events (such as paid employment). The first use of 'unconditional' in the passage, in 'unconditional transfers', might suggest that none of these kinds of conditions apply – although in fact they might. The second usage of 'unconditional' is more explicit. Here one condition does apply: age, which we cannot affect. Another condition, the payment of contributions, is separately stated not to apply, suggesting that in the author's mind 'unconditional' by itself does not necessarily imply that a particular condition related to past actions – the payment of contributions – does not need to be met. 'Unconditional' here must therefore imply that some other conditions do not need to be met: presumably conditions related to income and wealth.

It would therefore appear that the word 'unconditional' can imply a variety of meanings and associated definitions within a single document, and that we might need to add to the dictionary a definition broader than those represented in the Oxford English Dictionary as follows:

> Not limited by or subject to conditions or stipulations; absolute, unlimited, complete; *or* not limited by or subject to a particular condition or stipulation either stated or understood.

Defining 'universal' in relation to its use

The Oxford English Dictionary defines 'universal' as follows:

> Extending over or including the whole of something specified or implied, esp. the whole of a particular group or the whole world; comprehensive, complete; widely occurring or existing, prevalent over all. ... Affecting or involving the whole of something specified or implied. ... *Of a service or facility: extended to, provided for, or accessible to all members of a community, regardless of wealth, social status, etc. ...*

I have italicized this last entry because of its particular relevance to social security. The most recent example given is from the *South China Morning Post*: 'By last year, 94 per cent of the mainland's populated areas had provided nine years of universal compulsory education.' Here it is clear, as with other parts of the definition given above, that any use of the word 'universal' requires the specification of the community within which something applies, from which it comes, or to which it is supplied. By 'all without exception' is meant 'all without exception within the specified community'.

We shall employ the same International Labour Organization publication as a case study:

> But despite the progress made in the materialization of the universal right to social security, very important gaps remain. ... Non-contributory schemes include a broad range of schemes including universal schemes for all residents, some categorical schemes or means-tested schemes. ... Categorical schemes could also be grouped as universal, if they cover all residents belonging to a certain category, or include resource conditions (social assistance schemes). They may include other types of conditions such as performing or accomplishing certain tasks. (International Labour Organization, 2010: 1, 39)

Here we find three different uses of 'universal'. The first use applies to everyone, globally; and the second and third to everyone within a particular country. However, the second and third uses have different meanings, and we can only deduce these from the context. The second use implies that a 'universal' scheme is neither means-tested nor categorical (that is, the payment depends neither on the level of other income nor on the recipient belonging to a particular category) and therefore that it pays the same income to everyone, whereas the third use implies that universal schemes can be categorical or means-tested. While 'universal' always means 'extending over or including the whole of something specified or implied', the different uses here warn us to be clear about what precisely is universal: Is it the provision of an income? Or is it the provision of an income on certain conditions? The UK's 'Universal Credit' is the provision of a means-tested and work-tested income to everyone who fulfils the conditions (and would probably be better designated 'Unified Benefit'), whereas in the context of 'Universal Basic Income' 'universal' means that 'every individual unconditionally receives an income as a right of citizenship, independent of labour-market status' (Painter and Thoung, 2015: 18). ('Independent of labour-market status' is strictly redundant, but is presumably added to emphasize the point.)

As with 'unconditional', the meaning of 'universal' is determined by its particular use, and care must be taken not to make untested assumptions about the word's meaning in a particular context.

'Universal' and 'unconditional' in the context of the Citizen's Basic Income debate

If we study uses of the word 'universal' in the context of the Citizen's Basic Income debate, then we generally find that it means 'everyone within a national boundary', or perhaps 'everyone within a regional boundary'. For those campaigning for a global Citizen's Basic Income, 'universal' means what it says (World Basic Income): but generally 'universal' does not in fact mean universal in this strict sense. Does that matter? Not if everyone understands what is meant.

If within a particular jurisdiction a benefit is 'unconditional', then by definition it is universal within that jurisdiction. If it is universal then it is not necessarily unconditional. This means that 'unconditional' cannot be replaced by 'universal'. It might be thought that 'universal' in the now common designation 'Universal Basic Income' is redundant. Strictly speaking, it is. Presumably 'Universal Basic Income' has become a common designation for a Citizen's Basic Income because it emphasizes an aspect of the income that its proponents wish to emphasize: the fact that everyone would receive it.

Defining 'Citizen's Basic Income' by its use
For the purposes of this discussion I shall study the term 'Basic Income', and then add a brief note on the 'Citizen's' in 'Citizen's Basic Income'. (The complex notion of citizenship receives a thorough discussion in Chapter 11 on politics, with additional discussions on who should receive a Citizen's Basic Income in Chapter 10 on social administration and in Chapter 13 on law.)

There is no entry for 'Basic Income', 'Citizen's Income', or 'Citizen's Basic Income' in the Oxford English Dictionary (which is interesting), but we do of course find both 'basic' and 'income'. 'Basic' used as an adjective is given a wide variety of definitions, the first two of which are as follows:

> a. Of, pertaining to, or forming a base; fundamental, essential: ... b. That is or constitutes a standard minimum amount in a scale of remuneration or the like.

The dictionary also offers the following definition:

> Providing or having few or no amenities, accessories, functions, etc., beyond the ordinary or essential; of or designating the lowest standard acceptable or available; rudimentary:

– of which it gives an example: 'Pastries and other sweets in the north can be pretty basic.'
English as spoken in the United States of America exhibits similar meanings:

> a. being the main or most important part of something ... b. very simple, with nothing special added: 'The software is very basic.' (Cambridge Essential American English Dictionary)

Whether the derogatory undertones are understood by a speaker using the word 'basic' in the context of 'Basic Income', or by someone hearing or reading the words, will depend on the speaker's, writer's, hearer's or reader's previous experience of the word 'basic' and the context in which the word is being used. It is in relation to such undertones that meaning and stated definition can diverge. When we hear the term 'Basic Income' we might define it as 'an unconditional and nonwithdrawable income for every individual': but we might also understand the term to mean that in some respects the income will not be a very good one. This is an aspect of our understanding that might not appear in the stated definition. So to attempt to define 'Basic Income' by reference to current usage will deliver a variety of different definitions and an even wider variety of understood meanings, with each definition and meaning depending on the particular uses of the words that the definer and the reader or hearer have experienced and the context in which the words are being used. Any family resemblances between the different definitions and between the different meanings might not be entirely obvious.

In relation to the global debate on Citizen's Basic Income, a significant additional question has to be that of the transferability of definitions between different languages. The German '*Grundeinkommen*' offers a useful example. 'Grund' in this context means 'foundation', so '*Grundeinkommen*' means a foundational income. There is no sense here that the income is not of good quality. '*Basiseinkommen*' has a similar meaning to '*Grundeinkommen*': it represents an income that provides a foundation on which people can build. So again, the question arises as to whether two people using a word will mean the same thing by it. An English speaker might translate '*Grundeinkommen*' as 'Basic Income' and might understand some derogatory undertones that a German speaker would not understand when they heard the same word. The relationship between the various definitions of '*Grundeinkommen*' and the various definitions of 'Basic Income' will therefore be an interesting one.

As for the 'Citizen's' in 'Citizen's Basic Income': It is partly because of the somewhat derogatory undertones of the word 'basic' in English that in 1992 the trustees of the Citizen's Basic Income Trust agreed with a suggestion from the Joseph Rowntree Charitable Trust that we should speak of a 'Citizen's Income' rather than a 'Basic Income'. The Green Party in the UK has often preferred 'Citizen's' to 'Basic' as well. The word 'citizen' does not necessarily include everyone who lives within a nation state's borders, so the word is not as all-encompassing as 'universal': but it does connect Citizen's Basic Income with a discourse about citizens' rights. 'Citizen's Income' avoids the negative connotations of 'Basic', but it does not include the word 'Basic' so it does not make it clear that a Citizen's Income relates to the global debate about Citizen's Basic Income. 'Citizen's Basic Income' retains the term 'Basic Income' in order to connect itself with the global debate; the position of 'citizen's' at the beginning of the term draws attention away from the unfortunate undertones associated with 'basic'; and adding the word 'citizen's' encourages debate about the meaning of 'citizen'. The new Scottish network, and the publisher of this author's 2016 book *Citizen's Basic Income: A Christian social policy* (Torry, 2016b), both independently asked that 'Citizen's Basic Income' should be used: and the trustees of what is now the Citizen's Basic Income Trust decided to do the same. The advantage of 'Citizen's Basic Income' is that it contains both 'Basic Income' and 'Citizen's'. The disadvantages are that it is longer than either 'Basic Income' or 'Citizen's Income', and that CBI can also mean the Confederation of British Industry.

b)   Definition by Characteristics

What is sometimes called the 'classical' way of defining a definition is to envisage a category defined by a list of characteristics. Thus a rectangle is a four-sided figure with opposite sides parallel and all four of its angles right angles: so a square is a rectangle because it has four sides, opposite sides are parallel, and the angles are right angles, whereas neither a triangle nor a circle are rectangles. Those entities that possess the characteristics are in the category, and those entities that do not are not. But for anything other than simple cases of definition this strategy quickly breaks down because there are frequently cases where we cannot determine whether the entity concerned is in the category or not. Thus if to be a 'bird' something needs to fly, then an ostrich is not a bird and a bat is one. The category 'table' is defined by the characteristics 'horizontal surface' and 'supported on legs'. A folded drop-leaf table is not a table, whereas a stool is a table.

Defining 'unconditional' and 'universal' by characteristics
So the question to ask is this: Is there a set of characteristics by which we can decide whether something belongs in the category labelled 'unconditional'? And similarly with the category labelled 'universal'? There are a number of ways to approach this:

- Each user of the terms 'universal' or 'unconditional' could select their own preferred characteristics. The individual's autonomy would thus be honoured, but at the risk of losing mutual comprehension.
- We could study a wide variety of actual usages of the terms and work out the lists of characteristics either stated or assumed by users of the terms. If we could find characteristics employed in *all* actual usages, then we would have discovered the 'family likeness' and would be able to list a definitive set of characteristics. However, that does not mean that everyone would agree with the list. It would only take one user of the terms 'universal' or 'unconditional' to insist that they understood a characteristic not in the list

to be essential to the definition of the category for the definition to become problematic in relation to attempts at mutual comprehension.

- An authority of some kind could decide on the list of characteristics that would qualify something as belonging to the categories 'universal' or 'unconditional'.

Defining 'Citizen's Basic Income' by characteristics

'Citizen's Basic Income' is frequently defined in relation to a list of characteristics. An income might belong in the category 'Citizen's Basic Income' if it is 'unconditional', 'nonwithdrawable', and paid to 'each individual' rather than to households. However, as we have seen, meaning might be richer than definition. Usually unstated, but generally assumed, are some additional characteristics:

- That the income will be paid monthly, fortnightly, or weekly (or perhaps daily?). The Alaska Permanent Fund Dividend (Goldsmith, 2012: 49–50), which pays an annual dividend to all citizens of Alaska, is therefore not a Citizen's Basic Income.
- That the income will not vary, although regular annual upratings will be expected. Again, the Alaska Permanent Fund Dividend, which is the payment of a varying dividend, is not a Citizen's Basic Income.
- That the income will vary with the recipient's age, with a 'standard' amount for working age adults, smaller amounts for children, and perhaps for young adults, and larger amounts for individuals over a defined state pension age. (See the case study about 'conditionality' at the end of this chapter.)

These three assumptions are generally understood to belong to the definition of a Citizen's Basic Income, but they are rarely stated. If 'definition' means a set of words that give some indication of the meaning of 'Citizen's Basic Income', then the definition will rarely include these three assumptions. If by 'definition' we mean the understood meaning of 'Citizen's Basic Income', then these characteristics do belong to the definition.

If we look for the words that generally accompany 'Citizen's Basic Income' then we will often find the words 'unconditional', 'nonwithdrawable', and 'individual'. We might find 'regular', which can encapsulate the first assumption above; we might find a statement that the payment will be at the same level each week or each month, reflecting the second assumption; and we will generally find different levels of Citizen's Basic Income for different age groups, reflecting the third assumption. So in the case of 'Citizen's Basic Income', usage delivers a fairly consistent set of characteristics and our first two definitional methods converge.

c) Definition by Comparison with a Prototype

Eleanor Rosch (Rosch and Lloyd, 1978; Rosch, 1999) has suggested that categories are not the clear-cut things that we often think they are, and that it is often not the case that entities are either in the category or not in it; and neither is it the case that entities belong equally. Thus a robin is more a bird than an ostrich is, and a bat is on the boundary of the category. Rosch points out that in the real world we define categories in terms of prototypes and then decide whether something is in the category by asking how similar it is to the prototype. For the category 'bird' the prototype might be 'robin'. Mark Johnson (Johnson, 1993) has argued that we categorize actions as moral or otherwise by comparing them with a prototype lie and then asking whether they are more or less like it. So in order to define an object as a table we would have in mind a particular table and ask how similar to it the object might be. To take an organizational example: Is a doctors' organization such as the British Medical Association a trade union? It has members who pay membership fees; it negotiates on behalf of its members; and it will represent members when asked to do so. When we compare this organization with organizations that call themselves trades unions, we can find a sufficient number of similarities to suggest that we ought to call the BMA a trade union, even if it chooses not to do so itself (British Medical Association).

To take a relevant example: Should we call an unconditional income for every 16-year-old a 'universal benefit'? An appropriate prototype of a universal benefit presents itself: the UK's Child Benefit (Spicker, 2011: 13). Child Benefit is paid for every child in the UK: but a residence condition needs to be satisfied; for children between the ages of 16 and 19 no payment is made if they are no longer in full-time education (HM Revenue and Customs, 2018); and the fact that a tax charge is now paid by individuals who pay higher rate Income Tax if they live in households in receipt of Child Benefit means that some women are withdrawing their claims. This suggests that the criteria for an income being defined as a 'universal' benefit are somewhat short of universality in the strict sense of that word; and that an otherwise unconditional income paid to everyone aged sixteen would have no trouble being defined as a universal benefit. The meaning of language is its use, and definition by prototype is as legitimate a method of definition as any other: so for an otherwise unconditional income for 16-year-olds to be called a 'universal benefit', on the basis that the similar but in practice less universal Child Benefit is already termed a 'universal benefit', would be entirely legitimate.

Similarly, in order to decide whether an income is a Citizen's Basic Income, we might ask whether it is similar to incomes that are already regarded as Citizen's Basic Incomes. Both Namibia and India have seen pilot projects that allocated unconditional individual incomes: in the case of Namibia, to everyone within a single large community; and in the case of India to everyone living in a variety of rural, urban, and tribal communities (Basic Income Grant Coalition, 2009; Davala et al., 2015; Haarmann and Haarmann, 2007; 2012; Osterkamp, 2013; Standing, 2015; 2017a: 232). These are the only genuine attempts so far at saturation pilot studies, although an existing small experiment in Kenya is now scaling up to a larger concentrated sample than that employed in India, and to Citizen's Basic Incomes being paid over longer periods (Bregman, 2017: 28–30; Douillard, 2017; McFarland, 2017).

In Namibia, every adult in the pilot community was paid an individual, unconditional and regular monthly income for a period of two years, and in the case of India the payments were for eighteen months. If with Young (2018) we distinguish between 'pilot projects', which test unconditional incomes, and 'experiments', which test incomes to which conditionalities of various kinds might be attached, then both the Indian and Namibian projects should be regarded as 'Citizen's Basic Income pilot projects'. Or should they be? Van Parijs and Vanderborght offer two reasons for believing that the projects suffer from defects that prevent them from being regarded as models for 'real-life schemes': they were for limited durations, which a real-life Citizen's Basic Income would not be; and they employed external additional funding, whereas a real-life Citizen's Basic Income would need to be funded from within a community's existing resources (Van Parijs and Vanderborght, 2017: 139–40). There is some justice in these observations: however, do they mean that we should not regard the incomes paid during the projects as Citizen's Basic Incomes? The incomes were unconditional and for every individual, which, as we have already discovered, is the normal definition in terms of characteristics; and they were regular monthly incomes, which satisfies a normal assumption. Neither the duration of the payments, nor the funding method, has been an issue so far in this chapter. Significantly, Van Parijs and Vanderborght are not arguing that the incomes paid in India and Namibia were not Citizen's Basic Incomes: instead, they are suggesting that the experiments did not model 'real-life schemes' (Van Parijs and Vanderborght, 2017: 139). This is true. So first of all we need to be clear about a distinction: a Citizen's Basic Income is always an unconditional regular income paid to every individual, whereas a Citizen's Basic Income *scheme* is a Citizen's Basic Income, along with the levels at which it will be paid for each age group specified, and along with a statement of the method by which it will be funded. The scheme might also specify that the Citizen's Basic Income will be permanent, but it might not. And second, the fact that a limited pilot project might not conform in all respects to what a nationwide Citizen's Basic Income scheme would look like does not mean that the project should not be carried out, and it does not mean that it would not be a pilot project if it was. If the pilot project is carefully planned to answer questions relevant to the current state of the debate, and if it tests a genuinely unconditional income, then the project could be well worth doing (Widerquist, 2018).

Van Parijs and Vanderborght are correct to suggest that there are differences between the characteristics of the Indian and Namibian pilot projects and those of a 'real-life scheme': but that does not stop us regarding the unconditional incomes paid in Namibia and India as prototype Citizen's Basic Incomes: and neither does it stop us comparing other proposed incomes with the incomes paid out during those pilot projects in order to decide whether the proposed incomes should be regarded as Citizen's Basic Incomes.

As we have seen, attempting to define by using prototypes has raised issues not raised by attempts to define by usage or by characteristics. There are both similarities and differences between the different methods, so perhaps the most fruitful approach will be to employ all three of them.

d)   Definition by a Recognized Authority

If a field of interest has related to it an organization that those involved in that field believe to have some standing or authority, then participants might look to that organization to supply definitions of terms. This will be by way of something like a social contract. In order to avoid the chaos of multiple definitions, participants might be willing to forego their autonomy and to grant authority to the recognized organization.

There are a number of ways in which the organization might construct the expected definitions. It might construct a list of characteristics that something has to have in order to be included in the named category; or it might collect examples of the use of the term and on that basis decide on a definition; or it might employ a mixture of those methods, constructing a list of characteristics and testing the list against current usage. There might be various ways in which an organization might go about the task. There might be an individual with the authority to make such decisions about lists of characteristics; a small body of people might be elected or appointed to decide; or the entire membership might decide on definitions by a democratic process (although this method might in practice come down to an individual or a small group making the decision, because a resolution will always be written by an individual or a small group).

There are now multiple organizations involved in the Citizen's Basic Income debate. In many countries we can find at least one organization facilitating the debate, and in some countries there will be more than one (in the UK the Citizen's Basic Income Trust has been facilitating the debate for thirty-five years; Basic Income UK is a more recent campaigning organization; and Citizen's Basic Income Network Scotland is now facilitating the debate in Scotland). The Basic Income Earth Network (BIEN) functions as something of a global umbrella organization. Some of the national organizations affiliate to BIEN, but BIEN has no control over the activities or views of the national groups.

Each of these organizations has the authority to construct its own definition of Citizen's Basic Income, but because each organization's definition reflects common usage, and because the organizations are in network relationships both with each other and with numerous writers on the subject, we might expect a certain amount of consistency. Quite often, 'unconditional', 'non-withdrawable' and 'individual', or similar words, will be found, and the three assumptions (regular payment, nonvarying but upratable payments, and payments varying with age) will also be found.

Because BIEN is an umbrella organization with affiliated organizations, its own definition of Citizen's Basic Income will need to reflect current usage, and in particular it will need to reflect current usage among its affiliated organizations. This is not difficult to achieve. The wording on its website runs as follows:

> A basic income is a periodic cash payment unconditionally delivered to all on an individual basis, without means-test or work requirement.
> That is, basic income has the following five characteristics:
> 1. Periodic: it is paid at regular intervals (for example every month), not as a one-off grant.
> 2. Cash payment: it is paid in an appropriate medium of exchange, allowing those who receive it to decide what they spend it on. It is not, therefore, paid either in kind (such as food or services) or in vouchers dedicated to a specific use.
> 3. Individual: it is paid on an individual basis – and not, for instance, to households.
> 4. Universal: it is paid to all, without means test.
> 5. Unconditional: it is paid without a requirement to work or to demonstrate willingness-to-work. (Basic Income Earth Network)

And a shorter form, last amended at the Seoul General Assembly in 2016, reads like this:

> A periodic cash payment delivered to all on an individual basis, without means test or work requirement. (Basic Income Earth Network)

Neither of these definitions conflicts with any affiliated organization's definition, and both of them represent the consensus among affiliates and, most importantly, they reflect common usage of the term 'Basic Income' (although note that 'without means test' is thought to be implied by 'universal' rather than by 'unconditional'). BIEN can therefore confidently function as a 'recognized authority' in relation to the definition of Citizen's Basic Income.

The amount of the payment

There would appear to be just one issue over which the national organizations disagree: the amount of the payment. A survey reveals that for some national organizations only an unconditional, nonwithdrawable, regular and individual income at 'subsistence level' can qualify as a Citizen's Basic Income, whereas for other organizations an unconditional, nonwithdrawable, regular and individual income of any amount can count as one (Torry, 2017b: 9–17). A similar division can be found in the literature on Citizen's Basic Income. Some of the literature assumes that the level of the Citizen's Basic Income must be above some poverty line (Pereira, 2017: 2), but other literature does not (Torry, 2017d; 2018c; Reed and Lansley, 2016; Lansley and Reed, 2019; Martinelli, 2017a; 2017b; 2017c).

First of all, we need to recognize the significant difficulties that any individual or organization that insists that 'Basic Income' or 'Citizen's Basic Income' implies payments at a particular level, and in particular at 'subsistence' level, will encounter:

- 'Subsistence level' is notoriously difficult to define. Every household behaves differently, and what one household counts as a subsistence income might be counted as utterly inadequate by another, and as over-generous by yet another. Qualitative research can construct a list of expenditures regarded as necessary for participation in society (as in the Minimum Income Standards annual survey conducted for the Joseph Rowntree Foundation) (Davis, Hirsch, Padley and Shepherd, 2018): but such an approach can only obscure the wide variation in understandings of 'subsistence'. Government-specified subsistence levels are precisely that, and are driven largely or partly by political considerations.
- Governments tend to be cautious, and social policy is path dependent, so it is more likely that a Citizen's Basic Income will start small, and will then grow, than that a large Citizen's Basic Income will be implemented in the first instance. Organizations that insist that 'Basic Income' or 'Citizen's Basic Income' means an income at subsistence level will not help a government to ponder the possibility of making a start with a small Citizen's Basic Income: and such an organization will not be doing the kind of research required to enable a government to think rationally about whether a small Citizen's Basic Income might be feasible.
- Any organization that decides that a payment is only a Citizen's Basic Income if it is at a predetermined subsistence level is at risk of depriving itself of research results from organizations that research Citizen's Basic Incomes at lower levels.

However one evaluates the significance of these difficulties, it might be thought that disagreement over whether or not the amount of the payment is intrinsic to the definition of Citizen's Basic Income leaves an umbrella organization such as BIEN with a dilemma. It does not. If BIEN were to include 'at subsistence level' in its definition of Citizen's Basic Income, then it would have to disaffiliate national organizations that did not require that (or they would disaffiliate themselves), whereas if it were not to include 'at subsistence level' in its definition of Citizen's Basic Income then every national organization would be able to remain affiliated. The fact that some of those organizations might choose to add an additional characteristic to their definition would only be relevant to affiliation if BIEN were to decide that it should be.

If BIEN did wish to say something about the level of Citizen's Basic Income that would be agreeable to every affiliate, then there is just one possibility. The survey shows that:

- Some affiliated organizations do not mention the issue, suggesting that the amount to be paid is not integral to the definition;
- Some say that a democratic process will be used to decide the amount;
- One organization mentions a particular amount;
- And some organizations offer descriptions of the kinds of life that the Citizen's Basic Income would be expected to fund ('subsistence', 'dignity', 'participation', 'poverty line') in relation to the national context, but without specifying the relevant level of Citizen's Basic Income.

BIEN could legitimately say that in each country the normal democratic process would determine the level of Citizen's Basic Income and the funding mechanism. This would be entirely uncontentious. A further suggestion might be to return to a set of terminology developed during the earlier period of the debate: a 'Full Citizen's Basic Income' meant a Citizen's Basic Income at subsistence level (somehow defined); and a 'Partial Citizen's Basic Income' meant one at a lower level (Parker, 1989: 4). Some organizations might find this terminology helpful: and, because it assumes that a Citizen's Basic Income can be paid at any level, no organization should find the terminology problematic.

The Word 'Guarantee'

During the early 1980s, at the beginning of the modern debate about Citizen's Basic Income, Hermione Parker and Brandon Rhys Williams MP called a Citizen's Basic Income a 'Basic Income Guarantee' (House of Commons Treasury and Civil Service Committee Sub-Committee, 1982; House of Commons Treasury and Civil Service Committee, 1983; Parker, 1989). The word 'guarantee' was confusing because to guarantee an income is not necessarily to provide one. A means-tested benefit can guarantee someone an income by filling a gap between other income and a specified minimum income level. When the British Government wanted a new name for its means-tested top-up for pensioners, it chose 'Minimum Income Guarantee': a rare example of accurate description. Because 'guarantee' can imply means-testing, the British debate soon dropped the word, preferring 'Basic Income', then 'Citizen's Income', and now 'Citizen's Basic Income'. The North American debate, however, retains the use of 'guarantee', causing occasional misunderstanding as to what is intended. Take, for instance, the wording on USBIG's website:

> The Basic Income Guarantee (BIG) is a government ensured guarantee that no one's income will fall below the level necessary to meet their most basic needs for any reason. ... The Basic Income gives every citizen a check for the full basic income every month, and taxes his or her earned income, so that nearly everyone both pays taxes and receives a basic income. (USBIG)

Here 'Basic Income Guarantee' can mean a means-tested benefit, whereas 'Basic Income' does not. Because 'Basic Income' appears in both designations, this is potentially quite confusing, because someone could easily think that 'Basic Income' and 'Basic Income Guarantee' mean the same thing, when in fact they do not. Similar confusion can be found elsewhere. When Bent Greve suggests that a 'guaranteed minimum income' should be implemented as a response to increasing automation, it is not clear whether what is to be guaranteed is a Citizen's Basic Income – an unconditional income for every individual of the same age – or a minimum net household income (Greve, 2017: 95, 127). (Greve is equally confused about the meanings of Citizen's Income and Basic Income: Greve, 2017: 96.) My recommendation is that the word 'guarantee' should be avoided altogether: but if it is to be used, then it would be helpful for anyone using the term 'Basic Income Guarantee' to say whether they mean a Minimum Income Guarantee or a Citizen's Basic Income.

Clear Definition, and Its Importance

Whichever way we arrive at it, Citizen's Basic Income has a clear definition: it is an unconditional income paid to every individual. It is as simple as that. It has a number of different names: Citizen's Income, Basic Income, Citizen's Basic Income, and Universal Basic Income. They all mean exactly the same. They mean an unconditional income paid to every individual. The amount received would never depend on the amount of any other income, on the level of someone's wealth, on household structure, on employment status, or on anything else. Every individual of the same age would receive exactly the same amount, every week or every month, automatically.

Older people might receive more than working age adults, younger adults less, and less for children. Does adjusting the amount with someone's age compromise Citizen's Basic Income's unconditionality? No, it does not. What is unique about Citizen's Basic Income, what matters, and what makes it work, is that it can be turned on at birth, and turned off at death, and no active administration would be required in between. Once the computer knows someone's date of birth, it never needs to ask about their age: it can seamlessly adjust the amount paid as the person's age changes.

Sometimes words are added, but they are not necessary. Citizen's Basic Income is unconditional, so within the jurisdiction in which it is paid everybody gets it, so it is universal. There is no need to say that it is. Citizen's Basic Income is unconditional, which means that it would not fall if other income rose, so it is nonwithdrawable. There is no need to say that it is. It is universal, and it is nonwithdrawable, but all we need to say is this: Every individual of the same age would receive exactly the same income, unconditionally.

Does any of this matter? Yes, it does. It matters particularly when an organization or individual calls something a Citizen's Basic Income and it isn't one. Take as an example the quickly curtailed Ontario 'Basic Income' pilot. The Ontario Government described its 'Basic Income' like this:

> The payment will account for other income and ensure a minimum level of income is provided. Participants will receive:
> * Up to $16,989 per year for a single person, less 50 per cent of any earned income
> * Up to $24,027 per year for a couple, less 50 per cent of any earned income
> * Up to an additional $6,000 per year for a person with a disability. (Ontario).

Such payments are neither 'individual' nor 'without means test' nor 'unconditional'. They do not constitute a Citizen's Basic Income, so they should not be called one. To call the payments a 'Basic Income' invites us to compare other household-based and means-tested incomes with the incomes paid during the Ontario experiment and to call those incomes 'Basic Incomes', which would lead to multiple individuals and organizations conversing at cross-purposes.

The same problems occur in the literature. Take three recent books: In his *Utopia for Realists* (2017), the journalist Rutger Bregman is an enthusiastic advocate for Citizen's Basic Income – or is he? Many of the examples that he gives have conditionalities attached to them, and there is no single definition against which he evaluates the different benefits that he discusses. Erik Brynjolfsson and Andrew McAfee, in *The Second Machine Age* (2014: 232–3), make no distinction between Citizen's Basic Income schemes and schemes for Minimum Income Guarantees. And in a book by a number of academics about the prospects for Citizen's Basic Income in Australia and New Zealand, 'Basic Income' is used with a variety of meanings within the same book (Mays et al., 2016). This matters. Without an agreed definition, participants in a discussion cannot be sure what someone means by 'Basic Income': Do they mean an unconditional payment, the same to every individual of the same age, or do they mean a household-based and means-tested payment? If such diversity of definition persists, then every time someone uses the term 'Basic Income' or 'Citizen's Basic Income' they will need to say what they mean by it if mutual comprehension is to take place. It might be thought that permitting minor variations in the definition that do not go as far as the contradictions to it represented by the Ontario scheme might be permitted (Smith-Carrier and Green, 2017): but then the problem to be faced is knowing where to draw the line between what is a Citizen's Basic Income and what is not one. The possibility of conversing at cross-purposes remains. Clear and agreed definitions really do matter. We might arrive at those definitions by a variety of routes, as we have discovered: but the aim must always be clarity.

A different question: Does it matter that there are a number of different *terms* in circulation? Is it not rather confusing that the same thing is called a Citizen's Basic Income, a Basic Income, a Citizen's Income, and a Universal Basic Income? It might be thought that it would be helpful to reduce this variety to a single agreed term. First of all, there is no organization with the authority to make the decision as to which that term should be; second, neither individuals nor organizations would be under any obligation to conform; and third, the diversity is helpful in that it enables different aspects of a Citizen's Basic Income to be emphasized: 'Basic Income' its foundational nature; 'Citizen's Income' its payment to each individual as a right; 'Citizen's Basic Income' both of those; and 'Universal Basic Income' its payment to everyone.

CONCLUSION

The reason that this chapter about language use is at the beginning of this book is because clear definition is essential to rational debate. Only if two people can agree on definitions of terms can they understand each other: so only if all of the individuals and organizations participating in a widespread debate can agree on the meanings of terms will mutual comprehension and useful research collaboration be possible. How we use language matters, and there is nothing more essential to the rationality and comprehensibility of the Citizen's Basic Income debate than attention to how language is used.

CASE STUDY

The Word 'Conditionality'

The noun 'conditionality' (or the adjective 'conditional') is singular, but in the context of the Citizen's Basic Income debate it represents at least two somewhat different meanings. This is most obvious in relation to the assumption that the level of Citizen's Basic Income would vary with the individual's age. This would appear to breach the 'unconditional' requirement, and, strictly speaking, it does: but because this conditionality is of a particular type, the breach is permitted.

In relation to social security benefits, conditionalities exhibit two variables: ease of administration, and whether or not enquiry has to be made into an individual's situation or activity. Two of the expected advantages of a Citizen's Basic Income are that it would be simple to administer, and that it would require no bureaucratic intrusion into the lives of recipients. Employment market status, household structure, and disability, are conditionalities about which enquiries have to be made. I shall call these 'type 1' conditionalities. On the other hand, nobody would ever have to enquire into someone's age. Their Citizen's Basic Income could begin at their birth, the computer could automatically increase their Citizen's Basic Income as they ceased to be children, when they became working age adults, and when they passed state retirement age, and it could turn off their Citizen's Basic Income when they died. There would be no bureaucratic intrusion, and, indeed, no active administration at all. Someone's age is a 'type 2' conditionality. Type 1 conditionalities cannot be allowed to influence the level of payment of Citizen's Basic Income, but type 2 conditionalities can be and are.

The difference between the two types of conditionality might appear to be a purely theoretical issue, but it is not. It has significant policy implications.

Conditionalities relating to factors that we might be able to influence, such as household structure and labour market status, can result in moral hazard and in disincentives, and they always result in enquiry having to be made. Someone whose means-tested benefits depend on them not being employed might be hesitant to seek employment if their employment income and any remaining means-tested benefits would offer them little additional net income, or even with a lower net income if they would have to pay fares to work. Moral hazard will be a risk under such circumstances, and there will certainly be a level of disincentive that would not be experienced in the absence of the conditionality. In addition, any enquiry, and any attempt on the part of the state to influence how someone reacts to the conditionality, will result in administrative and other costs.

Factors relating to events in the past, such as paying social insurance contributions, do not act as a direct disincentive, and they exhibit no moral hazard: and a disability, however originated, does not either. However, both the payment of contributions and the existence of a disability require bureaucratic enquiry. This can create stigma, and it certainly creates complexity and administrative cost. So while it might be thought that conditionalities relating to events in the past or present that we cannot now affect would not be a problem, they can be.

Conditionalities relating to factors over which we have no control, such as age, cause no problems at all. Except when a child is born, or perhaps when a Citizen's Basic Income is paid to someone about whom the state holds no information, no enquiry would be required.

This all suggests that when social policy is made, conditionalities about which enquiry has to be made should be avoided, whereas conditionalities that require no enquiry to be made are not a problem.

In relation to the Citizen's Basic Income debate, clarity is essential if discussion is to be rational. It is therefore potentially a problem that 'unconditional' has not always meant the same thing. For instance, the word has been taken to mean 'not conditional on a work test', rather than 'not conditional on either a work test or a means test'. If the word is used in this restricted sense (Young, 2018), then an income will only be a Citizen's Basic Income if 'nonwithdrawable' is added to the definition. As with any other word, an author can mean what they wish by it: but it will always be essential to say what is meant if the reader might have in their mind a different meaning of a word. In relation to Citizen's Basic Income, a reasonable assumption to make is that a reader will think that 'unconditional' means that no work test or means test will be applied, and that the payment will not depend on the structure of the household. The reader might also correctly assume that different age groups might receive Citizen's Basic Incomes of different amounts.

3. Histories of Citizen's Basic Income

History: The branch of knowledge that deals with past events; the formal record or
study of past events, esp. human affairs.
(Oxford English Dictionary)

INTRODUCTION

In this chapter we shall discuss how history is created, we shall construct
a list of questions based on the understanding of history that emerges, and we
shall ask how histories of Citizen's Basic Income suggest that their writers
might have answered those questions. We shall conclude by asking what the
discipline of history might offer to the Citizen's Basic Income debate, and also
what the Citizen's Basic Income debate might contribute to our understanding
of history.

It is not my intention to offer a history of Citizen's Basic Income – a number
of histories already exist, of varying degrees of comprehensiveness (Duverger,
2018; Sloman, 2018; Torry, 2013: 17–47, 65–80; Van Parijs and Vanderborght,
2017: 51–98; Van Trier, 1995; Widerquist, 2017a) – but of course, as the
structures of a number of different histories are described, a certain amount of
Citizen's Basic Income's history will be told. The main aim of this chapter is
to discuss how history is written, and how histories of Citizen's Basic Income
have been written, with the intention of informing any future such histories.

As will become clear from our discussion of how history is written, histories
are always in the plural. There is never a single history. 'Never again shall
a single story be told as though it were the only one' (Berger, 1972: 133).
Hence the plural in the title of this chapter; and hence the main body of the
chapter being constituted by discussion of a number of different histories of
Citizen's Basic Income. So unusually for this book, most of the chapter is
a series of case studies. Conclusions are drawn at the end, on the basis of the
collection of case studies.

One aspect of there being 'never again ... a single story' is that a historian
has to take numerous decisions as to what to include and what to omit. For
instance, geographical limits might be set (as for instance when Walter Van
Trier's and Peter Sloman's histories, discussed in this chapter, focus on the
United Kingdom, and Timothée Duverger focuses on France); and chronological limits might be set, with one historian concentrating on the modern period,

somehow defined, and another tackling a longer period of history. In order to explore the boundary-setting undertaken by the historians that we study in this chapter, a set of questions will be put to their histories of Citizen's Basic Income.

HOW HISTORY IS MADE

I shall be taking as my guides to the discipline of history the four historians Robert Harrison, Aled Jones, Peter Lambert, and Philipp Schofield (Harrison et al., 2004a; 2004b; 2004c; Schofield, 2004), and in particular the first few chapters of their book *Making History* (Lambert and Schofield, 2004). They show how during the eighteenth and nineteenth centuries, first in Germany, and then elsewhere, historians came to see themselves as a distinct body of writers and teachers with a defined and increasingly autonomous task, 'history', and that this growing network of scholars professionalized the discipline by creating institutional structures: university departments, journals, libraries, and archives. The revolutions and wars of the late eighteenth century made problematic an earlier shaping of history as 'progress' (Harrison et al., 2004a: 11), so during the nineteenth century, instead of the past being judged in relation to a present understood to be better, it came to be understood more on its own terms. The two understandings have continued to jostle for position. Historians might wish or need their craft to prove its usefulness, so they draw lessons from the past, which assumes that we can to some extent understand the past in terms of the present: but in order for history to understand itself as a scientific discipline, each period of history needs to be understood as objectively as possible on the basis of documentary and other evidence (Harrison et al., 2004b: 33). Understandably, all history-writing is an amalgam of the two approaches. Whether to a greater or lesser extent, historians' agendas have always been informed by the concerns of their own times: but a desire to uncover the truth about a period has always driven historians to grapple with data. The result has generally been historians arguing for a particular story, with the story backed up by evidence (Harrison et al., 2004b: 26). It cannot be otherwise. As Immanuel Kant recognized, experience is always the outcome of our own minds shaping the raw data of our sense perceptions; and similarly, history – both our general understanding of the past, and what we might write about its detail – is always an ordering of data undertaken in the context of some agenda or other. If it were not, then the data would be incomprehensible. Von Below describes the iterative process that emerges:

> Everywhere, our work proceeds as follows: we begin our research with particular conceptions, revise the latter according to the results obtained, then approach the

issues anew with the findings we arrive at in order once again to approach a revision
of our conceptions on the basis of new research work. (von Below, [1925] 2004: 22)

This is a scientific method which makes history into a science (Harrison et
al., 2004b: 33), although it remains an art in the sense that imagination is
employed to construct the story for which evidence is then sought.

Because the scientific method relies on documentary evidence, history has
generally been the history of states and their rulers, simply because the activities of states and their rulers have been more adequately documented than the
activities of farmers and artisans (Harrison et al., 2004c). About a century ago,
the new subdiscipline of social history – 'the analysis of economic, social,
cultural and political institutions from the perspective of the social subjects
meaningfully interacting with one another' (Welskopp, 2003: 218) – set
about righting this imbalance, and more recently such data as sixteenth- and
seventeenth-century hearth tax records have enabled us to explore the lives of
artisans, farmers, and other inhabitants of towns and villages (Wrightson and
Levine, 1979): but still history tends to be the history of kings, queens, presi-
dents, and prime ministers, and it continues to be told from the standpoint of
a relatively privileged group in society: salaried university teachers (Harrison
et al., 2004c: 46, 49). Given that the subject matter of such history is politics,
and that the historian's selection of material, and their interpretation of it, will
inevitably favour some current political agendas and implicitly criticize others,
the history that is written cannot help being political (Harrison et al., 2004c:
40–1, 51). As the twentieth century progressed, historians were increasingly
aware that the same data could be used to support widely differing interpretations of events, meaning that the ideal of 'objective' history looked increasingly unrealizable; and we have also become increasingly aware that data from
different directions about the same events can result in very different accounts.
As Stedman Jones has pointed out, the Chartists of the mid-nineteenth century
saw themselves as reformers who respected such social institutions as private
property and were making a political case for political reform: but the fears that
the movement inspired caused a very different narrative to become dominant.
'Whatever Chartism's official self-identity, contemporary observers could not
refrain from projecting onto it deeper, unavowed motives and sentiments …
Analysis of Chartist ideology must start from what Chartists actually said or
wrote' (Stedman Jones, 1983: 90, 94). As the 'new political history' saw it,
it was important to place 'a strong premium on the reconstruction of culture
and on the importance of taking political rhetoric and political ideas seriously,
rather than treating them as codes for more fundamental class or personal
interests' (Lawrence, 2003: 193). The language used – whether the language
used by the Chartists, or the language used by commentators at the time – was
shaping the meaning of the event: hence the 'linguistic turn' in social history

(Welskopp, 2003: 216, 218). And clearly, because the meaning of language is dependent on the context in which language is used (on this, see Chapter 2 of this volume on language and Citizen's Basic Income), the language that was used at the time must be understood in its historical context, and the historian must not assume that what a word means now is what it would have meant in a different period. As Quentin Skinner suggests, the meaning of a text from a previous era is neither to be discovered purely in the text itself, nor in some attempted reconstruction of the context in which it was written, but instead, when reading any text from the past, 'the essential question ... is what its author writing at the time that he did write for the audience he intended to address, could in practice have been intending to communicate by the utterance of this given utterance' (Skinner, 1969: 48–9). Texts from the past are responding to the questions of their own context, and not necessarily to our questions (Skinner, 1969: 50), so our language, questions, and context might seriously mislead our attempts to understand. This poses something of a challenge in relation to any attempt to write a history of Citizen's Basic Income, as it might be difficult to identify whether anything like a Citizen's Basic Income, as we might understand it, is in an author's mind and is intended to be communicated.

This all goes to show that 'history does not have an inner structure, an immanent pattern, other than that imposed by the historian' (Harrison et al., 2004c: 51). History writing is the construction of a narrative written by individuals with preformed ideas and questions. If history remains a science, then that is only because we now recognize that all science is an interpretation of reality based on preformed agendas imposed by scientists.

ECONOMIC HISTORY

Inspired by an increasing interest in social history, and building on previous work by German historians, the end of the nineteenth century saw the birth of the subdiscipline of economic history (Harrison et al., 2004c: 47). This development was both a recognition that a variety of different kinds of history could be written on the basis of different kinds of data, and a reaction against the state-centred history that was now being seriously challenged by economic shocks, political turmoil, and labour and other social movements that were looking at least as significant as the political institutions and individuals previously of interest to historians (Schofield, 2004: 69). The new subdiscipline established itself first of all in more recent institutions such as the University of Manchester and the London School of Economics, then in more traditional universities such as Cambridge and Oxford, and then beyond the traditional academy in such contexts as Workers Educational Association evening classes. In all of these contexts, and particularly at the London School of Economics, economic historians were interdisciplinary by default, and would often be found working with economists and sociologists. The methods employed by sociology and economics exhibited complex iterative processes, whereby hypotheses might be reshaped by the evidence, causing new sources of evidence to be sought, leading to further reshaping, and so on. Economic historians employed the same method. They often had available rich sources of data, and were as keen as any other historians to base their work on robust evidence (Schofield, 2004: 65, 69, 71); and at the same time, as we might expect, their work was just as driven by contemporary agendas. It was those agendas that informed hypotheses, which in turn determined the kinds of evidence that were sought. As with other historians, the economic historian's strategy might best be described as argument backed up by evidence (Schofield, 2004: 72–3). As the twentieth century progressed, an increase in the diversity of agendas led the subdiscipline into increasing contact with such contemporary ideologies as Marxism. Marxist economic historians might have been one of the clearer cases of an existing pattern in the scholar's mind setting the agenda for the collection and interpretation of data (Schofield, 2004: 74), but that does not mean that other economic histories have not been shaped by equally influential but less explicit agendas.

As with any history-writing, the writing of economic history is always the telling of a story. It might be a story about the evolution of an idea or a set of ideas, or it might be a story about the process by which a social policy changed: but it will always be a story constructed by a historian. That story might be informed by evidence of various kinds, but the evidence will have been sought and discovered because a story needed to be backed up by evidence: it is always that way round. Yes, of course, the shape of the story might to some extent be the result of evidence previously discovered: but that evidence too will have been sought and discovered on the basis of an existing set of questions – and behind every question there is an agenda. This is all at least as true of economic history as it is of any other kind. So for the rest of this chapter we shall be looking for the same method: the telling of a story, and the seeking of evidence for it.

HISTORIES OF CITIZEN'S BASIC INCOME

What kind of history would a history of Citizen's Basic Income be? Citizen's Basic Income is an idea – it is an unconditional income paid to every individual: so we should expect a history of Citizen's Basic Income to be the history of an idea. However, as we have seen, the further back in history we go, the more difficult it will be to decide whether what an author's text is referring to is what we might mean today by a Citizen's Basic Income. And would we regard the story that emerged from our history-writing to belong in the category 'economic history'? Yes, with economic history understood as a history of economic ideas. But it would also be a philosophical history and a social history.

Because today Citizen's Basic Income is the subject of policy debates, policy actions, pilot projects, and the like, a history of Citizen's Basic Income will be a policy history and a political history, and the economic history of Citizen's Basic Income will be as much a history of economic policy change as it is a history of an idea.

These two strands – the history of an idea, and the history of policy actions – will of course overlap, because ideas and practical policy action constantly interact, so although one history of Citizen's Basic Income might be more a history of ideas, and another more a history of practice, they will both be both. We should therefore expect any history of Citizen's Basic Income to be a complex multidisciplinary history.

In order to study the methods employed by a number of historians of Citizen's Basic Income, we shall attempt to answer a series of questions in relation to a number of different histories. Three questions are inspired by our study of history-writing:

1. Is the history of Citizen's Basic Income a subdiscipline of history, or a sub-discipline of social history, or a subdiscipline of economic history? This can be two separate questions: (a) How *should* we think of the history of Citizen's Basic Income in relation to these other disciplines, and (b) how *do* historians understand those relationships? I shall ask the latter question before tackling the former.
2. What are the agendas that historians of Citizen's Basic Income bring to their work?
3. What are the data that historians of Citizen's Basic Income seek as evidence to back up their arguments?

Two further questions, not raised by our previous discussion on how history is made, are nevertheless important in the context of the history of Citizen's Basic Income:

4. To what extent should a history of Citizen's Basic Income be the history of the idea of a regular unconditional income for every individual, to what extent should it be a history of policy debates, and to what extent should it be a history of Citizen's Basic Incomes being paid or trialled?
5. To what extent should the history of Citizen's Basic Income be told in the context of the history of existing tax and benefits systems – that is, as a subdiscipline of that historical subdiscipline – and to what extent should it be regarded as a subdiscipline in its own right?

And Chapter 2 on the language of Citizen's Basic Income requires us to add one further question:

6. To what extent should historians of Citizen's Basic Income restrict themselves to studying the history of the idea of regular and unconditional incomes for every individual, and of implementations of that idea, and to what extent should they include such close and less close cousins as Negative Income Tax and Minimum Income Guarantee?

I shall now study a number of histories of Citizen's Basic Income and ask how those histories suggest that their writers would answer those questions. I shall begin with Peter Sloman's study of the history of Citizen's Basic Income in the UK, as this will best enable us to locate the other histories that I shall discuss.

Peter Sloman's 'Five Waves of Enthusiasm' (Sloman, 2018)

In an article in the *Journal of Social Policy*, Sloman charts the history of Citizen's Basic Income in the UK over the past two hundred years, and he finds a pattern: five waves of enthusiasm, each one occurring at the same time as concern about the future of employment was increasing.

The story begins at the end of the eighteenth century with Thomas Paine (who suggested one-off payments to 21- and 50-year-olds, which constitutes Citizen's Basic Capital rather than Citizen's Basic Income) (Paine, [1796] 2004: 4–7; Prabhakar, 2018) and Thomas Spence (who suggested something closer to a Citizen's Basic Income) (King and Marangos, 2006; Spence, [1797] 2004: 87). The first wave of enthusiasm was then constituted by various proposals made between 1918 and 1939 to pay a dividend to all citizens, funded by government-created credit (the Social Credit movement), a tax on earned and unearned income (the State Bonus League), or the proceeds from national assets (James Meade) (Heydorn, 2016; Sloman, 2018). An important characteristic of waves is that in the open sea they can take a long time to merge: and so, in the case of Sloman's first wave, the use of 'dividend' language was not finally submerged until the mid-1980s (Van Trier, 2002). The second rather smaller wave consisted of Juliet Rhys Williams' 1943 proposal of a regular income that would have been a Citizen's Basic Income if it had not depended on evidence of job-search (Rhys Williams, 1943; Sloman, 2016): a condition that she later abandoned.

Citizen's Basic Income proposals were not entirely absent from Sloman's third wave, but mostly it consisted of a variety of proposals made between 1965 and 1974 that were for what we are calling 'cousins' of Citizen's Basic Income, and not for Citizen's Basic Income as it is normally defined. The proposals were for Minimum Income Guarantees (and thus for means-tested benefits), Negative Income Tax, and Tax Credits (real ones, which would have functioned in the same way as a Negative Income Tax).

Sloman dates the fourth wave of enthusiasm from Claimants' Union interest in the idea of Citizen's Basic Income during the early 1970s, and from a variety of individual writers taking an interest around the same time: but it was Juliet Rhys Williams' son Brandon Rhys Williams MP's submission of a proposal for a genuine Citizen's Basic Income to a House of Commons select committee in 1982 (a significant event not mentioned by Sloman) that might be a better starting point for this wave, because it was that event that more than anything else inspired a small group of diverse individuals to form the Basic Income Research Group (now the Citizen's Basic Income Trust) in 1984, and that stimulated debate among both Conservative and Liberal Members of Parliament. As Sloman suggests, this was a period during which individuals with political allegiances across a broad political spectrum found themselves working together to research and debate Citizen's Basic Income: but momentum slackened as first the Conservative Government, and then a new Labour Administration, committed themselves to means-tested benefits alongside 'active labour market' policies.

As Sloman suggests, it is difficult to date the beginning of the fifth wave of enthusiasm. From the early 2000s a number of developing countries experimented with cash transfers of various kinds, and Citizen's Basic Income pilot projects in Namibia and India cemented the connection between Citizen's Basic Income and a growing debate about the best way to defeat global poverty. Various other experiments have followed – some genuine Citizen's Basic Income experiments, others not: and Silicon Valley entrepreneurs getting involved has more firmly connected the debate with deepening concern about the future of employment. All of this, alongside the government's difficulty with the implementation of Universal Credit, and the availability of microsimulation tools to research feasible Citizen's Basic Income schemes, has stimulated debate in the UK and led to a particularly powerful fifth wave from about 2013 onwards. Sloman identifies as a particularly significant element of this fifth wave an increasing interest in Citizen's Basic Income on the Left of British politics: not something so obvious during the previous waves of interest.

Sloman concludes that waves of enthusiasm for Citizen's Basic Income have occurred during periods of uncertainty in relation to employment. There is certainly a correlation, though to what extent we can deduce causality must as always remain an open question. In relation to the current wave of enthusiasm, Sloman might well be right to suggest a causal effect: that a combination of concern about the possibility of rapid job loss due to new technology, and current experience of increasing fluidity, diversity, change and fragility in relation to people's experience of employment, might be a significant cause of the upturn in interest in Citizen's Basic Income since 2013.

In answer to the six questions:

1. Sloman's history of Citizen's Basic Income in the UK is political history, and so firmly within the historic mainstream of the discipline of history.
2. Sloman brings several agendas to his work. He is a career academic, so needs to publish papers, and the history of Citizen's Basic Income is a relatively unresearched field; and he has personal interests in history, politics, social policy, and Citizen's Basic Income in particular, so to research the political history of Citizen's Basic Income is an attractive task. Sloman identifies the centre-right as the political location of many of the main players in the UK Citizen's Basic Income debate; he argues that Juliet Rhys Williams' antipathy to socialism meant that she was unable to engage with the Labour Party and trades unions (Sloman, 2016: 215); and he recognizes in the final paragraph of his history that really for the first time the Left in British politics is now becoming seriously engaged with Citizen's Basic Income (Sloman, 2018). Whether all of this reveals a personal political agenda must remain an open question.
3. The data that Sloman has employed is the now considerable literature on Citizen's Basic Income, along with archive material and interviews with individuals who have been involved in the debate in the UK during the past thirty-five years.
4. Sloman's history is a history of ideas. Namibian, Indian and Finnish experiments are mentioned, but not Alaska or Iran's accidental implementation of something close to a Citizen's Basic Income; and the experiments are discussed because they have fuelled the debate in the UK, not because they are of interest in their own right.
5. Citizen's Basic Income is the clear focus for Sloman's 'five waves' history, as it should be. Other aspects of the debate that relate in some way to that history are carefully described (for instance, the Beveridge Report, and the Tax Credit proposals of the early 1970s), and relevant trends in contemporary discussion of social security are discussed: but the history is not explicitly located within the broad context of British social security history. This is understandable, as to describe the history of social security in the UK during the past two hundred years before locating the history of Citizen's Basic Income within that context would have required greater length than a journal article would have permitted.
6. On the second page of his history Sloman is clear about the definition of Citizen's Basic Income, but he frequently mentions both close and distant

cousins of Citizen's Basic Income, and during his third wave of enthusiasm they take centre stage.

This raises the question as to what extent a history of Citizen's Basic Income should also be a history of cousins of Citizen's Basic Income. Perhaps we should construct a spectrum, with a regular unconditional income for every individual at one end, and means-tested benefits at the other. We could then arrange policy proposals along the spectrum in relation to their characteristics, and identify a cut-off point, which would of course constitute a somewhat arbitrary choice. Everything to the Citizen's Basic Income side of the cut-off point would be included in the history, and everything to the other side would not be. But this just proves the point: once we stray from a strict definition for Citizen's Basic Income, deciding what goes into the history would be a somewhat arbitrary decision. It might be better to write a history of Citizen's Basic Income, properly understood, and only mention such mechanisms as Negative Income Tax when policy activity in relation to them can be shown to have had a direct impact on the Citizen's Basic Income debate either at the time or subsequently. Whatever decision is taken, what matters is clear definition of the terms used, along with a recognition that the same phrase might mean different things in different places and at different times.

This is in fact the policy that Sloman appears to have followed. The various suggestions made, projects organized, and campaigns held during the third wave do appear to have had a significant impact on subsequent debate on Citizen's Basic Income (– a position also taken by Yannick Vanderborght (2017) in a brief history of Citizen's Basic Income). This suggests that these income maintenance provisions can legitimately be placed in a third wave of support for the idea of a Citizen's Basic Income, and in the context of a history of Citizen's Basic Income more generally.

Walter Van Trier's 'Three Sets of Writings' (Van Trier, 1995: 3)

Van Trier's published doctoral thesis, *Every One a King*, is a study of three particular 'sets of writings': by the founders of the State Bonus League, by those involved in the social credit movement, and by James Meade and his colleagues: the first two sets from the early years of the twentieth century, and the third from mid-century. Rather than employing the image of successive waves, Van Trier describes the situation in terms of Lewis Carroll's Cheshire Cat, that was 'able to suddenly emerge on the scene and to disappear part by part, leaving only the mark of its broad grin before fading away completely' (Van Trier, 1995: 19). He draws a significant conclusion:

> At particular times in history, someone discovers this attractive and simple idea of paying everyone unconditionally a cash sum of money. Apparently without knowing that, prior to his, older similar proposals existed, he presents his idea to the wider public and explains the good things that could spring from it. The professionals and politicians scrutinize the idea and find wanting some of its major characteristics, cutting it loose from the view that it could appear simple or even unequivocally attractive – except to its dedicated followers. Finally, the idea fades away, leaving only the slightest of marks on the policy process. Until, at another particular time in history, another person discovers this attractive and simple idea of paying everyone unconditionally a cash sum of money. Apparently without knowing that, prior to his, older similar proposals existed, he presents ... etc., etc.
>
> ... the problem is not only particularly intriguing but also fundamentally troubling (and not only for basic income advocates) because the message can be given two completely contradictory meanings. The 'eternal return' element could be seen as indicating a deep rooted link between basic incomes and the present (post)modern or (post)industrial human condition. Thus, it may signal the promise of a prosperous future full of basic income proposals. The 'inevitable downfall' element may be seen as suggesting that under the present (post)modern or (post)industrial human condition its implementation proves ultimately impossible. Thus, it may signal a future full of disillusioning experiences. (Van Trier, 1995: 19)

Turning to our six questions:

1. Van Trier's *Every One a King* might best be described as economic biography. It is focused on a small number of individuals, the ideas that they discussed, and the institutions that they founded. To some extent it is social and economic history, but still economic biography is the best description: a description that might suggest that we should extend our list of historical subdisciplines to include biography, and also that we should decide that biography is an important subdiscipline of the subdiscipline of Citizen's Basic Income history.
2. Important clues to the agendas that Van Trier brought to his work can be found in the third section of the thesis' epilogue. He 'constructs Basic Income's identity' in two different ways: as a social movement, and as an economic research programme. Van Trier was at the time firmly embedded in the social movement that had the concept of a Citizen's Basic Income at its heart, and his doctoral thesis on the subject served both his personal interest in the subject and his future academic career: a combination of factors that must have constituted a personally integrating experience.
3. There was a lot less secondary literature available to Van Trier than there was to Sloman, so Van Trier's only option was to employ primary liter-

ature and interviews. The thesis bears witness to a vast amount of data having been collected.

4. This history is a history of ideas. The Alaska Permanent Fund had already been established and was paying dividends, and in his prologue Van Trier regrets the fact that the dividend's unconditionality had been an accident and not connected with previous debate about Citizen's Basic Income (Van Trier, 1995: 2). It is of interest that the UK's unconditional Family Allowance, and its unconditional successor Child Benefit – which were argued for, by Beveridge as well as by others, partly on the basis of their unconditionality – are not even mentioned in the prologue. To have employed Family Allowance and Child Benefit as the focus of the prologue would have enabled the idea and the practice of unconditionality to be connected at the beginning of the thesis, whereas the separation between ideas and practical policy exemplified by Van Trier's history of the Alaska dividend is maintained throughout the thesis.

5. The thesis is essentially a discussion of economic ideas, with the social security context playing only an occasional walk-on part. This is as true of the UK's unconditional Family Allowance as it is of other social security policies of the times.

6. The first part of the thesis is a very thorough discussion of the definition of Citizen's Basic Income, and where the thesis discusses close or distant cousins Van Trier is generally clear about the differences between those cousins and Citizen's Basic Income. Again, it is of interest that Family Allowance does not play a significant role in these discussions.

Karl Widerquist's 'Three Waves of Support' (Widerquist, 2017a)

Karl Widerquist employs the same image of waves as Peter Sloman, but in a more international context. For Widerquist, the first wave is the same as Sloman's first wave of enthusiasm in the UK: individuals' proposals for unconditional incomes paid for out of government money creation or the profits of nationalized industries: but he extends the wave to include James Meade's theoretical work and the social credit movement's brief and some-what unproductive political success in Alberta, Canada.

Widerquist's second wave of support is located in the US and Canada, and is constituted by a variety of individuals' and groups' proposals for a variety of different policy reforms: Citizen's Basic Income, Minimum Income Guarantees, and Negative Income Tax. Widerquist credits this second wave with stimulating a number of experiments in the US and Canada: but these were Minimum Income Guarantee trials, and not Citizen's Basic Income trials; and also with inspiring the Alaska Permanent Fund Dividend and the US Earned Income Tax Credit: a version of a Minimum Income Guarantee for households with members in employment. As with Sloman's third wave, this second wave might best be described as a diversion around Citizen's Basic Income between two waves of support for it.

Following what he calls the second wave, Widerquist identifies a fallow period in which the Citizen's Basic Income idea disappeared from mainstream political debate but was taken up by a number of academics and other authors, leading to the establishment of the Basic Income European Network (BIEN: now the Basic Income Earth Network) in 1986.

Widerquist dates the third wave of support from the Citizen's Basic Income pilot project in Namibia, first proposed at the BIEN congress in South Africa in 2006. The first International Basic Income Week was held in 2008, and 2010 saw a large pilot project in India, a campaign for a referendum in Switzerland, and the European Citizens' Initiative petition across Europe. The third wave is now characterized by increasing media interest around the world, and a growing number of experiments and promises of further experiments. Widerquist is correct to identify both the global nature of the debate and the growing number of vigorous attacks on Citizen's Basic Income as significant characteristics of the current wave of support; to recognize that the research and debate that continued between the second and third waves has contributed to the strength of the third wave; and to understand that continuing concern about growing inequality, increasing recognition of the deficiencies of a conditional social security system, and anxieties about the future of employment, might continue to strengthen the third wave.

In response to our six questions:

1. Widerquist's history is a mixture of political, social, and economic history, with the social history taking centre stage as he discusses the importance of social movements and of citizens' and voluntary organizations' initiatives in the third wave of support.
2. Widerquist is an academic, and his books and articles about Citizen's Basic Income and related subjects have constituted a significant aspect of his career, as has his involvement with BIEN, of which he was Co-chair and then Vice-chair from 2008 to 2018. He is also heavily committed personally to the idea of Citizen's Basic Income as a means of enhancing 'republican freedom': the freedom not to be dominated (Birnbaum, 2019; Widerquist, 2013).
3. Widerquist employs both primary and secondary literature to write his history.
4. Pilot projects, other experiments, and other practical activity, such as petitions and referenda, have a more significant place in Widerquist's history than in Sloman's, and he is happy operating across the entire spectrum

from the very practical to the most abstract political and philosophical ideas.

5. Only those aspects of the tax and benefits contexts that have direct relevance to the history that Widerquist wants to tell get a mention. This is inevitable as Widerquist operates across a global context as opposed to Van Trier's and Sloman's single country focuses.

6. Widerquist locates Citizen's Basic Income as one kind of Basic Income Guarantee (BIG), and he suggests that Negative Income Tax is another kind. While he is sometimes clear that for him Basic Income Guarantee is a broader category than Citizen's Basic Income, it is somewhat confusing to use a term that includes the word pair 'Basic Income' to describe a category of policy proposals that includes policies that are not Citizen's Basic Incomes. As with Sloman's history, one of the waves of support is constituted more by proposals that are not Citizen's Basic Incomes than by proposals that are.

Van Parijs and Vanderborght: A Philosophical History (Van Parijs and Vanderborght, 2017: 51–98)

In their book *Basic Income: A radical proposal for a free society and a sane economy*, Philippe Van Parijs and Yannick Vanderborght offer two historical chapters: a 'prehistory', that relates the history of public assistance and social insurance, and a 'history'. This begins with Thomas Paine and Thomas Spence; adds a section on Joseph Charlier, who in 1848 made the first known proposal for a national Citizen's Basic Income; discusses other nineteenth-century individuals who proposed either a Minimum Income Guarantee or a Citizen's Basic Income; offers more detail on Bertrand Russell's Citizen's Basic Income proposal than do the other histories that we have studied; and then follows the same route as other histories through the State Bonus League and social credit to James Meade and Juliet Rhys Williams. A detour through US Minimum Income Guarantee and Negative Income Tax proposals during the 1960s takes us to Senator George McGovern's proposal for a 'demogrant': an annual Citizen's Basic Income. Along the way we encounter the two editions of J.K. Galbraith's *The Affluent Society* – on which see below. Van Parijs and Vanderborght traverse territory familiar to Sloman and Van Trier during their treatment of the 1970s: Minimum Income Guarantee experiments in Canada and the US, and the Alaska Permanent Fund Dividend; they find a number of authors and organizations advocating a genuine Citizen's Basic Income during the 1970s; and they then recount the founding of both the Basic Income Research Group in the UK in 1984 and BIEN in 1986.

In relation to the six questions:

1. This is philosophical history, with elements of political, social and economic history attached.
2. The authors are career academics. One of them is nearing retirement and probably has an eye to his legacy, and so wanted to publish a summary statement to represent the vast proportion of his life that he has dedicated to the Citizen's Basic Income debate; and the other still has an academic career to nurture, for which the book will no doubt be important. Philippe Van Parijs is a philosopher for whom the concept of 'real freedom' is pivotal, and Yannick Vanderborght teaches sociology, ethics, economics, and politics. All of the authors' interests are represented in the book.
3. The data employed is almost entirely primary and secondary literature, but in Van Parijs' case in particular much personal knowledge has found its way into the book.
4. The historical sections of the book are almost entirely histories of ideas, and those ideas are more philosophical than in the other histories that we have discussed. We find pilot projects and other experiments discussed elsewhere in the book, but they are not permitted near to the history sections.
5. The authors have provided an entire previous chapter on the history of social security as a context of the history of Citizen's Basic Income.
6. Another previous chapter defines Citizen's Basic Income and also discusses the characteristics of some of its 'cousins'. Negative Income Tax is studied, as is the US's Earned Income Tax Credit. The latter has some similarities to a Minimum Income Guarantee (or minimum income scheme), but is not one. Early in the book, 'minimum income schemes' are carefully compared to Citizen's Basic Income, but by the time we get to the history chapter, various writers' treatments of Citizen's Basic Income and Minimum Income Guarantee schemes are often discussed within the same section without these very different mechanisms being carefully distinguished from each other. The most acute case of this problem can be found in the discussion of J.K. Galbraith's proposals, which are vague in the extreme. What exactly does Galbraith mean by 'a basic source of income', by 'the provision of a regular source of income to the poor', by 'for those who are unemployable ... the immediate solution is a source of income unrelated to production', and by 'provision of a basic income as a matter of general right and related in amount to family size but not otherwise to need'? (Galbraith, 1969: 264, 243). Citizen's Basic Income? Minimum Income Guarantee? The question is not raised.

A Highly Selective History (Torry, 2013: 17–47, 65–80)

In his *Money for Everyone* (Torry, 2013) this author wrote a highly selective history across three chapters: the first historical chapter is a history of means-testing in the UK, and of the non-means-tested Family Allowance and its successor Child Benefit; and the second is an account of the UK's 1970s Tax Credit proposals, a brief summary of some of the early history of Citizen's Basic Income, a longer discussion of both Juliet Rhys Williams' and Brandon Rhys Williams' attempts to get the idea taken seriously, and an account of the Pensions Minister Steven Webb's navigation of the UK's Single Tier State Pension from idea to implementation, the result of which will be that the UK will find itself with something like an unconditional pension (Torry, 2013: 17–42). A later chapter recounts practical activity elsewhere in the world: the Alaska Permanent Fund Dividend; something like a Citizen's Basic Income in Iran; pilot projects in Namibia and India; and cash transfers in South America (Torry, 2013: 65–80).

The six questions:

1. The three historical chapters contain a somewhat untidy mixture of political and economic history.
2. Each of the three historical chapters has a distinct and stated agenda. The first historical chapter recounts the histories of means-tested benefits, of Family Allowance, and of Child Benefit, in order to reveal the complexity and inappropriateness of much of the UK's current tax and benefits structure, and to set the stage for the rest of the book. A second historical chapter is about the UK's 1970s Tax Credit proposal, the history of Citizen's Basic Income in the UK, and the Single Tier State Pension, and it addresses the question: Why do some policy reform proposals succeed, and others fail? The later historical chapter, on Alaska, Iran, pilot projects, and cash transfers, is designed to ask whether a pilot project could be conducted in the UK.
3. The data was primary and secondary literature, archive material, and the author's long experience of the Citizen's Basic Income debate in the UK.
4. The history is mainly an account of activity: of what people and institutions have done, of policies planned and implemented, of policies planned and not implemented, and of projects undertaken.
5. The history of Citizen's Basic Income in the UK is firmly located in the context of the development of the UK's tax and benefits systems.
6. A long section on terminology at the beginning of the book defines a variety of terms, and in particular Citizen's Basic Income, Negative Income Tax, and means-tested benefits. The book is always clear as to whether what

is being discussed is a Citizen's Basic Income, and the concept is never confused with means-tested benefits or with Negative Income Tax. In the British context, Minimum Income Guarantee was once the name of a means-tested benefit for pensioners, so the book avoids using the word 'guarantee'.

The second historical chapter had a clear purpose: to discover the conditions under which policy change can occur. Three conclusions were reached. The proposals that have changed the system

- have been for identifiable groups of people;
- have benefited from longstanding and widespread debate and a reasonable level of public understanding of what was intended (although more recent experience in the UK suggests that public understanding and debate are no longer prerequisites for the implementation of changes to the benefits system (Torry, 2013: 45));
- and are those that did not reduce the number of civil servants, whereas those that would have done so have not progressed through the policy process (Torry, 2013: 42–6).

Additional Histories

Two further quite short histories might have been included. Guy Standing, in his *Basic Income: And how we can make it happen*, offers a short 'waves' story, with the four waves somewhat differently organized to Widerquist's 'three waves' and Sloman's 'five waves' versions. Some of the questions that we have asked might have been answered in ways similar to the ways in which we have answered them for Sloman and Widerquist, except that a social justice agenda is clearly visible in Standing's history, and particularly a social justice agenda focused on the plight of the growing precariat (Standing, 2017a: 9–18).

In her *A Basic Income Handbook* Annie Miller includes a chronology in an appendix (Miller, 2017: 261–8). The unique aspect is mention of Quaker engagement with Citizen's Basic Income and related debates. The agenda behind the chronology might be as Miller herself suggests in her own discussion of the appendix: 'Readers may notice that I like lists' (Miller, 2017: 27).

A final history that might have been included is Timothée Duverger's *L'Invention du Revenu de Base: La fabrique d'une utopie démocratique* (Duverger, 2018). The book is rather short of references, but it appears to have relied on secondary literature for the parts of the history that it mentions, and on primary research and the author's involvement in the situation for the large sections of the book on the Citizen's Basic Income debate in France.

CONCLUSIONS

We can draw a number of conclusions in relation to the answers that we have given to the questions that we have put to each of the histories that we have studied:

1. Historians of Citizen's Basic Income employ a variety of the history sub-disciplines – political history, economic history, social history, philosophical history, and biography.
2. They bring a variety of agendas to their history-writing: academic agendas, philosophical agendas, social policy agendas, and political agendas. Historians of Citizen's Basic Income are to a greater or lesser extent committed to the Citizen's Basic Income proposal and to the social movement that has gathered around it, and such commitments generate significant agendas as they write their histories of Citizen's Basic Income.
3. A wide variety of different data are employed – primary and secondary literature, archive material, interviews, and personal experience – in different proportions, depending on their availability and on the agenda to be pursued.
4. Each history can be located somewhere along an ideas/practice spectrum. A history might be a history of ideas; it might be a history of events; or it might contain elements of both. The agenda pursued by the historian will generally determine where their history lands on the spectrum.
5. A similar spectrum can be drawn between an author providing a history of a country's benefits systems as a context of the Citizen's Basic Income debate and telling the story of Citizen's Basic Income with very little reference to the benefits context: but this particular spectrum is far from simple, because at the 'describes the context' end the author might locate the contextual history either within their history of Citizen's Basic Income or as a preamble to it. Where the context is debated within the history of Citizen's Basic Income itself, those parts of the context most relevant to the particular aspects of Citizen's Basic Income's history that the author wishes to discuss might be emphasized, whereas where the contextual history is located in a separate chapter, the history of the benefits system might be more general and less connected to the agenda of the Citizen's Basic Income history chapter.

   I say 'benefits system' here advisedly. We find discussion of the histories of means-tested benefits, social insurance benefits, and unconditional benefits, but rarely any mention of tax systems, except occasionally in relation to such cousins of Citizen's Basic Income as Negative Income Tax or the US Earned Income Tax Credit. This is all part of a trend. In the UK, the Mirrlees review of the tax system took no notice of the benefits system, even though for many households the benefits system is more relevant to domestic budgets than the tax system (Adam et al., 2010; 2011); and whereas study of the benefits system is frequently regarded as a proper subdiscipline of social policy, study of the tax system might not be.

Unconditional and therefore universal public services other than unconditional benefits tend not to be mentioned. This is probably as it should be, as the unconditionalities related to different public provisions might well be different: for instance, the unconditionality related to the UK's National Health Service is an unconditional free access at the point of need, whereas Child Benefit is, and Citizen's Basic Income would be, unconditional equal provision (Torry, 2017c).

As with our previous responses, the author's agenda might determine how much of the benefits system context is described, which parts of it are described and how, and where that description is located.

6. Some authors are clearer than others about the definition of Citizen's Basic Income, and some are more careful than others to use terms consistently and in accordance with normal usage. All of the authors find themselves discussing alternatives to Citizen's Basic Income, and some authors are better than others at distinguishing the alternatives both from Citizen's Basic Income and from each other. A particular problem relates to the way in which Citizen's Basic Income and Minimum Income Guarantee (with its accompanying means-tested benefits) are not always sufficiently distinguished from each other. The ways in which authors do or do not distinguish between Citizen's Basic Income and its various cousins might be determined by authors' agendas, with authors with clearer social policy agendas being most careful about definitions and distinctions.

We might also draw a number of further conclusions:

a. Each of the authors that we have studied has in mind some agenda-driven pattern as they write their history, and such patterns, as well as the agendas, will have determined to some extent what is researched and written. So, for instance, a 'several waves' structure – like the one through which historians of feminism understand its evolution (Tjitske, 1994) – can lead authors to fill chronological gaps with material that in fact has little connection with Citizen's Basic Income; a more philosophical author who patterns their history around the perceived progress of an idea might broaden the definition of the idea in order to find the desired progress; an episodic 'sets of writings' pattern might fail to grasp the continuities that have characterized the Citizen's Basic Income debate; and a social policy agenda might encourage the author to structure their history around a conflict between means-testing and Citizen's Basic Income, and that pattern might make it difficult to understand that means-testing and Citizen's Basic Income might in practice complement each other.

b. Apart from Duverger's recent history of Citizen's Basic Income in French and from a French point of view (Duverger, 2018), the only histories so far are chapters in books and articles in journals, their contents frequently overlap, and when we put them all together we have to recognize that all that they offer is a series of snapshots. This suggests at least one reason for there being no comprehensive full-length history of Citizen's Basic Income: that we know quite a lot about a small number of contexts, periods, events, and sets of literature, because those have been researched, but that we know very little about Citizen's Basic Income debate that has taken place in a lot of other contexts, and over long periods of time. A huge research effort would be required before anything like a comprehensive history of Citizen's Basic Income could be written (Van Trier, 2017). If someone were to be brave enough to do the research and to set out to write a comprehensive history: what agendas would they bring to the task; what patterns would they impose on the history; what kinds of history should it be; to what extent would they describe the social, economic, and social policy contexts; to what extent would they record academic debate and literature, and to what extent events; and to what extent would they include Citizen's Basic Income's many cousins in the history? As we have seen, the answers to many of those questions would depend on the answer to the first: the question of agenda – for on the answer to that question will depend the search for data, and then the data will alter the agenda, and so on.

c. To answer a question asked at the beginning of this chapter: The discipline of history contributes to the Citizen's Basic Income debate an understanding of the agenda-driven nature of any and every history of Citizen's Basic Income, and therefore of the agenda-driven nature of the movement's own self-understanding. In the other direction: the history of Citizen's Basic Income might offer to the discipline of history a useful case study on the agenda-driven nature of history, and a reminder, if ever we need one, of the inadequacy of any and every history.

4.   The ethics of Citizen's Basic Income

Ethics: The branch of knowledge or study dealing with moral principles.
(Oxford English Dictionary)

INTRODUCTION

Are moral philosophy and ethics the same discipline? Bernard Williams distinguishes between the two, with moral theory focusing on the notion of obligation, and ethics having a broader remit (Williams, 1985: 182, 196). However, as the definition above from the Oxford English Dictionary suggests, we might be justified in connecting them sufficiently closely that for the purposes of this chapter we can regard the questions 'Is Citizen's Basic Income moral?' and 'Is Citizen's Basic Income ethical?' as being identical. Given that all tax and benefits policy is value-driven, at least to some extent, and is therefore a moral issue (Spicker, 2014: 182–3), this is an important question to answer.

Ethics is a discipline as broad as many of those tackled in this book. It encompasses the history of ethics, ethical theories, and consideration of capacious and contested concepts such as justice; and it tackles in a highly detailed way many of the issues facing our society, such as abortion, euthanasia, sexual morality, pornography, censorship, hate speech, sexism, racism, oppression, affirmative action, economic justice, world hunger, global justice, animals, and the environment (Mappes and Zembaty, 1997). Many of the issues that we might expect to find discussed by sociologists, social psychologists, and political economists, will have significant ethical aspects.

In this chapter I shall take an approach often taken elsewhere in this book and will tackle aspects of the relationship between ethics and Citizen's Basic Income that would be less likely to be found discussed in other chapters. This constraint suggests that the subjects that I should tackle here should be ethical theories, and the concepts of freedom, justice, and reciprocity. A multiplicity of guides will be employed as guides to these subjects.

ETHICAL THEORIES

Behind any response to the question 'Is it ethical?' will lie some kind of ethical theory: perhaps consequentialist (– are the consequences of the action good?), deontological (– is the action good in itself?), foundationalist (– does the action follow a given axiom?), Aristotelian (– does the action promote wellbeing and happiness, particularly in the person doing it?), or virtue ethics (– does the action stem from a virtuous character?). An institution is a set of connected actions, so we can ask of an institution: Is it ethical? – and behind any verdict that we might offer will lie an ethical theory, or perhaps several of them.

In this section of the chapter I shall ask whether a Citizen's Basic Income would be ethical, and in order to attempt an answer I shall discuss the ways in which a number of ethical theories might understand an unconditional income.

Actions Good in Themselves

My action is good in itself (a deontological ethical position) if it conforms to a 'categorical imperative', that is, an experienced imperative that I cannot help regarding as a universal law. So for instance: I do not lie because I cannot help regarding it as a universal law that people should not lie. I would not want someone to lie to me, and our society would be a most unpleasant place in which to live if we thought it right to lie. It is wrong for me to lie because I cannot help regarding lying as universally wrong. As Kant puts the condition for ethicality: 'I ought never to act in such a way that I could not also will that my maxim should become a universal law.' So the only question to be asked is this: 'Can you will that your maxim should become a universal law?' (Kant, [1785] 2002: 202–3).

The argument breaks down, of course, because there might be occasions on which I might want someone to lie to me; there might be occasions when I could not help thinking it right for someone to lie to someone else; and in a particular situation I might experience a categorical imperative to lie. Donegan offers an alternative phrasing that does not break down so quickly: 'Act so that the fundamental human goods, whether in your own person or in that of another, are promoted as may be possible and under no circumstances violated' (Donagan, 1977: 61). However, in relation to both phrasings of the idea, the 'categorical imperative' does not by itself offer rules for ethical behaviour. In fact, it offers nothing specific. If we experience a decision as one that we can feel to be based on an inner law that is in principle universalizable, or that we know will benefit another individual, then we know that we have obeyed a categorical imperative: but before the act, we could not have known that we would be able to make that decision about our action. In any case, Kant's categorical imperative relates to an individual's behaviour, and Donagan's to a relationship between two individuals, whereas what we need to discuss here is institutional activity, and, in particular, social policy.

A variant of the process of universalizing a positive imperative is Scanlon's suggestion that

> an act is wrong if its performance under the circumstances would be disallowed by any system of rules for the general regulation of behaviour which no-one could reasonably reject as a basis for informed, unforced general agreement. (Scanlon, 1982: 110)

As Scanlon points out, 'many non-equivalent sets of principles will pass the test of non-rejectability' (Scanlon, 1982: 112), because it allows for principles that we find to be nonuniveralizable. And the theory is intuitive, as we do in fact try to justify our actions on grounds that we hope others will not be able to reject. So

> individual well-being will be morally significant, ... not because it is intrinsically valuable or because promoting it is self-evidently a right-making characteristic, but simply because an individual could reasonably reject a form of argument that gave his well-being no weight. (Scanlon, 1982: 119)

Scanlon's morality is 'a device for our mutual protection' (Scanlon, 1982: 128), rather than one for mutual benefit.

> The desire for protection is an important factor determining the content of morality because it determines what can reasonably be agreed to. But the idea of general agreement does not arise as a means of securing protection. It is in a more fundamental sense what morality is about. (Scanlon, 1982: 128)

Such a 'negative' version of 'acts good in themselves', which generates rules that it would be difficult to object to, provides a clear basis for arguing that Citizen's Basic Income would be an ethical social policy. Because it would be entirely secure, it would be quintessential protection. It is certainly true that numerous individuals object to the idea of a Citizen's Basic Income, but once it was in place it would be a lot more difficult to object to it, because abolition would tip many of those households who had escaped from other problematic benefits systems back onto them.

Returning to the positive version of 'acts good in themselves', let us take it on its own terms and ask what it might have to offer to a debate on income maintenance, and in particular to a consideration of the questions as to whether we would want to live in a society in which everyone received an equal foundational income, and as to whether we would want to live in one in which, if we found ourselves in a relatively impoverished situation, we might be able to improve our financial position. Both could be regarded as a rational choice. We would therefore wish to live in a society in which additional earned income was withdrawn only slowly, or not at all, and in which everyone had an equal foundational income to live on. We would be unlikely to wish to live in a society in which additional earned income was withdrawn through a stigmatizing means test, in which we might be subject to sanctions-infested work tests, and in which we could not be sure that our basic needs would be met. It therefore rather looks as if Immanuel Kant's ethical theory would have led him to think seriously about an income maintenance system based on an unconditional income if he had lived in today's society.

Actions Good in Relation to Good Outcomes

A very different ethical tradition, consequentialism, counts actions to be good if their consequences are beneficial: although perhaps rather than seeing this tradition as being radically different from deontological ethical theory, we ought to see it as a particular example of deontological ethics, because at the heart of such a consequentialist ethical theory lies a single obligation: to pursue the best consequences somehow defined.

The particular version of consequentialism that I shall study here is John Stuart Mill's 'utilitarianism', which seeks the greatest happiness of the greatest number, and which takes as evidence for the desirability of any state of affairs the fact that people desire it. 'Actions are right in proportion as they tend to promote happiness. By happiness is intended pleasure, and the absence of pain' (Mill, [1861] 1993: 7). As Schneewind puts it:

> It cannot be the case that some factual property of acts makes them right, and that this entails that doing them must maximize goodness. It must rather be the case that bringing about the most good is what makes right acts right. ... the utilitarian principle is that the conduct which is objectively right is that which will produce the greater amount of happiness on the whole. (Schneewind, 1977: 308, 327)

Underlying utilitarianism are three main assumptions: that we can know what makes other people happy; that we can know the levels of happiness that other people experience; and that we can know the consequences of our actions. Quite apart from our difficulty in defining what we mean by 'happiness' (Hare, 1963: 119–21), the first and second assumptions are well demolished by Richard Hare when he suggests that not only can we not know the objects of others' desires, but also that we cannot know the intensity of those desires (Hare, 1963: 119–21); and, in a similar vein, by Bernard Williams, when he writes that utilitarianism has 'too few thoughts and feelings to match the world as it really is' (Smart and Williams, 1973: 149). The theory also suffers from the objection that we would not be able to decide whether a considerable increase in happiness for just one individual should be counted as more significant than slight increases in happiness for many. As for the third assumption:

while it might be true that we cannot work out all of the consequences of possible actions before we have to decide what to do, Mill recommends a practical approach and suggests that we have learnt 'by experience the tendencies of actions' (Mill, [1861] 1993: 24) and that we can develop that knowledge of tendencies into 'rules of morality' (Mill, [1861] 1993: 25). Hare systematizes these suggestions when he distinguishes between 'act utilitarianism' and 'rule utilitarianism'. The former refers to the outcome of a rational process applied to a particular situation in order to discover the course of action that would promote the greatest happiness of the greatest number. The latter consists of principles or rules constructed on the basis of multiple examples of act utilitarianism (Hare, 1963: 130–6; 1981: 43). Any society needs a set of rules, and individuals, households, and other associations, similarly; and to develop a set of rules that might promote the greatest happiness of the greatest number is bound to be regarded as an ethical approach. However, we can rarely tell beforehand what the consequences of our individual actions will be, and we can predict with even less accuracy what the long-run complex consequences of institutional activity, or of the rules that we might make, might be. The point is well put in a sermon by a former Vice-Chancellor of the University of Cambridge:

> What we actually achieve is never wholly in our power to determine; it is influenced, in all manner of ways and degrees, by factors beyond our control. But the methods we use in pursuing our purposes are largely within our own power to choose and to determine. For what results from our actions we are only partly responsible; but for the means we decide to employ we carry the responsibility on our own shoulders. Again, the future ... we can never clearly or certainly foresee, still less determine; but the methods we choose to use in seeking to mould the future are our own choice. These we can determine. And by these, very largely, we make or mar the world, and ourselves. (Boys Smith, 2003: 277)

It will clearly be difficult for a consequentialist outlook to enable us to choose actions that we can reasonably believe to be ethical, so maybe we shall have to be content with trying to avoid actions that we might decide to be unethical. We and our institutions do in fact function with what I would call a 'negative consequentialism': that is, we would regard an individual or an institution as acting unethically if they knew that their actions might result in greater unhappiness. A strong version of negative consequentialism would regard as unethical any set of actions that would cause any one person greater unhappiness; a weaker version would regard as unethical any set of actions that would cause additional misery for the least happy members of a society. A 'rule negative utilitarianism' would therefore regard as potentially ethical any set of institutional activities that did not decrease the welfare of the least well off in society.

There are several respects in which means-tested benefits decrease the welfare of the least well off in society. They make it difficult for households on low earned incomes to earn their way out of poverty; and they impose complex dilemmas on poorer households, and acute dilemmas for households with fragile and diverse employment patterns. For instance: if someone is on means-tested out-of-work benefits and they are occasionally employed for a few hours a week, should they declare the additional earnings? To declare them would subject their household to weeks of income uncertainty and to hours coping with administrative complexity: not to declare them is illegal and might result in worse consequences. The rules can also make it financially advantageous for the parents of children to live apart. A 'negative consequentialist' criterion for ethical action would suggest that it is unethical to means-test benefits. None of these problems apply to people not on means-tested benefits. To misquote John Rawls, means-tested benefits could legitimately be termed 'injustice as unfairness'.

None of these problems apply to the UK's Child Benefit. Child Benefit is not withdrawn as earnings rise (– there might now be an additional tax charge, but that is a different matter); it does not change if employment status changes; and it does not encourage parents to live apart. A Citizen's Basic Income would behave in much the same way as Child Benefit. A Citizen's Basic Income would not be withdrawn as earnings rose; it would not change if employment status changed; and it would not encourage the parents of children to live apart. Child Benefit is not unethical. A Citizen's Basic Income would not be unethical. By the same argument, any universal benefit would be more ethical than means-tested benefits.

Interestingly, a critique of utilitarianism suggests a positive argument *for* Citizen's Basic Income. Because it is impossible to compare one person's desires with another, that desires can be mistaken, that moral systems have a variety of psychological roots, that it is generally impossible to know what the outcomes of actions will be, and that we invent and support moral codes for pragmatic reasons (Brandt, 1979), the default position ought to be an equal distribution of resources to every individual. Scheffler comes to a different conclusion, and asks for an ethical system in which 'the lower a person's level of relative well-being is, the greater the weight that is given to benefiting him' (Scheffler, 1994: 31). Needless to say, a Citizen's Basic Income would provide a level of equal distribution: and because a revenue neutral system that redistributed slightly from rich to poor could on average increase the net household incomes of poorer households by a proportion greater than the proportion of net household income that more highly paid households would lose (Torry, 2017d; 2018c; 2019a), it could increase a poor person's level of wellbeing at a faster rate than it would decrease the level of wellbeing for a wealthier family.

We have experienced a number of critiques of consequentialism in general, and of utilitarianism in particular. These are all valid, and we have to conclude that utilitarianism has limited usefulness. However, as a contribution to ethical debate it remains important: and it will continue to be important in relation to the Citizen's Basic Income debate. A 'negative utilitarianism', which might help us to decide that one set of actions might be more ethical than another, would suggest that we should ensure that as many people as possible should be able to escape from means-testing. More positively, one of the tests of whether a Citizen's Basic Income is ethical has to be whether it would fulfil its promises (Torry, 2016a: 143–66), and in particular whether it would be possible to implement a scheme that would maximize the happiness of the greatest possible number. If a Citizen's Basic Income scheme were found to decrease happiness rather than to increase it, then we would have to conclude that it might not be ethical to pursue it.

Aristotle's Good Life

Aristotle was well aware that if we aim at the good, then evil consequences can be the result: but that did not stop him from wanting to 'live well', or from wanting others to do so, each one in relation to their own understanding of happiness (Aristotle, 1987: I, 3–4). Aristotle was not concerned with 'what is good essentially, but [with] how we are to become good men' (Aristotle, 1987: II, 2), and the statesman's task – and, in our terminology, the state's task – is to help citizens to form such a moral character (Aristotle, 1987: I, 8) – a character characterized by wisdom and prudence (Aristotle, 1987: VI, 5–13) – and to enable someone to realize 'in action a goodness that is complete and that is adequately furnished with external goods, and that not for some limited period but throughout a fully rounded life spent in that way' (Aristotle, 1987: I, 10). As Broadie puts it in her commentary on Aristotle's *Nichomachean Ethics*, 'virtue has to be cultivated and happiness depends on that cultivation' (Broadie, 1991: 50).

We have discovered above that means-tested benefits do not encourage the kind of character that will lead to happiness and to living well. They discourage people in part-time employment from seeking full-time employment, particularly if they are low-paid; they discourage the gaining of new skills and responsibilities in order to increase earned income; they discourage unemployed people from seeking occasional or part-time employment; they discourage people from saving for their old age (because savings reduce the amount of means-tested pension that elderly people receive); they discourage the formation of permanent households; and they discourage honesty between citizens and government agencies (Parker, 1995). Unconditional benefits exhibit none of these drawbacks. They actively encourage people in part-time employment to seek out additional hours of employment, they encourage the seeking of new skills and responsibilities, and so on. Unconditional benefits therefore encourage the habits that enable citizens to 'live well' and to experience 'complete goodness in a complete lifetime', which, in Aristotle's view, it is a government's task to ensure can happen (Aristotle, 1987: I, 8).

Incommensurable Unique Human Beings?

The flaw at the heart of every ethical system is that they do not recognize the incommensurability of human beings. The utilitarian is unable to compare one person's happiness or welfare with another's; people behind the veil of ignorance at John Rawls' original position (see the case study at the end of this chapter) will think different kinds of society will be the kind in which they would not mind what position they would find themselves in; and Aristotle's statesman can never know how to act in such a way that he will encourage habits that will promote every citizen's happiness. We are all different. There is no universal 'interest' or 'utility'.

Every human being is of course a member of the human species: a concept that assumes that we belong to the same category and therefore share a number of characteristics, and in particular that we share a variety of needs: both needs that have to be met if we are to survive, and also a variety of other needs that constitute our humanity (Dean, forthcoming 2020: Chapter 2 and the end of Chapter 4). Because we share such needs, and because we are interdependent as a species and individually conscious, we are not entirely opaque to each other. However, we remain opaque to each other in a variety of ways, and in particular we are incommensurable in relation to the utility that we might gain from some good or service: that is, the characteristics of another person's personal projects, and the extent to which an individual other than ourselves would exchange one good for another, can only be discovered by seeking information from the action or words of the other person. All of this means that Immanuel Kant, John Rawls, John Stuart Mill, and Aristotle, cannot make assumptions about other people's opinions, plans, emotions, and much else. Such things are hidden, too, from Emmanuel Lévinas, but he knows that they are, because for him the person he is with is 'other'. In the face of the other there is nothing that we can pin down in terms of ideas or categories: but there is revelation, and there is an invitation to responsibility – that is, to ethics (Lévinas, 2000: 9–11, 111–12, 184–7).

None of this is to say that ethical theories are not useful, or that there is nothing in common between my morality and yours. There clearly are commonalities, particularly in relation to such needs as creative work and social interdependence (Dean, forthcoming 2020: last page of Chapter 2), and we need to know them and to act on them if we are to live together in the same society. Whilst each of us has an identity that is radically different from anyone else's, and whilst we will often share an aspect of our identity with some but not with others, we share our humanity, our membership of society, and some basic needs (Ferguson et al., 2002: 179–82). What will not work ethically is any category of people smaller than the human race. This suggests that only a benefits system with both universal and individual provisions, and without any other categorization, can be ethical (Ferguson et al., 2002: 187), and this implies a system with unconditional and universal benefits at its heart. A consequence of there being only one ethical category – the human race – is that 'individualism' becomes a moral concept: 'a belief that, regardless of social relationships, every person should be treated as an individual' (Spicker, 2014: 26) rather than being placed in a category. This is not a statement that we should not address social structures, but is rather a commitment to release each and every individual from social structures that categorize and oppress (Spicker, 2014: 26–7).

Child Benefit treats every individual child in exactly the same way, it does not impose any constraints on the individual, and it is not altered in any way by the individual's characteristics or choices. This means that it can live happily alongside children's radical diversity and with the radical diversity of their situations. It is no surprise that Child Benefit is highly popular and (a slightly different point) that it attracts almost no unpopularity.

So not only does each of the ethical theories that we have studied suggest that universal benefits are more ethical than means-tested benefits: but the failure of all ethical systems, except for one with radical otherness at its heart, draws us to the same conclusion.

The same will surely be true of the UK's National Health Service. Not only would we choose a health service free at the point of use if we did not know what our position in society would be, but such healthcare provision also takes account of our radical diversity by treating us all the same. If we are ill then we will be treated. Keeping within budgets in the context of an ageing population, and the increasing availability of expensive treatments for increasing numbers of illnesses, will continue to be a challenge, and maintaining both consistency across the country and a measure of local governance will be another: but for the same reasons that unconditional and universal benefits are more ethical than means-tested benefits, a health service free to every citizen will be more ethical than one available on the basis of means-tested payments or on the basis of voluntary or obligatory insurance (Torry, 2017c: 377–84).

Foundationalist Ethics and a Gift Relationship

A further ethical theory is foundationalist ethics: the idea that ethics is based on something beyond itself – that is, it has a foundation of some kind: for instance, a single idea treated as an axiom, a set of human rights established by a multinational organization, or a religious tradition. The concept of 'gift' can function as such a stand-alone axiom, and it can also function as a central component of a religious tradition.

As Richard Titmuss has suggested, 'the gift relationship' can be a perfectly adequate basis for social policy (Titmuss, 1970). In the UK, blood donation is precisely that: it is a donation from one person to another, and it is received as a gift. Titmuss employs this relationship as a model on which social policy can be based: that is, each of us gives what we can, and each of us receives what we need, as a gift. There is no contract involved here: it is altruism; and altruism is something that we do. As Nagel suggests, altruism is an attitude depending on the recognition of the value of other persons, 'and on the equivalent capacity to regard oneself as merely one individual among many' (Nagel, 1977: 1). Nagel founds the possibility of altruism on Kant's categorical imperative, which assumes our freedom, determines our motivational structure, and makes possible both prudence and altruism, both of which discount present desires in favour of something reasoned and not felt: our future interest in the case of prudence, and others' interests in the case of altruism (Nagel, 1977: 90, 107, 127).

However, in a complex society, individual to individual relationships of altruism are no more adequate than individual to individual barter, and just as the market in goods and services is constituted by such institutions as money and contracts, so blood donation and other donations and gifts occur through social institutions, and particularly through the mechanism of government organizations and taxation: but they are still in essence donations, and they are still in essence received as gifts. And yes, taxation is still a donation. We vote for governments that we know will impose an Income Tax, so in any democratic country it is our collective act to make practical provision for the giving of such gifts as free healthcare, free education, and unconditional benefits.

It is of course an open question as to the extent to which such an ethical foundation for social policy has religious roots – in the case of the UK, Christian roots – and it is another open question as to whether it still needs that foundation or can now manage perfectly well without it. Jean-Luc Marion's philosophy (Marion, 1997) is a meditation on the gift relationship, with that relationship treated as a foundational axiom rather than as a consequence of a historic tradition: but the Christian roots of Marion's philosophy are everywhere to be seen.

The problem with trying to disentangle a gift ethic from its Christian roots is that there is a long and entirely opposed ethical tradition rooted in a Protestant Christian tradition that expects individual effort to precede the granting of resources of any kind, whether those resources are spiritual or material (Michaelsen, 2018). The 'response' is expected before the gift can be given; or rather, the granting of resources is conditional on our correct behaviour. While this tradition can of course be supported from within the Christian tradition, it is open to question whether it reflects the grace-shaped heart of it (Groves, 2012). A detailed discussion of reciprocity will be found in Chapter 7 on social psychology: but here we are treating it as an ethical question, in which context we need to suggest that because an understanding of reciprocity as an expectation of correct behaviour on the part of a supplicant claimant before resources will be granted continues to draw on deep historical and religious roots, a reciprocity that gives first and then invites a response might also need to continue to draw on deep historical and religious roots if it is to counter an increasing conditionality in social policy. An alternative basis for altruism could be the fact that much current wealth is a gift to us from the resources of the planet and the work of previous generations (Birnbaum, 2019). Whatever the roots of the gift relationship, and however it is sustained as an ethical position, it is an essential ethical foundation of our welfare state, and it is going to need all the help that it can get: and the greatest help that we could offer to it would be the implementation of more social policies informed by the gift relationship. There could of course be no clearer example of such social policy than a Citizen's Basic Income, which would be simply a gift: universal, and unconditional. In Christian theological terms, it would be 'grace': an unmerited gift (Preston, 1992; Torry, 1988b: 7, 21; 1988a: 25–6; 2016b), recognizing in the fiscal sphere the fact that the earth and its resources are a gift to us, and that all of our creative activity is a response to God's original gift (Walter, 1989: 81–2). We do not create wealth out of our ingenuity alone, but by co-operating with a creator; and it is the 'given' nature of the natural resources with which we work that gives theological grounding to a Citizen's Basic Income understood as a social dividend: as an equal sharing of the wealth generated by a created order that we did not ourselves create. However, only by loosening the connection between work and income shall we be able to enter into such a covenant relationship with the created order, and to understand it as a gift to be cherished. Our current economic ideas persuade us that wealth is the product of our own effort and intelligence, and that those who do not work are morally inadequate, and so need to suffer sanctions and stigmatizing means tests, and to be provided with as little of the workers' wealth as possible. Only when we share a common source of income shall we understand that wealth is a gift of God and that it belongs to all of us, and that work of all kinds is a response to God's invitation to take responsibility for the world (Torry, 1988b: 17).

The UK's society is now better described as multifaith than as Christian, so if we wish to retain religious roots for the gift relationship, we shall now need to ask about the centrality of grace in a variety of religious traditions (Phillips, 2018; Woodhead et al., 2002: 85, 187, 207): but however it is sustained, whether by religious means, secular means, or both, the gift relationship ought to remain at the heart of policymaking, and a Citizen's Basic Income should be as near to the top of the agenda as Child Benefit and the National Health Service. Similarly, if the churches or other religious institutions are looking for a social policy to advocate, then it would be difficult to find one more appropriate than a Citizen's Basic Income: an unconditional, nonwithdrawable income that mirrors the unconditional and nonwithdrawable love of God. But whether or not we are Christians, or adhere to any other faith for which the gift relationship is a theological foundation, we can recognize the value of the gift relationship as the foundation for a humane social policy, we can understand how true to that foundation a Citizen's Basic Income would be, and we can understand the extent to which a Citizen's Basic Income would recognize both our radical diversity and our equality as human beings.

CONCLUSION

Philippa Foot suggests that 'if we accustom ourselves to the thought that there is simply a blank where consequentialists see "the best state of affairs", we might be better able to give other theories the hearing they deserve' (Foot, 1988: 242). There is no reason to commit ourselves to only one ethical theory, so a 'pluralistic welfare-maximizing moral system' (Brandt, 1979: 286) would be a rational choice and might be of more use than any conceivable single-basis code. As Michael Stocker suggests, 'plurality and conflict are absolutely commonplace and generally unproblematic features of our everyday choice and action. They had thus better not be a bar to sound judgement, resolute informed action, and a sound and rational ethics' (Stocker, 1990: 2). Life in society is always a complex whole made up of 'disparate and incommensurable values and emotions' (Stocker, 1990: 3). In recognition of the ubiquity of plurality and conflict, and of the disparate and the incommensurable, and in the cause of Brandt's 'pluralistic welfare-maximizing moral system' (Brandt, 1979: 286), we have found utilitarianism to be still of limited usefulness in relation to the Citizen's Basic Income debate; we have found that a Citizen's Basic Income could facilitate the good life that Aristotle envisaged; and we have found that a Citizen's Basic Income would both represent and facilitate a gift relationship.

This chapter has studied a number of philosophical ideas. Some of the chapters in this book – for instance, Chapter 9 on social policy, and Chapter 10 on social administration – study the fine detail of particular proposals for Citizen's Basic Income schemes. This diversity reflects the diversity of the literature on Citizen's Basic Income, in which there is everything from books that relate Citizen's Basic Income to a wide variety of broad themes (Walker, 2016) to the working papers and reports referenced in the sections on financial and administrative feasibility in Chapters 9 and 10. An interesting correlation emerges: The broad-brush approach is more in evidence in such large countries as the USA, and attention to detail more prevalent in small countries such as the UK, with continental Europe somewhere in between: so perhaps the pre-dominant approach to the debate in each country is determined at least partly by the size of the country. Whether or not that is the case, the evidence of this book is that a multidisciplinary approach to Citizen's Basic Income requires that the whole spectrum of the literature needs to be studied.

We close this chapter with considerations of two of the broadest possible philosophical ideas.

CASE STUDIES

The three case studies in this chapter tackle concepts central to any discussion of the ethics of Citizen's Basic Income: freedom, justice, and reciprocity.

A 'Justice as Fairness' Argument for a Citizen's Basic Income

The idea of justice has a complex history, and diverse meanings. There is not the space here to provide a thorough treatment of the subject from Plato's seeking the meaning of justice by discussing the concept of the just State, with its different social strata, as an analogy for the just individual (Plato, 1903/1969: II, §§368–76; IV, §444d; V, §472b), to Amartya Sen's attempt to build a pluralistic concept of justice that can encompass a variety of theories, viewpoints, and experiences (Sen, 2009), and to debate how that history might relate to the Citizen's Basic Income debate (Widerquist et al., 2013: 39–78). Here I shall select a single author's treatment of the idea of justice and ask how that treatment might relate to Citizen's Basic Income.

John Rawls, in his *A Theory of Justice*, posits an 'original position' in which all parties are equal: 'all have the same rights in the procedure for choosing principles'. In this original position, Rawls posits a 'veil of ignorance': that is, he asks us to think of ourselves as citizens choosing principles while not knowing which position we might hold in society, and then to choose the kind of society in which we would wish to live (Rawls, 1971: 19). We might object that we cannot assume that everyone behind Rawls' veil of ignorance will think in the same way about criteria for a fair and just society in which they might find themselves in any social position, and that some people might find other people's positions in society to be as significant as their own (Brandt, 1979: 286): but leaving those entirely legitimate objections to one side, we shall consider what Rawls' theory might have to offer in terms of the ethics of Citizen's Basic Income.

In relation to the conceptual structure that Rawls offers to us, would we want to live in a society in which everyone receives the same income, or would we want to live in one in which, if we found ourselves in a relatively impoverished situation, we would be able to improve our position? Either would be rational. We shall study the latter option first.

Assuming, for the sake of this exercise, that above an income I_0 I would pay tax and receive no benefits, and below it I would receive benefits and pay no tax: If I did not know in which position I would be in society, then I would want a society in which I would be able to change the position in which I found myself if my income was below I_0 and I found myself in a relatively impoverished position. In more practical terms: If I was earning a low wage, then I would want social policy to offer the maximum possible increase in income for every additional pound that I earned.

If I were earning wage w per hour, working h hours per week, and receiving a means-tested in-work benefit, then my income I would be given by:

$$I = wh + B - \alpha wh \qquad (4.1)$$

where B is the amount of benefit received if $wh = 0$ and α is the withdrawal rate, that is, the *proportion* of a pound withdrawn from benefit B for every additional pound of earnings.

I would want w and B to be as high as possible, and α as low as possible. Similarly, if my income was above I_0, and all earnings above I_0 were to be taxed at rate t, then my income I would be given by:

$$I = I_0 + (wh - I_0)(1 - t) \qquad (4.2)$$

I might want to be able to improve my position, so I would want t to be as low as possible.

For a population of m benefits recipients and n taxpayers, and a balanced budget, the amount spent on benefits must equal the revenue gained through taxation:

$$Bm - \alpha \sum_{i=1}^{m} w_i h_i = t \sum_{j=1}^{n} (w_j h_j - I_0) \qquad (4.3)$$

Consider individuals with incomes just above and just below I_0, and a requirement that they should be treated fairly in relation to each other. For the benefits recipient with earned income just below I_0: $I_0 = wh + B - \alpha wh$, and for the individual just above I_0, $I_0 = wh$, so $B = \alpha I_0$. The benefits recipient will want α to be as low as possible. If α tends to zero, then either B also tends to zero (which isn't what the possibly impoverished citizen will want as they stand at the original position), t will rise, which might not be what taxpayers want, or I_0 rises, which would generate less tax revenue and mean more people receiving B, meaning a rapidly decreasing B. If B does not tend to zero, α does tend to zero, and I_0 is located where sufficient tax revenue can be collected to pay a B of a reasonable size, then, at I_0, B is still being paid in full, and the only way to ensure fairness and therefore justice between the taxpayer just above I_0 and the benefits recipient just below I_0, will be to pay B to the taxpayer. I_0 will then become the earned income at which tax begins to be paid, rather than that at which benefits cease to be paid. For a balanced budget, equation (4.3) becomes:

$$B(m + n) = t \sum_{i=1}^{m+n}(w_i h_i - I_0)   \tag{4.4}$$

and the distinction between taxpayer and benefits recipient disappears – an eventuality which could potentially please everyone standing at Rawls' original position.

So for a Rawlsian 'justice as fairness' society, a Citizen's Basic Income – an unconditional, nonwithdrawable income paid to every individual as a right of citizenship – is indicated. But that is all. This is the conclusion that Rawls himself drew: although Rawls scholars have drawn a variety of conclusions from some of Rawls' multiple principles of justice, with Weale finding that they privilege social insurance over Citizen's Basic Income, Waldron finding that providing a bare minimum to keep people alive is all that is indicated, and Fukuma arguing that Rawls' requirement that people should be able to do meaningful work and have fulfilling lives is best served by a Citizen's Basic Income (Rawls, 2001: 128; Waldron, 1986; Weale, 2013; Fukuma, 2017).

Our argument has assumed that everyone behind the veil of ignorance will think the same way about a variety of social possibilities. They might not. If one of them begins with the assumption that it would be wrong for the state to give a benefit to high earners, then they might not be willing to follow the argument above, and would instead be left thinking that fairness requires means-tested benefits. This might not be rational, but it would be their legitimately held view. All we can say is that those who accept the argument will prefer a Citizen's Basic Income to means-tested benefits.

Arguing from the 'justice as fairness' which results from considering the positions of individuals behind a veil of ignorance at the original position, Rawls suggests two 'principles of justice':

> First: each person is to have an equal right to the most extensive basic liberty compatible with a similar liberty for others. Second: social and economic inequalities are to be arranged so that they are both (a) reasonably expected to be to everyone's advantage, and (b) attached to positions and offices open to all. (Rawls, 1971: 60)

This last proviso is later strengthened to require 'conditions of fair equality of opportunity' in relation to positions and offices (Rawls, 1971: 302).

As Dworkin suggests, this second principle implies that 'inequalities in power, wealth, income and other resources must not exist except in so far as they work to the absolute benefit of the worst-off member of society' (Dworkin, 1977: 150). We might prefer to reformulate this condition in line with the idea of Pareto efficiency: that inequalities in power, wealth, income and other resources should be so arranged that no other arrangement of inequalities can increase any individual's resources.

Because there are multiple inequalities, with roots in the deep structures of society (Torry, 2010; Wilkinson and Pickett, 2009; Bergh et al., 2016), the benefits system can never be the only answer to poverty – and given the means-tested scenario envisaged in the equations above: If a high earner increased her earnings by e, then she would pay additional tax te, and the government would be able to increase benefits B by te/m, where m is the number of recipients of B. From equations (4.1) and (4.3), the lowest earner will benefit from a high α. Conversely, an earner with earnings just below I_0 will benefit from a lower α. We can therefore see that to strengthen Rawls' principle in what I have called a 'Pareto' direction might give us different preferences.

The above discussion assumes that the lowest earner will remain the lowest earner, and the earner with earned income just below I_0 will remain in that position. We are employing what we might call a 'static' definition of poverty. The situation changes if we employ a more 'dynamic' definition in which we define 'poverty' as an inability to earn one's way out of a low income (Lister, 2004: 94–7, 145–6, 178–83). As we have already discovered, this will be the definition of poverty with which individuals behind a veil of ignorance at Rawls' original position might be working. If they were to find themselves with few resources and low earnings, then they would want to live in a society in which it would be possible to change that situation. If our definition of poverty were to be a dynamic one, and if we wished to alleviate poverty, then we would require α to tend to zero, and we would be heading towards the scenario envisaged in equation (4.4), where an increase in a high earner's earnings will generate additional tax revenue and thus a higher B for everyone. Everyone would benefit, including the earner who was paying more tax, because she would still receive an additional $e(1 - t)$. Thus our strengthened Rawlsian principle would be satisfied.

Returning to Scanlon's 'an act is wrong if its performance under the circumstances would be disallowed by any system of rules for the general regulation of behaviour which no-one could reasonably reject as a basis for informed, unforced general agreement' (Scanlon, 1982: 110), we find an ethical theory that does not presume to judge how others will view the situation; that does not assume ignorance, or that we can be impartial; and that does not pretend to know how we will feel in someone else's position. Accepting a principle because someone cannot easily reject it is less problematic than accepting a principle because it would be the choice of everyone behind a veil of ignorance. Similarly, Rawls' 'maximin', which maximizes the resources of the least well off, is difficult to envisage, let alone to calculate, whereas Scanlon's morality is 'a device for our mutual protection' (Scanlon, 1982: 128) rather than one for mutual benefit.

Whether or not we accept the presuppositions on which Rawls' theory of justice is based, we can find reasons for wishing to see a Citizen's Basic Income implemented.

The Reciprocity Norm

The reader will find a discussion of social norms in Chapter 7 on social psychology: an appropriate place for it because social norms are social interactions, and social psychology is 'the study of social interactions, including their origins and effects on individuals and groups' (Oxford English Dictionary). However, a social norm can often be termed a 'moral repertoire' (Dean, 1998: 150), because social norms can manifest as social values. Such a moral repertoire is the reciprocity norm: that is, our expectation that people will reciprocate (Svallfors, 2012a: 10). If I do something for you, then I might legitimately expect you to do something for me if the need arises, or even if it does not. We might feel that a legitimate extension of this kind of interpersonal reciprocity might be reciprocity between an individual and the state: if the state is to provide something for an individual, then the state might legitimately expect the individual to reciprocate. However, there are two ways of understanding such reciprocity. Either we can require or expect an individual to do something for the state *before* the state provides something for the individual, or we can expect or require someone to do something for the state *after* the state has provided. There would thus appear to be four types of reciprocation between the state and an individual: (1) ante/required; (2) ante/expected; (3) post/required; and (4) post/expected. Means-tested benefits that apply sanctions if work-conditions and other conditions are not met are an example of ante/

required reciprocity, which translates as an explicit attempt to control benefits' recipients' behaviour (Dean, 2012c: 51). The expectation that someone might contribute to society if granted a Citizen's Basic Income would be an example of post/expected reciprocity.

Stuart White suggests that

> where institutions governing economic life are otherwise sufficiently just, e.g., in terms of the availability of opportunities for productive participation and the rewards attached to these opportunities, then those who claim the generous share of the social product available to them under these institutions have an obligation to make a decent productive contribution, suitably proportional and fitting for ability and circumstances, to the community in return. I term this the fair-dues conception of reciprocity. (White, 2003: 59)

Note that this is a 'contribution ... in return' which people have an 'obligation' to make. This is post/expected reciprocity, and not the kind of ante/required reciprocity represented by the UK's means-tested benefits work test and sanctions regime.

White offers a number of arguments for the importance of such reciprocity. He argues that self-esteem is a good thing, and that self-esteem depends on reciprocity; that non-reciprocation burdens other people with providing for our needs; that to expect not to reciprocate is a statement of superiority; that to expect others not to reciprocate is a statement of servility; and that a welfare state is more likely to remain politically acceptable if it is founded on reciprocity. Individuals can reciprocate in a variety of ways – paid labour, care work, and voluntary community activity – all of which count as the kind of 'civic labour' that reciprocity requires. They are all 'work' (Uhde, 2018). It is this civic labour that provides the 'civic minimum' – of income, healthcare and other resources – that provides the basis for both a viable society and the expectation of continuing reciprocity (White, 2003: 99, 131, 132).

As White suggests, 'in a context of otherwise sufficiently fair economic arrangements, everyone should do their bit' (White, 2003: 18): but this in turn suggests that if economic arrangements are *not* otherwise fair, then it is difficult to sustain the obligation to reciprocate. In the context of an adequate civic minimum, *and* in a context in which obligations apply equally to all, including the asset-rich, a work test 'can be defended as a necessary device for protecting citizens against the unfair resource claims of those who are unwilling to meet the contributive obligations they have to the community' (White, 2003: 152). If some can live without providing a contribution of some kind to the community, and others find it hard to contribute because paid employment has disappeared from their communities, then it is difficult to regard economic arrangements as 'sufficiently just' (De Wispelaere, undated).

It is therefore clear that reciprocity is not the only value that should determine the distribution of resources, however deeply felt the need for reciprocity might be. As White goes on to suggest,

> some resources are properly seen as belonging to a common citizens' inheritance fund, and it is implausible that the individual's entitlement to a share of this fund is entirely dependent on a willingness to work. (White, 2006: 13)

It would therefore make sense to peg the amount of a Citizen's Basic Income to the estimated per capita value of the commons (Cogolati and Wouters, 2018; Standing, 2019), that is, natural resources, and the wealth generated by previous generations: but White argues for a Citizen's Basic Income of a larger amount than that on the grounds that:

1. Even if basic income is bad for reciprocity, this is outweighed by its positive effects on other concerns of fairness, such as the prevention of market vulnerability.
2. Even if basic income is bad for reciprocity in one way, it is also likely to have positive effects in terms of this same value. (White, 2006: 14)

As White recognizes, a Citizen's Basic Income would establish one of the main criteria for a *just* reciprocity (White, 2003: 168).

Freedom for the Surfer?

Philippe Van Parijs recommends a Citizen's Basic Income on the basis of the 'real freedom' that it would offer: 'real freedom' because a Citizen's Basic Income would offer the financial security to turn what Van Parijs regards as a right to freedom into the reality of freedom. That practical freedom would extend to the ability to spend one's days surfing (Reeve and Williams, 2002; Van Parijs, 1995: 2, 89, 96, 133; Widerquist et al., 2013: 1–37).

First of all, it might not be financially feasible to pay a Citizen's Basic Income of a high enough amount to enable someone to live on it without seeking additional income, which would normally be earned income; and second, even if that were possible, there would be few who would wish to spend their whole time surfing. Most of us want to make some sort of contribution to society: and one of the important effects of a Citizen's Basic Income might be that it would enable us more easily to make the kind of contribution that we might wish to make. But Van Parijs is right to emphasize one of the freedom-enhancing effects of a Citizen's Basic Income: that it would provide everyone with at least an element of real freedom – that is, it would give to everyone more ability to choose what we do with our time, and the kinds of gainful employment that we might decide to undertake. In particular, a Citizen's Basic Income would begin to democratize the workplace: although additional measures, such as collective bargaining, would still be required (Casassas, 2016; Gourevitch, 2016).

As we have seen, others might wish to see a bit more reciprocity in the situation: whether the onerous behavioural requirements of many means-tested benefits systems; the lighter behavioural requirements of a Participation Income (which would impose conditions that required some sort of evidenced participation in society); an invitation to respond to a Citizen's Basic Income by voluntarily undertaking unpaid caring or community work, or by seeking new or additional paid employment or self-employment; or Stuart White's 'just reciprocity': as already discussed, an expectation of contribution to society on condition that the context is just, which would be more likely to be the case if a Citizen's Basic Income were in payment. From White's point of view, if free riders fail to reciprocate and fail to contribute to a context of just reciprocity, then a small number of people not fulfilling those obligations would be a small price to pay for a secure income floor that would establish one of the main criteria for an overall just reciprocity (White, 2003: 168; Widerquist et al., 2013: 79–140). It is easy to find grounds for objecting to Van Parijs' 'real freedom' argument for Citizen's Basic Income (Piachaud, 2016), but less easy to object to White's 'just reciprocity' arguments for it, or to Henderson's finding that Citizen's Basic Income would enhance both real freedom and social reciprocity (Henderson, 2017).

A somewhat different concept of freedom is described by Karl Widerquist: 'freedom as the power to say no' (Widerquist, 2013): that is, freedom as the right not to be dominated by any person or institution. This might be regarded as a lesser freedom than the 'real freedom' advocated by Van Parijs – it is a negative freedom from something, rather than being provided with the resources that would give us the freedom to do whatever we might wish – but although the ideas might be framed differently, the practical outcome would be much the same. If a Citizen's Basic Income that was enough to live on were to be provided, then the individual would be free from domination (by an employer, as they could say no to any job that they thought undesirable; or by a government's means-tested benefits sanctions regime), and they would be free to do as they wished with their time. If a Citizen's Basic Income of a lesser amount were to be paid, then both freedom as non-domination and 'real' freedom would be diminished: but the individual would still be able to experience more of both kinds of freedom than if there were not a Citizen's Basic Income in payment, as they would have more ability to decline or to leave an undesirable, 'lousy' or 'pointless' job (Goos and Manning, 2007; Graeber, 2018: 9), as at least some of their weekly income would be totally secure; and they would have more choice over what to do with their time: for instance, they might be more able to seek the part-time employment that would suit them, or to start a business that would enable them to spend more time caring for others or volunteering for a community project. Contextual factors will always be important, of course. It might be that only one kind of employment is readily available in an area, thus reducing the ability to exit one job and find another; or it might be that one group of workers' ability to exercise additional power in the workplace reduces the solidarity required to enable all of a workforce to do so (Birnbaum and De Wispelaere, 2016). But whatever the additional factors in play, a significant contextual factor will always be the situation prior to the implementation of a Citizen's Basic Income. If a secure layer of income has replaced insecure in-work means-tested benefits, then the worker will know that not all of their income is permanently at risk. This difference cannot fail to enhance both kinds of freedom (Birnbaum, 2019).

However similar the practical effects of the two freedoms that Citizen's Basic Income would deliver, it might be important to maintain the two different framings of freedom. For some people, Van Parijs' 'real freedom' might be more important, and to others Widerquist's 'freedom as non-domination' might be what is required. Both of them can properly be described as freedom, and both would be enhanced by the implementation of a Citizen's Basic Income.

5. The economics of Citizen's Basic Income

Economics: The branch of knowledge (now regarded as one of the social sciences) that deals with the production, distribution, consumption, and transfer of wealth; the application of this discipline to a particular sphere; (also) the condition of a state, etc., as regards material prosperity; the financial considerations attaching to a particular activity, commodity, etc.
(Oxford English Dictionary)

INTRODUCTION

For the purposes of this chapter, I shall be taking as my guide *Economics*, by Lipsey and Chrystal (2004), and on welfare economics I shall be relying on *Intermediate Public Economics*, by Hindriks and Myles (2006).

Economics is the social science that tries to understand how a variety of goods are created and distributed, where 'goods' can mean anything from which individuals or society might benefit: machinery, leisure, employment, money, financial assets, land, water, computer code … . The science's practitioners build hypotheses or models, then test them, and hopefully discard them in favour of new models when they fail the test of experience. Whether what might be called the 'classical' model has properly stood up to testing in the real world of complex individuals, monopolies, inequality, the financial crisis, and austerity, is of course a matter for debate: a debate that has given rise to varieties of so-called 'heterodox' economics, some of which might become new orthodoxies until those too are eventually and reluctantly swept away when they fail the test of real world experience. In this chapter we shall employ elements of the classical model such as indifference curves; and we shall explore some of the branches of economics, such as welfare economics and labour market economics. We shall then discuss the concept of efficiency, and then the relationship between Citizen's Basic Income and climate change: a relationship that sets an essential question to every future Citizen's Basic Income researcher: that is, could Citizen's Basic Income contribute to the reduction of carbon emissions, or might it exacerbate the problem? It might have been thought that 'behavioural economics' might belong in this chapter, but because it is a science of human economic behaviour, discussion of it will be found in

Chapter 6 on psychology. A case study at the end of this chapter studies the difference between Citizen's Basic Income and Negative Income Tax.

In a single chapter it is of course impossible to do justice to the whole of the discipline of economics, or to all of the possible relationships between economics and Citizen's Basic Income. What this chapter hopes to achieve is to provide examples from across much of the breadth of the discipline as a stimulus to readers to contribute their own explorations in economics to the Citizen's Basic Income debate.

Readers might wish to read this chapter in conjunction with Chapter 12 on political economy. That chapter relates the economy to values and institutions, and particularly to the institutions of government. One way of reading the current chapter would be to see it as a progression towards political economy, with the first two sections leaving values and institutions largely to one side; the section on welfare economics taking institutions seriously; the fourth section, on efficiency, introducing some ethical values; and the final section, on climate change, leading us to questions related to the survival of life as we know it. This theme is taken up again in the section on sustainable growth in Chapter 12; and in that chapter the reader will also find a discussion of how money creation might fund Citizen's Basic Incomes.

CLASSICAL ECONOMIC MODELS: INDIFFERENCE CURVES, CONSUMPTION, AND EMPLOYMENT CHOICES

Hours not spent in paid employment ('leisure') are useful to us (they have utility); and consumer goods, and thus earned income, also have utility. Each combination of leisure and earned income will yield utility, or satisfaction, and there might be a number of combinations of leisure and earned income that for a particular individual would yield equal utility: that is, we are indifferent as to which of the combinations we are presented with. If we plot those points on a graph, then we can draw through them an 'indifference curve'; and we can draw a series of such indifference curves on each of which utility will be equal (Lipsey and Chrystal, 2004: 108–15).

In Figure 5.1, if at the three combinations of leisure and earned income represented by points a, b, and c, we regard ourselves as having equal levels of utility, then along the indifference U_1 our utility is constant. The curve at U_2 represents a similar series of points of equal utility, all at a higher level of utility than those on U_1.

For a given wage rate w, we can draw a line (a 'budget constraint'), as in Figure 5.2, showing what our earned income will be for each hour worked, that is, for each hour subtracted from our leisure.

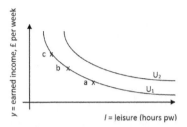

Note: At every point on each of the curves the combinations of the levels of leisure and income provide the individual with equal levels of utility. The level of utility along curve U_2 is higher than the level of utility along curve U_1.
Source: Torry, 2008.

Figure 5.1   Indifference curves

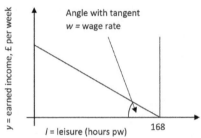

Note: Points above the line are not feasible.
Source: Torry, 2008.

Figure 5.2   Budget line, showing the relationship between the number of hours of leisure and the earned income

The combinations of earned income and leisure represented by points to the right of the budget line are unobtainable, so our utility will be maximized where an indifference curve is at a tangent to the budget constraint (as this is the highest utility available to us under the circumstances), as in Figure 5.3.

Now suppose that on all earnings up to the amount y_0 tax is charged at rate t, then the wage rate net of tax will be $w(1 - t)$ per hour for the first y_0/w hours of employment per week (that is, between $(168 - y_0/w)$ and 168 hours of leisure).

In Figure 5.4, with this particular tax system, the person whose utility was previously maximized at a high number of hours of employment (a low number of hours of leisure) now has utility maximized at a lower number of hours of employment (a higher number of hours of leisure, and possibly at 0 hours of employment). This somewhat unusual tax system mirrors the effect of the rapid withdrawal of means-tested benefits on the utility of low-earning

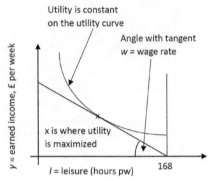

Source: Torry, 2008.

Figure 5.3   *Utility is maximized where the budget constraint is at a tangent to an indifference curve*

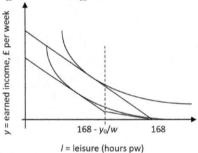

Source: Torry, 2008.

Figure 5.4   *The utility that can be achieved with untaxed income is higher than the utility that can be achieved when income is taxed*

households. The result is reduced utility and reduced incentive to seek employment or to seek additional hours of employment.

For any specified tax and benefits system, and for any particular type of household, we can create a graph to show the household's net income for a variety of numbers of hours of work. The graphs that follow show net income for the very simple case of an individual with no partner or children, no housing costs, and receiving the UK's National Living Wage and the means-tested Universal Credit. Because the horizontal axis is now showing hours worked rather than hours of leisure, the budget constraint has a positive

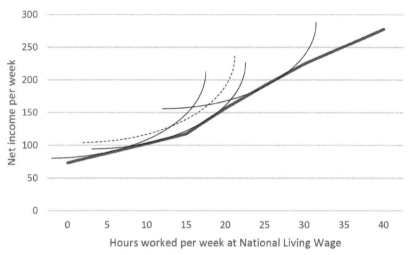

Note: Graph constructed by the author.

*Figure 5.5   A variety of indifference curves in relation to the budget
constraint generated by Universal Credit*

slope rather than the negative slope generated by a horizontal axis showing
leisure hours as in previous graphs. Notional indifference curves can now be
drawn – again, reversed. Figure 5.5 shows the budget constraint for the UK's
current tax and benefits system. The graph reveals a shallow poverty trap for
someone with a particular indifference curve. This situation is an improvement on the UK's legacy system of Jobseeker's Allowance and Working Tax
Credits, where employment between 0 hours and 12 hours per week could
make almost no difference to net income: but it can still be clearly seen that
one of the indifference curves is at a tangent to the budget constraint at both
10 hours and 17 hours, suggesting that any individual who experiences the
relationship between leisure and net income represented by such a curve will
gain no utility by increasing their employment hours from 10 to 17.

Figure 5.6 shows both the current system and a scheme that pays a Citizen's
Basic Income of £63 per week, charges Income Tax of 23 per cent and
National Insurance Contributions of 12 per cent on all earned income,
and treats Citizen's Basic Incomes in the same way as other income when
Universal Credit is calculated.

The graph shows that this particular Citizen's Basic Income scheme would
not only offer to individuals with low earnings an increase in utility, but it

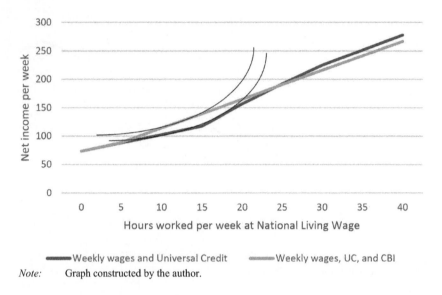

Note: Graph constructed by the author.

*Figure 5.6   Budget constraints for both the current UK tax and benefits
                system and a system containing a Citizen's Basic Income,
                with associated indifference curves*

would also release the previously trapped individual from their poverty trap.
Whatever the shape of an individual's indifference curves, the Citizen's Basic
Income scheme would not impose a poverty trap because there would always
be just one number of hours of employment at which the individual would
maximize their utility, and for much of the working hours range utility would
be higher than under the current system (Atkinson and Flemming, 1978;
Brown and Levin, 1974; Deaton and Muellbauer, 1980: 282; Deaton, 1992:
193; Shone, 1981: 1–24; Torry, 2018b).

This exercise raises some interesting questions. First of all, the exercise has
assumed that the only relevant relationships are between time spent in gainful
employment, the wage rate, and disposable income. In reality, there will be
multiple factors in play (Mideros and O'Donoghue, 2015), complicating the
situation. Second, the concept of an indifference curve suggests that every
point below or on the budget constraint is feasible. However, if only jobs at
a particular number of hours are available, then only that point on the curve
will be feasible. So, for instance, if only full-time jobs at 40 hours per week
are available, then utility will be maximized at point A in Figure 5.7, and
not at x: so the individual might find themselves on a curve lower than the

tangential curve, and therefore on a lower level of utility. Third, the concept of an indifference curve suggests that the bundles of such goods as income and leisure that generate particular levels of utility for an individual have some kind of consistency over time, and that they remain relatively unaffected by external influences. However, the ways in which an individual's choices affect someone else's levels of utility will alter over time, and that person's choices and levels of utility will affect the individual's indifference curves. This means that the assumption that an individual experiences relatively stable indifference curves might be a long way from reality. Between them, the complicating factors that we have discovered suggest that if we are to employ the concept of indifference curves at all, then we shall need to recognize them as *dynamic*, and as constantly shifting in both shape and position; and this in turn suggests that the tax and benefits system needs to avoid the kind of trap represented by Figure 5.5, because even if at time t_1 someone's indifference curve does not fall into it, at time t_2 it might do so (Torry, 2008). The radical diversity of human experience, and therefore of the utilities experienced by different individuals in relation to different goods, means that it is impossible to design a benefits system that will suit every individual in a population; and the complexity of the policy process means not only that careful design is essential (Peters, 2018), but also that only a system with minimal design features is likely to prove useful. The nearest benefits system to one without design features has to be Citizen's Basic Income.

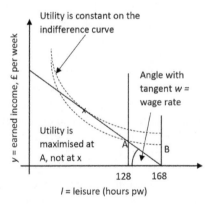

Source: Torry, 2008.

Figure 5.7   *If only full-time jobs at 40 hours per week are available, then utility is maximized at point A, and not at x*

Indifference curves are at the heart of classical economic models. As we have seen, they can provide insight into why individuals might make the employment market decisions that they do, and like other elements of classical economic theory they have their uses: but at the same time this particular part of the classical model raises some questions that suggest that reality might not be as simple as the model makes out, which means that other parts of the model, and the model as a whole, might not be as connected to reality as we might have thought.

In an exercise similar to the one just described, Meghnad Desai and Ana Helena Palermo (2019) make a variety of assumptions commonly made in classical economic theory, and use mathematical methods commonly employed, in order to evaluate the effects that Citizen's Basic Income schemes might have on individuals' consumption of goods, the amount of paid work that they might choose to undertake, and the amount of time that they might spend on leisure and unpaid work, and also in order to evaluate the effects that Citizen's Basic Income schemes might have on a society's aggregated consumption and on its income distribution. They study two different funding methods – an additional income tax, and an undefined source of revenue from outside the current tax and benefits system; and they study Citizen's Basic Incomes paid at three different levels: a 'partial' Citizen's Basic Income, which would not meet basic needs; a 'freedom-enhancing' Citizen's Basic Income, which could meet the most basic of needs, but would still require most people to seek additional income; and an 'emancipatory' Citizen's Basic Income, which would be sufficient for life in society, and would enable people to choose whether or not to participate in the employment market.

The authors find that if they make the reasonable assumption that consumption and unpaid (leisure) time have 'subsistence amounts' for an individual – that is, that there are levels below which the two goods cannot fall – then the amounts of consumption and unpaid time that people experience will depend on the subsistence amounts of the two goods, and each of leisure and consumption will be negatively correlated with the subsistence amounts of the other.

For the emancipatory Citizen's Basic Income, the Citizen's Basic Income equals the subsistence level of consumption, and Desai and Palermo (2019) find that consumption depends on the amount of the Citizen's Basic Income and on how much paid work the individual chooses to do. Because with a Citizen's Basic Income equal to the subsistence level of consumption the subsistence amounts of both consumption and unpaid time can always be met, the amount of unpaid time becomes independent of the level of the Citizen's Basic Income. However, if the Citizen's Basic Incomes were to be funded by an additional income tax, then the additional taxation could negatively affect both consumption and unpaid time: something that would not occur if funding were to be external to the income tax system (although some kinds of taxation would negatively affect the subsistence amounts of consumption).

When Desai and Palermo (2019) study aggregate societal economic effects, they assume that the marginal propensity to consume (Lipsey and Chrystal, 2004: 413) declines as income rises – that is, poorer people spend more of any additional income than wealthier people do: and they therefore find that if a Citizen's Basic Income scheme were to redistribute income from rich to poor, then aggregate consumption would rise. When they come to discuss redistribution, they find that a Citizen's Basic Income funded by an additional income tax would be likely to redistribute from rich to poor, whereas one funded externally would not necessarily do so – and it is of course possible that if Citizen's Basic Incomes were to be paid for by consumption taxes then inequality could increase.

Classical economics still has its uses, but because of the numerous assumptions that it makes about how people behave, it can no longer be regarded as the whole of the discipline of economics. Other kinds of economics will now be essential to the Citizen's Basic Income debate.

WAGE LEVELS

We have already discussed some of the factors that might govern the number of hours for which individuals might choose to be gainfully employed. Another important aspect of the subfield of labour economics is discussion of the factors that determine wage levels (Lipsey and Chrystal, 2004: 259–61, 267–82): so here we need to ask about the possible effects of a Citizen's Basic Income on wages.

In the absence of an existing tax or benefits system, and assuming no consumption or income effects of the funding method (admittedly an unlikely assumption), the Citizen's Basic Income would provide every worker with a secure financial floor on which to build. Depending on the level at which the Citizen's Basic Income was paid, workers in some occupations might be in a position to leave employment that had little intrinsic value for them, or they might choose to work fewer hours. Wages would have to rise to attract workers, or the tasks would be automated. Similarly, Citizen's Basic Incomes would either take households off means-tested benefits or would bring them closer to coming off them. The increased possibilities of leaving a bad job, leaving means-tested benefits, or both (Handler, 2005: 120), and living on household members' Citizen's Basic Incomes and a variety of part-time and self-employments, could be life-enhancing. In paid work that workers found intrinsically valuable, workers' Citizen's Basic Incomes might enable wages to fall (Pech, 2010). The direction in which wages moved would therefore be an indicator of the intrinsic desirability or otherwise of the employment.

However, in a more developed country, no Citizen's Basic Income would ever be implemented in isolation: there would always be existing tax and benefits systems that would need to be adapted or replaced. Let us assume a revenue neutral Citizen's Basic Income scheme that retained and recalculated means-tested benefits. Anyone no longer on means-tested benefits would experience lower marginal deduction rates and so would be likely to seek more employment hours, whereas for some, the security of the Citizen's Basic Income might lead to a reduction in hours of employment. For a revenue neutral scheme with small household gains and losses, there would be little incentive for those in employment to leave it, so the latter effect would be small. This suggests that for an introductory level Citizen's Basic Income there would be increased employment market activity, the amount of which would depend on the number of households taken off means-tested benefits by the Citizen's Basic Incomes coming into their households. If in addition the scheme brought more families within striking distance of coming off means-tested benefits – that is, the values of their claims fell to levels at which it would be feasible to add employment hours that would take them off means-tested benefits – then again we would see increased employment market activity. In this situation, we would also expect to see an increase in self-employment and new small businesses. If the Citizen's Basic Income then started to grow, initially more people would experience lower marginal deduction rates, so we would continue to see an increase in employment market activity: but as the Citizen's Basic Income continued to grow towards subsistence level, we would see additional withdrawal from employment. A classic upside down U shaped curve would represent the rising and then diminishing employment market activity, as in Figure 5.8. Empirical data would determine when the maximum employment market activity had been achieved. It would then be important not to increase the Citizen's Basic Income any further. The logic suggests that this point would only be reached when anyone previously on means-tested benefits was no longer on them, and sources of revenue from outside the income tax system were being used to fund the Citizen's Basic Income. That's a long way off.

A question often asked is whether Citizen's Basic Incomes would have a subsidy effect on wages: that is, because the Citizen's Basic Incomes would meet a proportion of households' subsistence costs, and wages would no longer be the only source of subsistence income, would employers take the opportunity to reduce wages? (Pitts et al., 2017). If there were no current means-tested benefits system then this would be a concern: but there is. In the context of means-tested in-work benefits, a fall in wages triggers an increase in the benefits, meaning that both employer and employee experience a lower

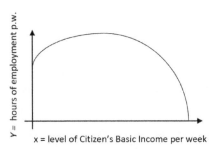

Note: Figure created by the author.

Figure 5.8   *An upside down U curve, representing the rising and then diminishing employment market activity generated by a rising Citizen's Basic Income*

disincentive to lower wages than would be the case in the absence of the means-tested benefits. Similarly, for any household receiving means-tested in-work benefits, an increase in wages triggers a fall in means-tested benefits, and the effect of the wage rise on disposable income can be minimal. Because in low-paid occupations a large proportion of workers might be on means-tested benefits, this effect will be particularly evident in such occupations. The outcome is that in low-paid jobs there can be little incentive to raise wages, and little incentive not to reduce them.

A Citizen's Basic Income would have none of these unfortunate effects. Yes, it would subsidize wages, but it would function as a static subsidy, not as a dynamic one. This means that any Citizen's Basic Income scheme that took a significant number of households off means-tested in-work benefits would reduce the incentive to lower wages, and would increase workers' incentive to see them rise (Torry, 2016a: 177). A National Minimum Wage would therefore become less necessary: but not unnecessary in low-paid occupations. Importantly, there would be no conflict between a National Minimum Wage and a Citizen's Basic Income, and they could work quite happily alongside each other (Dolton, Bondibene and Wadsworth, 2010; Gilbert et al., 2019; Parker and Sutherland, 1996: 8).

We can conclude that Citizen's Basic Income would confer rights to a foundational income, better employment terms and conditions for less desirable jobs, and more choice over employment options.

WELFARE ECONOMICS: CLUB THEORY

Welfare economics is

> the branch of economics concerned with the effects of economic activity on the welfare of the individuals that compose society ... economic theory or practice aimed at improving the welfare of the individual. (Oxford English Dictionary)

At its heart lie distinctions between public goods, private goods, and club goods. Private goods are those goods, such as machinery, financial assets, and intellectual property, which are owned by and are under the control of individuals or private sector organizations. Only those who own the goods can benefit from them. Public goods, such as the atmosphere and public parks, are goods that are available to everyone, and from which no-one can be excluded. Between these two can be found 'club goods': that is, goods available to members of a club (Hindriks and Myles, 2006: 143–69). So an angling club might build a fence around a lake that it owns in order to ensure that only members of the club can fish in it.

Buchanan (1965) suggests that goods can be located along a spectrum between the purely private and the purely public. If the quantity of a good per unit of time that is available for each individual remains the same however many individuals have access to the good, then the good is a purely public good. Those goods that cannot be shared with even one more individual are purely private goods. Goods near to the purely public end of the spectrum might be termed 'mainly public', those goods near to the private end might be termed 'mainly private', and those goods that are at some distance from both ends of the spectrum are 'club goods'. Here a single person would not be able to afford to purchase the good; if a number of people join together to purchase the good then it becomes affordable and they all gain utility from consuming it: but as more people consume the good it becomes of less value to each of them (– think too many anglers around the lake), and membership will cease to climb when the value of the good to each member equals the membership fee. If more members were to join, then although the fee would fall, the good would be of less value to each of the members, and members would withdraw until equilibrium was regained. Similarly, for any given club size there will be an optimum provision of the club good. Having conceived of the relationship between amount of club good, level of membership fee, and number of members, in this way, we can now look again at the extreme positions. A private good can now be understood as a club good for which the optimal size of the club is one individual and the membership fee is the price of the good; and a public good can be understood as a club good for which the size of the club can be infinite and for which the membership fee is zero.

In practice, the fee is not zero, of course. Cleaning up pollution costs money, and maintaining a public park costs money: so in terms of club theory what we have is club goods for which the optimal size of the club is the size of the local, national or global community, and the membership fee is the tax paid to maintain the goods. Problems occur of course when some members of the community that consumes the good are not paying the tax required to maintain it. Such members are 'free riders', benefiting from the good while not contributing to the cost. Only nation states can collect taxes, so free riding occurs if a club larger than a nation state is consuming a good that costs money to maintain. The obvious example is the global environment.

As Buchanan puts it, club theory is 'a theory of optimal exclusion, as well as one of inclusion' (Buchanan, 1965: 13; Cornes and Sandler, 1986: 157–243; Foldvary, 1994: 62–5, 69). It is this insight that Bill Jordan employs in order to understand global, national and local societies as made up of competing clubs, each of which regulates its own members in order more effectively to compete with other clubs for scarce resources (Jordan, 1996: 62–77). Jordan suggests that Buchanan's ideas have enabled us to understand the way in which previously public goods have become club goods: for instance, leisure centres that charge for membership and admission (Jordan, 2008: 92) – but this latter example suggests that before the term 'club goods' was invented, admission charges for publicly owned swimming pools had already constituted such facilities as club goods: which, as Wicksell suggests, is only fair if particular individuals are benefiting from the service and others are not, and if the fee equals the marginal cost (Wicksell, 1958: 98). This means that to treat hospitals as club goods is inappropriate: we all have need of them, so they must be treated as public goods, they must be supplied to everyone who needs healthcare, and they must be paid for by taxation (Jordan, 2008: 104–5).

Club theory can prove to be a most useful lens through which to understand how the world works. For instance, we can view the European Union as a club that provides benefits for its members, and that then regulates those members so that it can more effectively compete with other clubs (Dean, 2016: 15; Jordan, 1996: 10, 73). Similarly, we can understand the society of a nation state as containing privileged communities that exclude more deprived communities in order to monopolize resources, often by building physical barriers around their housing areas, or by voting for policies that either explicitly or implicitly exclude more vulnerable groups (Jordan, 1996: 9). More privileged communities are 'communities of choice', whereas more deprived communities are 'communities of fate', with more constrained options open to them (Jordan, 1996: 161–88; Dean, 2016: 16).

> Individual and collective actors ... face strong incentives to exclude the most vulnerable members of their societies from compulsory public welfare systems, as

well as powerful incentives to form private welfare clubs through exit from State schemes ... this fragmentation process, consisting of exclusion of the vulnerable from so-called 'universal' benefits and services, and the formation of more new mutualities for those with lowest social risks, is characteristic of the development of social relations in the final quarter of the twentieth century (Jordan, 1996: 65)

– and since then, of course.

We might legitimately develop this conceptual framework in the context of the detail of the tax and benefits field. Thus large corporations form a privileged 'community of choice' that enables them to compete with governments and thus reduce the amount of tax that they are required to pay. Employees, on the other hand, constitute a 'community of fate' because they have their tax automatically deducted by their employers and sent to the tax authorities. In countries that run social insurance systems, employees with stable full-time jobs build up contribution records and receive the benefits to which those records entitle them; and wealthier households will often provide themselves with private insurance cover and private pensions. They are all members of privileged clubs: that is, communities of choice. Those prevented from belonging to such clubs for whatever reason are left to rely on means-tested and work-tested benefits. They belong to a community of fate because they have no choice.

As Jordan suggests, to treat education as a club good is no way to run an education system because we all have a need for an education: and it would be equally legitimate to suggest that to employ clubs to provide a nation state's population with an income is no way to run an income system, because we all have similar subsistence needs. It is therefore arguable that a foundational income should be treated as a public good and not as a club or private good. Additional income can of course be regarded as a private good, and possibly as a club good, just as it is perfectly legitimate for parents to provide their children with music lessons as an addition to the education that they receive in publicly provided schools: but that is no reason to deny the possibility that a foundational income is a public good that should be paid for by taxation.

EFFICIENCY

What do we mean by an efficient economy? Arguably it means one in which every individual and every household is able to obtain, by purchase or public service, the resources that they need for a dignified life in society. So-called developed economies like the UK's are clearly failing in this respect (Corlett et al., 2018; Cribb et al., 2018). Before the economic crisis of 2008, consumption fuelled by household debt increased the level of Gross Domestic Product (GDP), whereas after the crisis the level of debt reduced consumption (Harari,

2018: 23). A compounding factor is the reduced level of public services now available because governments bailed out banks that had bundled bad debt into valueless financial 'commodities', blamed the level of public debt for causing the crisis, whereas private debt and the behaviour of the banks had been to blame, and used the crisis as a pretext for austerity measures.

Income inequality measured by the Gini coefficient across the whole population of the UK is at much the same level as it was in 1990, but this masks some significant changes. Inequality has reduced slightly across most of the population, but top earners now receive a larger share of national income than they did in 1990. Following the financial crisis, earnings growth has been strongest in the mid-range of earnings, which has increased inequality in the lower part of the earnings range – an effect exacerbated by cuts in means-tested benefits. Cribb, Keiller and Waters (2018: 32–4) predict a somewhat complex picture for the future.

But perhaps it is not the short-term changes in inequality that really matter. Before 1979, inequality in the UK had been stable for thirty years, but between 1979 and 1990 a significant increase took place (Cribb et al., 2018: 30). This is what matters. And it is during the same period that the share of national income going to labour decreased, so that by 1995 it was below the level of Gross Domestic Product (Crocker, 2019), meaning that consumption was bound to drop, or household debt was bound to increase: and that if the latter happened – as it did – then that too would eventually cause consumption to fall. The imbalance in the rewards to capital and labour has resulted in both lower demand and increased inequality (Lansley, 2011a: 12; 2011b). Apart from the social and political effects of debt and inequality, the economy's efficiency is put at risk:

> Sufficient equality in the distribution of income, within a country, is a proper goal of efficient economic policy, and is part of a strategy for shared prosperity and full employment; it is both effect and cause. (Galbraith, 2002: 224)

If we can assume that in an economy without taxation or benefits all markets operate efficiently (– that is, prices balance supply and demand in a context of perfect competition and perfect information), then the economy will be efficient: and if we choose to introduce taxation in order to fund public services, then a lump sum tax (which could not be affected by our behaviour) would be the only taxation option that could redistribute income in such a way that the highest possible welfare could be achieved (Hindriks and Myles, 2006: 38–9, 373–80). This might suggest that a Citizen's Basic Income – which would not be affected by our behaviour, and could therefore be regarded as a reverse lump sum tax – could be the most efficient way of redistributing resources so as to obtain the highest possible amount of total welfare.

But how large should such a Citizen's Basic Income be in order to achieve the maximum available welfare efficiency? Efficiency requires that demand should match supply, which suggests that the Citizen's Basic Income should be set at subsistence level, somehow understood (Spicker, 2000: 169). However, because such a level of Citizen's Basic Income would need to be paid for, and the rate at which a lump sum tax would have to be charged to fund that level of income for every member of the population would be impossible to collect, a progressive income tax would probably be required, which would impose inefficiencies on the economy. However, in response to the objection that the outcome of implementing a Citizen's Basic Income scheme could be as ineffi-cient as the current benefits system, it is of course possible to reply that at least the Citizen's Basic Income element of the scheme would be efficient, whereas with a system based largely on means-tested benefits neither the benefits nor the taxation to pay for them can be efficient. A Citizen's Basic Income could be a rare achievement: it could both improve the efficiency of the economy and reduce inequality (Zelleke, 2005: 14–15).

But now let us question our original presupposition, and ask whether an economy with no tax or benefits system really is necessarily efficient.

> When we allow for real-world phenomena like incomplete information and the absence of markets, it is conceivable that the payment of basic incomes, and the levying of the associated tax, may improve the allocation of resources. (Atkinson, 1989: 13)

> Many versions of the 'equality-efficiency trade-off' … do not survive closer scru-tiny; … abdication of the insurance function of the welfare state produces efficiency losses in our second-best world; … progressive redistributions may not entail effi-ciency losses or higher costs because the alternative system of order maintenance, namely disciplinary enforcement, is also costly; … distributive policies … produce dynamic efficiency gains if, by reducing poverty and inequality, they positively influence the welfare and the cognitive abilities of children and hence human capital formation; … the under-provision of [care] services acts as an 'inactivating influence' on market participation and employment, particularly for women … . (Costabile, 2008: 225–31)

In relation to the factors that Costabile lists, a Citizen's Basic Income imple-mented in the context of a progressive tax system would appear to be more likely to improve economic and welfare efficiency than a system based on means-tested benefits. A means-tested system contributes to inequality, has to pay for coercion and surveillance, and disincentivizes informal care work, whereas a Citizen's Basic Income implemented in the context of a progressive tax system could facilitate informal care work, increase equality, and confine the use of coercion and surveillance to any residual means-tested benefits required to smooth the transition to a Citizen's Basic Income scheme that can manage without them. Whether or not the Citizen's Basic Income made people better off at the point of implementation, anyone currently on means-tested benefits would eventually benefit from the lower marginal deduction rates, and everyone would benefit from the more secure income floor and the more efficient economy that would result from implementing a Citizen's Basic Income (Levitas, 2012: 451; Rathbone [1930] 2012).

Perhaps the issue in relation to which the question 'Efficient for what?' is at its most acute is that of climate change. Here the efficiency question is this: What kind of economy would be most efficient in relation to the economy's ability to reduce carbon emissions and provide the planet and its multitude of species with a sustainable future?

CLIMATE CHANGE

Climate change: an alteration in the regional or global climate; esp. the change in global climate patterns increasingly apparent from the mid to late 20th cent. onwards and attributed largely to the increased levels of atmospheric carbon dioxide produced by the use of fossil fuels. (Oxford English Dictionary)

The most serious issue facing us today is climate change: the warming of the Earth's surface because an increasing concentration of carbon dioxide in the atmosphere prevents heat from leaving the planet's surface. This is not the place for a general discussion of climate change: but it is the place for a discussion of the relationship between climate change and Citizen's Basic Income.

A fundamental problem is economic growth. Economies that grow use more energy – which often means more fossil fuels – and they use up natural resources, which too often results in the destruction of such carbon sinks as the Amazon rainforest. First of all we need to ask a question about what we mean by economic growth; and then we need to ask how we can reduce the growth that damages the climate and facilitate growth that does not.

In Chapter 12 on political economy we discuss economic growth in terms of Gross Domestic Product: but it is also important to ask the question: What other kinds of growth might we wish to see in our society? Gross Domestic Product measures only those goods and services that are exchanged for money, and there is a lot of useful production of both goods and services that never gets anywhere near the money economy. For instance, as John Bowlby has put it:

Man and woman power devoted to the production of material goods counts a plus in all our economic indices. Man and woman power devoted to the production of happy, healthy and self-reliant children in their own homes does not count at all. We have created a topsy-turvy world. (Bowlby, 1988: 2)

It is from insights such as this that wellbeing economics sets out. It recognizes that some kinds of economic growth can harm wellbeing, for instance, by polluting the environment and causing climate change, and that the task of the economy and of economics is to serve people's wellbeing rather than Gross Domestic Product for its own sake. Dalziel, Saunders and Saunders (2018) argue that wellbeing economics requires attention to seven different types of capital: human, cultural, social, economic, natural, knowledge, and diplomatic (Dalziel et al., 2018: 10); that decisions should be taken about how to build and employ these different capitals at the personal, household, civil society, market participation, local government, nation state, and global community levels (Dalziel et al., 2018: 11); and that the two lists cohere with each other, with decisions about human capital being taken mainly at the personal level, decisions about cultural capital being taken mainly at the household level, and so on (Dalziel et al., 2018: 13). Take as an example of this approach the impor- tance of parents being able to take decisions over their use of time (Dalziel et al., 2018: 24), and in particular over how much time they can spend with their children. Citizen's Basic Income's potential for providing parents with greater choice over their allocation of time to both paid employment and unpaid caring work might prove to be of far more benefit to society than any of the economic growth that we might measure by calculating Gross Domestic Product.

However, whilst we might be able to see how a variety of different kinds of growth might be facilitated, it is more difficult to work out how to reduce the kinds of economic growth measured by Gross Domestic Product (GDP). Unfortunately, if we were to reduce the money supplied by governments in an effort to restrict economic growth, then the gap between GDP and the money available to pay for it would probably be filled by consumer credit. However, at some point both public opinion and government action might seek a degrowth agenda, in which case providing a Citizen's Basic Income would ameliorate the inevitable turbulence in household economies. Citizen's Basic Income would not by itself serve up a degrowth economy – different ways would have to be found to do that – but if a Citizen's Basic Income for every individual were already in place, then we could have some confidence that the poverty and inequality that might otherwise result from a degrowth process might to some extent be avoided.

In the meantime, an important problem has to be faced. Because marginal propensity to consume is higher among low income households than among high income households, if inequality is reduced then more money will flow towards low income households and less towards high income households, so consumption will increase, which would be likely to exacerbate climate change. This is an unfortunate conclusion to have to draw. In one sense this is not a problem for Citizen's Basic Income: it is a problem for any mechanism that reduces inequality. However, if a Citizen's Basic Income scheme were to reduce inequality, then care would have to be taken that climate change would not accelerate. One way to do that would be to put in place financial measures that would reduce carbon dioxide emissions, which means measures that would reduce the use of fossil fuels. An obvious mechanism to achieve this would be carbon taxes. Carbon, in the form of fossil fuels, is easy to tax, because the raw material enters the economy at relatively few entry points, and the fuel is used locally and not elsewhere in the world. Very little of the tax base would be out of reach of taxation. Unfortunately, poorer households spend higher proportions of their incomes on heating their homes than wealthier households, so if carbon taxation were to be used to reduce the use of fossil fuels, then the incomes of poorer households would have to be increased. The obvious solution is to combine carbon taxation with a Citizen's Basic Income that redistributed sufficiently from rich to poor to ensure that the living standards of poorer households would not be reduced by the combination of carbon taxation and the Citizen's Basic Income scheme (Cato, 2010; Fitzpatrick, 1999: 201; Howard et al., 2019). This is the solution agreed by the Government of Canada (2018): to put a price on carbon use, and to return 90 per cent of the proceeds directly to households as a dividend. The dividend is not quite a Citizen's Basic Income because it is household-based and not based on the individual, but it isn't far off. Canada's solution to the problem needs to be tried elsewhere. Carbon taxes on their own could disadvantage poorer households, and a redistributive Citizen's Basic Income scheme could increase global warming, but the combination of the two could reduce the speed of climate change and at the same time protect the incomes of poorer households – and of course provide them with all of the other advantages of a Citizen's Basic Income. As Ian Gough suggests, 'the goal must be to respect biophysical boundaries while at the same time pursuing sustainable wellbeing: that is, wellbeing for all current peoples and for future generations' (Gough, 2017: 37); and as he recognizes, a Citizen's Basic Income

… would provide more freedom of choice over citizens' life courses; it would promote a better work–life balance, enhance gender equality and expand choices between paid and unpaid work. It might enable more people to contribute to the 'core economy' … [it would] reduce division and stigma and enhance social solidarity. … [it would contribute to] a realistic transition strategy from the present to a post-growth society. (Gough, 2017: 184, 185, 186)

CONCLUSIONS

Employing several aspects of economic science has provided us with insights that might be useful as the Citizen's Basic Income debate continues. We have learnt that a Citizen's Basic Income would not interfere in employment market decisions in the same way that means-tested benefits do; and that different methods of funding Citizen's Basic Incomes, and different levels of payment, would result in different effects on consumption and income distribution. We have found that club theory provides a useful lens through which to see the difference that Citizen's Basic Income might make to our society; and we have discussed the concept of efficiency. Perhaps most importantly, we have discovered that an appropriate Citizen's Basic Income scheme alongside a tax on carbon use would reduce carbon emissions and at the same time protect household net incomes. In this chapter's case study, we shall discover that while Negative Income Tax and Citizen's Basic Income might appear similar to an economist, they look very different to an administrator.

Alongside the insights that economic theory of various kinds has given us into Citizen's Basic Income and its possible effects, we have found that the exercise of relating economic theory to Citizen's Basic Income has posed some questions to economics, particularly in relation to the assumptions and methods employed by classical economic theory.

We have found the building of relationships between economics and Citizen's Basic Income to be a fruitful activity. More such relationship-building should be attempted.

CASE STUDY

Is Negative Income Tax the Same as Citizen's Basic Income?

The relationship between net income and earned income in the context of a Citizen's Basic Income can be expressed as in Figure 5.9. This figure assumes a single rate of income tax and no means-tested benefits. In the absence of income tax and of a Citizen's Basic Income, the relationship between earned income and net income is shown by the line OA. If a Citizen's Basic Income of £x were to be paid, and income tax were to be collected on earned income, then the relationship between earned income and net income would be as shown by the line BC.

Income tax paid increases as earned income increases. Negative Income Tax (NIT) is the reverse of income tax: that is, as earned income decreases, increasing amounts of NIT are added to earned income.

In Figure 5.10, income tax is deducted from earnings above an earnings threshold £y, and a Negative Income Tax pays money to the employee below the threshold.

As we can see from Figures 5.9 and 5.10, if the amount of NIT paid to someone with no earnings is £x, and in the context of a Citizen's Basic Income the net income and earned income are equal at £y, then the relationship between earned income and net income is exactly the same for both the Citizen's Basic Income and the Negative Income Tax. The purely theoretical

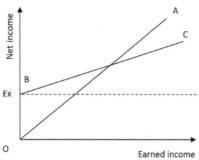

Source: Torry, 2015a.

Figure 5.9   *Graphical representation of a Citizen's Basic Income*

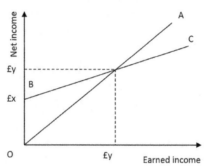

Source: Torry, 2015a.

Figure 5.10   *Graphical representation of a Negative Income Tax*

approach adopted here would suggest that Negative Income Tax and Citizen's Basic Income are really the same thing, and unfortunately this has sometimes led to the two being confused with each other (Pereira, 2017: 2–3; Sommer, 2016). They are not the same. Citizen's Basic Income pays out to everyone and then taxes it back, so everyone is both receiving Citizen's Basic Income and paying income tax, whereas Negative Income Tax pays out to individuals below an earnings threshold and collects tax from those above it. These differences really matter.

To the advantage of Negative Income Tax, a laboratory experiment in Japan suggests that Negative Income Tax provides a materially greater work incentive than Citizen's Basic Income, even if the relationship between earned income and net disposable income is the same in both cases, probably because the loss of a greater amount of tax creates a larger psychological effect than the receipt of the Citizen's Basic Income (Thaler and Sunstein, 2009: 36–7; Thaler, 2015: 33–4). An argument also offered is that a Negative Income Tax would involve less 'churn' – that is, less money would need to be moved (Story, 2015: 37–8) – and that because no money would be paid out to individuals above a threshold, the idea might be palatable politically in contexts in which a Citizen's Basic Income might not be (Torpey, 2017: 77).

To the advantage of Citizen's Basic Income: the administration of a Negative Income Tax would be far more difficult for governments, employers, individuals and households than the administration of a Citizen's Basic Income, because administration of the latter could not be simpler. In tax systems in which employers collect tax and send it to the government, employers would also pay out Negative Income Tax. They would therefore need to know about their employees' other employments or self-employments; if someone became unemployed for a period, then the administration of their NIT would need to be returned to the government; and then when they found employment the administration would need to be transferred to the new employer. Similarly, because the Negative Income Tax would vary during the year, if either the Negative Income Tax or net disposable income (of which the Negative Income Tax would be a component) were to be taken into account when other benefits were calculated, then constant recalculation would be required: which would not be the case with Citizen's Basic Income (Honkanen, 2014). A Negative Income Tax would be just as difficult to administer as the UK's means-tested Universal Credit. A Citizen's Basic Income would simply keep on arriving in every individual's bank account, and no active administration would be required (Story, 2015: 37–8; Torry, 2015a; 2016a: 126–30). The fact that more money would need to be moved than with a Negative Income Tax would hardly be relevant.

This exercise shows that formal graphical description can usefully reveal similarities between different policy options, but also that study of how different options would need to be administered can reveal significant differences that do not show up in the formal models.

6.   The psychology of Citizen's Basic Income

Psychology: The scientific study of the nature, functioning, and development of the human mind, ... the branch of science that deals with the (human or animal) mind as an entity and in its relationship to the body and to the environmental or social context, based on observation of the behaviour of individuals or groups of individuals in particular (ordinary or experimentally controlled) circumstances. ... The psychological aspects of an event, activity, phenomenon, etc., esp. considered as a subject for study.

(Oxford English Dictionary)

INTRODUCTION

The discipline of psychology is capacious: inevitably so, because every aspect of our lives as individuals or as a society relates to the human mind. To attempt a comprehensive view of what might normally be included under the label 'psychology' for the purposes of teaching or researching it would clearly be impossible. Instead, this chapter will offer a number of aspects of the discipline that appear to the author to be the most relevant to studying the desirability, feasibility and implementation of Citizen's Basic Income.

PSYCHOLOGY

I shall take as my first guide to the discipline of psychology the textbook *Psychology*, by Ronald Smith (Smith, 1993b). The contents page reveals the breadth of the discipline. The first chapter describes psychology as the science of behaviour, and following chapters study research methods, and the roots of behaviour in biology and in the influences encountered during infancy, childhood, adolescence, and adulthood. Sensation, perception, states of consciousness, learning, memory, reasoning, problem-solving, and intelligence, are then discussed; and then follow chapters on motivation, emotion, personality, stress, coping, and wellbeing. There are then chapters on psychological disorders and their treatment, and finally chapters on social influences on behaviour, and on social interaction, which are the subject matter of social psychology. The final chapter is about how the insights of the discipline of psychology are applied in a variety of contexts.

Although in this chapter the material will relate closely to the behaviour of the individual human mind, nobody is an island, and each individual mind relates to many others in society and cannot help being influenced by them. This means that some of the material in this chapter might have been located in Chapter 7 on social psychology, and some of the content of that chapter might legitimately have been placed here.

My second guide will be a briefing paper by the UK collective Psychologists for Social Change, *Universal Basic Income: A psychological impact assessment* (Psychologists for Social Change, 2017). This discusses a number of psychological consequences of the structural changes that a Citizen's Basic Income would be likely to bring about.

Psychological Indicators of a Healthy Society

A briefing paper from Psychologists for Social Change, *Universal Basic Income: A psychological impact assessment*, begins by setting out a number of structural changes that the authors believe a Citizen's Basic Income would bring about: fewer people would suffer the bureaucratic intrusion intrinsic to means-tested benefits; the quality of jobs would improve because people would have more choice over whether or not to take a particular job; and there would therefore be fewer jobs with poor psychosocial characteristics. The paper lists 'five evidence based psychological indicators of a healthy society' (although it might have been better to title the section 'five evidence based psychological indicators of healthy minds in a healthy society'), and it argues that the way in which Citizen's Basic Income would affect these indicators suggests that the outcome would be a healthier society.

The five indicators, along with the ways in which they would be affected by Citizen's Basic Income (termed here a Universal Basic Income) are as follows (I make no apology for quoting at length):

Agency

A sense of agency and mastery over one's life is crucial for positive mental health and well-being (Ryan and Deci, 2000) … A key argument for a UBI is that it gives people more agency over their lives, with less interference from others, such as the state or employers. There is strong evidence, for example, that low control is associated with work stress (Karasek, 1979; Van der Doef and Maes, 1999). … The UBI could have the effect of motivating employers to create more desirable jobs, with a better balance between demands on employees and the control they are able to exert at work, in order to recruit and retain employees. … UBI would change the role of the state in people's lives. There would be no requirements for citizens to 'sign on', attend job centres or be assessed for their capability. If the UBI, as hoped, could allow people to make more autonomous choices, which are not simply driven by financial need or coercion, then this is likely to increase life satisfaction ... (Psychologists for Social Change, 2017)

– an outcome somewhat different from the 'sanctions and other measures experienced as punitive by welfare recipients' (Friedli and Stearn, 2015: quoted in Psychologists for Social Change, 2017). This section of the Psychologists for Social Change paper could have been summed up in the words of the National Mental Wellbeing Impact Assessment Collaborative: 'The extent to which individuals and communities have control over their lives has a significant influence on mental health and overall health' (National MWIA Collaborative, 2011: 18; cf. Wallerstein, 1992).

Security

Employment insecurity is associated with a range of individual and family psychological difficulties, including distress (Dekker and Schaufeli, 1995), depression (Meltzer et al., 2010), strained relationships, and overall poorer life satisfaction (Silla et al., 2009). Similarly, insecure housing resulting in frequent house moves impairs academic performance and probably other aspects of child well-being, particularly for low-income families. Financial insecurity worries often form a basis for family stress, which can contribute to poorer outcomes for children, including their mental health. (Psychologists for Social Change, 2017)

The paper goes on to reference the recent increase in zero hour contracts, and the section concludes that

a social policy that enables a less stressful financial context for families is arguably an investment in the nation's future mental health. The UBI means that there is a minimal threat of falling into absolute poverty, ensuring people experience greater security and thus overall better physical and mental health. (Psychologists for Social Change, 2017)

Connection

Positive mental health and well-being is deeply connected to our relationships with others and is a core psychological need. One of the greatest protective factors for positive mental health is social support, and indeed its opposite, loneliness, is very bad for our health; having an impact on mortality rates equal to smoking and alcohol (Holt-Lunstad, 2018). (Psychologists for Social Change, 2017)

Now that employment is less secure, relationships at work are less likely to provide the sense of connection that we need, so we shall be more reliant on family and community relationships, both of which could be enhanced by a Citizen's Basic Income, because it would give people more choice over how to spend their time.

> Affording citizens more time to participate in wider community agencies, governing and political processes could enable a virtuous cycle of an increasing sense of agency, empowerment and control over the social environment, further predicted to improve mental health. … (Parsfield, 2015). (Psychologists for Social Change, 2017)

Meaning

A Citizen's Basic Income would mean that

> the population could have more time to spend on activities that connect to values, potentially creating more meaningful lives that are more psychologically fulfilling. … people could choose to prioritize spending time on creative projects, volunteering or other nonpaid work (such as caring) that has meaning for them. … meaningful work and activities could become more accessible and equitable across different demographics within society. (Psychologists for Social Change, 2017)

A sense of meaning matters, because it correlates with quality of life. (We discuss later in this chapter the increased motivation that can result from activities being pursued for their intrinsic value rather than for extrinsic reward.)

Trust

'Social relationships are important determinants of mental health' (Psychologists for Social Change, 2017), so social cohesion, trust, and involvement in community life are essential.

> The psychological impact of means tested benefits, as per the current system in the UK, inherently produces a 'deserving' and 'undeserving poor', generating stigma and mistrust of 'outgroups'. … social policies that improve social cohesion and trust are likely to reduce mental health problems. (Psychologists for Social Change, 2017)

(A corroborating research result is that surveillance can be demotivating because it represents distrust, particularly when the surveillance belongs to a strategy of control, or when its purpose is not clear (Enzle and Anderson, 1993). This suggests that work tests and sanctions regimes are likely to be counterproductive.)

An assumption made in *Universal Basic Income: A Psychological Impact Assessment* is that the Citizen's Basic Income implemented would be large enough to enable current means-tested benefits to be abolished. If this were not the case then the psychological improvements experienced by individuals and households still on means-tested benefits would not be as significant as the effects on individuals and households able to come off them; and the effects on the employment market might not be as significant. However, a Citizen's Basic Income of any size would be able to reduce the number of households on means-tested benefits, and to bring many households within striking distance of coming off them, and so could begin to improve the range of employment market decisions for all of those households. As the Citizen's Basic Income increased in size, those effects would become larger, slowly creating a more healthy society.

Psychologists for Social Change summarize their findings thus:

> Evidence from previous Basic Income-oriented experiments indicates the potential for UBI to increase all five psychological indicators of a healthy society: agency, security, connection, meaning and trust. The security and flexibility of a UBI is likely to give citizens a stronger sense of agency, greater personal mastery and more control over their lives, which evidence shows would lead to an increase in life satisfaction. The population could have more time to spend with friends, family and in their communities and would experience higher levels of social support as a result, which is incredibly important for well-being. People might gain a renewed sense of purpose and meaning through activities outside of currently constructed 'paid' employment, leading to a weakening of the current over-importance placed on paid work as part of the 'good life'. UBI is likely to lead to a general increase in social trust and a lessening of the shame, humiliation and devaluation that comes with relying on means-tested welfare benefits or being occupied in unpaid caring. In the light of all these positive social impacts of UBI, its introduction has the potential to be a hugely significant and beneficial public health intervention. (Psychologists for Social Change, 2017)

And they conclude

> that the UBI has great potential as a policy proposal for improving psychological health and wellbeing and reducing emotional distress. It is likely to have a sig-nificant impact both on the social determinants of mental health and on the five psychological indicators of a healthy society, namely security, connection, meaning, trust and agency. ... can we afford not to explore, rigorously test and implement it? (Psychologists for Social Change, 2017; cf. Watkins, 2010)

We shall now scour the psychology and social psychology literature for themes, insights and evidence that might be relevant to the Citizen's Basic Income debate, before drawing together our discoveries and the conclusions drawn by Psychologists for Social Change.

Motivation

An objection often raised in relation to both the desirability and feasibility of Citizen's Basic Income is that giving people an unconditional income would mean that they would be less likely to work, with 'work' here meaning paid employment. Motivation is a psychological issue, so this is a natural subject for this chapter.

Motivation is 'an internal process that influences the direction, persistence, and vigor of goal-directed behavior' (Smith, 1993b: 367): so the study of human motivation is an attempt to discover 'why human ... organisms think and behave as they do' (Weiner, 1992: 1). Intrinsic motivation, which 'is the energy source that is central to the active nature of the organism' (Deci and Ryan, 1985: 11), is enhanced when the psychological needs for 'competence, autonomy, and relatedness' are met (Ryan and Deci, 2000), and is 'vulnerable to the continued encroachment of environmental forces' (Deci and Ryan, 1985: 43). We might therefore expect the intrusive and stigmatizing processes connected with means-tested benefits to reduce motivation, and the competence-assuming, autonomy-enhancing, and relatedness-facilitating Citizen's Basic Income to enhance motivation. A pressured environment – such as that created by a combination of insecure employment and uncertain in-work means-tested benefits (Hilton, 2014) – might reduce intrinsic motivation (Reeve and Deci, 1996). The less pressured environment that a Citizen's Basic Income would foster would increase motivation.

More specifically, in relation to income and work, 'expectancy x value theory' suggests that motivation is a function of both the strength of someone's expectation that an activity will result in a particular goal being met, and the value that the person ascribes to the goal (Smith, 1993b: 369), as well as being a function of the difficulty of the task and of the individual's skill level (Brehm and Self, 1989; Weiner, 1992: 219). If a household receiving means-tested benefits decides to seek an increase in disposable income, then in the context of means-tested benefits, and particularly benefits subject to multiple regulations and sanctions, experience of attempting to increase disposable income by someone in the household seeking additional paid employment will soon reduce the expectation that the goal can be achieved. In a context in which a Citizen's Basic Income has replaced all or most of a household's means-tested benefits income, the relationship between disposable income and earned income will be far more transparent, so the expectation that a higher disposable income can be achieved will be at a higher level, which means that the motivation to achieve the goal will be higher.

An important distinction is that between intrinsic and extrinsic motivation: the former generated by our own needs, and the latter by external causes (Pittman and Heller, 1987). A classic example of the latter is the research result that 'children who are expected by their teachers to gain intellectually in fact do show greater intellectual gains after one year than do children of whom such gains are not expected' (Rosenthal and Jacobson, 1992: 121). However, alongside the distinction, we need to recognize that any particular action might be motivated by a connected combination of the two kinds of motivation. Because we need an income if we are to sustain ourselves and any dependents, we experience an intrinsic motivation to seek paid employment; and because paid employment can be experienced as a disutility – that is, it can have an adverse effect on our wellbeing – a monetary reward might be required to induce us to go to work (Bryson and MacKerron, 2013): that is, as an extrinsic motivator. Our employer's provision of the income that we need is therefore a combination of extrinsic and intrinsic motivators.

If we are rewarded for something that we were doing for its own sake, and the extrinsic reward is then withdrawn, then motivation might drop below the level that it was at before the reward was offered (Brehm et al., 1999: 62; Lepper and Greene, 1978: xi; Smith, 1993b: 369). However, if rewards are experienced as recognition of performance, rather than as an incentive to undertake a particular task, then they can be motivating; and if the task is initially undertaken for reward, then the reward might also be motivating (Brehm et al., 1999: 62; Cameron and Pierce, 1994; Smith, 1993b: 370): although all of these effects are in fact quite small, they often depend on the social environment in which tasks are undertaken, and some of the relationships have been questioned (Eisenberger and Cameron, 1996; Tang and Hall, 1995). Research has shown that 'widely differing external constraints will undermine creativity, as long as those constraints can lead people to view their work as extrinsically motivated rather than intrinsically motivated' (Amabile, 1996: 171), and that

> positive effects of reward ... appear when intrinsic motivation is kept salient, when extrinsic motivation becomes less salient ... and when rewards signify competence or enable performance of interesting new activities – rather than signifying external control of behavior ... A considerable body of ... evidence suggests that constraint placed on task engagement has consistent negative effects on creativity. (Amabile, 1996: 177)

While Citizen's Basic Income would be unlikely to be experienced as a reward for particular behaviours, it might give to some individuals and households the ability to take on tasks in a voluntary capacity that they would previously only have been able to take on if they were paid to do them. Such activity, undertaken for its own sake and not for reward, can be highly motivating. It would, of course, be essential not then to reward it: and, in particular, it would be important not to reward it with a Participation Income (an income conditional on fulfilling a participation condition) (Atkinson, 1996; Torry, 2016a: 124–6, 134–9).

As Pech points out, if a Citizen's Basic Income were to provide more of the income security that households need, then employment would not need to provide so much of it. This would mean that there would be less need to accept undesirable jobs simply because a wage was required, and a greater ability to accept more desirable jobs with lower financial rewards. In order to attract workers, undesirable jobs would need to pay more, and the larger number of workers seeking more desirable jobs would mean that those jobs could pay less (Pech, 2010: 9–10).

A particularly interesting research result is that, in relation to employment, the level of pay is not a significant motivator, and that 'only procedural justice [is] related to intrinsic work motivation ... how people's compensation is determined and communicated has implications for employees' need satisfaction' (Olafsen et al., 2015: 455). If a household's employment income changes, then they might find changes in the calculation of their in-work means-tested benefits (such as the UK's Working Tax Credits, Child Tax Credits and Universal Credit) to be opaque, and that the communication of the changes and the reasons for them might be by way of a demand for repayment of an overpayment. Demotivation might be the result. How a Citizen's Basic Income would be calculated could not be more transparent.

Motivation is a complex field, but we can already see that there would be a variety of ways in which a Citizen's Basic Income could improve motivation.

During the Second World War, Juliet Rhys Williams, a member of the committee charged with reforming the UK's social insurance system and chaired by William Beveridge, objected to the Beveridge report's recommendations because she believed that the means-tested aspects of the proposals would damage the will to seek employment (Rhys Williams, 1943: 13, 45, 141). Any household on means-tested benefits would experience a significant marginal deduction rate – that is, as their earnings rose, benefits would be withdrawn, so there might be very little increase in disposable income. If someone is already in employment then they are in the 'poverty trap'; and if they are not, and on entering employment they find that they receive little additional disposable income, then they are in the 'unemployment trap' (Parker, 1995: 27). In a household-based means-tested system, depending on the detail of the regulations, a second earner entering employment might find that the household reaps almost no financial benefit from their initiative. They too are in an 'unemployment trap'. Part-time employment in particular can end up adding very little to household disposable income (Cory, 2013; Torry, 2008). There are of course numerous motivating factors in relation to employment or self-employment because they can generate self-esteem, companionship, and skills development, as well as financial reward, so it is no surprise that full-time employment is fairly inelastic in relation to marginal deduction rates: that is, as marginal deduction rates change, employment does not change very much. However, there *is* an effect, especially in relation to part-time employment; and if one earner in a household loses their job, and the household ends up on means-tested benefits, then another earner might give up their job or reduce their employment hours (Atkinson and Mogensen, 1993: 191; Emmerson et al., 2014: 161). When someone is unemployed and seeks a job, or they leave or lose a job and seek a new one with a higher wage, they might not be aware of the effect of the unemployment and poverty traps, so those traps might not influence their decisions. However, we learn from experience, so the more such transitions take place, the more someone will be aware that increasing earned income does not necessarily translate into increasing disposable income. Effects can be cumulative. In the context of a means-tested system, governments are trapped between two undesirable alternatives: raising the levels of means-tested benefits in order to assist poor families, or lowering them to incentivize employment; or, alternatively, either reducing the taper rate, which extends the disincentive effects higher up the earnings range and draws more families into means-testing, or increasing the taper rate in order to take families off means-tested benefits more quickly, which deepens the poverty and unemployment traps for those still subject to means-testing (Adam et al., 2006: 1). One way or another, demotivation is inevitable.

Burchardt and Le Grand suggest that several factors are involved in any employment market decision: (1) Factors over which someone has no control, such as age; (2) Factors over which someone has no control at present, such as educational achievement; (3) Factors that someone can change in the near future, such as place of residence; and (4) Factors that someone could change easily, such as doing voluntary work. Burchardt and Le Grand conclude that 'just 1 in 10 of non-employed men, and a similar proportion of non-employed women, can be unambiguously classified as voluntarily out of work' (Burchardt and Le Grand, 2002: 24): that is, none of the factors listed are in play. Some of the factors a Citizen's Basic Income would not change: but we can see that it might enable someone to seek a few hours of employment each week alongside voluntary work, both of which would enhance their skills, or that it might enable them to repair an educational deficit. To be provided with additional options for the use of time would increase motivation (Palermo Kuss and Neumärker, 2018).

A very large Citizen's Basic Income would enable some people to leave the employment market, but even with a large unconditional income lots of individuals would stay in the much-improved experience that their job would become, or they would move to a better job. With the smaller Citizen's Basic Income that would be feasible in the short to medium term we would see some increased motivation in relation to both paid and unpaid activity. Even a Citizen's Basic Income scheme that left means-tested benefits in place and recalculated them in relation to changed net earnings and the Citizen's Basic Incomes that household members would be receiving, would float lots of households off means-tested benefits, and would bring many households within striking distance of coming off them, enabling them to seek a few hours of employment to escape from them.

One of the real problems with in-work means-tested benefits is that they cope even less well with self-employment than they do with employment. Escape from complex means-tested benefits would mean release from the high marginal deduction rates as well as from the bureaucratic intrusion that means-testing involves, and it would more easily enable workers to combine with others to form co-operatives in order to benefit themselves, their families, and their communities. Such enterprises can be highly motivating (Carmen, 2000). The overall effect of a Citizen's Basic Income could therefore be positive for positive motivation, thus reducing governments' felt need to impose such techniques as benefits sanctions which, as we have seen, can be counterproductive. No longer would the entire benefits system be designed to control workers at the same time as maintaining household incomes (Dean, 2012c: 51). The Citizen's Basic Income elements of household incomes would for the first time provide a solid financial floor on which every household could build, and it would both increase employment motivation and reduce the level of government control over workers.

A possible objection to Citizen's Basic Income is that people would stop working – in the sense of seeking gainful employment – if they were given an unconditional income. The argument that we have outlined suggests that this would not be the case. Empirical research has come to the same conclusion by showing that almost no withdrawal from employment takes place when workers are given unconditional incomes (Gilbert et al., 2018).

Behavioural Insights

Whether we call it behavioural economics, behavioural science, or behavioural insights – where does it belong? In a chapter on economics, in a chapter on psychology, or in a chapter on social psychology? (Egan, 2017: 58–61). This section of the book is located here because behavioural science is less about how money or society functions, and more about how the human mind works.

What are governments to do when faced with such large and complex problems as growing inequality? The foundational insight of behavioural economics is that such problems are rooted in individuals' behaviours that damage both those individuals and the society to which they belong. As the roots are psychological, governments need to 'nudge' in order to shift current behaviour patterns towards new ones, and private sector organizations might choose to employ similar methods. This insight has generated an industry of experiments in order to discover the roots of behaviours and the most effective nudging mechanisms. As behavioural scientists understand the situation, the problem to be overcome is that for the individuals concerned there might be no short-term gain to changing their behaviour, even if many individuals changing their behaviours would benefit society as a whole and therefore each person as an individual. A secondary problem is that in an era in which governments are less trusted, a government explaining to individuals how changed behaviour would benefit themselves and others might be counterproductive. This situation requires governments to tailor messages so that they will be heard, and to adjust the 'choice architecture' facing individuals in such a way as to encourage more beneficial behaviour: so instead of telling people to keep their doctors' appointments, the message might state how much more money would be available to the National Health Service if everyone kept their appointments; instead of telling people to pay their taxes on time, a government might inform taxpayers that nine out of ten people have already paid their taxes, thus reinforcing a social norm; and to change the choice architecture for pension contributions from opt-in to enforced enrolment accompanied by an opt-out option might again reinforce an existing social norm. Someone is more likely to agree to a medical operation if they are told that 90 per cent of people survive than if they are told that 10 per cent of people die (Thaler and Sunstein, 2009: 37): and, in general, how a question is framed will partly determine the response.

> Framing works because people tend to be somewhat mindless, passive decision makers. Their Reflective System [as opposed to their Automatic System] does not do the work that would be required to check and see whether reframing the question would produce a different answer. One reason they don't do this is that they wouldn't know what to make of the contradiction. This implies that frames are powerful nudges, and must be selected with caution. (Thaler and Sunstein, 2009: 40)

This approach has understandably been labelled a 'new paternalism' (Abdukadirov, 2016). It raises other questions, too. Does it divert policymaking energy from potentially beneficial evidence-based interventionist policy? (Egan, 2017: 44–7, 65; Thierer, 2016). And is it entirely ethical to 'nudge' people without explaining that that is what is happening? An important difference is between nudges that enhance someone's ability to reach self-selected goals, and nudges that make it more likely that individuals will serve other people's goals (Rizzo, 2016); and another important difference is between nudges that work without the nudged being invited to think, for instance, putting sweets next to the supermarket checkout; and nudges that require the nudged to think, for instance by putting fruit by the checkout: a nudge that might initiate a thinking process that the 'five a day' slogan might already have initiated (Citizen's Basic Income Trust, 2018b; John, 2018a; White, 2016).

And perhaps another question needs to be raised: even though academics have often made their behavioural science as easy to understand as possible, and governments have publicly and institutionally committed themselves to behavioural approaches in policymaking, there can be institutional constraints to the extent to which policy can reflect behavioural insights, and policymakers, and those who implement policy, are as likely to behave irrationally as those for whom they are making and implementing policy, resulting in conflicts of interest between the nudgers and the nudged (Williams, 2016: 326). The behavioural sciences might have handed the wealthy and powerful elite yet one more means of controlling society to their own benefit; or it might have provided the internet-connected public with a means of nudging policymakers and public policy. Who will ensure that nudgers question the goals that their nudges seek to meet? (Smith and Zywicki, 2016: 245) Who will nudge the nudgers? Behavioural economics, by problematizing the rational utility-maximizing individual, constitutes an attack on the classical economic model at its heart (Thaler, 2015: 50), and mainstream economics is already shifting towards a recognition that we might wish to maximize others' utilities as well as our own. Who will nudge economists towards new economic models that align with behavioural insights? And will the models they create be any less prescriptive than current rational utility-maximizing ones? (Citizen's Basic Income Trust, 2018b; John, 2018a).

A behavioural economics finding that is particularly relevant to a discussion of Citizen's Basic Income is the 'endowment effect': the research result that the loss of something already possessed is felt more keenly than a gain of the same value (Thaler and Sunstein, 2009: 36–7; Thaler, 2015: 33–4). A result that has confirmed this more general finding is that loss of benefits income is felt more keenly than the taxation of earnings, even if the monetary values concerned are the same (Avram, 2015): so, as earnings rise, the loss of benefits will be more keenly felt than the Income Tax charged on the additional earned income, because the combination of additional earned income and tax deducted will be experienced as an increase in net earned income and not as additional tax. This suggests that replacing means-tested benefits with Citizen's Basic Incomes could increase employment incentives, and that that effect would not be seriously blunted by manageable increases in income tax rates, although we would need to recognize that if tax allowances were reduced to pay for the Citizen's Basic Income then net earned income would fall, which might be felt more keenly than the gain of a new Citizen's Basic Income of the same value.

A second finding of behavioural science is that the certainty of not losing is preferable to uncertain gain or loss. This suggests that a system that contains an unconditional income would be more motivating than one that does not (Thaler, 2015: 33–4).

A further research result is that small gains that have no noticeable effect on our wellbeing have little impact on us, whereas larger gains that increase our wellbeing do. This suggests that the small gains in net income that result from the high marginal deduction rates associated with means-tested benefits will have little impact on us and will therefore not be experienced as motivators, whereas larger gains associated with the lower marginal deduction rates experienced by individuals and households no longer on means-tested benefits would act as motivators (Thaler, 2015: 20–30, 33).

Behavioural science such as this also offers lessons in relation to the Citizen's Basic Income debate. A particularly important result in this respect is that we are not always consistent: so, for instance, an individual might approve of both a Citizen's Basic Income along with a higher rate of income tax, and means-tested benefits along with a lower rate of income tax (Thaler, 2015: 47–9): and there would be nothing wrong with that because the two structures could work together quite happily.

As we have seen, we might have legitimate concerns in relation to the uses that might be made of behavioural sciences, but to employ some of their theories and research results might be useful as a means of understanding some of the potential effects of implementing a Citizen's Basic Income.

CONCLUSION

In an article in *The Guardian* in 2014, Oliver Burkeman asked why unconditional cash transfers, which in practical experiments have proved to be useful, have been implemented so rarely. He suggests that it is simply that the idea is 'too obvious'. As behavioural scientists constantly show, we are not always rational. 'The obvious options actually become non-obvious, because it's hard to remember they're options in the first place ... Sometimes, the surprising truth about the truth is that it isn't surprising at all' (Burkeman, 2014: 45).

CASE STUDY

Stress

'Stressors' are situations that make demands on us where there is an imbalance between the demands made and the resources to meet them (Smith, 1993b: 466), particularly in situations of complexity and uncertainty (Bekker et al., 2000). In prehistory, stress was usually momentary and was evolutionarily useful, as it prepared the hunter for a flight/fight response: but today's long-term stress, such as the stress related to poor job quality, has been shown to be correlated with damaged psychological and physical health (Paterson and Neufeld, 1989: 8). Research shows that support from colleagues, management, and trades unions, makes almost no difference, which suggests that only changing the situation itself would do so (Dekker and Schaufeli, 1995). Poverty and inequality create stress, and that affects families' wellbeing and therefore children's wellbeing (Jones et al., 2013: 4; Murali and Oyebode, 2004); and the World Health Organization has found that 'the greater the inequality, the higher the inequality in risk' (World Health Organization and Calouste Gulbenkian Foundation, 2014: 9). At least one of the mechanisms involved is that inequality correlates with failure to meet basic psychological needs, which in turn affects health (Di Domenico and Fournier, 2014). The same process operates in relation to unemployment, employment insecurity, underemployment, and poor quality jobs. Particularly in situations of uncertainty and ambiguity, psychological needs are not being met, and the unmet needs affect health (Butterworth et al., 2011; Dooley, 2003; Fryers et al., 2003: 236; Murphy and Athanasou, 1999; Paterson and Neufeld, 1989: 8; Sverke et al., 2002).

It is not just the actuality of insecure employment that creates stress (Quinlan et al., 2001): perceived employment insecurity has been shown to be negatively correlated with life satisfaction, and the strength of that correlation is found to be negatively correlated with the generosity of government provision for unemployed individuals (Carr and Chung, 2014). This means that where provision is ungenerous and grudging, life satisfaction will be reduced for individuals in insecure employment, underemployed individuals, and unemployed individuals. Similarly, stress related to poverty reduces cognitive function, because attention has to be paid to resource constraints, meaning that less attention is available for other cognitive tasks. Uncertainty over resource levels also requires attention, which means that when poverty and uncertainty over resource levels are experienced together, the cognitive load might leave little cognitive capacity for other tasks: so scarcity creates more scarcity (Mani et al., 2013; Mullainathan and Shafir, 2013: 47, 64–7).

A compounding factor is that mechanisms related to the benefits system can generate their own additional stresses. The administration of means-tested and work-tested benefits constitutes 'microstressors', or 'daily hassles' (Kohn et al., 1991; Smith, 1993b: 467). The problem with this kind of stressor is that over time, and often quite quickly, the situation saps the energy required to tackle demands, and the gap between 'demands' and 'resources' grows: so then the demands grow, and so on. The prolonged stress that is the result can manifest as 'alarm, resistance, and exhaustion' (Taylor, 1999: 200), can cause 'persistent psychological distress, reduced task performance, and over time, declines in cognitive capabilities' (Taylor, 1999: 201), and can permanently affect psychological wellbeing and worsen someone's health (Cohen and Edwards, 1989: 235; Cohen and Williamson, 1991; Epstein and Katz, 1992; Smith, 1993b: 474–5).

> Events that are negative, uncontrollable or unpredictable, ambiguous, overwhelming, and threatening of central life tasks are likely to be perceived as stressful. ...

any event that forces a person to make change increases stress and the likelihood of illness. The daily hassles of life can also affect health adversely, as can chronic exposure to stress. (Taylor, 1999: 201)

So, for instance, missed or reduced means-tested benefits payments, or the knowledge that benefits will be stopped or reduced if yet again a sick child makes attending an interview at the benefits office impossible, can be highly stressful when there is a family to feed, rent to pay, and a loan shark at the door demanding his money. The usual coping strategies, such as reappraising the situation and developing behavioural skills (Smith, 1993b: 487), might not be available. It is impossible to change the situation; it is not easy to reinterpret, accept, deny, repress, escape, or avoid the situation, or to control one's feelings; and, in a fragile community, help, guidance, emotional support, affirmation of worth, and such tangible aids as more money or a job, will be in short supply (Smith, 1993b: 477). Being able to cope can enhance wellbeing, and not being able to cope can do the opposite (Folkman and Lazarus, 1988).

It might have been thought that 'differences in social support systems, skills, attitudes, beliefs, and personality characteristics' could achieve a certain amount of 'stress buffering': but there is little evidence for that (Cohen and Edwards, 1989: 236). There can be no substitute for ameliorating the situation that is causing the stress, and any strategy likely to reduce stress needs to involve the relationships and social structures in which the stressed individual is involved (Meichenbaum, 1985: 12, 52). We need to reduce the 'risk' in today's 'risk society' (Dean, 2012c: 119–20). If a household were to transition from means-tested benefits to unconditional incomes, then not only would their situation have changed, but reappraisal would become more possible because income security would have enhanced a sense of security. 'A simple perception that one is in control of a situation is sufficient to reduce stress levels' (Neufeld and Paterson, 1989: 64).

At the same time as financial security would be increased, a greater variety of employment pattern options might reduce the stress experienced by parents, and particularly by women, as families attempt to balance employment and caring responsibilities (Lundberg and Frankenhaeuser, 1999). If part of the solution to stressful jobs and employment insecurity, and to parents not having sufficient time with their children, might be a shorter working week, then, as Coote, Franklin and Simms suggest, 'radical restructuring of state benefits' will be required (Coote et al., 2010: 4). A Citizen's Basic Income would clearly constitute an appropriate restructuring; and as an unconditional cash transfer programme in Kenya is showing, unconditional incomes can have some very positive effects on mental health (Haushofer and Shapiro, 2016). Marmot has shown that 'the social gradient in health is influenced by such factors as social position; relative versus absolute deprivation; and control and social participation'. The solution is to 'change society' (Marmot, 2003: S9, S21; cf. Marmot, 2013: 24, 32–3; Yuill, 2009).

7.   The social psychology of Citizen's Basic Income

Social psychology: The study of social interactions, including their origins and effects on individuals and groups.
(Oxford English Dictionary)

INTRODUCTION

The discipline of social psychology is as capacious as that of psychology: inevitably so, because every aspect of our lives as individuals or as a society relates to human minds functioning in a society. To attempt a comprehensive view of what might normally be included under the label 'social psychology' for the purposes of teaching or researching would clearly be impossible. Instead, this chapter will offer a number of aspects of the discipline that appear to the author to be the most relevant to study of the desirability, feasibility and implementation of Citizen's Basic Income. To do this is to contribute to a psychosocial approach to social policy, which recognizes 'the psychological dimension to welfare issues and ... the deep implication of the social and psychological sciences in the regulation and governance of welfare and well-being' and attempts 'to understand the expressive component of the social relations of welfare and their moral and ethical dimensions' (Stenner et al., 2008: 411).

SOCIAL PSYCHOLOGY

I shall take as my guide to the discipline of social psychology the textbook *Social Psychology*, by Sharon Brehm, Saud Kassin and Steven Fein (Brehm et al., 1999). The book is divided into chapters on the history of social psychology, social psychology research, self-esteem and the concept of the self, how we relate to other people, how we relate to groups, the formation of attitudes and how they change, social conformity, group processes, relationships, helping others, aggression, and applications to law, business, and health. As we can see, social psychology overlaps considerably with psychology, because the individual mind relates to society and is significantly influenced by it, and society is made up of individual minds. Just as Chapter 6 on the psychology of Citizen's Basic Income contained material that might legitimately have been placed in this chapter, so some of the content of this chapter might properly have been located in that one.

Social Norms

The Zimbardo prison study, in which college students were allocated roles as prisoners and guards and began to behave in very different ways, showed the extent to which 'social systems exert profound influences on our thoughts, emotions, attitudes, and behavior' (Smith, 1993b: 570). Whether it was the constructed social situation, or the students' clinging to group norms in a situation of uncertainty, that motivated their behaviour, the result stands: social systems influence our attitudes and behaviours (Haslam and Reicher, 2012; Zimbardo, 1972). Social systems are constructed out of 'rules of the game', that is, culturally transmitted social norms that regulate our behaviour (Staerklé et al., 2012: 81–3). Two particularly relevant examples of 'rules of the game' are the norm of reciprocity, and the related norms of taxpayer and benefits recipient.

We take our norms from 'reference groups' – the family, colleagues, and so on – in order to navigate a complex world; and we purposely seek out social environments that will help us to preserve existing attitudes: again, in order to navigate a complex world (Newcomb, 1963). Psychological experiments carried out by Sherif during the 1930s showed that, in a group situation, group members will conform to an evolving norm:

> Stereotypes, fads and fashions, customs, traditions, and attitudes are, psychologically, cases of the establishment of socially determined norms and values serving as frames of reference. (Sherif, 1935: 53)

If we are benefits recipients, then we will occupy roles that other benefits recipients occupy, and we will share that group's norms and attitudes. Similarly with taxpayers who are not benefits recipients, and with taxpayers who are.

However, social norms are precisely that: they are socially constructed norms, and they can be contested. So, for instance, the 'wages for housework' movement of the 1970s campaigned for wages for housework in order to locate housework as paid employment alongside other kinds of paid employment, and to dislodge it as a definition of a woman's role in society (Federici, 1975). Similarly, to argue for a Citizen's Basic Income would be to contest the social norm of 'benefits recipient'. Where a benefit or service is universal, the only source for norms, attitudes and roles is universality. We might all have opinions about the UK's National Health Service, but there are no distinct social groups with distinctive attitudes and roles in relation to it, and the only behavioural norm is turning up, using it, and not paying when we do so. The same is true of the UK's Child Benefit, although the new tax charge has somewhat complicated attitudes to it, and therefore norms that relate to it, with a new norm emerging among mothers living with high-earning men who are not the fathers of their children. Members of this group are tending to withdraw their Child Benefit claims: a new social norm. (The author bases this knowledge on families that he has known. He is not aware of any research on the issue.)

The Deserving and the Undeserving

Across Europe, and in other countries too, welfare provision, broadly defined to include health and education services as well as social security benefits, serves everyone's needs: particularly during childhood and old age, but also across the lifecycle. The idea that there is a clear division in society between 'them and us', with some households receiving from the state, and others paying for it, is an untenable myth: but it is persistent, and in the public mind it divides the welfare state from the rest of society (Blomberg et al., 2012: 75–7; Hills, 2014; Staerklé et al., 2012: 86; Svallfors, 2012b: 222–6). But the fact that there is in fact no clear division between taxpayers and the recipients of public expenditure; that there is considerable diversity across Europe in relation to the deserving/undeserving categories and people's attitudes towards them (van Oorschot et al., 2017); that inequality, insecure employment, and low pay, are the main causes of poverty, and not personal moral failings; and that inefficiency, errors, and disincentives are bigger benefits system problems than fraud and idleness, does not stop the press from sensationalizing individual abuses of social security benefits (Golding and Middleton, 1982: 129) and perpetuating the deserving/undeserving divide in the language of 'strivers' and 'skivers' perpetrated by politicians and 'orchestrated' in the print and other media (Golding and Middleton, 1982: 67, 75; Mau, 2003: 127; van Oorschot and Meuleman, 2012: 51–3). Those newspaper readers who are most likely to buy into the headline myths are precisely those in the most precarious economic situations (Golding and Middleton, 1982: 168, 181). As Runciman has shown, it is the inequalities closest to our own situations that we feel most keenly (Runciman, 1966).

A further factor might then come into play in perpetuating the deserving/ undeserving divide: a 'confirmation bias', or a 'self-fulfilling prophecy'. This is the situation in which two people given different information about an individual, and identical experiences of that individual, will draw evidence from the experience in such a way that it confirms what they have already been told (Darley and Gross, 1983; Murdock-Perriera and Sedlacek, 2018). The situations that have led to someone claiming means-tested benefits, and the ways in which they have been treated subsequent to their claim, can combine into a severe psychological challenge that completely demotivates the individual, enabling the non-claiming majority to blame the victim for their demotivation, to stigmatize them, and thus to make their situation even worse (Dean, 2012c: 104–6).

A connected factor is the 'fundamental attribution error', now often called 'correspondence bias', which occurs when we attribute behaviour to personal factors when it is the social situation that has been determinative (Hogg and Vaughan, 2014: 93; Smith, 1993b: 60; Weiner, 1992: 232–6). Someone might be demotivated in relation to job-search, not by personal factors, but by a debilitating sanctions regime (Fenger et al., 2016): but if the demotivation is then regarded as the moral failure of the jobseeker, then the individual might find themselves even more demotivated (Smith, 1993b: 609).

So would there be a psychological problem if a government were to attempt to implement a Citizen's Basic Income? Yes, because the deserving/undeserving divide is deeply embedded in our social psychology (van Oorschot et al., 2017: 341), and the reciprocity norm (see Chapter 4) is generally understood as ante/required: that is, a working age adult claimant must fulfil specified conditions before a payment can be made – and this attitude, like all such welfare regime attitudes, can be found right across the social class spectrum (Coughlin, 1980: 123–4) and so will be difficult to dislodge (Taylor-Gooby and Leruth, 2018), however often individuals tell opinion pollsters that they approve of the idea of a Citizen's Basic Income (European Social Survey, 2017).

An important connection between the reciprocity norm and the deserving/ undeserving divide is that we do not expect the reciprocity norm to apply to those deemed 'deserving'. Van Oorschot suggests that the 'deserving' are seen as 'personally responsible … people with greater need … closer to "us" … likeable, grateful, compliant and conforming to our standards … who have contributed … or who may be expected to be able to contribute in future' (van Oorschot, 2006: 26; cf. Larsen, 2006: 47–8); and Berg finds that territorial attachment is also an important deservingness criterion, which means that a Citizen's Basic Income at the European level would be difficult to establish (Berg, 2007: 100–6, 126–7; Levy et al., 2014; McKnight et al., 2016: 67–8, 80; Torry, 2013: 61–3; Van Parijs and Vanderborght, 2017: 230–41).

> Welfare conditionality … [is] ethically unjustifiable, because it disproportionately punishes poor people, is socially divisive, and, by primarily focusing on the responsibility to undertake paid work undermines other valid forms of social contribution, such as informal care. … it is largely ineffective in promoting paid employment or personal responsibility, and … it exacerbates social exclusion among disadvantaged populations. … welfare conditionality is really about blaming and punishing poor people for their marginalization, while simultaneously justifying their exclusion from ever-reducing support, offered via collectivized, publicly financed welfare rights. The behaviour change agenda is a smokescreen that obscures this much harsher reality. (Dwyer, 2019: 4, 177)

Deservingness criteria, along with the effects of a largely means-tested benefits system, mean that unemployed working age adults are not 'deserving' unless they fulfil some fairly rigorous conditions, or they are older, disabled, or looking after young children (Saunders and Pinyopusarek, 2001: 161). Implementing an unconditional income for the 'undeserving' would be difficult for the UK's and many other countries' policy processes to achieve. This suggests that the implementation of a Citizen's Basic Income might have to begin with unconditional incomes for demographic groups that fit the deservingness criteria: that is, older people and children, and, to some extent, individuals between the ages of 16 and 21 whom we expect to be in education or training (van Oorschot and Meuleman, 2012: 51).

It might have been thought that one possibility might be to start with an enhanced Child Benefit. However, although the National Health Service achieves significant public approval, unconditional Child Benefit experiences less than we might have hoped (Coughlin, 1980: 124): hence the ease with which the unadministrable proposal to means-test it was received, and the ease with which the associated additional tax charge for high earners living in households in receipt of Child Benefit was achieved (Torry, 2018a: 19–20). A possible reason for the UK public's ambivalence towards Child Benefit is that, although it is intended for children, it is paid to households that might contain 'undeserving' unemployed working age adults; and another possible reason is that it compromises the wealthy's self-concept as deserving of the entirety of their income and wealth.

This means that enhanced Child Benefit might be difficult to achieve, which leaves as possibilities a genuine Citizen's Pension – an unconditional pension for every older person – and a Citizen's Basic Income for individuals between their sixteenth and twenty-first birthdays, or perhaps between their eighteenth and twenty-first birthdays: and of course there is no reason why these two options should not both be attempted at the same time. The particularly interesting one would be the Citizen's Basic Income for young adults. Because this age group is not already enmeshed in the existing system, in the UK they could be charged Income Tax and National Insurance Contributions on all of their earnings, and paid a Citizen's Basic Income of the same value as the Income Tax Personal Allowance and the National Insurance Contributions Primary Earnings Threshold. The net cost would be minimal (Torry, 2016e).

How social policy issues are 'framed' – the framework of concepts within which they are expressed – will always have a significant effect on attitudes towards them and therefore on the policy process (6, 2018); and to frame policy issues in relation to values widely held in society can be particularly persuasive (Botterill and Fenna, 2019: 151). So to frame social security benefits in relation to an existing 'them and us' narrative, and to frame recipients as 'scroungers', is inaccurate (McKenzie, 2015: 13), but it will embed the deserving/undeserving narrative even deeper into our social consciousness. There would be many ways of framing a Citizen's Basic Income – as redistribution, as incentivizing work, and so on (Perkiö, 2012) – but it could never be framed in terms of 'them and us', or in terms of the deserving and the undeserving. Such a mismatch between contemporary societal values and values underlying Citizen's Basic Income could pose a problem, so a strategy would be required: for instance, to implement a Citizen's Basic Income for 'deserving' groups, which would begin the process of dissolving the deserving/undeserving distinction, so that by the time a government got round to extending the new provision to demographic groups previously thought to contain undeserving individuals, the categorization might have lost sufficient of its force to enable implementation of a Citizen's Basic Income for a whole population to be relatively easy to achieve.

The 'them and us' narrative is not the only available social value or norm. Unconditionality might also be a prevalent social value, particularly in countries that already have social policies characterized by unconditionalities, as in the UK, meaning that in such contexts Citizen's Basic Income can be framed in relation to its unconditionality.

In the Nordic countries, giving everyone some money is experienced as to some extent immoral, and at the same time it is possible to discuss ideas similar to Citizen's Basic Income such as a Participation Income or a Negative Income Tax. In this context, Citizen's Basic Income will need to be framed to fit the mindset that rejects it: for instance, as an investment in the skills that the next generation will need – 'venture capital for the people' (Bregman, 2018); or as the financial security required for children's wellbeing; or as a minor development of the existing welfare state (BIEN Nordic Day, 2018).

Different framings can be found in different kinds of media: for instance, in academic texts and in more popular media (Perkiö et al., 2019), possibly because popular media believe their readers to be more interested in immediate social problems than in longer term policy issues (Tiffen, 2018). In any particular context one metaphor might work better than others, or one argument might have more appeal than another (Legein et al., 2018): so different narratives might be required for different groups and organizations, particularly if a group of people for some reason opposed to the idea of Citizen's Basic Income might find the idea more acceptable if it were to be framed in terms of the group's own concerns, or if it were to be framed as the most acceptable of a number of options that they might not wish to take (Drew and Fahey, 2018). How the concept is framed is a particularly important issue in relation to opinion surveys, as are the ways in which different aspects of Citizen's Basic Income are connected with each other in the questioning (Chrisp, 2018; Pulkka, 2018). The name given to Citizen's Basic Income is an equally important issue. Precisely what a Citizen's Basic Income is called at different stages of the policy process should be decided by how different interest groups will experience different names. For instance, if the name 'Basic Income' were to become problematic, either because of the 'inadequacy' undertones of the word 'basic' (see Chapter 2), or because the name had become too firmly attached to infeasible implementation proposals, then another name might be more helpful: for instance, 'Weekly National Allowance' (Stirling and Arnold, 2019) or 'Fair Allowance' (see the case study in Chapter 13).

How both Citizen's Basic Income and the problems that it would help to solve are framed (6, 2018) will be important as the global debate continues to evolve, and it will be interesting to see whether a widespread 'narrative' emerges (Lejano et al., 2018): that is, a story that can be told (Botterill and Fenna, 2019: 151) that expresses ideas with which large numbers of individuals and institutions can identify, either within a particular context or globally. Whether that occurs might depend on whether a new general narrative or paradigm emerges from the problems now facing the neoliberalism narrative (see the first case study in Chapter 12).

Stigma

> When an individual appears before others, he will have many motives for trying to control the impression they receive of the situation ... A status, a position, a social place, is not a material thing, to be possessed and then displayed; it is a pattern of appropriate conduct, coherent, embellished, and well articulated. (Goffman, 1969: 13, 65–6)

Such self-presentation requires someone for the individual to play to: a 'team' in opposition to our 'team'; and we find ourselves 'in the grip of one of our types of reality' (Goffman, 1969: 147, 223–4). It is such self-presentation that is at the root of stigma, as one group of people 'others' another by judging it against its own set of criteria (Spicker, 2014: 39; Lister, 2017). The social and institutional context then reinforces the judgement, and the members of the judged group internalize the judgement and experience the stigma imposed on them. In the context of the employment market and the benefits system, for the winners to feel successful, the poor must be made to feel guilty and ashamed (Golding and Middleton, 1982: 244). It is no surprise that regarding poverty as people's own fault is an attitude more prevalent among people who express insecurity about their own lives (Knight, 2013: 16).

Erving Goffman lists three types of stigma: 'physical deformities', 'blemishes of individual character', and 'the tribal stigma of race, nation, and religion' (Goffman, 1990: 13–14). There are elements of both the second and third types in the stigma experienced by people in receipt of means-tested benefits. We might believe them to have character flaws, and we might regard them as a 'tribe' separate from the rest of society. So, if we are not on means-tested benefits, we might stigmatize people who are because we fear being in their situation; and someone on means-tested benefits might experience the stigma applied to them by others, and might stigmatize themselves, because they are in a situation that they do not wish to be in.

A contributing factor to stigma is 'deindividuation' (Festinger et al., 1952; Mullen, 1986; Prentice-Dunn and Rogers, 1982). Deindividuation can occur in a large crowd, whether in the same physical space or in the same social space, when a victim – in the case of means-tested benefits, the claimant – is not known personally to members of the crowd. Abnormal behaviour is the result. A historic classic case is the lynching of black people in the United States. Today's classic case is inhumane treatment of migrants. Equally significant are the 'psycho-policy interventions' (Friedli and Stearn, 2015) that are more commonly known as 'active labour market policies' – that is, work tests and benefits sanctions – which are both an increasing reality across Europe and seriously counterproductive (Haagh, 2019a: 25–7). In a study in Salford, the UK's benefits sanctions were found to be characterized by

> inconsistencies in sanction activity between ... offices. ... [and] a degree of inappropriate and unreasonable sanctioning of claimants in Salford who appear to have made minor breaches or had genuine reasons for failing to meet their work related requirements ... The conditionality and sanctions regime is leading to a myriad of problems affecting both claimants and their families. A review of the evidence collated through case studies and reports from service managers place the main impacts for claimants under four main headings which relate to: finance, health and wellbeing, skills, training and employability, and offending. (Partners in Salford, 2014: 6–7)

The UK's benefits system can legitimately be described as 'broken' (Royston, 2017), and the 'indecency, humiliation, stigma, and depression' (Fryer and Fagan, 2003: 94) associated with it might well be the kind of 'inhuman or degrading treatment' banned by the European Convention on Human Rights (Adler, 2018): 'treatment' which deindividuation makes possible. The stigmatized individual or group becomes a victim twice over: of the situation that has caused them to become a victim and stigmatized in the first place, and of the stigmatizing and victimizing practices then applied to them (Smith, 1993b: 576–7).

A particularly important factor in the stigmatizing process is the print and other media. The idea that benefit recipients are scroungers and fraudsters is an inaccurate media characterization that has a direct stigmatizing effect on benefits recipients who read such media opinion, and that increases the stigma by providing ammunition to those who already have a tendency to stigmatize benefits recipients (Coughlin, 1980: 117; Hills, 2014; Whiteford, 2015a; 2015b).

The extent of the stigma imposed on people on means-tested benefits by others and by themselves might seem out of proportion to the regulations relating to such benefits, but once we study how means-testing works in practice, we might begin to understand why those on such benefits feel them to be so demeaning (Greener, 2018: 174–6). A significant factor is the bureaucratic intrusion required by means-testing: an intrusion that someone on means-tested benefits simply has to suffer. A claim for a means-tested benefit might begin with a face to face interview with someone younger than the claimant, to whom the claimant will be expected to divulge details of their sources of income and, even more painfully, details of their intimate relationships. Claimants are required to provide evidence, which suggests that they are not believed. And then it is not always clear why benefits have been permitted or disallowed, or how a payment might have been calculated. 'Discretion' has been exercised (Hill, 1990: 110), which puts the claimant in a subservient position in relation to the bureaucrat. However much the law on social security benefits might be framed in terms of rights, and however often the claimant might be termed a 'customer', the entire process says to them and to others that the claimant is a supplicant (Wagner, 2007: 196). Once benefits are in payment, 'work-related' interviews might take place in connection with the government's 'active labour market policies' (Handler, 2005: 117). An underlying assumption is that the claimant cannot exercise intrinsic motivation and has to be coerced into it, whereas it is often lack of employment opportunities that has demotivated them; it is the complexities of the benefits system that make them hesitate to seek change in their labour market status in case such change leaves them with insufficient money to live on; and it is the 'active labour market' policy itself that cements the demotivation (Welfare Reform Team, Oxford City Council, 2016: 51). 'Active labour market' policies represent a contradiction: 'external surveillance and sanctions, and encouragement to internal motivation and effort – [whereas] genuine empowerment can only come from freely exercised choice' (Carpenter et al., 2007: 5, 6). In contrast: no stigma attaches to such universal services as the UK's National Health Service: a service that protects the vulnerable without attaching any stigma to them (Dean, 2012c: 65; Spicker, 2014: 39–40). National Health Service hospital admissions, outpatient appointments, and visits to a General Practitioner, are free at the point of need for everyone legally resident in the UK. There is no 'tribe' that receives the service, nor a majority that do not; and there is no scrutiny of intimate personal details by an official, unless required for medical reasons. We used to be able to say this of the UK's Child Benefit, because the Child Benefit claim process is not intrusive, and everyone with a child receives the income: but now the failed attempt to means-test it in 2010, and the additional Income Tax eventually charged to high-earning individuals in households receiving Child Benefit, have begun to include Child Benefit in the stigmatized and stigmatizing benefits category.

An interesting example of an income mechanism lying between unconditionality and means-tested and work-tested benefits was the Mincome experiment in Dauphin, Canada, during the 1970s. This was a Minimum Income Guarantee experiment that guaranteed an income of a specified level to every household, with the level of the guaranteed income varying with household structure. Households without other income were given payments that equalled the guaranteed income, and households with other income had their payments reduced by 50 cents for every $1 of other income. Wealthier households therefore received no payments. The difference between the guaranteed income and means-tested benefits was that the guaranteed income payments were not work-tested, and so were located between unconditional incomes and the means-tested benefits experienced in liberal welfare regimes. Alongside significant increases in health indicators, and particularly in mental health indicators (Forget, 2011), a significant result of the Mincome experiment was that

> the design and framing of Mincome led participants to view payments through a pragmatic lens, rather than the moralistic lens through which welfare is viewed. … Mincome participation did not produce social stigma. … The social meaning of Mincome was sufficiently powerful that even participants with particularly negative attitudes toward government assistance felt able to collect Mincome payments without a sense of contradiction. By obscuring the distinctions between the 'deserving' and 'undeserving' poor, universalistic income maintenance programs may weaken social stigmatization and strengthen program sustainability. (Calnitsky, 2016: 27)

While it is important not to confuse guaranteed income experiments with Citizen's Basic Income (Torpey, 2017: 73), to employ the term 'universalistic' for mechanisms that do not provide incomes to everyone, or to assume that the results of guaranteed income experiments can reliably predict the effects of a Citizen's Basic Income, it might still be possible to draw tentative conclusions from guaranteed income experiment results in relation to Citizen's Basic Income. For instance, Baumberg, Bell and Gaffney find that 'international evidence suggests that countries with benefit systems based on contribution or on citizenship, rather than on a means test, are less likely to see high levels of benefits stigma' (Baumberg et al., 2012: 3). This evidence, alongside the results of the Mincome experiment, suggests that a Citizen's Basic Income – a nonwithdrawable income with *no* conditions attached, so that *every* individual would receive it – would be entirely without stigma, and would begin to repair the legitimacy of the social security systems which have been seriously damaged by means-testing, work-testing, and the associated stigma (Staerklé et al., 2012: 111; Torry, 2016a: 8–9). As Tony Walter puts it, a Citizen's Basic

Income would 'replace structural guilt with a universal structure of acceptance and forgiveness' (Walter, 1989: 133). If everyone of the same age were to receive the same income, then the deserving/undeserving distinction would be obscured out of existence; stigma would be impossible; social cohesion would be enhanced; social and individual welfare would improve, particularly in relation to the self-worth of individuals and households able to come off means-tested benefits (Birnbaum, 2012: 48–51; Jordan, 2010; Lundvall and Lorenz, 2012: 347); and the social bonds that would be generated by improved wellbeing would provide an essential foundation for the maintenance of the Citizen's Basic Income (Jordan, 2010) and for the social and economic prosperity of communities (Jones et al., 2010). A 'social multiplier' effect would generate a level of positive outcomes for individuals and households beyond what we might expect (Glaeser et al., 2002); and the absence of stigma, along with Citizen's Basic Income's simplicity, would ensure almost 100 per cent take-up (Darton et al., 2003: 33; Spicker, 2011: 14–15).

> Means-testing can stigmatize potential recipients and prevent their taking up the [means-tested] benefit. The take up of means-tested benefits is often low because of that stigmatization and because of administrative complications in qualifying for the benefits. In some instances it may be more effective for governments to provide universal benefits and then claw back the money from the more affluent through taxation. (Peters, 2018: 97)

Attitudes and Conversions

If a social policy change from a system based largely on means-tested benefits towards one based largely on unconditional incomes would require a substantial number of individuals to change their minds about the change's desirability and feasibility, then is such a widespread mind-change possible? Perhaps the sheer logic of the situation will enable a sufficient number of individuals to change their minds; or perhaps a changing context – for instance, a more precarious employment market – will enable Citizen's Basic Income to make sense (Lister, 2017). But individuals changing their minds might be purely that, and might not have any social consequences. So how might the mind of a whole society be changed? Research on group behaviour suggests how this might occur.

Our attitudes – that is, our 'evaluative reactions' to people, objects, ideas, values, and norms (Smith, 1993b: 578) – are our way of organizing our relationships with other people, objects, ideas, values, and norms. Attitudes are shaped by a society's normative beliefs; they can be learned, often simply by exposure to them (Hogg and Vaughan, 2014: 152–3; Smith, 1993b: 580; Staerklé et al., 2012: 114); and they can become deeply embedded: but they can also be changed by a credible persuader, particularly if we have not embraced the deeper conceptual structures underlying our existing attitudes, and if we have not developed counterarguments against alternative attitudes. Simple, emotionally based arguments can work against attitudes held on rational grounds, and vice versa (Hogg and Vaughan, 2014: 192–206; Millar and Millar, 1990; Smith, 1993b: 581): so we can in fact find our minds changing about the people, objects, ideas, norms, and values most important to us.

Since William James wrote *The Varieties of Religious Experience*, we have known quite a lot about individual conversion experiences, both religious and otherwise (James, [1902] 2012; Sargant, 1976): but it is Moscovici's work on how groups of people change their minds that will be of more relevance to us here.

As Moscovici found, agreement expressed publicly might initially side with social norms – that is, with majority opinion (Moscovici, 1985: 348–9). Individuals will sometimes conform to erroneous majority opinion because they are seeking public approval, or because the opinion accepted by the majority originated with a recognized authority figure (van Avermaet, 2001: 408–10). However, our private thoughts might have moved in a different direction:

> A minority, which by definition expresses a deviant judgment, a judgment contrary to the norms respected by the social group, convinces some members of the group, who may accept its judgment in private. They will be reluctant to do so publicly, however, either for fear of losing face or to avoid the risk of speaking or acting in a deviant fashion in the presence of others. (Moscovici, 1980: 211)

A further reason for someone hesitating to reveal their change of mind might be a fear of being asked to explain their new position when they know that in a field such as tax and benefits they might struggle to respond adequately to questions.

So in public we might see 'compliance' behaviour, and in private 'conversion' behaviour: and it is only when a majority of the group is behaving in this way, and in an act of courage one member expresses their conversion, that everyone in the group can understand that a widespread conversion has in fact taken place. An additional effect of someone's declaration of conversion might be that it breaks a social norm, which reveals to everyone that a norm exists. By drawing attention to the norm, the declaration makes it both possible and necessary to engage with it, which makes it possible to question and change it (Ulmer, 2018).

Moscovici finds that

> a consistent minority can exert an influence to the same extent as a consistent majority, and … the former will generally have a greater effect on a deeper level,

while the latter often have less, or none, at that level. (Moscovici, 1980: 214–16; cf. Nemeth et al., 1990)

For the conversion to take place, the minority's message has first of all to be consistent and persistent: but if it wishes to generate the 'admiration and trust' and 'perception of stability and confidence' (Nemeth et al., 1974: 61) required to enable the majority to change its mind, then at the same time as offering a distinctive and consistent alternative perspective (van Avermaet, 2001: 418) the minority will have to ensure that the difference of opinion with the majority does not exceed a certain threshold (Moscovici, 1976: 81), and that the message is flexibly expressed, and not simply repeated in the same form all the time (Moscovici, 1985: 401). Too much rigidity in the minority can cause the majority to reject its message (Migny, 1982: 84–5). The required combination of consistency and flexibility – the required 'behavioural style' (Moscovici, 1976: 109) – constitutes a 'dual process' model in which the minority's view exerts direct influence on the majority, and both the disagreement and the flexibility in the expression of the message loosen the majority's minds so that they allocate cognitive resources to integrating new information with existing belief systems and become more receptive to alternative views (Petty and Cacioppo, 1986: 7–9; Turner, 1991).

We need to retain a certain hesitancy when applying the results of Moscovici's, van Avermaet's, and Nemeth's, Swedlund's and Kanki's research on group behaviour to the behaviour of entire societies, but we can understand how the same mechanisms might operate to create not just a social psychological change, but also what might better be called a cultural change; and we can certainly see how the mechanisms might operate in relation to such groups as governments, parliaments, and political parties. We can therefore envisage how a consistent definition of Citizen's Basic Income, alongside a diverse debate about the details of Citizen's Basic Income schemes, might facilitate opinion change in both individuals and organizations, and how a political party, a government, or a whole society, might shift its opinion on the desirability and feasibility of Citizen's Basic Income; and we can also see how such a shift might appear to have been rapid when in fact the conversion had been a long slow process that had suddenly come to light. The same process occurs within scientific communities when existing theory no longer makes sense of empirical evidence, new theories come and go, and eventually a new consensus emerges that for a while explains the evidence: until again theories cannot explain the evidence, and new theories have to be sought. Sometimes the process appears to have been rapid, whereas in fact the change had been happening in people's minds over a long period and had then suddenly emerged into the public realm (Kuhn, 1962; Torry, 2013: 56–61).

The characteristics of different welfare states have deep historic roots in long-run social evolutions and élite ideologies of the nineteenth and early twentieth centuries, and these characteristics are constantly 'reinforced by the attitudes and behaviour of élites' (Coughlin, 1980: 54, 156). At the same time, public opinion is often ill-informed and incapable of being influenced in relation to the detail of social policy: a factor particularly important in relation to complex benefits systems. This is why the UK has ended up with the highly problematic means-tested 'Universal Credit' with almost no public debate; and it is why, if the UK does ever implement a Citizen's Basic Income, it will be because a number of policy process factors have arrived together to create that effect (Torry, 2016a: 195–246). Public attitudes, and attitude conversions, might have been crucial: but they might not have been.

A further interesting conclusion that we might draw from Moscovici's research is this: No country has implemented a genuine nationwide Citizen's Basic Income, so no country is willing to do so. If just one country were to implement a Citizen's Basic Income scheme, then after a decent interval other countries would follow (Dunlop et al., 2018).

Institutional Influences

We have seen how changing attitudes might begin the process of changing welfare provision: but might changing welfare provision then result in a change in attitudes? It would appear that it could.

Institutions are organized patterns of norms and roles, and the norms represented by an organization will to some extent determine individuals' attitudes and behaviours (Mau, 2003: 28–35): so a social security system constituted by a system of contributions and contribution-based benefits – however disconnected the contribution rates and conditions might be from those of the benefits paid out (Golding and Middleton, 1982: 243) – will encourage participants to invoke reciprocity-based norms shaped by the system's regulations (Mau, 2003: 42); and a system based on means-testing will inevitably generate a 'them and us' attitude (Larsen, 2006: 4–5, 23; Taylor-Gooby and Leruth, 2018: 21).

> The perception of the poor and unemployed [is] most negative in liberal [means-tested and selective benefits] regimes (maybe moderated by the fact that the recipients really are in need), more positive in conservative [that is, contributory] regimes ... and most positive in social democratic [more universal] regimes (maybe moderated by the fact that many of the potential poor have rather good living conditions) (Larsen, 2006: 141);

and similarly,

> where social welfare institutions are most developed – as measured by relative budgetary effort, program coverage, and program duration – the collectivist components of mass ideology are strongest. In contrast, where institutional development lags, the mix of ideologies is either evenly balanced (as in Canada) or individualism predominates (as in the United States). (Coughlin, 1980: 51)

Louise Humpage charts the growth of neoliberal economic and welfare policies –

> significant cuts/targeting, leading to extensive welfare state retrenchment ... reductions in benefit eligibility/generosity, introduction of conditionality ... citizens framed as responsible for their own wellbeing, active citizenship focused on citizen responsibilities, especially participation in the labour market (Humpage, 2015: 26)

– and finds 'a generally negative impact on public beliefs about the social right to economic and social security ... the public rolled over and accepted the need for further social security reform' (Humpage, 2015: 143). It is no surprise that in this context recipients of means-tested benefits do not feel themselves to be legitimate recipients (Humpage, 2015: 228). However, recipients of unconditional benefits do believe themselves to be legitimate recipients; 'the public tend to support universal social programmes more than targeted ones because they are visible and proximate to a wider range of citizens' (Humpage, 2015: 240); and 'universal encompassing programs such as pensions and health care receive strong support, while more targeted or selective programmes such as unemployment benefits and social assistance receive much lower support' (Svallfors, 2012a: 6). So the UK's National Health Service receives strong support (Coughlin, 1980: 118–19), and although there would be objections if new unconditional benefits were to be proposed in the UK, once implemented, such provision would be more popular than means-tested and work-tested benefits.

But what of the effect of a Citizen's Basic Income on attitudes? As Kellow has found, 'policies continue to have effects on politics beyond the process by which they are adopted' (Kellow, 2018: 469), and we have discovered that welfare regime affects public attitudes, that a contributory system reinforces a reciprocity norm, and that means-testing entrenches an attitude of 'them and us' and a particular kind of ante/required reciprocity norm. For the benefits system to move away from these regime types would reduce those effects, and for it to move towards a more universalist character would promote more solidaristic public attitudes (Larsen, 2006: 57).

Three particular examples might be given:

1. Growing up in poverty can lead to financial success being highly valued and social relationships less so (Kasser et al., 1995), which is a problem, because materialistic attitudes are negatively correlated with wellbeing (Kasser et al., 2014). However, if economic security increases, then attitudes become less materialistic, and wellbeing increases (Kasser, 2016: 502). This is yet another reason to encourage the implementation of a Citizen's Basic Income. It would make households' disposable incomes more secure, which would reduce materialistic values, which would in turn enhance wellbeing. So on top of the normal list of advantages of Citizen's Basic Income, we would find a variety of useful psychological and social psychological effects.

2. Jane Gingrich has found that

   > as individuals pay more direct taxes, they are more likely to vote based on their redistributive preferences. Receiving tax breaks, by contrast, actually reduces the weight that individuals attach to their preferences, even though they have important distributive implications. (Gingrich, 2014: 109)

   Because a likely way of paying for a Citizen's Basic Income in the UK would be the removal of the Income Tax Personal Allowance, Income Tax would be paid on all earned income, so more Income Tax would be paid. One consequence would be that individuals would be more likely to vote according to their redistribution preferences.

3. A country's existing welfare state affects attitudes to Citizen's Basic Income. For instance, in countries with weak social security safety nets approval rates for Citizen's Basic Income are higher than in countries with more universalistic welfare states, as in Norway and Sweden (Lee, 2018). There are two ways of looking at this. People in countries with stronger safety nets might worry that implementing a Citizen's Basic Income would put at risk a system that they already value; and people in countries with less well developed welfare states would like to move in a more universalist direction.

To implement a Citizen's Basic Income could have a profound effect on the way we think – on our psychology, and perhaps even more on our social psychology. Humpage's research suggests that, once implemented, Citizen's Basic Income would become popular: so if an unconditional income were to be paid to 16- to 20-year-olds, or to 18- to 20-year-olds, not only would the initial cohort wish to keep it, but each new cohort of 16- or 18-year-olds would wish to receive it, and cohorts above the initial cohort would also want it. The ante/required reciprocity norm would have been successfully bypassed.

CONCLUSION

The material in this chapter on the 'deserving/undeserving' and 'them and us' narratives, and on the often insulting language employed in relation to them, has been treated in terms of social psychology. It could equally well have been described in terms of hegemonic moral discourses (Gramsci, 1971: 145, 373, 507): that is, narratives or discourses perpetrated and perpetuated by groups within society able to exercise hegemony. Interpretations of the world are imposed on society by social groups with the power to do that. The neo-liberal narrative researched by Humpage is an example of such a hegemonic discourse. Such hegemonic discourses and social norms matter, because they form the 'moral economy' that enables high levels of poverty and inequality to persist in a society (Rowlingson, 2019). The obvious question in relation to Citizen's Basic Income is this: Citizen's Basic Income is an unconditional income for every individual, so however much a Citizen's Basic Income scheme might reduce poverty and inequality, and however much it might offer all manner of other advantages, it would be difficult to implement because it would be anathema to the deserving/undeserving discourse, and to the reciprocity social norm as that is normally understood. Tackling such deeply embedded hegemonic discourses and social norms head on is probably a waste of energy in the short term. As we have already suggested, implementation of a Citizen's Basic Income scheme would need to be constructed in such a way as to circumvent the discourses; and it might also be necessary to frame Citizen's Basic Income in such a way as to conform both to the neoliberal dis-course and to the increasingly salient but still less well co-ordinated discourses in opposition to it. This is of course perfectly possible, and, once implemented, Citizen's Basic Income might begin to change both existing and future hegem-onic discourses in interesting ways, and might form an important element in a new unconditionality narrative.

Material in this chapter could have been included in chapters on organiza-tional behaviour, hegemonic discourses, sociology, or psychology, so it is no surprise that in these fields disciplinary boundaries are particularly fluid and contested. We are in the field of the 'psychosocial', of a 'second order psychol-ogy' (Brown and Stenner, 2009: 5) in which we are 'hybrid creatures with mul-tiple forms of heritage: creatures of biochemistry, creatures of consciousness, creatures of communication' (Brown and Stenner, 2009: 6).

The final section of this chapter on social psychology has been framed as a case study about self-concept, which is how Hofstede's research is described in social psychology texts (Brehm et al., 1999: 67). The research and its results are also employed in research on organizational behaviour, which is how Hofstede would have described it; and Esping-Andersen's categorization is understandably and correctly regarded by social policy academics as central to the discipline of social policy. So here again we experience the boundary-crossing that this chapter has been largely about. Perhaps the most important function that the Citizen's Basic Income debate has performed for the field of social psychology is to have revealed the fuzziness of its boundaries.

CASE STUDY

The Self-concept and Inequality

The concept that each of us has of ourselves has multiple roots, it is heavily influenced by prevailing attitudes in the society in which we live and by the ways in which other people relate to us, and it significantly influences our behaviour (Brehm et al., 1999: 55; DePaulo, 1992; Markus and Kitayama, 1991; Smith, 1993b: 603; Swann et al., 1992). We might therefore speak of a prevailing self-concept to which each individual self-concept will tend to conform; and we might also speak of the many similar self-concepts that constitute the prevailing self-concept of a society (Rhee et al., 1995). Both individual and collective self-concepts can be either conscious or subconscious; an individual self-concept can be purposefully or subconsciously projected (Schlenker and Weigold, 1992); and, whether conscious or not, a collective self-concept might be experienced and described as a culture. And so, for instance, in one culture, that is, in one collective self-concept, an individualist self-concept, more concerned with the self than with relationships, might be prominent, whereas in another culture a more collectivist self-concept, more concerned with connections and relationships, might be pervasive (Singelis, 1994).

> The cultural syndromes of individualism and collectivism are the consequences of a number of different influences ... including affluence, family structure, cultural complexity, [broad philosophical and political] situations, and demographic factors. (Triandis, 1995: 105)

So an individual can experience either an individualist or a collectivist self-concept, and a society can experience either an individualist or a collectivist collective self-concept, or culture.

In 1980, Geert Hofstede published the results of research on the self-concepts and resultant behaviours of 116,000 employees of the global company IBM (Hofstede, 1980; Brehm et al., 1999: 67). He ranked countries along four spectra related to prevailing self-concepts: from individuals' tendency to assertiveness to their tendency to more modest behaviour; from individualism to collectivism; from behaviour designed to avoid ambiguity and uncertainty to a more welcoming attitude to them; and according to 'power difference', where power difference is

> the extent to which the less powerful members of institutions and organizations within a country expect that power is distributed unequally. (Hofstede, 2001: 98)

Each country was ascribed a Power Difference Index (PDI) constructed on the basis of answers to such questions as: How often is there a problem in express- ing disagreement with managers? (Hofstede, 1997: 27). When individuals are responding to questionnaires, we must always keep in mind the distinction between perception and reality – for instance, between a perception of power difference and actual power difference: but with such a vast research sample, average perception is fairly likely to match reality.

Hofstede concluded that power difference is socially determined, and he found that '43 percent of the variance in PDI can be predicted from the geo- graphical latitude of the country's capital alone ... 51 percent can be predicted from a combination of latitude and population size' (Hofstede, 1980: 122). He also found that wealth was a factor, and that latitude, population size and wealth together predict 56 per cent of the variance in power difference (Hofstede, 2001: 79, 115). This suggests that our self-concepts have roots deep in history, with those roots possibly related to the kinds of social organization required to enable a population to survive in a colder climate. A similar pattern emerges in relation to populations' preferences in relation to government expenditure: more northerly European populations expect higher government expenditure, and therefore higher taxes, than more southerly European popu- lations (Janky, 2012).

As well as locating each country along each of the four spectra, Hofstede also sought correlations with other variables, and, in the case of the PDI, with income and wealth inequalities. In relation to OECD countries, he found a particularly close correlation between PDI and the ratio of the average net income of the top 20 per cent of earned incomes and the average net income of the bottom 20 per cent of net incomes, with a correlation coefficient of 0.85 if just one outlier, Japan, is removed (– the nearer to 1 the correlation coefficient is, the closer is the correlation) (Hofstede, 1980: 147–8). As Hofstede writes: 'We can take the data as proof that income inequality is larger in high PDI than in low PDI countries' (Hofstede, 1980: 147).

Correlation does not prove causality, so we need to consider a number of possibilities. Self-concept could influence the level of inequality; the level of inequality could influence self-concept; latitude and population size might influence both self-concept and level of inequality; and there might be some additional factor that influences both self-concept and level of inequality. These possibilities are not mutually exclusive.

One possible mechanism for income inequality affecting self-concept might be the changing institutional context. Both positive life evaluation and experienced wellbeing correlate with income (except that for particularly high incomes, increases in income result in higher life evaluation but not in enhanced wellbeing) (Kahneman and Deaton, 2010). In a context of robust public services and an active civil society, income will have less influence on wellbeing and life evaluation than in a context of crumbling public services and failing voluntary and public institutions: but now public services *are* struggling, and public and voluntary institutions *are* less robust than they were, so income has to provide a greater proportion of a household's resources, which means that income inequality and poverty have a more significant impact on wellbeing than we had previously thought (Hout, 2016: 218–19).

A possible additional factor might be the structure of the welfare state. Welfare states are all different, with the character of each one having been formed by a wide variety of factors across long periods of time (Spicker, 2014: 159–79). A more recent ranking of income inequalities than the one available to Hofstede looks like this: From low inequality to high inequality: Finland, Norway, Sweden, Germany, Austria, Denmark, Belgium, Switzerland, France, the Netherlands, Canada, Italy, Australia, United States (United Nations, 2009: 195). An interestingly similar list emerges from Gøsta Esping-Andersen's research on welfare state regimes (Esping-Andersen, 1990: 69–77; Dean, 2012c: 30–31). Esping-Andersen scores welfare states for corporatism (the number of large occupationally distinct public pension schemes), étatism (expenditure on pensions for government employees), means-tested poor relief, private pensions (as a proportion of total pensions), private health spending (as a proportion of the total), universalism (social security benefits available to every citizen, excluding income tested schemes), and average benefit equality (the ratio of the legal maximum benefits possible to the guaranteed minimum income). By combining these scores, each country is then scored for conservatism (corporatism), socialism (universalism and equality), and liberalism (private provision, with a residual, means-tested welfare state). Some clear clusters of countries emerge, and Esping-Andersen is able to characterize their welfare states as in Table 7.1.

The countries listed in the right hand column of Table 7.1 are those which score 'strongly' for each of the welfare regime types. The same countries will also score 'medium' or 'low' for the other welfare regime types. Some countries do not score strongly for any particular type (Dean, 2012c: 31): the UK, for example, scores 'low' for conservatism (corporatism), and 'medium' for both liberalism and socialism. Similarly, in relation to PDI, income inequality, and preference for government expenditure, the UK finds itself around the

Table 7.1   Three types of welfare regime

Type of welfare regime	Character	Represented by
Social democratic regime / 'socialism'	The state is committed to full employment, generous universalist welfare benefits, income redistribution, etc.	Denmark, Finland, the Netherlands, Norway, and Sweden
Conservative / corporatist regimes	Occupationally segregated benefits	Germany, France, Austria, Belgium, and Italy
Liberal welfare regimes	Private provision, selective provision, and a residual safety net for the poor	Australia, Canada, Japan, Switzerland, and the United States

Source: Table constructed by the author on the basis of Esping-Andersen, 1990: 73–5.

middle of each range: perhaps as a result of its northern latitude and of the Gulf Stream's creation of a warmer climate uncharacteristic of that latitude.

A pattern is beginning to emerge: a country's prevailing self-concept, its income inequality, and its welfare state regime type, would appear to be strongly correlated with each other. An important root causal factor might be the latitude of a country's capital, but we can also theorize a variety of other causal mechanisms that might connect the different factors that have been shown to be correlated with each other. Self-concept is likely to influence income inequality because (employing Hofstede's categories) a tendency towards modest behaviour, collectivism, behaviour designed to reduce uncertainty, and low power difference, are likely to reduce income inequality. There might also be influence in the other direction, with greater income equality reducing aggressive behaviour. Welfare regime type is likely to influence both self-concept and income inequality, because a more liberal welfare state regime will tend to stigmatize and demotivate recipients, and to make it difficult for them to lift themselves out of poverty, whereas the other regime types would be less likely to have these effects (Torry, 2018a: 41–5; Welfare Reform Team, Oxford City Council, 2016), and a more universalistic welfare state is more likely to create the 'imagined community' that every nation needs if it is to thrive (Gregory, 2018: 92). What is difficult to see is how either self-concept or income inequality could cause a country's welfare regime type. We can see how they might reinforce an existing welfare regime type – for instance, individualism might result in tax reductions, and in more independent decision-making and less collective provision: but welfare regime types have deep historic roots, and if any self-concepts at all are causal then it will be the self-concepts of previous eras, not those of today. We can therefore reasonably suppose that a primary cause of the various correlations that we have found are the deep social structures of our societies (Dorling, 2017: 262), and particularly the welfare regime type; that welfare regime types have deep historic roots; that welfare regime types influence both today's self-concepts and today's income inequalities; and that a country's capital's latitude and its population size might be the root cause of all of this.

What has all of this to do with Citizen's Basic Income? We cannot change the latitude of our country's capital, nor its population size: but what we can do is change the structure of the welfare state. If we were to move a liberal welfare state in a more universalistic direction, then we would expect to see a positive change in self-concept and a positive change in levels of inequality.

Wilkinson and Pickett, in *The Spirit Level*, suggest that income inequality is the cause of a variety of social ills, but they offer no proof of that causal link (Bergh et al., 2016: 48–71; Torry, 2010; Wilkinson and Pickett, 2009). There is no more reason to suppose that lower income inequality on its own would reduce offending, teenage pregnancies, and mental illness, than to suppose that those social ills cause income inequality. Indeed, to attempt to reduce income inequality by increasing means-tested benefits would cause even deeper poverty traps and unemployment traps, would hinder people from emerging from poverty, and would draw more households into stigmatizing means-testing. The structure of the UK's welfare state would be even further embedded, which would be likely to cause even greater inequality and even more disempowering self-concepts. A Citizen's Basic Income, on the other hand, would reduce means-testing, and would provide a significant financial floor on which to build, and would therefore reduce income inequality and improve our collective and individual self-concepts.

8.   The sociology of Citizen's Basic Income

> Sociology: The study of the development, structure, and functioning of human society.
>
> (Oxford English Dictionary)

INTRODUCTION

This chapter will contain a discussion of some of the aspects of the history of sociology, among which we shall hope to find useful connections with the Citizen's Basic Income debate. We shall then tackle a number of issues related to the development, structure, and functioning of human society, and we shall again ask how they might relate to Citizen's Basic Income. We shall conclude by asking whether the Citizen's Basic Income debate might offer some lessons that might be useful to the discipline of sociology.

This is one of the chapters for which the boundary of the discipline, and therefore the boundary of the subject matter, remains somewhat insecure. Sociology is a social science that studies society (Hamilton, 1992): but so do economics, political economy, social psychology, and social policy. It is therefore no surprise that social policy as an academic discipline relies heavily on sociology, and that economics, political economy, and social psychology, all overlap with it. We shall therefore give most space in this chapter to those subjects that are least likely to find a place in chapters on social policy, economics, or political economy.

I shall be taking as my guides to sociology *Principles of Sociology* by Gosling and Taylor (2005), *Sociology* by Giddens (2001), and *Perspectives in Sociology* by Cuff, Sharrock and Francis (1998).

EXPLORING SOCIETY WITH THE SOCIOLOGISTS

How are we to understand our society? The description of sociology at the beginning of this chapter contains two words that imply change or action – 'development' and 'functioning' – and one that does not – 'structure'. Here I shall be particularly interested in how our society changes: that is, how society develops, how the way it works changes, and how the structure changes. I shall explore these more active aspects of society with the help of the founders of sociology: Karl Marx, Emile Durkheim, and Max Weber, and also with some more recent thinkers: George Herbert Mead and Herbert Blumer. As with all of the descriptions and histories of the disciplines studied in this book, the history of sociology offered here will have to be brief. This is of course to misrepresent the history of sociology, because it was far more complex, and involved far more individuals, than the brief summary contained here would suggest: but I hope that the brief summary of the discipline's earliest period offered here will provide sufficient of a basis for studying the discipline's relationship with the Citizen's Basic Income debate.

Karl Marx

While for Karl Marx society changes constantly via a dialectical method (thesis and antithesis in conflict giving rise to a new situation, a synthesis), class, alienation and capital function as unchanging universals. In Marx's system capitalism is ultimately abolished: it does not change or evolve – which of course it does. In the real world, classes change as well (– is there now a clearly identifiable working class?). Alienation from the product of our labour might still be a real experience for many, but for increasing numbers in the service industries proximity to the product of one's labour is an equally valid way of describing our experience of work – which is not to say that capitalists are not extracting surplus value from areas of the economy from which they were not extracting it before.

For humanistic Marxists the superstructure of human activity is not entirely determined by the class conflict substructure. Human activity can cause societal change. The scientific Marxist thinks that the substructure entirely controls the superstructure. The humanistic Marxist is right. Every action affects every other. Marx will remain useful to us if we recognize that the boundary between the superstructure and the substructure changes constantly (Giddens, 2001: 11–13, 283–5).

Emile Durkheim

Durkheim sought social facts. He, like Marx, believed that social facts significantly influence individual facts, and his research led him to the conclusion that industrialization, the division of labour, different household structures, and especially different religious traditions, are the reasons for different suicide rates in different places. For Durkheim, society's structures are what shape individuals, not vice versa.

While subsequent social scientists have questioned Durkheim's methods, as a snapshot of European society in his own time Durkheim's work on suicide rates was a huge achievement. But now the aspects of society that Durkheim studied have all changed: religion has changed, industry has changed, and households have changed: and they and everything else continue to change constantly. Customs, economic structures, and social structures, do indeed influence our behaviour, but they are here today and gone tomorrow: and we influence customs and social structures just as much as they influence us. After all (to take but one example), money is what we make it, and apart from our actions, neither money nor anything else societal can exist.

Durkheim wrote that 'When I fulfil my obligations as brother, husband, or citizen, when I execute my contracts, I perform duties which are defined externally to myself and my acts, in law and in custom' (Durkheim, 1938: 1). Yes. And when I act as a brother, husband, or citizen, I influence the social structures to which those terms relate; and when I execute contracts I create or expunge money, and I create or change organizational and personal relationships.

Social facts change, and we change them (Durkheim, 1938; 1952; 1961; 1984; Giddens, 2001: 8–11, 382; Taylor, 1982).

Max Weber

For Max Weber we are indeed free agents. There are no universal laws, and society is social action rather than structures. We attach our own meanings to our social action, and we change society as much as it changes us.

Weber is interested in changing patterns, and particularly in the reasons for the emergence of the capitalism of his time. His research suggested that Protestantism (and particularly Puritanism) had transformed a religious understanding of asceticism as signs of certainty of salvation into an ascetic lifestyle as an end in itself, and had therefore created the conditions for cap-italistic industry: for if we don't spend all of the proceeds of production on consumption, then we shall have sufficient surplus for investment in capital; and if people trust our contracts, our promises, and our stated prices, then we shall have customers.

Weber also studied authority types, and in a broad survey of the histories of societies he found three of them: (1) Traditional (ruled by custom, with authority residing in hierarchically appointed leaders); (2) Charismatic (the leader-personality whose word is law); and (3) The bureaucratic or rational (in which postholders keep an external law, tasks are defined by posts, and post-holders fulfil their roles only while they are in their posts). This last type made large industrial enterprises possible, and Weber might have been right to link bureaucratic authority to the concept of 'the calling' found in Protestantism: but it is equally possible that technology gave rise to industrial possibilities, that the bureaucratic structures were the ones that worked and therefore sur-vived, and that bureaucratic roles encouraged the concept of 'the calling'.

Weber was no doubt right to seek for religious roots of the social trends that he discovered, but he also knew that we change things: so he could equally well have suggested that our religion is partly the result of the economic positions in which we find ourselves. He sought '*Verstehen*', 'understanding', although it is not surprising that, having found a particular connection between Puritanism and capitalism, he allowed that connection to control his method and to close off other possibilities. The kind of capitalistic industry that emerged in the UK did not emerge in Calvinistic Geneva, and it did emerge in Catholic Italy. Maybe such facts should have had more influence on Weber's conclusions (Giddens, 2001: 11–13, 348–9; Weber, 1963; 1992).

Symbolic Interaction

For George Herbert Mead, who worked into the twentieth century, society is its individual members, interacting with each other through symbols: and he also recognized that it is through linguistic and other symbols that we represent ourselves to ourselves (Cuff et al., 1998: 123–6; Giddens, 2001: 17–18; Gosling and Taylor, 2005: 130–2): and in this sense he was as much a social psychologist as a sociologist. On the basis of Mead's work on the individual, Herbert Blumer constructed a model of society as a diverse network of interacting individuals. Society does not exist apart from the individuals that constitute it. Blumer recognized that patterns can be discerned within this hugely diverse construction, and that such patterns might conform to Marx's and others' theories about society: but still society can only in the end be understood by studying actual interactions within groups of individuals: and, inspired by Blumer, subsequent sociologists, such as Erving Goffman (1968), have studied individuals' and groups' behaviours in institutions in order to understand society and its activity (Cuff et al., 1998: 125–33; Gosling and Taylor, 2005: 132–4). 'It is the social process in group life that creates and upholds the rules, not the rules that create and uphold group life' (Blumer, 1969: 18).

Changing Structures

For Marx, Durkheim and Weber, society has a reality of its own, it has a continuing existence, and it changes. They differ in the extent to which certain fixed ideas determine their methods and conclusions, but for all of them certain fixed patterns constrain the field of action. For Marx, class, alienation and capitalism are unchanging universals, and dialectic is a permanent method; for Durkheim, social facts determine action – so nothing can change them (although other social facts can explain them); and for Weber, the Puritan-capitalist connection and his three authority types function as unchanging universals. But real societies move through these so-called universals, leave them behind, and move into new patterns. Nothing is fixed. Class, capitalism, religion, and authority types, all change all the time. We change them, they change us, they change each other, and they are changed by other changing aspects of the field of action that we call society. For Mead and Blumer, action within society is more important than any fixed structures. Mead understood the human self as evolving through a process of symbolic interaction with its environment, and Blumer extended this insight into an understanding of society as a network of symbolic interactions. If we combine these two insights, then both individuals and society become complex changing bundles of symbolic interactions. Any society is a society of constantly changing individuals in constantly changing relationships with each other; and within this chaos patterns emerge. This is what creates temporary social facts (Benedict, 1935; Berger, 1966; Blumer, 1969).

The fact that any social fact is inherently temporary is of particular significance for the Citizen's Basic Income debate. If a benefits or tax system – or, indeed, any other bureaucratic system – is based on society understood in any particular way – that is, on society understood as constituted by a particular set of social facts – then, as society changes, the benefits, tax, or any other system, will need to be changed accordingly. Then comes the dilemma. Each time society changes, the systems have to change, which means that they become more complex, because the changes made have to take account of the way the system was as well as the way in which it needs to change. This process can only lead to increasing complexity. And the more complex a system, the more difficult it will be to change it in order to conform it to social change, particularly if social change becomes rapid. The only way to escape the dilemma is to construct a benefits, tax, or other system, that will cohere with any set of social facts. This can only mean a radically simple system. A Citizen's Basic Income is the obvious candidate.

FAMILIES ARE CHANGING

A particular example of the ways in which social facts change is the way in which families and households are changing (Dean, 2012c: 94–6; Giddens, 2001: 172–93). In many of the more developed countries, it is now difficult to define either 'family' or 'household', and the two terms can often be used interchangeably. In 1961, 38 per cent of families in the UK consisted of a married couple with two or more children: but by 2011 'just 16 per cent of the UK population believe[d] that they fit[ted] the "traditional model". In short, there has been a meltdown in the traditional nuclear family' (Centre for the Modern Family, 2011: 4). This is a significant social fact. Increasing numbers of households involve individual adults sharing the same accommodation (Hughes, 2010: 14; Office for National Statistics, 2014), reductions in average household size (Office for National Statistics, 2017a), and women waiting longer before they have children (Office for National Statistics, 2015; 2016), often for financial reasons. We have seen the advent of civil partnerships in 2004, and same-sex marriage in 2014 (Office for National Statistics, 2017b); increases in extramarital births; and, following a period of increasing divorce rates, a stabilization of the number of divorces because fewer couples are getting married (Beaumont, 2011: 2, 6; Office for National Statistics, 2018a).

There are clearly multiple factors underlying these trends, but one signifi-cant factor might be a less secure employment market (Brittan, [1995] 2013). As Patricia Morgan suggests, this can result in 'whole communities in which it is very difficult to establish and maintain families, with almost insuperable obstacles to family formation at the bottom of the socioeconomic ladder' (Morgan, 1995: 61). The myth of the nuclear family might survive, but the reality will often be different (Bittman and Pixley, 1997: 14–15).

Here a similar but more focused point needs to be made in relation to the conclusion drawn above following our discussion of social change in general. The tax and benefits systems serving the populations of more developed coun-tries often have deep roots in history, and they have evolved by the addition of new elements rather than by the replacement of existing policies. In the UK, the current benefits system is still based on the Beveridge Report of 1942 (Beveridge, 1942), which was more a tidying up of existing systems than a new direction. Beveridge assumed that each family would consist of a full-time employed man, a woman who was either employed or not, and a number of children; that families would remain stable over time; and that governments would ensure sufficient full-time employment. In such a context it made sense for social insurance benefits to be at the heart of the benefits system (with unemployment benefit time-limited), and to hope that the accompanying means-tested system would be needed by only a few families, and only occa-sionally. In today's context of shifting family patterns, and increasingly inse-cure and badly paid employment, those presuppositions no longer hold, and the system is a lot less fit for purpose than it was. In the UK, the Income Tax system has followed social trends and has changed from being couple-based to being individual-based: but this has not happened to the benefits system, in which joint claims still have to be made, which means that the person making the claim has to know their partner's income. Both partners' earned incomes influence the level of payment to the household, so a change in one partner's earned income will affect the employment decisions made by the other; and administrators can still ask questions about the intimate details of a relation-ship in order to determine whether two people should be treated as individuals or as a couple. Children benefit from their parents living together, from their parents having sufficient time to care for them, and from their parents being gainfully employed (Cusworth, 2009: 195–7), but the current benefits system can reduce parents' incentive to live together (Griffiths, 2017: 555; Miller, 2017: 68), it can treat parents as workers rather than as parents (Muijsson and Liebermann, 2018), and it can reduce the employment incentive experienced by the partner of someone employed full-time. Individualizing current benefits would be a step in the right direction (Esam and Berthoud, 1991: 71), but only a Citizen's Basic Income could recognize the needs of families, be coherent with today's social trends, and remain relevant in the context of the currently unknown social trends of the future (Torry, 2013: 99–103).

THE STATUS OF WOMEN

A significant and ongoing social change relates to the status of women (Giddens, 2001: 104–23; Gosling and Taylor, 2005: 192–211). No longer do we regard women as the property of men, and to regard women and men as of equal status is today the default position. Unfortunately, that is not how the UK's benefits system sees the situation. Means-tested benefits can further disadvantage an already disadvantaged woman, because even if the mother receives Child Benefit for a family's children, if there is already a power imbalance that privileges the man (Bittman and Pixley, 1997: 42, 144, 170, 209) then means-tested benefits payments will be made into a single account over which he might have more control. His wife or partner has no right to an independent income in these circumstances (Miller, 2017: 66–7), and the power imbalance will be exacerbated (Addabbo et al., 2010; Adelman et al., 1999; Pahl, 1983). The way in which poverty statistics have generally regarded the household as the relevant unit to study is therefore somewhat flawed, as it assumes that within the household resources will always be shared equally. A recent exception to poverty surveys based purely on the household is the Poverty and Social Exclusion Survey 2012 in the UK, which as well as studying poverty at the level of the household also studied poverty at the level of the individual. A complex set of findings was the result, among which was the interesting discovery that 'poor men and women engage in economizing behaviours in largely equal measure ... Gender inequality affects the non-poor to a greater degree, with more women taking the lead in economizing' (Dermott and Pantazis, 2018: 98, 110).

Adding a Citizen's Basic Income to the mix of income types would not solve all of the problems related to the intra-household distribution of income, but because of its individualized nature it would begin to make a difference. Research has shown that

> if unconditional benefits for children continue to be allocated to the mother, then a fairly modest Citizen's [Basic] Income scheme that leaves in place means-tested benefits and recalculates them by taking into account each household's total

Citizen's [Basic] Incomes achieves a significant reallocation of resources from men to women. (Torry, 2016d: 9)

A Citizen's Basic Income would shift the balance of power within any household currently in receipt of household-based benefits paid to one individual within the household, and it would also shift the balance of power within any household with one main earner and one non-earner or secondary earner. With a Citizen's Basic Income, neither the woman nor the man would be totally financially dependent on the other (Miller, 2016: 173; Pahl, 1986; Zelleke, 2008), and the income would not constitute a financial incentive for either partner to leave the relationship.

Women now have more choices than they once had: full-time or part-time employment; time spent caring for children, and possibly for other relatives; and often now a varying mixture of the two during working age adulthood. Different social policies might privilege different options to different degrees (Hakim, 2003). We can therefore make what is now a familiar point. Because it would be entirely unconditional, and would never alter, Citizen's Basic Income would neither privilege nor discourage any particular household structure or employment choices that members of a household might decide to make. It might be objected that by providing an unconditional income, Citizen's Basic Income might make the caring role more financially viable, and because that role is normally fulfilled by women, it might exacerbate existing gender inequality (Bittman and Pixley, 1997: 114, 209, 268; Gheaus, 2008). This might happen: but at the same time, because Citizen's Basic Incomes would be paid to individuals and not to couples, women's financial independence would be enhanced, and any woman whose household is currently on means-tested benefits would find it more financially beneficial to seek employment than before, thus providing them with new opportunities for diverse activity (Elgarte, 2008). The unconditional and individualized payments would also provide each couple with additional choices, so both members of a couple might find that it has become viable for them to share both employment and caring roles, whereas previously this might not have been possible (Vollenweider, 2013). In this sense, it might be possible to solve Wollstonecraft's dilemma. This asks the question: Should women be treated the same as men, or differently? In practical terms: If we define men primarily as workers, and as parents in a secondary manner, then should women be treated differently from men: that is, primarily as mothers; or should they be treated the same as men: that is, primarily as workers? The current situation in many countries can be characterized as a 'male breadwinner model', which implies a caring role for women. For gender equality, should we now be seeking a gender-neutral 'universal breadwinner' model, or a gender-neutral 'caregiving parity with breadwinning'? (Miller et al., 2019). If part-time employment were to pay better, and if both women and men were to have available to them the same range of options, then both men and women would be able to carry out both employment and caring roles, and no longer would there be a dilemma to resolve (Bambrick, 2006; Parker, 1993: 10, 21; Widerquist et al., 2013: 141–88), and the whole of what women contribute to society and the economy could be properly recognized (Campbell and Gillespie, 2016: 205). While it is true that neither conditional nor unconditional cash transfers on their own would be able to transform the current gendered division of labour (Enríquez, 2016: 46–7; Levasseur et al., 2018), any household taken off household-based means-tested benefits by their Citizen's Basic Incomes would be better able to make new decisions about the division of labour if it wanted to do so (Fitzpatrick, 1999: 174; Mullarney, 1999: 32; Yamamori, 2014).

Our treatment of the status of women has so far assumed that we are discussing working age women. However, because women tend to live longer than men, because they need pensions for longer periods, and because their employment income is on average lower than that of men, women might have poor contribution records in relation to state, occupational and private pensions, and their relative poverty is likely to continue into old age, and particularly into very old age (Alstott, 2001; Ginn, 1993: 47; 2003; Rein and Schmähl, 2004; Twine, 1996: 16–17). To provide an equal and unconditional state pension of a reasonable size to every older individual would go a long way towards remedying the problem of poverty among elderly women (James et al., 2008: 30, 195).

Citizen's Basic Income would not put an end to gender inequality (O'Reilly, 2008), but, as we have seen, and as the pilot projects in Namibia and India discovered (Haarmann et al., 2019; Davala, 2019; Miller et al., 2019), it would begin to make a difference (Torry, 2013: 104–9).

In relation to our discussion of the status of women, we need to ask a question related to the boundaries of academic disciplines: should we regard 'gender studies' as a separate discipline? If gender is understood as

> the state of being male or female as expressed by social or cultural distinctions and differences, rather than biological ones; the collective attributes or traits associated with a particular sex, or determined as a result of one's sex. Also: a (male or female) group characterized in this way, (Oxford English Dictionary)

then we can see that the study of gender fits within the discipline of sociology – 'the study of the development, structure, and functioning of human society' (Oxford English Dictionary). We can also see the argument for regarding gender studies as a separate discipline that employs methods drawn from sociology, psychology, social psychology, economics, biological sciences, social policy, history, and so on. For the purposes of this book, the discussion of the status of women has been located within a chapter on sociology: but a different decision could have been made.

STIGMA

In Chapter 7 on the social psychology of Citizen's Basic Income we have tackled in some detail the subject of stigma. Here we ask briefly about the sociological aspects of the subject, because it is not only individuals and groups within society that can experience stigma: social institutions can be stigmatized as well.

Individuals and families on means-tested benefits experience stigma, so the benefits themselves are stigmatized (Baumberg et al., 2012: 4, 11; Larsen, 2006: 141), which makes it easy for a government to reduce the levels of benefits, to apply sanctions to their recipients (Hirsch, 2015: 4–5), and generally to construct regulations that communicate a derogatory verdict on recipients (Tonkens et al., 2013). A vicious circle is therefore established: stigma is imposed on the recipients, and they impose it on themselves; the institution suffers stigma; this makes it easy for a government to construct the institution's regulations so that they communicate stigma: for instance, by permitting detailed bureaucratic intrusion into personal relationships; the regulations stigmatize recipients; and so on. A particularly pernicious root of this institutional stigma is the 'active labour market' policies attached to benefits receipt. The regulations communicate the assumption that recipients are unwilling to contribute to society unless they are pushed into doing so. A verdict of moral weakness is communicated, both to the recipients and to society at large. This can only be demotivating (Patrick, 2017b: 123–44; Welfare Reform Team, Oxford City Council, 2016: 51). In this context Hartley Dean wonders whether combining the UK's in-work and out-of-work means-tested benefits in the new Universal Credit might have the unintended consequence of increasing the stigma attached to means-tested benefits for people in employment. With the legacy system of in-work Tax Credits, the 'virtuous worker', who believes that work is a virtuous taking of responsibility, can receive a means-tested benefit, described as Working Tax Credits, and still separate their self-image from that of the out-of-work means-tested benefits recipient, because Working Tax Credits have a name different from those of the out-of-work benefits Jobseeker's Allowance and Income Support, and they operate with different regulations (Baumberg, 2016: 196). With Universal Credit, the employed worker will attract, and will impose upon themselves, the stigma that attaches to means-tested benefits paid to unemployed workers (Dean, 2012a: 355).

The only way to break out of the stigma cycle is to construct benefits with regulations that simply do not allow stigma to operate. The UK's unconditional Child Benefit remains relatively unstigmatized, as does the National

Health Service. A Citizen's Basic Income would have the same effect. Any household taken off means-tested benefits by their Citizen's Basic Incomes would experience an increase in motivation generated by their removal from the stigmatized portion of society, and any family still on means-tested benefits would be on less of them and would have a significant incentive to get off them, without being pushed.

One very useful outcome would be an increase in the kind of interpersonal trust on which a society relies for its cohesion, and that is required to maintain a welfare state. Research has shown that means-tested benefits reduce levels of interpersonal trust, whereas universal benefits increase them (Gamble, 2016: 109; Hyggen, 2006: 507; Mulligan, 2013; O'Hara, 2014: 5, 15; Searle, 2008: 129; Svendsen and Svendsen, 2016; Taylor-Gooby, 2009). To implement a Citizen's Basic Income would therefore have significant beneficial effects for society as a whole, as well as for individuals currently on stigmatizing means-tested benefits.

CONCLUSIONS

A country's benefits system is bound to have an impact on society, and the way in which any particular society functions will influence the form and functioning of its benefits system. Society and the ways in which taxes and benefits are structured and administered are inextricably linked. We have studied the social science of sociology by discussing five of its early practitioners, and we have asked about the relationships between the Citizen's Basic Income debate and a number of social phenomena frequently studied by sociologists. We have found the insights of sociologists helpful to us in relation to the changing family, the status of women, and stigma, and a case study on globalization follows this set of conclusions. But there are far more aspects of society studied by sociologists, so a sizeable research agenda remains to be tackled: for instance, in relation to different demographic groups. To take one example: A study of elderly people would note that most societies are ageing, which is drawing attention to the significance of elderly people as an element in society, and is leading to an understanding that elderly people are active members of society rather than passive recipients of pensions and healthcare, and to an 'active ageing' social policy perspective: 'a comprehensive approach to the maximization of participation and well-being as people age and one that, ideally, operates simultaneously at the micro, meso and macro levels' (Walker and Maltby, 2012: S128). Such a study would of course find that a Citizen's Pension – an unconditional pension for every older person in society – would provide precisely the right financial basis for facilitating a wide variety of caring, voluntary, employed and leisure activities in old age.

But here we have only one chapter in which to study the relationship between sociology and Citizen's Basic Income. In it we have found that sociology has much to offer to the Citizen's Basic Income debate. We have also found that Citizen's Basic Income would cohere with a number of current social changes, suggesting that if a Citizen's Basic Income were to be implemented then any study of society following the implementation would find the new tax and benefits system to be more coherent with a changing society than the current one.

As for what the Citizen's Basic Income debate can offer to the discipline of sociology: we have found that the tax and benefits systems constitute a significant sociological issue, which suggests that they should be more firmly on sociologists' agendas than they might be today.

CASE STUDY

Globalization

Globalization is 'the social process in which the constraints of geography on economic, political, social and cultural arrangements recede, in which people become increasingly aware that they are receding, and in which people act accordingly' (Waters, 2001: 5). As Waters' description of globalization offered here suggests, this case study could have been located in Chapter 5 on economics, Chapter 9 on social policy, Chapter 11 on politics, or Chapter 12 on political economy. The case study is included in this chapter on sociology because globalization is a 'social process', and because sociologists study globalization (Waters, 2001).

We know that globalization is happening. We can text from one mobile phone to another across the world; McDonald's is everywhere; and when a young man kicks in a shop window during an anti-globalization demonstration, he is wearing Nike trainers. The time taken to get from one geographical point to another is still decreasing, so the world appears to be shrinking; we trust people on the other side of the world whom we have never met with intimate details about ourselves; and we are increasingly reflexive: responding, as individuals and collectives, to anything anywhere. Social collapse anywhere in the world (whether it be the economy of a South American country, or the rule of law in a European one) affects us all, and we know the world's news instantaneously (the censored version on television news, and an uncensored but maybe equally erroneous version on the internet) (Giddens, 2001: 50–76; Gosling and Taylor, 2005: 159–77).

However, globalization has different effects in different arenas, and Waters suggests that 'material exchanges localize; political exchanges internationalize; and symbolic exchanges globalize' (Waters, 2001: 20), which means that in the economic arena the local remains important (because the action is mainly material exchange, and is only power relationships and symbolic exchange to a smaller extent); in politics, international action is important (because politics is mainly power exchange, and only material or symbolic to a smaller extent); and in the cultural arena the global is the field across which action takes place (and only to some extent is it local and international). But the trend is towards symbolic exchange in the economy (because money is increasingly electronic, and the economy is increasingly constituted by information rather than objects); in politics (because the trend is towards regional blocs such as the European Union – in spite of the Union's current travails – and towards human rights as a controlling idea); and in culture – for it is the cultural arena which now dominates both the economy and politics. The result is that, to different degrees, there are now local, national, regional, international, and global elements to each of the economic, political, and cultural arenas, with the trend firmly set towards the global. (It is no accident that all of economics, politics and culture now create media stars.) Describing globalization in this way reveals the reason for the nation state's declining importance in the economic, political and cultural spheres, and explains the backlash against this trend in the recent elections of protectionist governments and in nationalist movements in Europe. An interesting question is whether the Chinese economy will remain significantly different from those of the USA and Europe (Gray, 2007). The answer is that it probably will, as long as it remains a predominantly manufacturing and construction economy, and that it will cease to be different once it joins the global information economy. In relation to the subject of this book: because social security policy is all three of economic, political, and cultural, it is no surprise that trends such as 'active labour market' policies are now to be found globally, and equally no surprise that the Citizen's Basic Income debate is now global.

However, globalization is by no means having it all its own way, for to every action there is a reaction. A globalizing culture has led to the resurgence of Welsh culture and language; a globalizing politics has led to moves towards Scottish independence and to the UK leaving the European Union; and Walmart has led to farmers' markets.

Globalization is not itself a paradigm: that is, it is not itself a set of ideas, but is rather a statement that whatever paradigms there are will be available globally, and will be combined locally with other ideas to produce a unique mixture of economic, political and cultural ideas and practices. This is the fundamental paradox of globalization: that the global creates radical diversity – so perhaps we should regard this combination of global ideas with local radical diversity as the definition of 'globalization'.

There is evidence of a wide variety of attitudes to globalization. Both doubters and sceptics quite rightly say that trade is international rather than global, with the doubters wondering whether globalization is in fact a significant reality, and sceptics being more aware of the globalization processes and wanting national governments to do more to protect their populations from the downsides of global corporations' activities: but perhaps all of them are taking too little account of cultural change and of the cultural aspect of the economy. Then there are the 'sponsors' who think that a global market will promote global wellbeing, and allied to these might be the hyperglobalizers, who think that a new global order is emerging in which everything will be globalized, including effective government: but all of these take too little account of the national and international aspects of the economy and of politics, and too little account of local reactions to globalization.

A further attitude is that of people who object strongly to globalization and demonstrate against global free trade, with a more moderate wing advocating 'fair trade' (Dean, 2012c: 28–9). And yet another attitude might be that of transformationalists, who regard 'globalization' as an umbrella term which has its usefulness within limits, rather like the other sociological term 'secularization'. They recognize that some patterns of national politics and personal and local life remain distinctive and local; that cultural flows are often personal, local, national, and global; that countries restructure in order to retain their identities; and that it is local culture that globalizes (as the culture of the United States has been doing for a long time, with considerable success). Economies will continue to be different in different places; and political patterns will continue to be unique to each country, like each other in blocs and close alliances, and less like each other otherwise. It is the cultural, religious and other ideational patterns that will exist everywhere, and that will then combine differently with other economic, political and societal patterns to create unique local patterns of action that will constitute *that* local society: and then the patterns will all change again, and the local mix will itself globalize and inform societies everywhere in one way or another (Waters, 2001).

Understood in this way it is clear that globalization has no obvious trajectory. New patterns will supersede old patterns, new combinations might look very unlike previous patterns, a pattern might emerge in one place which looks very like one somewhere else – and then the next moment it will be different again. 'Globalization' is a useful term if we recognize it for what it is: a partial description of what is going on in the world.

All of this raises the question as to the appropriate territoriality of Citizen's Basic Income. It is economic, it is political, and it is cultural, which suggests that it is local, national, regional, international, and global. So should we be seeking to implement a national Citizen's Basic Income? Or a Eurodividend (Cowen, 2002: 53; McKnight et al., 2016: 67–8, 80; Van Parijs and Vanderborght, 2017: 230–41)? Or a global unconditional income (Torry, 2013: 61–3)? Or perhaps a local one?

Any of these would be a possibility, which means that the question then becomes: Which would it be possible to implement first? Given that tax and benefits policy is everywhere under the control of national governments, with almost no co-ordination at regional or global level, and very little decision-making at the local level, it is clear that we should be attempting to implement Citizen's Basic Income in a small number of nation states before tackling the regional and global contexts. Once we have established some national Citizen's Basic Incomes, then will be the time to explore the possibility of a European Citizen's Basic Income: a Eurodividend; and then after that a small global one. Or perhaps we might first see subnational Citizen's Basic Incomes before we see national ones: with perhaps individual states in India, Canada, or the US, or maybe Scotland, implementing Citizen's Basic Income schemes before anyone else does (Barclay et al., 2019).

9. Citizen's Basic Income as social policy

Public policy: Policy, esp. of government, that relates to or affects the public as a whole; social policy.
(Oxford English Dictionary)

Policy science: The systematic study of the making and implementation of policy, esp. social policy; any of the academic disciplines which deal with this study.
(Oxford English Dictionary)

Social administration is the study of the development, structure and practices of the social services ... the social services are mainly understood to include social security, housing, health, social work and education ...
(Spicker, 2014: 477, 1)

INTRODUCTION

There is no entry for 'social policy' in the Oxford English Dictionary, although the entry for 'public policy' refers to 'social policy' as if the reader is bound to know what that means.

The London School of Economics defines social policy as

an interdisciplinary and applied subject concerned with the analysis of different societies' responses to inequality and social need. The Department's teaching and assessment approach builds on LSE's commitment to connecting theory with empirical research, and the application of research to 'real world' policy problems. (London School of Economics, 2018)

As guides to the subject for the purposes of this chapter I shall be using Paul Spicker's *Social Policy: Theory and practice* (Spicker, 2014) and Hartley Dean's *Social Policy* (Dean, 2012c). I choose both of these guides because they understand the discipline of social policy in rather different ways. Hartley Dean takes a broad approach, seeing the task of the discipline of social policy as

the study of human well-being and of systems for achieving well-being; in a way that celebrates human interdependency, that embraces diversity, etc. Of course, it is concerned with policy responses to social problems and strategies to combat social disadvantage, but it is also concerned with the means of providing or underpinning the things upon which a good life depends: health, learning, security, care, etc.; with the things that everybody should/can enjoy. (Dean, 2004)

And for Dean, social policy is never simply a matter of studying. He expects the social policy academic to exhibit a 'highly specific commitment to the cause of human wellbeing' (Dean, 2012c: 5). It is therefore no surprise that when he co-edited a book about *Social Advantage and Disadvantage*, it included chapters on poverty, capabilities, human rights, equalities, class, capitals, social mobility, the family, education, income distribution, wealth, labour, work, ageing, gender, race, ethnicity, citizenship, migration, religion, place, crime, and punishment (Dean and Platt, 2016). There are no chapters specifically on health or housing, but apart from that the book is a comprehensive exploration of what is required for human wellbeing and of what prevents it.

Paul Spicker understands the discipline of social policy more narrowly.

Social policy, as it was initially conceived, was study for a purpose. It was aimed at future public and voluntary sector administrators who needed to know about the problems and processes they would be dealing with. The core of the subject was Social Administration ... Social Administration studies the structure and operation of services, the process of service delivery, and the effect that services have on the people who receive them. This is as central now as it's ever been. (Spicker, 2004: 8)

So somewhat differently from Dean's view, the discipline as Spicker understands it is 'concerned with people who lack wellbeing – people with particular problems or needs – and the services which provide for them' (Spicker, 2014: 6). The discipline is interested in 'policy and practice', and only in social and economic relationships and institutions insofar as they are relevant to that: and so, for instance, 'it is not concerned with physical health, but it is very much concerned with policies to promote health and the provision of medical care' (Spicker, 2014: 6).

It is certainly true, as Spicker suggests, that the modern discipline grew out of the earlier discipline of 'social administration', which was intended to be a practical training in the management of such public services as public housing, education, and social security benefits (Spicker, 2014: 1). The shift to 'social policy and administration' and then to 'social policy' twenty years ago (Spicker, 2004: 8) reflected the increasing importance of social theory (Spicker, 2014: 15–18): but this chapter will show that empirical research (Spicker, 2014: 381–407) and the study of real-world problems are still just as much in evidence as they ever were.

Related to the different approaches taken by Spicker and Dean are two methods for discussing policy change: one is to ask about social problems and then to seek policy solutions; the other is to ask what society is like, and what we might wish it to be like, and then to construct social policies that might take us from the former to the latter. There will of course be some overlap between the two approaches, because in solving problems we might find ourselves creating the kind of society that we might wish to see; and to seek policy that both reflects today's social reality and moves us towards society as we might wish it to be might solve some of today's social problems. So, for instance, we might want to see a far simpler social security system that would better serve an increasingly complex society, and that would enable social change to be more easily accommodated. The same simpler system would also help to solve some of the problems associated with the complexity of current social security systems. But however much some policy prescriptions might cohere with the two different approaches to policy change, the different approaches might also generate different prescriptions. For instance, there might be a bundle of problems faced by a particular type of family. The problem-centred approach might try to adjust regulations to alleviate the problems, or might implement a new benefit or a new addition to a benefit. The alternative approach would recognize the problem as symptomatic of an increasingly diverse society, and would seek a new benefits and tax system that would be more likely to serve any individual and any household type. The problem-centred approach will always ask how we can alleviate today's problems. The alternative approach will instead ask how a system might be designed so that it would continue to serve our society and economy whatever changes might take place in the future. The problem-centred approach, by tackling today's problems, might make it more difficult to tackle tomorrow's. The alternative approach is more likely to result in policy that would serve *any* society, today and in the future (Torry, 2013: 81–2).

An additional guide for this chapter, on the process by which policy is made, will be Michael Hill's *The Public Policy Process* (Hill, 2009). This will be of particular interest to us in relation to Citizen's Basic Income. Paul Spicker suggests that study of the policy process belongs in the discipline called 'public policy' rather than in social policy, which for him is focused on the content of policy and the problems to which it is addressed (Spicker, 2014: 13–14). However, in relation to the definition of public policy quoted at the beginning of this chapter, it might be best to view 'social policy' as the discipline related to those social problems and aspects of wellbeing addressed by state provision, and 'public policy' as the discipline related to social problems and aspects of wellbeing addressed by private and voluntary provision regulated by public authorities. This understanding of the difference between the two suggests that study of the policy process is intrinsic to the discipline of social policy as well as to the discipline of public policy.

As with disciplines such as 'law' and 'history', and unlike disciplines such as 'economics' and 'psychology', the name of the discipline called 'social policy' is the same as the name of the reality studied: social policy. That in itself is not a problem: but what might be a problem is that, as the London School of Economics' definition at the beginning of this introduction suggests, the discipline named 'social policy' is 'interdisciplinary': that is, it employs methods from a variety of disciplines (Dean, 2012c: 5; Spicker, 2014: 10–14), the corollary being that it does not have a distinctive method of its own. And although 'responses to inequality and social need' might to some extent define the field across which methods from a variety of disciplines are employed, it cannot tell us what to include in this chapter, simply because anything that we might include could equally well have been included in the chapter on the discipline to which the methods employed belong.

The reader will find that a large volume of material is categorized under social policy in this book: material on how social policy is made, on feasibility, on administration of social security benefits, and on implementation. Far more of the material in this book could have been located in a discussion of social policy: in fact, all of it could have been, simply because all of the subject matter has been chosen because it relates to the Citizen's Basic Income debate, and Citizen's Basic Income is a social policy. The issues that the reader will find in this chapter are located here first because they are concerns that have always been at the heart of the academic discipline that we call 'social policy', and second, because they are issues that do not fit quite so easily into other chapters.

The extent of the material categorized under social policy means that two chapters are required to contain it. The first of the two chapters, Chapter 9, is labelled 'social policy', and discusses how social policy is made, the complexity of social policy, and the question of feasibility. The second of the two chapters is labelled 'social administration', and discusses questions of administration and implementation. In this context, 'social policy' and 'social administration' should be understood as two aspects of a single subject area: social policy; and the subdiscipline of social policy and the subdiscipline of social administration should be understood as two aspects of a single discipline: social policy. Because both chapters contain reflection on the discipline of social policy, and because they both contain subject matter that relates the discipline of social policy to the Citizen's Basic Income debate, the allocation of subject matter between the chapters is bound to be somewhat arbitrary: although an attempt has been made to locate under 'social administration' those aspects of the subject that might best be described as administrative in character.

Because the two chapters on social policy and social administration are both about social policy, this introduction serves as the introduction for both of them.

HOW IS SOCIAL POLICY MADE?

Any policy process – by which we mean the way in which new or changed policy is made – will be constituted by a number of elements: participants, perspectives, situations, values, strategies, outcomes, and effects (Dunn, 2018: 115). However, once we leave such broad generalizations, the subject becomes highly context-specific, as is generally the case with social policy, and with much of the content of this book. As well as facing its own unique socio-economic situation (Blomquist, 2018), each country will have its own set of institutions, and they will relate to each other in unique ways; and in each country the relationships between the policy process, that is, the process by which policy is made, and the country's legal structure, history, psychologies, social psychology, economy, and so on, will be different from those of any other country. An important complexity, and one that will be particularly context-specific, is the informal structures operating within each institution. To take the UK as an example: Parliament, the government, think tanks, the civil service, trades unions, and a wide variety of other institutions involved in policymaking, will relate to each other in ways that conform to their stated structures, but also in highly complex ways through their changing informal relationships; and both their formal and informal structures will be changed by new social policy (Birkland, 2005: 97–103; Ham and Hill, 1984: 124; Hill, 1990: 4; Hodge and Lowe, 2009: 160; Smith, 1993a; Spicker, 2014: 137–50; Torry, 2016a: 226; Zahariadis, 1999: 74). All of this means that studying how the different stakeholders in the policymaking process actually behave will be essential to any understanding of the process as a whole (Bartels, 2018). In the UK, the changing nature of the relationship between the government and the civil service – between government ministers' 'heroic' policymaking, and civil servants' 'humdrum' contributions to policy change (Page, 2018) – is particularly significant. The centralization of power in the Prime Minister and the Prime Minister's office, the growing number of advisory staff who are not career civil servants, and an increased expectation that civil servants will actively campaign on behalf of the governing party's policies, is dissolving the previously quite rigid division between governments fulfilling political agendas and the civil service offering objective policy advice to ministers (Diamond, 2018: 13, 31–3).

An interesting case that epitomizes this change in the policy process is the UK's Universal Credit policy. While the Conservative Party was in opposition, Iain Duncan Smith established a think tank, the Centre for Social Justice

(CSJ). He had recognized some of the problems posed by the UK's complex system of different means-tested benefits, so the CSJ appointed a working group to develop new policy. The result was the document *Dynamic Benefits* (Centre for Social Justice, 2009), which recommended that the existing benefits should be replaced by a single 'Universal Credit'. When Duncan Smith became Secretary of State for Work and Pensions in 2010, he brought the idea of Universal Credit and associated advisors from the CSJ into the department, and the civil service was then expected to implement the policy recommended in *Dynamic Benefits* (– an interesting example of the centrality of documents to the policy process (Sedlačko, 2018). A similar example would be the Beveridge Report of 1942 that gave birth to the current shape of the UK's welfare state). The problem for the civil service was that as well as implementing a policy on which it had no influence, it was expected to take responsibility for its failings: failings exacerbated by an increased expectation that civil servants would actively support government policy rather than offer objective advice that might suggest that the policy should be changed (Diamond, 2018: 43). The problem was exacerbated by changes made to the policy as it progressed through implementation, such as the change from long-term stable awards of Universal Credit, with withdrawal through the tax system as earned income rose (Centre for Social Justice, 2009: 27, 269–72), to real-time monthly calculation of Universal Credit. As Colebatch suggests, policy design happens throughout implementation as well as during the initial stages of policy formation (Colebatch, 2018a).

It is not only the policy process that constantly changes. The social problems to which the different players address themselves will always be socially constructed and so will constantly change; and what look like sensible solutions will be similarly socially constructed and thus constantly changing, and those solutions will also be constantly pushed around by often unrelated political factors (Anglund, 1999: 151; Dean, 2012c: 99; Gregory, 1997: 189; Minogue, 1997: 12, 15; Spicker, 2014: 63–9; Turnbull, 2018). The system is more like a 'primeval soup' (Hill, 2009: 88, 108, 157) than a rational system (Gordon et al., 1997: 5, 7), and the whole tangled web of individual and institutional players constantly evolves in complex and often unpredictable ways (Colebatch, 2018b; Morçöl, 2012: 90). Any one part of the policymaking system can block change (Hill, 2009: 68, 73), the media find it difficult to understand or to explain major policy shifts (Jacobs and Shapiro, 1999: 136), we think that we understand the way things are (Richardson, 1999: 67; Rose, 2006: 57), none of us find it easy to understand major paradigm shifts (Jacobs and Shapiro, 1999: 136; Hill, 2009: 159), changing more than marginally the systems about which we have some understanding can feel like too much of a risk (Smith and May, 1997: 166; Rose, 2006: 51), and interorganizational communication channels ('policy networks'), and particularly policy networks with tight-knit groups of knowledgeable individuals at their heart ('policy communities'), can often pull in different directions: so it will always be easier to maintain the status quo (Hill, 2009: 58–66; Hodge and Lowe, 2009: 155, 160–1; Marin and Mayntz, 1991: 16; Smith, 1993a: 56–65), to make only small changes, or accidentally to generate a pendulum effect – for instance, between means-tested and less conditional benefits – than it will ever be to make major changes to the basic structures of a social policy field (Barkai, 1998; Hill, 2009: 156–7, 164, 188). The results are 'path dependency' – that is, a policy field is more likely to continue in the direction in which it is moving than to take some major new direction, even if major change would be a better response to society's problems (Majone, 1989: 77; Zahariadis, 1999: 90) – and 'satisficing': that is, policymakers study a narrow range of possible changes, all of them close to the status quo, and choose the one that looks the safest (Richardson and Jordan, 1979: 21–2). Policymakers 'muddle through' (Botterill and Fenna, 2019: 82).

A compounding factor is 'governance capacity': the ability of a government to create change. In a country with high social inclusion – whether through high and stable employment, a more universalist welfare state, a sizeable and diverse tax base, low inequality, or a combination of these, such as in the Nordic states – a government's capacity to legislate change, particularly in a more universalist direction, will be higher than in countries with low governance capacity such as the UK, where a lack of governance capacity can result in policy drift and neglect. The result is a paradox: in those countries more in need of Citizen's Basic Income, the government is less likely to legislate for it; and in those less in need of it there is a greater capacity to make it happen. A further result is a dilemma: in high governance capacity countries, income maintenance will generally be via employment and social insurance, rather than means-tested social assistance, and in such a context Citizen's Basic Income can meet resistance from social insurance institutions (Haagh, 2019b: 252–3, 259; Martinelli and Pearce, 2019: 269). All of this means that in more developed countries, whatever their level of governance capacity, legislating for Citizen's Basic Income will be problematic.

The combination of path dependency and satisficing will not necessarily result in the policy change that the country needs, and might make matters worse, as the UK's combination of several means-tested benefits into the new Universal Credit has done. Because the UK has been means-testing benefits for four hundred years, it carries on doing so (Martin, 2016). A further consequence of path dependency, low governance capacity, and satisficing, and a significant contributor to the complexity of the tax and benefits systems, is the tendency to add rather than subtract: that is, new provisions are bolted on to existing provisions, which are left largely intact. This means that genuine change will only be possible if a proposal can be understood as in continuity with existing provision. So, for instance, an extension of unconditional benefits could be understood as an extension of Child Benefit. This means that the UK might experience future

> multi-layered reforms to our tax and social security system with tiers of financial support working in combination: universal as well as means-tested; unconditional as well as conditional; non-contributory as well as contributory. Along the way, these reforms should embrace elements of the UBI [Citizen's Basic Income] idea – and modest, partial basic incomes may have their place in the eventual toolkit. (Harrop and Tait, 2017)

However, path dependency, satisficing, and governance capacity, are not the only factors involved in the policy process, and the fact that in many policy fields, in a variety of countries, incremental policy change is giving way to more deliberate and wide-ranging policy change suggests that path dependency might be losing its grip on the policy process (Hoppe, 2018). Botterill and Fenna (2019) might be right to suggest that the idea that the policy process can be rational and evidence-based has always been something of a 'dream' (Botterill and Fenna, 2019: 63, 78), and that values held by members of society, and communicated to policymakers through democratic processes, have always been more important than we might have thought (Botterill and Fenna, 2019: 96, 110): so if values are now more diverse, and are held with more conviction, then policymaking might become less path dependent. We might therefore see more of a balance between change and the status quo (Grin, 2018). If a small coherent group finds itself at the heart of a policy community, it holds with a conviction a set of values prevalent in society, its message is consistent, it has access to multiple communication channels, and other parts of the policymaking system are distracted, then major change can sometimes occur. The obvious example is William Beveridge, whose 1942 report, as well as conforming to the British social policy tradition by tidying up existing means-tested and contributory benefit provisions, employed values that had evolved during the Second World War in order to make significant changes to UK social policy, and in particular the implementation of unconditional Family Allowances for the second and subsequent children in every family, which led eventually to unconditional Child Benefit for every child (Harris, 1977). The operative phrase here is 'the heart of a policy community', because however competent a policy network or community might be, only government ministers can propose major policy change, civil servants have to permit it (– that is, they have to decide not to brief ministers against it), and Parliament has to vote for it. Policy change requires 'élite' (Presthus, 1974: 67) members of the relevant policy network to line up (Hill, 2009: 87; Kenis and Volker Schneider, 1991: 48; Wu et al., 2010: 4, 13, 18). This can be particularly difficult to achieve if more than one government department is involved and the balance of power is shifting between them (Basu, 1980: 44,

86; Marinetto, 1999: 7, 10–11; Richardson and Jordan, 1979: 28). If all of the relevant institutional and individual players *do* line up, and they successfully exchange research and other resources, then major useful change can occur. If they do not, then it never will (Smith, 1993a: 56–65).

In the UK, the US, and a growing number of other countries, some of the important relevant players will be think tanks. This is simply because they are institutions, which means that they can better relate to other institutions, such as the civil service, than individuals might be able to do; because civil servants often move to work in think tanks and vice versa (Hill, 2009: 88; Stone, 1996: 1, 47–8); and because think tanks can enable politicians to float new ideas that might be difficult to discuss within political parties because such internal party discussions risk internal and external accusations of disunity (Abelson, 2002: 163–4; Birkland, 2005: 88–9; Day, 2000: 132; Zahariadis, 1999: 75). Think tanks that build positive relationships with legislators and government departments, by providing them with safe opportunities for discussion and with information that they might not possess, might then be able to insert into the policy process ideas that might be more difficult to contribute from alternative directions (Presthus, 1974: 209). However, think tanks tend to assume that the policy process is rational, which might not be the best description of it (Birkland, 2005: 191; Denham and Garnett, 1998: 195): so their prescriptions might sometimes be tolerated rather than heard.

An important characteristic of the entire policy process is the self-interest of every individual and institution involved. Every government minister, member of parliament, and political party, will to some extent be influenced by their own interests – both ideological interests, and interests related to their electability and their political careers (Majone, 1989: 76; Natili, 2019). Every civil servant will similarly have their eye on their career, and on their ability to maintain the considerable areas of freedom that they possess by virtue of their expert knowledge and the time that they can spend gaining and deploying it (Ham and Hill, 1984: 124, 146); and, because civil servants have to work with whatever government is in power, they will always have an interest in policy that will be broadly acceptable to all of the main political parties, which will normally be somewhere near to the status quo (Hill, 2009: 186). Similarly, every think tank's main aim is to survive and thrive. So if senior staff members of a think tank believe that supporting a policy proposal that they were not the first to think of might draw attention away from an idea that only they had developed, then they might be unlikely to support the proposal; and similarly, senior civil servants might decide to brief ministers against a policy change that might reduce the size of their own departments (Hill, 2009: 19, 90, 102, 105). The question that policymakers might ask themselves is how much 'credit' they might gain or lose by implementing a Citizen's Basic Income (Natili, 2019). The relevant questions might therefore be: What credit would be gained by policy actors if they implemented a Citizen's Basic income? And just as importantly: What credit would be gained by abolishing a Citizen's Basic Income?

Because so much social policy is now managed via communication and information technology – computers, mobile phones, and other similar devices – the manufacturers, installers, and programmers of computers and telephone systems have become major players in the formation of social policy. They possess expert power, and once a contract has been signed, they can possess economic power because they can have a government department over a financial barrel. A company's insistence on a policy change that would be easier and cheaper to computerize than the democratically determined policy proposal, and that might make it easier to keep the project within budget, would be difficult to resist (Hill, 2009: 191; French and Raven, 1959).

But having said all of that, it is still true that values and ideas remain an essential aspect of any policy process, and particularly values and ideas related to political ideologies (Botterill and Fenna, 2019; Dowding, 2018): so the battle of ideas related to Citizen's Basic Income might be as important as the individual and institutional interests involved. This means that if a Citizen's Basic Income scheme is ever to be legislated and implemented, then a substantial policy community will be required, made up of think tanks, academic departments, and a wide variety of civil society organizations, including trades unions, and then members of parliament, government ministers, and civil servants (Baggott, 2000: 6, 80; Heyman, 2008: 114–17). Widespread public education will be required, so engagement with a wide variety of media will be needed (Hogwood and Gunn, 1997): and one element of the content of that education must be that Citizen's Basic Income would conform to values widely held in society, and at the same time would be a minor rearrangement of the current tax and benefits system, even though it might also constitute a major paradigm shift (Deeming and Smyth, 2017: 324). A careful eye would have to be kept on whether Citizen's Basic Income as a concept could be aligned with the stated and unstated priorities of the government of the day, on whether it could be fitted into the ideological commitments of major political parties (Hill, 2009: 291), and on the kinds of evidence, and framings of evidence, that might be appropriate under the political circumstances of the time (Strassheim, 2018). Whereas in some policy areas a certain amount of compromise can be both permitted and useful (Richardson, 1969: 107), in the case of Citizen's Basic Income it would not be useful and it must not be permitted. To compromise on the definition of Citizen's Basic Income would mean that something other than a Citizen's Basic Income would be implemented, would make the resultant compromise difficult to implement and to administer, and would not deliver the social and economic benefits of Citizen's Basic Income.

For policy change to occur, the current policy 'agenda' (John, 2018b) – that bundle of (socially constructed) problems and policy ideas currently tacitly agreed as the field within which policy debate occurs – must include the idea of Citizen's Basic Income as a discussable idea; and a 'problem stream', a 'policy stream', and a 'politics stream', might need to come together (Ritter and Lancaster, 2018). The 'policy stream' related to Citizen's Basic Income is of an unusually consistent character, simply because the definition of Citizen's Basic Income is clear and no compromise with that definition can be permitted – although of course a variety of feasible illustrative Citizen's Basic Income schemes might be on offer. The consistency of the policy stream means that it ceases to be a shifting variable, and the alignment required is for the value- and interest-driven political stream and the socially constructed problem stream to travel in the same direction as the existing Citizen's Basic Income policy stream.

COMPLEXITY

Complexity studies is now a well-developed academic discipline in its own right. There has not been space to include an entire chapter on the relationship between complexity and Citizen's Basic Income, but because at least a recognition of the relationship needs to be offered, a decision has had to be made as to the chapter in which that belongs. Chapter 5 on economics and Chapter 10 on social administration would both have been candidates. A discussion of complexity is located in this chapter on social policy because the most direct connections between complexity and the Citizen's Basic Income debate probably relate to the complexities of benefits policy and of the policy process.

Whilst its simplicity is generally reckoned to be one of a Citizen's Basic Income's major advantages, complexity theory might lead us at least to ask the question: Is simplicity necessarily the right direction in which to take our benefits system? Complex physical systems often experience both chaos and self-organization (Davies, 1989: 4; Nicolis, 1989: 316–47; Prigogine and Stengers, 1984); and living organisms are likewise 'the result of the unfolding of many developmental mechanisms that have become integrated with one another. ... such integrated complexity generally yields simplicity; [and the process whereby viable forms evolve] may be inherently robust, not exquisitely fragile' (Kauffman, 1993: 642). Geoffrey M. Hodgson has extended the methods and insights of Kauffman into the field of economics, and has suggested that the discipline needs to remain diverse if it is to develop new usable theory (Hodgson, 1999: 13). We might similarly extend the same insights and methods into the social policy field, and suggest that tax and benefits systems are complex, that they evolve in company with evolving social processes, and that they will need to remain diverse if they are to continue to evolve creatively. This suggests (counter-intuitively) that simplification of the system *as a whole* is *not* what is required, and maybe that a combination of universal provision, private provision, and means-tested provision, is what is needed. A complexity theory approach also suggests that the total social system will develop most creatively if it is not overcontrolled by any one part or parts of the tax and benefit structure. This suggests that disincentives and coercion should be reduced to a minimum, and that the number of elements that might enable other parts of the system to develop freely should be increased (Torry, 2002).

There are of course limits to the ways in which tax and benefits systems might evolve. As we have seen, social policy is path dependent: that is, its current trajectory will determine to a large extent where it goes. The process also experiences feedback loops: that is, a policy change will provoke reactions that themselves cause policy change. So, for instance,

> as structural change alters the landscape of positional competition, it is … in general those who are already advantaged who are best placed to take advantage of the new opportunities and to avoid the new insecurities. (Room, 2011: 7, 209–10)

Households are agile institutional entrepreneurs, finding their way around the social policy landscape (Jordan et al., 1992). In the employment market, 'agile creativity accrues disproportionately to the advantaged' (Room, 2011: 265). Only a flat landscape can mitigate against such entrepreneurial inequalities, which means that a Citizen's Basic Income would do so, and that the higher the Citizen's Basic Income, and the less substantial the other elements of the system, the less will financial resources belong to the already wealthy.

Initially a Citizen's Basic Income would be added to the existing structure, and the existing tax and benefits systems would be adapted to pay for it (see the case study at the end of this chapter). Policy change always carries a risk of unintended consequences (Capano et al., 2019), so a gradual implementation achieved by establishing a Citizen's Basic Income for one demographic group at a time might be a useful precaution. However, because the Citizen's Basic Income would be added to the existing system, it would contribute to complexity, and therefore to creative evolution, and therefore to self-organization; and, because the Citizen's Basic Income itself would be extremely simple, it would relate to the complexity of the system as a whole in a predictable way. A Citizen's Basic Income could therefore help the whole system to pass the 'creative complexity' test, as well as passing the 'simplicity' test itself.

THE FEASIBILITY OF CITIZEN'S BASIC INCOME

The question of feasibility generally breaks down into a set of feasibility questions, with the implication that a policy change has to be feasible in all or most of the subsidiary senses in order to be generally feasible. In relation to Citizen's Basic Income, we can identify at least seven different feasibilities, and in each case a feasibility question or test can be formulated (De Wispelaere and Noguera, 2012; Torry, 2014; 2016a: 25–37). The feasibilities are as follows:

- financial (Would it be possible to finance a Citizen's Basic Income? And would implementation avoid substantial financial losses for households? – which suggests that there are in fact two different financial feasibilities)
- psychological (Is the idea readily understood, and understood to be beneficial?)
- administrative (Would it be possible to administer a Citizen's Basic Income? Would it be possible to manage the transition?)
- behavioural (Would a Citizen's Basic Income work for households and individuals once it's implemented?)
- political (Would the idea cohere with existing political ideologies?)
- policy process (Would the policy process be able to process the idea to implementation?).

We shall tackle each type of feasibility in turn; and where arguments against feasibility are discovered, we shall have to ask whether it might be possible to formulate and then implement strategies to turn non-feasibility into feasibility.

Financial Feasibility

The obvious answer to the question 'Would a Citizen's Basic Income be financially feasible?' is of course 'yes' if we mean by the question 'Could a Citizen's Basic Income be funded by reducing tax allowances and means-tested and contributory benefits?' A revenue neutral Citizen's Basic Income would always be possible if the Citizen's Basic Income was constructed in that way (Torry, 2017d; 2018c; 2019a). But the question that we have answered is only the first of two. The second and equally essential financial feasibility test is represented by the question 'Would implementation avoid substantial financial losses for households?' We might somewhat arbitrarily decide that feasibility in this sense might be defined as: No more than 2 per cent of households in the lowest original income quintile should suffer losses at the point of implementation of more than 10 per cent, and no more than 10 per cent of all households should suffer losses of more than 5 per cent (Torry, 2017d; 2019a).

While a calculation method that employs the national accounts and census data can calculate the net cost of a Citizen's Basic Income scheme (Miller, 2017: 192–215; Ortiz et al., 2018; Painter and Thoung, 2015; Pereira, 2017; Widerquist, 2017b), this method cannot calculate the effects of illustrative Citizen's Basic Income schemes that leave in place and recalculate existing means-tested benefits, nor can it calculate the number and extent of net disposable income losses that low income households would suffer in relation to a particular Citizen's Basic Income scheme, or the overall redistributional effects of different illustrative schemes (Reed, 2019; Citizen's Basic Income Trust, 2019a). For the UK, and for European countries generally, we are fortunate that we can use the EUROMOD microsimulation programme and Family Resources Survey or similar data to discover the gains and losses that would be experienced by a 0.1 per cent sample of the population if a specified benefits system reform were to be implemented – although even when this method is employed, Citizen's Basic Income schemes that would result in substantial losses for a significant number of low income households are still published without sufficient commentary relating to the sizeable number of large losses (Badenes-Plá et al., 2019). Research using EUROMOD shows that in the UK a Citizen's Basic Income of between £65 and £70 per week for working age adults, and different amounts for other age groups, could be paid for by reducing to zero the Income Tax Personal Allowance, increasing Income Tax rates by three percentage points, making changes to National Insurance Contributions, and leaving means-tested benefits in place and recalculating them in relation to households' Citizen's Basic Incomes and changed net earnings, and that a Citizen's Basic Income of £50 per week for working age adults would be possible if an Income Tax Personal Allowance of £4,000 per annum were to be retained. The research also shows that these particular schemes would either meet or come close to meeting the criteria that we have chosen in relation to the second financial feasibility test; and it further shows that both poverty and inequality would be reduced, and that significant numbers of households would be taken off means-tested benefits and that even more households would be brought within striking distance of coming off them (Torry, 2019a). Similar schemes have been researched using similar microsimulation programmes (Reed and Lansley, 2016; Lansley and Reed, 2019). Citizen's Basic Incomes of different levels, and paid for by different adjustments to tax thresholds, tax rates, and means-tested and contributory benefits, would deliver different patterns of gains and losses (Martinelli, 2017a; 2017b; 2017c; Stirling and Arnold, 2019), but some of the schemes researched in this way could increase rather than reduce poverty (OECD, 2017). The reason for fixing criteria for the kind of Citizen's Basic Income scheme required, and then seeking a scheme that fits the criteria, is that if just one such scheme can be found then the conclusion can be drawn that Citizen's

Basic Income is feasible in relation to both kinds of financial feasibility test (Torry, 2017d; 2018c; 2019a), and that the objection that Citizen's Basic Income would either be unaffordable or would impose large losses on lots of low income households (Knight, 2017: 146; Sage and Diamond, 2017: 26) no longer stands up. Choosing a variety of schemes and then researching their effects cannot achieve this result. The suggestion that 'most defenders of basic income do not tend to be very specific regarding how it would be financed' (Wehner, 2019: 4) might or might not be correct, but the idea that 'the present debate has failed to make clear the winners and losers under an unconditional basic income regime' (Wehner, 2019: 4) is simply wrong in relation to the significant volume of research results now available for the UK.

There will of course be debate as to how to frame the detail of the feasibility tests. In relation to the first financial feasibility test: Should we be quite so strict about the requirement that the Citizen's Basic Incomes should be paid for out of rearrangements of the current income tax and benefits systems? Should we not rather assume that some of the revenue required might be available from elsewhere? That would always be possible of course: but the question has then become a question about policy process and politics. This shows that different feasibility questions can be intimately connected with each other, with inverse relationships between them. One particular Citizen's Basic Income scheme, funded entirely from within the current tax and benefits system, might be financially feasible, policy process feasible, and politically feasible, whereas an alternative scheme that hopes for additional funding from outside the current tax and benefits system (Major, 2016; Špeciánová, 2018) might be even more financially feasible in a theoretical sense, but it might be less feasible in terms of both the politics and the policy process (Torry, 2014; 2016a: 39–86).

A general conclusion that we might draw is that high quality research is required in relation to a variety of feasibility criteria, and particularly in relation to the two different financial feasibilities. A particular conclusion that we might draw is that scholars who pick on a particular Citizen's Basic Income scheme, find that it fails one or other of the financial feasibility tests, and then declare Citizen's Basic Income to be infeasible, have confused 'Citizen's Basic Income' and 'Citizen's Basic Income scheme'. The former is an unconditional income paid to every individual. The latter is a Citizen's Basic Income, with its levels specified for different age groups, the funding method fully specified, and in particular any changes to the current income tax and benefits systems fully specified. To find a particular scheme to be financially infeasible is not to find Citizen's Basic Income financially infeasible: a piece of logic too often not understood (Centre for Social Justice, 2018; Rothstein, 2018; Torry, 2018d). To generalize the point: to find a particular Citizen's Basic Income scheme lacking in any particular respect is not to find Citizen's Basic Income lacking in that respect (Disabled People Against Cuts, 2019; Citizen's Basic Income Trust, 2019b). Conversely, to find just one Citizen's Basic Income scheme to be financially feasible is to find Citizen's Basic Income to be financially feasible (Torry, 2019a).

Psychological Feasibility

Psychological feasibility is a subject that we tackle in some depth in Chapter 6 on psychology and Chapter 7 on social psychology: but for the purpose of offering a complete set of feasibility considerations here, it might be worth including here a brief section on the psychological issues particularly relevant to the question of Citizen's Basic Income's feasibility.

There are some policy fields in which public opinion plays only a small part in policymaking (Richardson, 1969): but in the benefits sphere public opinion matters, and in the UK and other developed countries it might be in relation to the public mindset in particular that a Citizen's Basic Income might struggle to achieve feasibility. A long history of means-tested and social insurance benefits has left us with a number of presuppositions, and two in particular: To reduce poverty we need to give money to the poor; and if you give money to the poor then they might not work. Responding with logic and evidence – that it is more efficient to give money to everyone and then to tax the rich (Torry, 2018a: 175); and that both logic and the evidence show that a secure financial platform is more likely to increase employment incentives than to reduce them (Torry, 2018a: 151–9) – might not work because the presuppositions are so deeply embedded. Similarly, asking people to consider a scenario in which we already had a Citizen's Basic Income, and then asking them whether they would wish a system based on means-tested benefits to be implemented instead, we might find that our deeply embedded presuppositions would swing votes away from Citizen's Basic Income and towards means-testing. And in a similar way, asking people to refrain from setting tests that relate to an existing means-testing system, such as 'Does it give more to the poor than to the rich?' – tests that Citizen's Basic Income would find it difficult to pass – and instead asking them to construct questions on the basis of unconditional incomes and then use them to test a means-tested system, would not necessarily persuade people that Citizen's Basic Income might be a good idea. For instance, asking them to test systems on the basis of employment incentives ought to favour a system based on a Citizen's Basic Income, because that would be likely to reduce marginal deduction rates, and therefore increase the incentive to earn additional income, which would in turn release people from poverty and unemployment traps (Torry, 2016a: 3–6): but if, contrary to the evidence, people already believed that giving people money unconditionally would reduce their employment incentives, then they would still vote for means-testing (Torry, 2013: 9–12, 149–60).

So the important question set by the difficulty of passing the psychological feasibility test is this: Is it possible to shift the public mindset? That is: is it possible for sufficient numbers of people to be persuaded that, in the context of a progressive tax system, a universal and unconditional benefit is a more constructive way of targeting money on the poor than means-testing could ever be? – that in general universal services remain more effective for the poor than services targeted at the poor? (Mackenzie et al., 2018)? – and that universal benefits make people more likely to work, and not less?

The answer that we give to this question in Chapter 7 on social psychology, relying on Serge Moscovici's research, is that yes, the minds of a group of people can be changed. However, Moscovici's research related to groups and institutions, and we ought not to assume that a whole society would function in the same way. However, in the UK and the Republic of Ireland, and elsewhere too, recent experience of rapid shifts in public opinion towards same-sex marriage suggests that the same process might also occur at societal level. That particular transition might be informative, particularly in relation to the incremental practical steps by which it occurred. In the UK, within just sixty years, we have seen the decriminalization of homosexual activity, anti-discrimination legislation, equalities legislation, civil partnerships, and now same-sex marriage. The same process occurred with equalities legislation generally. Starting with the Race Discrimination Act in 1965 and the Equal Pay Act in 1970, the UK Government has legislated for various equalities when doing so has been somewhat ahead of public opinion. Each legislative step changed public behaviour and propelled an already changing public opinion more quickly along its trajectory, thus preparing the ground for the next legislative step that was slightly ahead of public opinion. The public opinion trajectory was always clear, so although it might have looked as if the government was taking a risk, in fact it was not. Where societies already experience unconditional benefits – as in the UK, with Child Benefit and the National Health Service – there might already be a silent majority in favour of unconditional benefits; and it is possible that such a tacit understanding of the advantages of unconditional provision could become more conscious and could be transferred from existing unconditional provision to what would still look like a new idea: an unconditional income for every legal resident. The only way to test this possibility would be for the UK's Government to argue for Citizen's Basic Income and then to make the change: preferably for an age group within society that the majority could regard as deserving in some way, so that the experiment becomes a test of public appreciation of unconditional incomes rather than a test of public attitudes towards groups within society.

There is a precedent in the UK. It was a slow and somewhat fraught process, but during the 1970s Family Allowance for every child except the first in each family became Child Benefit: an unconditional benefit for every child. The mechanism by which the change occurred is that Child Tax Allowances were abolished, and Family Allowance was extended to the first child in each family. Effectively, a tax allowance became a new universal benefit. The change was achieved with almost no public opposition (Torry, 2013: 22–5). There is therefore no reason for not making similar attempts, and every reason for doing so.

Groups regarded by the public as deserving, and for whom the government might therefore attempt transitions from tax allowances and means-tested benefits to unconditional and nonwithdrawable benefits, might be young adults (Martinelli and Pearce, 2019: 273; Torry, 2019a: 10, 13, 15) and pre-retirement working age adults (perhaps with National Insurance Contribution records functioning as a gateway for the latter group, as they will do for the new Single-Tier State Pension).

We might then see the same process as we have seen for same-sex marriage, with the popularity of the changes for young and pre-retirement adults revealing and embedding a public opinion shifting towards understanding the advantages of universal, unconditional and nonwithdrawable benefits. The silent majority will have become conscious of their approval of unconditional provision, and might become vocal about it; and the minority willing and able to express the advantages of Citizen's Basic Income will have converted the rest of society (Torry, 2014; 2016a: 87–117).

Administrative Feasibility

We discuss the administration of Citizen's Basic Income in Chapter 10, so here we shall simply raise briefly the question of administrative feasibility.

The UK has been paying Family Allowance to every family with more than one child since 1946; and it has been paying Child Benefit for every child since the 1970s. Administration is simple and efficient; almost no fraud occurs; and error rates are negligible (Torry, 2013: 22–5). To pay a Citizen's Basic Income to every adult would be even easier, because every child who leaves school is allocated a unique National Insurance Number. Just as importantly, it would be easy to administer an unconditional and nonwithdrawable benefit for any particular age cohort; and whether for the entire population, or for a particular age cohort, the unconditional and nonwithdrawable nature of the benefit would make computerization simple in the extreme (Torry, 2016a: 118–42).

Behavioural Feasibility

This is both an essential and a somewhat complex feasibility test to pass because the behavioural feasibility of Citizen's Basic Income can only be evaluated several years after implementing a Citizen's Basic Income scheme for a sizeable population. The long-run effects of policy changes can sometimes be surprising, and it will be important to evaluate what a Citizen's Basic Income has achieved (Spicker, 2014: 241–2; 409–27). Pilot projects can help to predict what the effects might be if they are properly planned (Widerquist, 2018), but their limited nature means that effects could emerge following the implementation of a Citizen's Basic Income for an entire population that would not be revealed by pilot projects.

We can of course predict the kinds of changes that we might expect to see. Households on means-tested benefits at the point of implementation would find themselves off them completely or on less of them, and they would find themselves with a solid financial floor that would be completely secure: and, in particular, each member of the household would find themselves with their own individual secure financial floor. New opportunities would open up, both for the household as a whole, and for each individual within it. We can therefore predict that useful and interesting changes could take place for those households: but precisely what they would be we would only find out following implementation of the Citizen's Basic Income scheme; and much would of course depend on the details of the scheme, and not only on the fact that a Citizen's Basic Income would be in payment. If new opportunities turned into advantageous outcomes, in terms of work–life balance, increased disposable incomes, new businesses, and so on, then Citizen's Basic Income will have been behaviourally feasible: but we would not have been able to demonstrate that in advance.

An important relationship between feasibilities would be the connection between behavioural and psychological feasibilities. If a Citizen's Basic Income were to be rolled out sequentially to different demographic groups, then the behavioural feasibility evidenced by the changes experienced by one group to which a Citizen's Basic Income was being paid could enable the next stage of the implementation to become psychologically feasible. So if a Citizen's Basic Income were to be paid to the pre-retired and to young adults, then a large number of working age adults would be aware of people with Citizen's Basic Incomes, and of the beneficial changes that had resulted, and they might want similar changes for themselves. And if details of the particular scheme that had been implemented were found not to be ideal, then those factors could be changed for the demographic groups already receiving Citizen's Basic Incomes, and also for the subsequent stages of the roll-out. Testing for behavioural feasibility would not be a one-off activity. It would be continuous, so that the details of the scheme could be reviewed in the light of experience. What would not be reviewed, of course, would be the definition of a Citizen's Basic Income. That is set in stone: and it is that set-in-stone Citizen's Basic Income that the behavioural feasibility test would be all about.

All of the feasibilities are important, so testing for all of them would be important. However, because behavioural feasibility could only be tested after implementation of a Citizen's Basic Income, we would need to have reasonable assurance that Citizen's Basic Income, and the particular scheme to be implemented, *would* be behaviourally feasible: but we would also need to launch into implementation without being certain that the predicted beneficial behavioural changes would follow.

This raises a further possibility: if behavioural feasibility cannot be tested until after implementation, then perhaps psychological feasibility testing can be postponed until after implementation as well. Just as we can predict behavioural changes, and can proceed without proof that the predictions will be accurate, so we can predict psychological acceptability once Citizen's Basic Incomes are in payment, and we can proceed without the test having been passed prior to implementation (Torry, 2016a: 143–66).

Political Feasibility

For the purposes of this discussion of the feasibility of Citizen's Basic Income, political feasibility is regarded as a separate issue from policy process feasibility. They are of course connected, but they are not the same. A political feasibility test is passed if Citizen's Basic Income can and does cohere with current political ideologies, which means that questions such as 'Can every main political ideology generate arguments for Citizen's Basic Income?' and 'Do adherents of each of the main political ideologies in practice base arguments for Citizen's Basic Income on those ideologies?' need to be answered in the affirmative. A policy process feasibility test is passed if we can see how Citizen's Basic Income can navigate its way through a country's policy process from idea to implementation. Passing a policy process feasibility test will of course normally require a political feasibility test to have been passed: but not necessarily. Policy accidents can happen, and we can find that a new social policy has been implemented without it having passed all of the feasibility tests (Torry, 2016a: 242): but they are less likely to happen without any testing for political feasibility.

Research undertaken for this author's *Money for Everyone* (Torry, 2013) found that the main political ideologies in the UK – the New Right, Socialism, One Nation Conservatism, Liberalism, Social Democracy, New Labour's 'Third Way', Old Labour (and the Co-operative movement), a post-war consensus, and a Green perspective – themselves generated arguments for a Citizen's Basic Income; arguments for a Citizen's Basic Income had in fact been offered by proponents of the different ideologies; and any arguments against a Citizen's Basic Income had been generic: that is, whatever the ideology to which the objector adhered, the objections were of the form 'We could not afford a Citizen's Basic Income', 'We should not pay people for doing nothing', 'Rich people do not need it', or 'A Citizen's Basic Income would discourage people from working' (Torry, 2013: appendix for Chapter 13).

Political ideologies are different in different places, so political feasibility would have to be tested separately in each country; and because political ideologies change over time, Citizen's Basic Income passing a political feasibility test at one point in time would be no guarantee that it would pass it two or three years later: but the broad range of political ideologies tested for the UK at least suggests that political feasibility might be generally possible, and that any arguments against Citizen's Basic Income offered by politicians might be only loosely attached to their political ideologies, and therefore that changing politicians' minds about those objections might be more possible than it might have been had their objections been deeply embedded in their ideological commitments (Torry, 2016a: 167–93).

The Policy Process

We have discussed the policy process at the beginning of this chapter, and we have already found that there are circumstances in which a Citizen's Basic Income scheme might be able to navigate its way through the process from idea to implementation (Torry, 2016a: 195–236).

Relationships Between the Feasibilities

Ivan Steiner has identified three types of group task:

- Additive: all group members do the same thing, and the outcome is the sum of all of their contributions (as in a tug of war).
- Conjunctive: the performance depends on the performance of the least talented. All members' contributions are needed for success, and the links between the elements are often crucial (as in a relay race).
- Disjunctive: here the result depends on the performance of the most talented member. The group remains better than that individual because even the best at something does not necessarily know all of the right answers (as in a pub quiz). Here the major requirement is that less talented members of the group should not be able to hold back the most talented member (Steiner, 1972).

A policy change needs to pass a number of different feasibility tests, and if a policy change struggles to pass one of the tests then it might not be implemented. This suggests that the different feasibilities are conjunctive. However, some of the feasibilities relate to each other – for instance, if a policy change is psychologically feasible then it is more likely to be both politically and policy process feasible; and if it is politically feasible, then it is more likely to be both psychologically and policy process feasible. This suggests that there is an element of additivity involved.

The order in which feasibilities are established might be as important as the number of feasibility tests that can be passed. For instance, financial and administrative feasibility tests might need to be passed before other tests can be attempted; and we have already recognized that behavioural feasibility tested and proved for one demographic group might facilitate the psychological feasibility required for the next.

But the main point is that the feasibilities are generally independent of each other, and none of them can be reduced to the others, which means that the feasibilities are conjunctive, and that work on facilitating and proving all of them is required. None can be neglected (Torry, 2016a: 31–2, 35). And given the difficulty of passing a psychological feasibility test, and that political and policy process feasibilities depend on that test being passed, we clearly need to make it as easy as possible for the psychological feasibility test to be passed. This in turn suggests that the implementation of Citizen's Basic Income might have to start with demographic groups that the general public regards as somehow deserving, which in turn suggests children, young adults, the elderly, and the pre-retired. Financial and administrative feasibilities would be easy to establish; and political and policy process feasibilities would be possibilities. Behavioural feasibility could then follow, and that would build the psychological feasibility required for the next phase of the implementation. Eventually only working age adults would be left without Citizen's Basic Incomes, and all of those would know people for whom Citizen's Basic Incomes were providing a level of income security that only they did not experience. It is likely that psychological feasibility for the whole population would then enable everyone to receive a Citizen's Basic Income.

Or, alternatively, a policy accident might occur. A government, committed to implementing a Citizen's Basic Income for everyone, might simply implement one, on the basis that once people had it they would not want to lose it.

CONCLUSIONS

More general conclusions relating to both this chapter and Chapter 10 will be found at the end of Chapter 10: but here it is worth saying that we have studied three central questions at the heart of social policy, with social policy understood both as a practical activity and as an academic discipline: the question of how policy is made, the question of the complexity of benefits policy, and the question of feasibility. We have found these three questions, and the contribution that the discipline of social policy has made to our understanding of them, directly relevant to our study of Citizen's Basic Income. And as Citizen's Basic Income is a social policy that has already generated a vast amount of social policy literature and debate, it is not difficult to argue that Citizen's Basic Income has contributed to the discipline of social policy.

A particular difficulty relating to the relationship between social policy as an academic discipline and the other disciplines employed in this book is that there is very little in this book, if anything, that could not legitimately have been included in this chapter. This in turn suggests that the discipline of social policy crosses the boundaries of all of the disciplines to which this book dedicates chapters. We have located the three particular issues of feasibility, complexity, and the policy process in this chapter, because these are issues that would have been more difficult to fit into any of the other chapters. This suggests that the discipline of social policy might in fact possess core subject matter, and that study of the policy process, understanding of its complexity, and the exploration of policy feasibility, might constitute three elements of that core.

CASE STUDY

Three Citizen's Basic Income Schemes for the United Kingdom Tested for Financial Feasibility[1]

The illustrative Citizen's Basic Income schemes tested here for financial feasibility are funded from within the UK's current tax and benefits system by reducing the Income Tax Personal Allowance and the National Insurance

---

[1]   I am most grateful to Paola De Agostini of the Institute for Social and Economic Research for assistance with the working paper on which this case study is based. The results presented here are based on EUROMOD version I1.0+. EUROMOD is maintained, developed and managed by the Institute for Social and Economic Research (ISER) at the University of Essex, in collaboration with national teams from the EU member states. We are indebted to the many people who have contributed to the development of EUROMOD. The process of extending and updating EUROMOD is financially supported by the European Union Programme for Employment and Social Innovation 'EaSI' (2014–20). The UK Family Resources Survey data was made available by the Department for Work and Pensions via the UK Data Archive. This case study is based on a EUROMOD working paper (Torry, 2019a). Please see the working paper for details of the method employed to obtain the results listed here. The results and their interpretation are the author's responsibility and not that of ISER.

Contributions Primary Earnings Threshold, charging National Insurance Contributions at 12 per cent on all earned income (rather than at 12 per cent up to an Upper Earnings Threshold, and then at 2 per cent above it), and increasing Income Tax rates slightly. Current means-tested benefits are left in place, with each household's means-tested benefits being recalculated to take into account household members' Citizen's Basic Incomes in the same way as earned income is taken into account. The list of requirements for financial feasibility is as follows:

- as few changes as possible are to be made to the current tax and benefits system, consistent with the other aims in view;
- revenue neutrality (Hirsch, 2015), taken here to mean a net cost or saving of no more than £2bn per annum;
- the avoidance of significant household net disposable income losses, particularly for low income households (with at least an aim of ensuring that no more 2 per cent of low income households should experience household net disposable income losses of more than 5 per cent);
- Income Tax rates to rise by no more than 3 percentage points (Hirsch, 2015);
- reductions in inequality (measured by the Gini coefficient) and in all poverty indices;
- significant numbers of households removed from means-tested benefits, or brought within striking distance of coming off them.

Three different levels of working age adult Citizen's Basic Income were tested – schemes that abolished the Income Tax Personal Allowance and paid Citizen's Basic Incomes of £65 per week and £70 per week for working age adults, and a scheme that retained an Income Tax Personal Allowance of £4,000 per annum and paid a Citizen's Basic Income of £50 per week for working age adults – and the other variables of the schemes (different levels for the Citizen's Basic Income for the different age groups, different increases for Child Benefit, different Income Tax rates, and so on) were altered until the conditions were met, or were as nearly met as possible. The illustrative Citizen's Basic Income schemes that emerged from the normal trial and error testing method (Torry, 2019a) were found to be as follows:

- For a scheme that pays a Citizen's Basic Income of £65 per week to each working age adult, Child Benefit is increased by £20 per week for each child. For a scheme that pays a Citizen's Basic Income of £70 per week to each working age adult, Child Benefit is increased by £5 per week. For the £50 per week scheme, Child Benefit is increased by £10 per week.
- Citizen's Basic Income levels for different age groups are as in Table 9.1. The existing National Insurance Basic State Pension is left in place. (In

these schemes the Education Age Citizen's Basic Income is not paid to someone still in full-time education, in recognition of the fact that their main carer is receiving Child Benefit on their behalf.)

Table 9.1 gives the detail of the schemes and the household net disposable income losses generated for all households and for the lowest original income quintile.

Table 9.1   *Three Citizen's Basic Income schemes and the losses generated*

CBI levels, tax rates, numbers of losses over various limits for all households and lower quintile, and total net cost of scheme	£65 p.w. scheme, ITPA zero	£70 p.w. scheme, ITPA zero	£50 p.w. scheme, ITPA £4,000
Citizen's Pension per week (existing state pensions remain in payment)	£40	£40	£35
Working age adult Citizen's Basic Income per week	£65	£70	£50
Young adult Citizen's Basic Income per week	£50	£60	£40
Education age Citizen's Basic Income per week	£40	£25	£30
(Child Benefit is increased by £20/£5 per week)	[£20]	[£5]	[£10]
Income Tax rate increase required for strict revenue neutrality	3%	3%	3%
Income Tax, basic rate (on £0 – 46,350)	23%	23%	23%
Income Tax, higher rate (on £46,350 – 150,000)	43%	43%	43%
Income Tax, top rate (on £150,000 –)	48%	48%	48%
Proportion of households in the lowest original income quintile experiencing losses of over 15% at the point of implementation	1.23%	1.59%	0.38%
Proportion of households in the lowest original income quintile experiencing losses of over 10% at the point of implementation	1.77%	2.29%	0.60%
Proportion of households in the lowest original income quintile experiencing losses of over 5% at the point of implementation	3.71%	4.19%	0.73%
Proportion of all households experiencing losses of over 15% at the point of implementation	0.41%	0.48%	0.35%
Proportion of all households experiencing losses of over 10% at the point of implementation	1.74%	1.52%	2.27%
Proportion of all households experiencing losses of over 6% at the point of implementation	7.11%	6.22%	6.58%
Proportion of all households experiencing losses of over 5% at the point of implementation	12.54%	11.59%	8.38%
Net cost of scheme	£1.41bn p.a.	£1.14bn p.a.	£0.21bn p.a.

Source: Torry, 2019a. Abbreviation: ITPA: Income Tax Personal Allowance.

Table 9.2   *Reductions in numbers claiming means-tested benefits and in numbers of claimant households within striking distance of coming off them, and reductions in average value of claim and total cost*

Reductions in numbers claiming means-tested benefits or within striking distance of coming off them	The existing scheme in 2018	The £65 p.w. Citizens Basic Income scheme, ITPA zero	% reduction	The £70 p.w. Citizens Basic Income scheme, ITPA zero	% reduction	The £50 p.w. Citizens Basic Income scheme, ITPA £4,000 p.a.	% reduction
Percentage of households claiming any means-tested benefits	32.86%	30.45%	7.35%	29.24%	11.02%	25.56%	11.79%
Percentage of households claiming more than £100 per month in means-tested benefits	28.98%	24.31%	16.11%	24.38%	15.86%	21.21%	19.15%
Percentage of households claiming more than £200 per month in means-tested benefits	26.23%	20.67%	21.20%	20.39%	22.26%	10.19%	21.95%
Reductions in total costs and average values of claims for means-tested benefits		Reduction in total cost	Reduction in average value of claim	Reduction in total cost	Reduction in average value of claim	Reduction in total cost	Reduction in average value of claim
All means-tested benefits		30.60%	22.00%	32.10%	23.69%	26.00%	16.84%

Source: Torry, 2019a. Abbreviation: ITPA: Income Tax Personal Allowance.

We can see that the schemes keep within the 3 percentage points allowed for increases in Income Tax rates; they are all revenue neutral; and the levels of losses for poorer households and for households in general would not make the schemes impossible to implement. (As the working paper on which this case study is based shows, household net income losses would be likely to be lower once the UK Government's new Universal Credit has replaced the existing benefits system, because Universal Credit would impose a single taper rate, and not the multiple taper rates which seem to be causing many of the household losses here. There are many problems with Universal Credit: the single taper rate is not one of them.)

Table 9.2 shows how many households would be taken off means-tested benefits for each of the schemes, how many would be within £100 per month of coming off them, and how many would be within £200 per month of coming off them. If a household is within £100 per month of coming off means-tested benefits, then one working age adult seeking half a day of additional employment each week at the National Living Wage would take the household off means-tested benefits. If the household is within £200 per month of coming off means-tested benefits, then one working age adult seeking an additional one day of employment per week would take the household off them.

We can conclude that all three schemes would be revenue neutral (that is, they could be funded from within the current income tax and benefits system); and that the increase in Income Tax rates required would be feasible. The schemes would remove large numbers of households from a variety of means-tested benefits; they would reduce means-tested benefit claim values, and the total costs of means-tested benefits; they would provide additional employment market incentives for the large number of households no longer on means-tested benefits to the extent that marginal deduction rates affect employment market behaviour; and they would avoid imposing significant numbers of significant losses at the point of implementation.

Discussion of the three schemes' effects on poverty and inequality forms the case study in Chapter 11.

Because the only changes required in order to implement this illustrative Citizen's Basic Income scheme would be:

- payment of the Citizen's Basic Incomes for every individual above the age of 16 (apart from those between 16 and 19 still in full-time education), calculated purely in relation to the age of each individual,
- increases in the rates of Child Benefit,
- changes to Income Tax and National Insurance Contribution rates and thresholds, and
- easy to achieve recalculations in existing means-tested benefits claims,

any of these three financially feasible Citizen's Basic Income schemes could be implemented very quickly.

10. The social administration of Citizen's Basic Income

> Social administration is the study of the development, structure and practices of the social services ... the social services are mainly understood to include social security, housing, health, social work and education ...
>
> (Spicker, 2014: 477, 1)

INTRODUCTION

As explained at the beginning of Chapter 9, this chapter is the second of two chapters that understand Citizen's Basic Income in relation to the discipline of social policy. In this chapter the reader will find those aspects of the material that most clearly belong to a 'social administration' understanding of the discipline.

ADMINISTRATION

To Whom Should Citizen's Basic Incomes be Paid?

Chapter 12 on political economy asks how the concept of 'citizen' might relate to deciding to whom Citizen's Basic Income ought to be paid. Here we take a more administrative approach to the question as to who should receive a Citizen's Basic Income.

Most countries develop a variety of categories for people living within the country's territory: citizen, asylum seeker, refugee, legal resident, illegal immigrant, and so on. The categories themselves, as well as the criteria that determine who should be placed in which category, will often be quite fluid, because these are matters of often visceral social and political interest. Categories can sometimes overlap, as with European and national citizenships in the European Union (European Union, 2018). In a country with a federal structure that permits regional governments to manage their own tax and benefits systems, each regional government would need to decide to whom Citizen's Basic Incomes would be paid, in the same way as Alaska had to decide to whom the Alaskan Permanent Fund Dividend would be paid, and chose to pay it to anyone who had lived in Alaska for at least a year and intended to remain a resident (O'Brien and Olson, 1991: 5). Any national government would have to make a similar decision, as would any group of nations, such as the European Union, that chose to pay a Citizen's Basic Income. At first sight, and in the light of the complexity of residence statuses with which many countries operate, the problem of deciding who should receive unconditional incomes might appear rather complicated. However, in practice this might not be the case, because there might be existing sets of regulations on which to build. So, for instance, in the UK there is already a set of regulations to determine who should receive unconditional Child Benefit, and it would be perfectly possible to extend those regulations to cover payments to every individual (UK Government, 2018b). An important question to answer would always be whether someone normally resident in a country and receiving Citizen's Basic Income should continue to receive it if they moved abroad. Regulations relating to this eventuality might be necessarily complicated, and bilateral or multilateral treaties might be relevant: but there might still be existing rules that could be employed (UK Government, 2018a). (See the case study at the end of this chapter on who might receive a Citizen's Basic Income in the UK.)

Once a decision has been made as to precisely who should receive a Citizen's Basic Income, a reliable list of names and bank account details would be required. A list of names of residents and their contact details might already exist, in which case that could be employed. Where this was not the case, existing lists of taxpayers, benefits recipients, passport and driving licence holders, health service numbers, and so on, could be combined and developed. What would be essential would be to ensure that the resulting list would be a list of individuals, and not of households or of heads of households, somehow defined. In some cultures there has been understandable resistance to the creation of complete lists of residents of a country, but a list designed to ensure that everyone eligible would receive their Citizen's Basic Income would be for a clearly positive purpose and so would be unlikely to meet with public disapproval.

A particularly significant list already available in any country with a functioning democracy is the electoral register: that is, the list of individuals registered to vote in elections. This raises the question as to whether electoral registers could be used as the lists of individuals to whom Citizen's Basic Incomes would be distributed. What might look like a problem is that such lists are often both incomplete and inaccurate. In countries such as Australia where voting is compulsory, electoral registers are more likely to be both accurate and complete. In countries where voting is not compulsory, there will always be some doubt as to how accurate and complete the registers are. An interesting indication of just how incomplete the United Kingdom's electoral register is was given by the natural experiment of the referendum on membership of the European Union in June 2016. A large number of individuals registered to vote for the first time, because although they were not interested in voting in local and general elections, they did want to vote in the referendum. A snapshot of the UK's electoral registers is taken each December, and in December 2016 there were 1 million more entries than in December 2015: an increase of 2.3 per cent of the adult population eligible to vote (Electoral Commission, 2017: 12). This suggests that normally the register is incomplete by at least 2.3 per cent. If the electoral register were to be used as the basis of the list of individuals to whom Citizen's Basic Incomes were paid, then we can envisage a significant increase in registrations.

So far we have assumed that at the point of implementation of a Citizen's Basic Income scheme the entire population would receive unconditional incomes: hence the need for a complete list. However, if implementation of the Citizen's Basic Income were to be one demographic group at a time (– on which see Chapters 9 and 11), then additional possibilities might present themselves. For instance, in the UK every individual should receive a National Insurance Number as they approach their sixteenth birthday (UK Government, 2018c). If initial Citizen's Basic Incomes were to be paid to everyone aged sixteen, or perhaps eighteen, then a fairly reliable list of names, dates of birth, and contact details, should already exist. Similarly, as a main carer ceased to receive Child Benefit for a child, either at age sixteen, or when they left full-time secondary education (UK Government, 2018b), payment could be increased and transferred to the relevant adult as their Citizen's Basic Income. A combination of the two methods should ensure complete and accurate coverage of the relevant age group. Similar methods would be available in other countries.

While it might sometimes be a challenge to construct a reliable list for the payment of Citizen's Basic Incomes, it would not be a challenge difficult to meet, and meeting it might offer additional benefits, such as higher rates of inclusion in health screening programmes, and, if the electoral register were to be used, an improvement in the proportion of the population voting in local and general elections (De Wispelaere and Noguera, 2012: 26).

Even if there might be minor difficulties related to creating the list of Citizen's Basic Income recipients, an unconditional and therefore universal payment such as Citizen's Basic Income would avoid an entire administrative problem that faces any other kind of social security benefit: the claiming process (Spicker, 2014: 333–40). Once someone's Citizen's Basic Income had started, whether at birth, or at say age sixteen or eighteen, in all normal circumstances the Citizen's Basic Income would simply keep on being paid until the individual died. No further active administration would be required.

How Would Citizen's Basic Incomes be Paid?

A second administrative challenge might be to ensure that every eligible individual had a means of receiving the Citizen's Basic Income to which they were entitled. Again, this might look like a problem, as in almost every country significant proportions of the population do not have access to a bank account, or do not have access to a bank account to which only they have access (De Wispelaere and Noguera, 2012: 26). However, this might be more of an opportunity than a problem. In a Citizen's Basic Income pilot project in India that involved 6,000 men, women and children, every adult in the pilot communities had to open a bank account within weeks of the experiment starting. Ninety-eight per cent bank account coverage was achieved (Davala et al., 2015: 34, 38), which suggests that in any country that chooses to implement a Citizen's Basic Income, providing every individual with a means for receiving the income would not be difficult.

In the UK, 96 per cent of households have bank or other types of account into and out of which payments can be made, and an additional one per cent have Post Office Card Accounts (used for withdrawing benefits payments at post offices, and particularly suitable for women who do not want benefits paid into a joint bank account to which they do not have sufficient autonomous access) (Department for Work and Pensions, 2018a; Lott, 2017). In a country such as the UK it would not be difficult to ensure that every individual had an account of some kind into which their Basic Income could be paid.

If both the UK and India could easily achieve nearly one hundred per cent bank account coverage, then every other developed and developing country should be able to do so. Areas such as sub-Saharan Africa might once have appeared to be more of a challenge, but between 2014 and 2017 the proportion of adults with some kind of bank account, often via mobile phone banking, increased from 54 per cent to 63 per cent. The proportion will continue to grow. The next challenge will be ensuring that women experience financial autonomy (World Bank, 2018). To require that Citizen's Basic Incomes should be paid into individual bank accounts and not into joint accounts would go a long way to meeting this challenge.

Administering a Citizen's Basic Income Scheme

We have seen that administering Citizen's Basic Incomes would not be difficult, and would certainly be a lot easier than administering means-tested benefits (Torry, 2013: 82–93). However, no Citizen's Basic Income would ever be administered on its own, because the incomes would have to be paid for, and the means by which that would be achieved would have to be administered alongside the Citizen's Basic Income, either by adapting existing revenue raising methods, by developing new funding methods, or by making savings elsewhere: for instance, by reducing subsidies.

During the Indian Citizen's Basic Income pilot project that ran for eighteen months from June 2011 to November 2012, pilot village residents were able to choose whether to buy food from the subsidized ration food shops or to use mainstream markets and shops. Fewer used the subsidized ration food shops, and more used the markets and mainstream shops. Nutrition improved (Davala et al., 2015: 32, 91). In Iran, subsidies on food and fuel were reduced, and unconditional incomes were paid to heads of households (Tabatabai, 2012: 290). Any other country that funded a Citizen's Basic Income by reducing subsidies would not find the transition difficult to administer, because there would be no administrative connection between the subsidies and the Citizen's Basic Incomes.

Similarly with other forms of revenue. Alaska's Permanent Fund, into which are paid oil extraction royalties, pays an unconditional annual dividend to every citizen (Widerquist and Howard, 2012), the administration of which remains separate from existing tax and benefits systems, and is therefore easy to achieve. If the proceeds from a social wealth fund were to be paid out as a Citizen's Basic Income (Lansley, 2016; Lansley et al., 2018; Lansley and Reed, 2019; McCain, 2017; Reed and Lansley, 2016), then administration would be easy to achieve, because any changes to the existing tax and benefits system would occur automatically: for instance, by people's Citizen's Basic Incomes being taken into account when their means-tested benefits were recalculated. The same would happen if government money creation were to be employed to fund a Citizen's Basic Income (Crocker, 2015; 2019), or if new kinds of taxation, unconnected with the existing tax and benefits system, were to be employed: for instance, financial transaction taxes, which are already collected on share purchases (New York State, 2018; UK Government, 2018d) and might one day be collected on currency transactions; or perhaps a tax on robots, on the basis that they will be earning the revenue previously earned by human workers (Bruun and Duka, 2018). In relation to all of these, the only changes elsewhere would be automatic changes to households' means-tested benefits claims brought about by household members' Citizen's Basic Incomes being taken into account when entitlements were calculated.

Complications would only occur if Citizen's Basic Incomes were to be funded by making savings in relation to existing tax and benefits systems: by reducing tax allowances (that is, the amounts of earned or other income on which tax is not charged), by raising the rates at which income tax or social insurance contributions are charged, or by reducing the levels of existing means-tested or other benefits. Making such changes would never in itself be a problem, and, as we have seen, administering the Citizen's Basic Incomes would not be a problem either. However, making a number of administrative changes all at the same time *can* be a problem, both for the government departments making them, and for households having to manage their domestic budgets while changes are being made to their sources of income. It would therefore be important to make as few changes as possible to the existing tax and benefits systems, and for the changes that were made to be as simple as possible; and it would also be important to ensure that for low income households the combination of paying the new Citizen's Basic Incomes and of changes to the existing tax and benefits system did not result in net disposable income losses, and that for no household would any net loss be unmanageable. This is bound to be difficult to achieve if a revenue neutral constraint is imposed, because in that context every household net gain must be balanced by a household net loss, and the complexity of existing tax and benefits systems can make it difficult to keep all net losses at manageable levels. However, the requirement remains essential, and only Citizen's Basic Income schemes that make as few changes as possible to the existing tax and benefits systems, that do not impose net household disposable income losses on low income households, and that do not impose unmanageable losses on any households, should be attempted (Torry, 2017d; 2018c; 2019a).

Administering Alternatives to Citizen's Basic Income

Means-tested benefits
Means-tested benefits have always been problematic, because they are reduced as earned income rises, creating poverty and unemployment traps: but in the context of a more flexible employment market the problems multiply, because the complexity of means-tested systems can make employment market transitions difficult to handle (Dean, 2012a; 2012b). Individuals, households, and the relevant government departments, suffer an administrative burden every time someone faces changed circumstances, whether that be a change in earned income, a change in employment status, a change in the structure of the household, or a change in rent level (Spicker, 2005). The time, psychological and financial costs can be substantial (National Audit Office, 2011: 21). The problems can be particularly acute, as with the UK's Universal Credit, when payments during periods of employment relies on employers reporting someone's earnings accurately and on time to a government department, and particularly when information on a variety of sources of earned income has to be merged. And on top of all of that, claimants have to handle 'active labour market' policies that mean significant, unaccountable and complex benefits sanctions rules (Edmiston et al., 2017). The difficulties that workers face if they experience employment market transitions when they are on means-tested benefits can become an unsustainable burden for themselves and their families (Standing, 2011), and can create a significant disincentive to seeking change

in employment market status (Jordan et al., 1992; Smithies, 2007). The ability to navigate transitions successfully in a context of complexity can require substantial organizational skills, and these might either be absent, or suppressed by the stigma and unpredictability imposed by the system. People end up 'getting by' by using 'coping strategies' (Edmiston, 2017: 266). All of this matters, not simply because it causes significant suffering to a lot of families, but also because it is the rules and administrative systems relating to benefits, and not the rates at which benefits are paid, that most affect the rate of employment (McLaughlin, 1994; Atkinson, 1985: 9; 1995: 130–53).

In the case of Citizen's Basic Income, household members' Citizen's Basic Incomes would form a secure platform on which a variety of employment statuses and income sources could be constructed, and it would not matter if any of them changed. The Citizen's Basic Incomes would keep on coming (Van Parijs, 1996: 65). For households previously on means-tested benefits, and whose Citizen's Basic Incomes took them off them, there would no longer be complicated and stigmatizing means tests or work tests to worry about, and no need to report changes in circumstances. For households brought closer to coming off means-tested benefits by their Citizen's Basic Incomes, there would be more ability to seek small amounts of additional earned income in order to come off means-tested benefits, whereas previously the level of earned income required to achieve that might have seemed impossible to reach (Torry, 2018c).

Social insurance benefits

Social insurance benefits are paid to individuals if they suffer a particular contingency – usually illness, unemployment, or old age; and whether or not the benefits are paid, and the levels at which they are paid, generally depend on contributions records: records of contributions deducted by employers and paid to a government agency, often along with income tax payments. There might or might not be a relationship between the amount of benefit paid and the contributions made (Centre for Economic Studies/Ifo Institute, 2008).

While social insurance benefits are easier to administer than means-tested benefits, unemployment and sickness social insurance benefits are often of short duration, meaning that the recipient will soon end up on means-tested benefits; social insurance benefits can have work tests imposed on them in the same way as means-tested benefits; and because the benefits rely on contribution records, individuals with less secure employment experiences are less likely to receive them.

Negative Income Tax

In Chapter 5 on economics, we discussed the fact that Negative Income Tax and Citizen's Basic Income can generate the same relationship between earned income and net income. On occasions, this has led to a Negative Income Tax being called a Citizen's Basic Income (Pereira, 2017: 2–3; Sommer, 2016). It is not one, because it is not an unconditional income for every individual. The amount of the Negative Income Tax would vary according to someone's earned income, so administration would be difficult, and particularly difficult in contexts in which employers collect income tax on behalf of governments. In that case employers would need to know about individuals' other employments and self-employments in order to calculate any Negative Income Tax that needed to be paid out; and if someone spent a period unemployed, then at the beginning of that period the administration of their Negative Income Tax would need to be transferred from the employer to the government, and at the end of the period of unemployment the administration of the Negative Income Tax would need to be transferred from the government to the new employer. The problems could be as significant as those relating to the UK's means-tested Universal Credit (National Audit Office, 2018a; Story, 2015: 37–8; Torry, 2015a; 2016a: 126–30).

Negative Income Tax represents an interesting paradox. It would be intuitive to assume that integration – for instance, by reducing the number of payment systems to one – should result in simplification: but this might not be the case. As we have seen, to integrate taxation and benefits into a Negative Income Tax could create new complexities, as the UK Government discovered when it proposed a form of Negative Income Tax during the 1970s (Torry, 2013: 29–32, 43, 90, 255–7, 260–2). Counter-intuitively, keeping systems separate might be the route to simplification, particularly if one of those systems is radically simple. By reducing the number of people subject to means tests, a Citizen's Basic Income would reduce the number of people having their income and other details assessed for both benefits and tax, and it would reduce the number of families subjected to complex means-testing and demotivating sanctions. Keeping things separate can be simpler (Parker and Dilnot, 1988).

Participation Income
Professor Tony Atkinson has played a number of significant roles in relation to the modern debate on Citizen's Basic Income. First of all, his research and publications on poverty, inequality, and the welfare state, have helped to locate these subjects at the heart of economic theory and practice (Jenkins, 2017: 1165). Second, Tony was instrumental in the development of microsimulation – first of all TAXMOD, and then POLIMOD, and now the EU-wide EUROMOD: a computer programme into which are coded the regulations of tax and benefits systems, and through which is passed financial data from a large sample of a population in order to discover what effects tax and benefits policy changes would have on household disposable incomes, poverty levels, inequality, and so on (see Chapter 9). Third, he proposed the implementation

of a 'Participation Income': an otherwise unconditional income that would be conditional on some kind of participation in society (Atkinson, 1993). He believed that 'participation' of some kind would be required because otherwise 'it will be difficult to secure political support for a Citizen's Income while it remains unconditional on labour market or other activity' (Atkinson, 1996: 67; cf. Fitzpatrick, 1999: 101, 111–22; White, 2003: 170–5). 'Participation' would not be required from people who were ill, disabled, retired, or looking for work, but otherwise the recipient would need to be employed, self-employed, in education or training, undertaking voluntary work, or caring for the young, older people, or disabled dependents.

While the idea might sound sensible as a means of making an otherwise unconditional income palatable to a British public keen on what we might call front-end, or ante/required, reciprocity (– the idea that someone has to do something for society before society will do something for them), Atkinson never factored in the difficulty of administering a Participation Income. The current author undertook research that showed that only about 1 per cent of the population would not fulfil at least one of Atkinson's participation conditions (– these results have been recalculated and confirmed more recently in Torry, 2016a: 134–9). This means that a Participation Income amounted to a proposal for a vast bureaucracy that would enable street-level bureaucrats (Dean, 2012c: 74–5; Lipsky, 1980) to impose intrusive detailed questioning on every member of the population in order to exclude a tiny number from receiving the otherwise unconditional income: and an even smaller number if some of those initially excluded were then able to exercise creative compliance (De Wispelaere and Stirton, 2008). Atkinson agreed that there would be significant problems with administering his Participation Income: but although this author was not the only one to indicate the administrative difficulties (De Wispelaere and Stirton, 2008), in his final book before he died, *Inequality*, Atkinson still thought the idea a realistic proposition (Atkinson, 2015: 219–21). It is not uncommon for academics to ignore administrative implications. It is less common for those of us who have spent time administering social security benefits to do so.

A further objection to the idea of a Participation Income might be the fact that it would turn all of us into claimants, whereas everyone receiving their Citizen's Basic Income would see themselves as members of society receiving equal and unconditional social provision, in the same way that we see the National Health Service as a service provided for the whole of society. Yet another objection to Participation Income is that the unpopularity of its administrative requirements might make it so unpopular that it would be quickly abolished and that the experience would ensure that Citizen's Basic Income would be off the agenda until the experience had faded from memory.

Yet another objection is that a Participation Income cannot be evaluated by microsimulation because it would not be possible to code the participation conditions into a microsimulation programme. In Atkinson's last book, microsimulation results for a Participation Income are presented (Atkinson, 2015: 297): but they are not results for a Participation Income. What has been subjected to microsimulation testing is a Citizen's Basic Income. The fact that a scheme cannot be tested with a microsimulation programme is a sure indication that its administration would be riddled with street level discretion (Lipsky, 1980), and that throughout the implementation of the policy it would be constantly redesigned in possibly significant respects (Hupe, 2018). Conversely, there are no problems related to microsimulating an illustrative Citizen's Basic Income scheme: a clear signal that no discretion could be exercised in relation to it, and that implementation would not become an opportunity for policymaking stakeholders to redesign it.

But perhaps the most interesting response to Atkinson's proposal came from Hermione Parker, who suggested that 'a major public education exercise is necessary before voters are likely to adjust their value systems to the problems of post-industrial societies. Fudging the issues could delay this process' (Parker, 1994: 9).

Job guarantee

Not a proposal for a benefits system, but rather a counterproposal to Citizen's Basic Income, a job guarantee would guarantee paid employment for anyone who did not have a job (Murray and Forstater, 2018; Piachaud, 2016: 18). Apart from the cost of creating jobs not created by the employment market, the difficulty of training and supervising the workers, and the problem of the subsidized competition that firms that obtained their labour from the market would suffer, job guarantee schemes trap individuals in a 'minimalist, make-work, low-wage program' (Tymoigne, 2013: 63), and have been shown to 'have produced little in the way of useful output and have in some instances actually delayed job entry and subsequent job retention rather than promoted it' (Gregg, 2009: 175). A Citizen's Basic Income would incentivize employment and the formation of new businesses, and so would do the same job as a job guarantee without the coercion and the related costs and other disadvantages. A job guarantee programme could be expensive. A Citizen's Basic Income scheme could be revenue neutral.

Why Does Simplicity Matter?

More than once the UK's House of Commons Work and Pensions Committee has asked the UK Government to

> establish a Welfare Commission to examine the existing benefits system and model possible alternative structures with the aim of creating a fair but simpler system

that claimants and their representatives are able to understand more easily and DWP staff are able to administer more accurately. (House of Commons Work and Pensions Committee, 2010: 44)

Unfortunately, means-tested systems are inherently complicated (Morris, 1982: 210; Parker, 1989: 285–6; Whiteford et al., 2003: 27). As we have already discussed, such complexity makes it difficult for households to manage their relationships with the benefits system. It also makes the system difficult and expensive to administer.

In 2015/16, the cost of administering the UK's Child Benefit was 0.49p per £1 paid out. Net expenditure was £11.7bn p.a. paid out to 7.4m families. Total administrative cost was £57.3m p.a., and administrative cost per family per annum was £7.75 p.a. The cost of administering Tax Credits was 1.60p per £1 paid out. Net expenditure was £20.45bn p.a. paid out to 3.8m families. Total administrative cost was £327m p.a., and administrative cost per family per annum was £74.32 p.a. (National Audit Office, 2016a: 36, 52, 148, 180, R60). (Unfortunately, subsequent sets of accounts do not say how many families receive Child Benefit, only how many children, so the same comparison cannot be undertaken. Subsequent years would also be substantially complicated by the slow transition of Tax Credits claimants onto Universal Credit) (National Audit Office, 2017; 2018b). It would appear that means-tested benefits cost a full ten times more to administer than unconditional benefits such as Child Benefit, mainly because once a Child Benefit claim is set up it can run for years without any active administration being required, whereas means-tested benefits claims require constant attention from both claimants and public servants. The administrative cost differential would be even larger between means-tested benefits and Citizen's Basic Income. If we conservatively assume that the annual administrative cost for each Citizen's Basic Income recipient would be equal to that for each Child Benefit claim, then for a working age adult Citizen's Basic Income of £63 per week the administrative cost would be 0.24 per cent of the total cost of all Citizen's Basic Incomes. Occasional updating of contact and bank account details might be required, but no other active administration would be needed.

An advantage sometimes claimed for the simplicity of Citizen's Basic Income is transparency: that is, everyone would understand it. Whether such transparency would translate into increased public approval of the idea is an interesting question, because for the first time each taxpayer would know how much tax revenue was being paid out to people who were not paying tax (Walter, 1989: 59). If UK Citizen's Basic Incomes were being funded by the abolition of the Income Tax Personal Allowance, then a lot more people would be paying Income Tax, and both this and the payment of Citizen's Basic Incomes to everyone would help to dissolve the existing taxpayer/benefits recipient divide: but education might still be required to persuade taxpayers that to use the tax they paid for unconditional incomes would make it more likely that recipients would seek additional earned income than if their taxes were used to pay for means-tested benefits that disincentivized employment.

An important question is whether simplicity would in fact be achieved if a small initial Citizen's Basic Income were to be implemented. The objection might be offered that 'either the level of [Citizen's Basic Income] is unacceptably low, or the cost of providing it is unacceptably high' (Kay, 2017: 72), and that a small Citizen's Basic Income would either leave a lot of people in poverty, or it would leave them on means-tested benefits, so the system as a whole would either increase poverty, or it would be more complicated than the current system and not less (Piachaud, 2016: 3–4, 10–11; Parker, 1988). Not so. Complexity is an experienced reality. Any household no longer on means-tested benefits because its Citizen's Basic Incomes had taken it off them would experience less complexity; any household still on means-tested benefits would be on less of them, they would be more able to come off them, and they would therefore be closer to experiencing the simplicity that Citizen's Basic Income would offer them; and any family that remained on means-tested benefits would not experience their Citizen's Basic Incomes as an added complexity, but rather as a new and secure layer of income with rules that they entirely understood. 'Simplifying the benefits system shouldn't be the goal – simplifying it for the claimant should be' (Royston, 2017: 350).

There is understandable debate about the extent to which implementing a Citizen's Basic Income scheme would reduce administrative costs (Stirton and De Wispelaere, 2009; Miller, 2009). The saving or additional cost would of course depend entirely on the details of the particular scheme implemented. If the Citizen's Basic Income were too small to take a significant number of households off means-tested benefits, then it would be likely to increase administrative costs (De Wispelaere and Stirton, 2011: 122): which is why it is important that one of the tests for the feasibility of a Citizen's Basic Income scheme should be that it would take a significant number of households off means-tested benefits, and should also bring a significant number of households within striking distance of coming off them (Torry, 2017d: 8; 2018c: 8).

Computerization

Means-tested benefits generally evolved as manual systems, and subsequent attempts have been made to computerize them. This was always going to be problematic. Families' circumstances have always been complex and fluid, so whether regulations have been more general, allowing for public servants' discretion in implementing them, or more detailed, in an attempt to prevent public servant discretion, it has always been the human element between the regulations and the claimants that has enabled the former to serve the latter. This author writes from two years' experience of being part of the human element that made the system work for claimants in a South London benefits office.

When computerization began – as it began with UK means-tested benefits during the 1980s – the computer became a memory and calculating machine, with the public servant translating claimants' interview responses so that they would answer the questions asked by the computer. The system continued to work in much the same way as the manual system that it replaced.

The big change, well represented in the UK by the Department for Work and Pensions' digital strategy, is 'digital by default' (Department for Work and Pensions, 2012), which means the claimant relating to means-tested benefits through a computer rather than through a member of staff. The paradox is that there is just as much human involvement, because the claimant has to translate the realities of their lives to make them acceptable to the computer programme; and there is even more human involvement in relation to Universal Credit, the new combined means-tested benefit, because its administration requires someone's employer to inform the tax authorities accurately and on time how much they have earned during the previous month, and how much Income Tax has been deducted. What is missing, of course, is public servants, which no doubt saves money, but it removes the relatively knowledgeable human element that used to interpret claimant circumstances to the regulations running on the administration's computer. The absence of a staff member poses all manner of problems for individuals who are not computer literate; and for the many claimants whose complex circumstances do not fit the questions being asked, anxiety about the possibility of being accused of fraud is a constant presence (Campbell, 2010).

A further concern relates to computerization's threat to the democratic process. The greater the difficulty of computerizing existing systems, the higher the probability that companies that win contracts to computerize benefits systems will suggest changes to the system that would make it easier to computerize. Once a contract has started, it is difficult for the client, the government department, to resist pressure for such changes, particularly if the department possesses little expertise, and the computerization company suggests that the changes are necessary to enable the project to stay within budget. In the UK, both Tax Credits and Universal Credit computerizations have been flawed (Campbell, 2010; Craig and Brooks, 2006: 7–11). The one exception is Child Benefit, with which there have been no computerization problems (Craig and Brooks, 2006): although of course there would have been if the Conservative Government's 2010 promise to means-test it had been carried out, rather than a tax charge being introduced alongside a still unconditional income. A Citizen's Basic Income would be as easy to computerize as Child Benefit.

Error and Fraud

The simplicity of Citizen's Basic Income would be good for its recipients, would aid computerization, would reduce administrative costs, and would reduce the possibility of error and fraud.

The complexity of means-tested benefits offers considerable scope for both error and fraud: and, because of the complexity, it is not always easy to decide which claimant errors are fraudulent and which are genuine mistakes or debatable interpretations of regulations. Because of this, the UK's National Audit Office declines to distinguish between error and fraud in its reports. The UK's HMRC (Her Majesty's Revenue and Customs) estimates that in 2016–17

> error and fraud resulted in overpayments of Tax Credits of 4.9% of expenditure, compared with 4.8% in 2015–16. Errors in Tax Credits resulting in underpayments increased to 0.8% of expenditure, compared with 0.6% in 2015–16. This equates to overpayments of £1.3 billion and underpayments of £200 million. (National Audit Office, 2018b: R47)

The Department for Work and Pensions estimates that overpayments of means-tested benefits during 2017–18 were as follows: Jobseeker's Allowance 6.3 per cent of total expenditure, Housing Benefit 6.5 per cent, Employment and Support Allowance 4.3 per cent, Pension Credit 5.8 per cent, and Universal Credit 7.2 per cent. Underpayments were of lower amounts: Jobseeker's Allowance 1.3 per cent of total expenditure, Housing Benefit 1.4 per cent, Employment and Support Allowance 2.6 per cent, Pension Credit 2.4 per cent, and Universal Credit 1.3 per cent (Department for Work and Pensions, 2018b: 3). Of the total Jobseeker's Allowance overpayments of 6.3 per cent, 4.3 percentage points is estimated to be due to fraud, 0.2 percentage points due to claimant error, and 1.8 percentage points due to official error (Department for Work and Pensions, 2018b: 7). Following some criticism in previous years that it was counting all Child Benefit claims in relation to which recipients did not reply to letters as necessarily fraudulent, HMRC now estimates that only 40 per cent of nonresponses represent fraud.

> Our central estimate of the overall level of error and fraud associated with claims where we have positive contact with the customer in 2017–18 is 0.4% of total Child Benefit expenditure (£50 million) ... the estimated level of error and fraud [among nonresponders] for 2017–18 was 0.9% of total expenditure (£110 million). (National Audit Office, 2018b: 34)

As we would expect, there is a substantial difference between the rate of error and fraud relating to means-tested benefits and the rate of error and fraud relating to unconditional benefits. Once we recognize that much of the fraud related to Child Benefit is caused by claims not being closed when children leave full-time education before the age of nineteen, as they should be (National Audit Office, 2018b: R56), we can see that error and fraud related to Citizen's Basic Income (which would change in value as someone's age changed, but would not cease), would be lower than for Child Benefit (Torry, 2013: 95; 2016a: 9–10).

Criminalization

Where a university does not have a department dedicated to criminology – 'the study of crime and criminals; this as an academic discipline' (Oxford English Dictionary) – the subject will sometimes be found in social policy departments (for instance, in the UK, at the University of Kent, the London School of Economics, and Bristol University). Because the significant relationship between the discipline of criminology and Citizen's Basic Income relates to the ways in which tax and benefits systems might or might not encourage fraud and therefore criminal activity, it seems appropriate to locate this discussion of criminalization in the chapter in which we have already discussed error and fraud.

Fraud is a crime. However, that is not all that needs to be said. The problem with actions relating to the benefits system that might count as fraudulent, such as failing to declare occasional earnings, is that they might be entirely rational, suggesting that the benefits system is at least as responsible for the criminal activity as is the claimant. This is a particularly clear example of crime being socially constructed (Dean, 2012c: 106–8). For someone on means-tested benefits, to declare occasional earnings might have consequences for the household's financial security, because to declare them can cause a claim to be recalculated in unpredictable ways, or to be stopped and started again, with the chaos that can follow from that. A dilemma therefore presents itself: either to promote the wellbeing of one's family, including one's children, by earning small amounts of additional income when the opportunity arises and not declaring it; or not to earn additional income.

During the 1980s, Bill Jordan and his colleagues studied the employment market decisions of low income families on a housing estate in Exeter. They discovered that each household had constructed a financial strategy out of a variety of employments and self-employments, and that casual cash earnings were not declared to benefits offices if they remained below a level tacitly agreed by the community (Jordan et al., 1992: 277). While this seemed sensible as far as the individuals and the estate community were concerned, the practice and the related community attitudes meant that workers on the estate could undercut law-abiding businesses (Noteboom, [1987] 2013); that not declaring earnings had become common practice, thus depriving society of

Income Tax that ought to have been paid; that people could find themselves with criminal records and the associated longer-term consequences of that; that the practice encourages print and broadcast media to pursue an anti-claimant agenda, which enables governments to cut the levels of benefits (Baillie, 2011: 67–70); and that social legitimation had been granted to criminal activity, and thus by implication to other criminal activity as well.

The answer is to make the benefits system fraud-proof: a strategy to which a Citizen's Basic Income would contribute. The most likely route by which someone might defraud Citizen's Basic Income would be through establishing two different identities. If a Citizen's Basic Income scheme for the entire population of a country were to be implemented in one go, then either existing identity cards would need to be used to access Citizen's Basic Incomes, or, in the absence of an existing identity card system, some new means of ensuring that someone had only one identity would be required. The kinds of technology now used at airports to match individuals with passport records could serve this purpose. If a scheme were to be rolled out gradually, then Citizen's Basic Incomes could be simply a matter of transferring Child Benefit claims to the individuals to which they applied. If this were done, then dual identities would have to have been established at a child's birth and the fraud not detected: a somewhat unlikely scenario.

Because the level of earned or any other income would never affect the level of someone's Citizen's Basic Income, and neither would someone's employment status, family relationships, housing costs, or anything else, none of the usual ways to defraud means-tested benefits would be available. Fraud, and accompanying criminalization, would be almost impossible; and because a lot of households would be taken off means-tested benefits by their Citizen's Basic Incomes, or their Citizen's Basic Incomes would enable them to come off them, the amount of fraud and criminalization related to the benefits system as a whole would decline (Torry, 2013: 95–6).

Could Citizen's Basic Income be Administered?

We have discovered that Citizen's Basic Income would be easy and cheap to administer – something generally true of services and benefits that are uncon-ditional and universal (Spicker, 2014: 218–19) – and that it would reduce levels of error, fraud, and criminalization. It is no accident that almost the whole of the chapter on 'the administrative process' in Paul Spicker's *Social Policy* would be entirely irrelevant to the administration of Citizen's Basic Income (Spicker, 2014: 353–77).

IMPLEMENTATION

In Chapter 9 we discussed the feasibility of Citizen's Basic Income, and inevitably found ourselves discussing issues related to implementation, and in particular questions related to the differential feasibilities of different ways of implementing a Citizen's Basic Income scheme. In this section of this chapter we are asking a somewhat different question, although feasibility will remain an important consideration.

Also in Chapter 9 we discussed how policy is made. Let us suppose that the general idea of a Citizen's Basic Income has made its way through the policy process. We know that an established Citizen's Basic Income could be administered quite easily: but that does not mean that managing the transition to a Citizen's Basic Income scheme would be easy. Essential to seamless implementation would be a requirement that the Citizen's Basic Income scheme would make as few changes as possible to any existing social security and tax systems, simply because trying to make lots of changes at once is a recipe for complexity and errors (as the implementation of the UK's Universal Credit has shown). This seamlessness would need to apply not only to the systems employed to introduce the Citizen's Basic Income, but also in relation to the experience of recipients. It would be essential to ensure that no gaps occurred in people's receipt of sufficient income: so, for instance, if a scheme in the UK were to abolish an Income Tax Personal Allowance at the same time as implementing the Citizen's Basic Income, then the two changes would have to happen at exactly the same time. Similarly, any reductions in means-tested benefits claims consequent upon the payment of Citizen's Basic Incomes would have to happen at the same time as well. Given the simplicity of the Citizen's Basic Income itself, none of this should be difficult, and in particular it should be nothing like as difficult as replacing one set of means-tested benefits with another, which is what the UK has attempted with its roll-out of Universal Credit.

As with any policy implementation, plans would have to be made to mitigate effects in other policy areas. So, for instance, any change in a country's benefits system might mean changes having to be made in other policy areas where there are existing relationships between the policy fields. In the UK, receipt of means-tested benefits gives a family access to free school meals, and the number of children receiving free school meals influences the amount of money that the school receives. If fewer households were to receive means-tested benefits, then fewer households would receive free school meals, and schools in more deprived areas would receive less money. Similarly, receipt of means-tested benefits gives access to free prescriptions and dental care, so if fewer households received means-tested benefits, then more households would have to pay for their prescriptions and dental care (Miller, 2012). Leisure centres can sometimes be free for people on means-tested benefits but expensive for people who are not. The problem here is not Citizen's Basic Income: it is the cliff-edge that households face when they come off means-tested benefits. Earning just enough not to receive them can mean losing free school meals and free prescriptions, and being unable to afford the local leisure centre. The household can end up a lot poorer. An obvious response would be to make school meals, prescriptions and dental care free for everyone, and to recoup the cost by increasing tax rates. Families at the lower end of the earnings range could benefit, while families at the upper end might find themselves paying a little more Income Tax. And of course to make school meals free for every child could be a most useful way of weaning children off packed lunches full of crisps, chocolate biscuits, and sugar-saturated drinks, and therefore of improving child nutrition if the school meals were of sufficient quality. And it would not be difficult to find a different and rather better way to ensure that schools in more deprived areas received additional funding. This set of examples relates to the UK. Other countries planning to implement a Citizen's Basic Income would need to consider the policy linkages in their own contexts, how the implementation of a Citizen's Basic Income scheme would impact other policy fields, and how any potential problems might be mitigated (Torry, 2018a: 166–7).

A genuine pilot project for an entire community would of course help to ensure that a nationwide transition would run smoothly. Such pilot projects have so far only taken place in developing countries. The recent experiment in Finland was not of this nature, as it was for 2,000 randomly selected unemployed individuals across the country (De Wispelaere et al., 2019; Halmetoja et al., 2019: 325); and the municipal experiments in the Netherlands are about a variety of mechanisms, none of which conform to the definition of a Citizen's Basic Income (Groot et al., 2019). For the UK to run a pilot project for a Citizen's Basic Income scheme with the same parameters as the intended nationwide scheme in a community containing say 20,000 people should reveal any administrative difficulties that might arise at the point of implementation. Admittedly such a pilot project would not be easy to achieve because it would mean changing a country's tax and benefits systems for a single community: but running such a genuine Citizen's Basic Income scheme for a relatively small group of people could enable any potential problems to be sorted out before a nationwide scheme was rolled out.

When new social policies are implemented, a common occurrence is that the policy design changes during implementation as compromises are made in order to save money or for political reasons (Spicker, 2014: 237–8). If a Citizen's Basic Income scheme were to be implemented, then the one thing that must not happen is that the Citizen's Basic Income itself should be changed in any way. It must not be means-tested, work-tested, based on the household structure, or in any other way made conditional. Different amounts would be paid for different age groups, but that would be the only conditionality permitted. Any other aspect of the scheme could be changed, of course: the amount by which the Income Tax Personal Allowance would be reduced, the way in which the Citizen's Basic Incomes were treated when means-tested benefits were calculated, and so on: although of course care would have to be taken that household net disposable income losses would not be imposed on low income households, and that poverty and inequality would be reduced by the scheme as a whole, and not increased by it. But the Citizen's Basic Income itself must never be compromised. As Paul Spicker suggests: an important question to ask when a new policy is implemented is this: What can go wrong? (Spicker, 2014: 240). What could go wrong with the implementation of a Citizen's Basic Income scheme is that we could find that it wasn't a Citizen's Basic Income that was being implemented, but something else instead.

CONCLUSIONS RELATING TO THIS CHAPTER AND CHAPTER 9

If more space had been available in this and the previous chapters, then we might have been able to tackle a variety of other matters frequently studied by social policy academics. To take just one example here: Individuals who choose to care for relatives who are disabled or ill would for the first time receive an income that was totally secure and was the same as everyone else's; and the person that they were caring for would experience the same unconditional income. Other benefits that they both received previously would be either reduced or no longer received. As always, the Citizen's Basic Income scheme would need to ensure that carers and those that they cared for should not find themselves worse off following implementation: but if this could be done – which it could be – then additional possibilities would follow. Because other benefits would be at lower levels, and because in the UK Local Authorities provide a variety of incomes and services for people with disabilities alongside central government benefits for people with disabilities and their carers, there might be a case for remaining disability benefits being administered by local rather than central government (Leaper, 1986; Fenger et al., 2016). The question is sometimes raised as to whether people with disabilities should receive higher Citizen's Basic Incomes (Martinelli, 2017a: 15; 2017b: 9–10). The answer has to be no. The Citizen's Basic Income has to be kept unconditional, otherwise it would become something else and would not offer the considerable social and economic advantages of a genuine Citizen's Basic Income. Any additions thought necessary for various groups of people should either be new benefits unconditional apart from being tested for appropriate recipients, or they should be enhanced versions of relevant benefits in the current system (Basic Income Research Group, 1988; Howard and Lawrence, 1996).

At the beginning of Chapter 9 we discussed Paul Spicker's and Hartley Dean's rather different understandings of the academic discipline that we call social policy: the former understanding the discipline as the study of policy designed to address social problems, and the latter seeing the subject as about everything related to human wellbeing. It is therefore no surprise to find that Dean has a longstanding interest in Citizen's Basic Income (– he was a trustee of the Citizen's Income Trust, and he endorsed three of this author's books on the subject: 'Citizen's Income is a big idea whose time might at last have come' (Torry, 2013: back cover)). It is equally no surprise that Paul Spicker can find little enthusiasm for the concept:

> If you limit the level of benefit you are still dependent on other benefits, so you'll get all the problems of the tapers, the poverty trap, the intrusion into people's lives and the complexity. If you increase the cost, then you can float people off those benefits – but what will you have achieved if you do that? ... those people who were formerly on benefits will find themselves on the equivalent in Basic Income, and you'll have spent nearly all the money to the benefit of people who weren't on benefits – to people who are better off. So you have really got to decide, is it worth putting large amounts of money into a scheme which isn't going to benefit the people you most want to help? (Spicker, 2017)

In relation to the detail of this quotation, it hardly needs to be said that it is irrelevant that money is spent on people who are better off if they will be paying additional Income Tax and National Insurance Contributions and might see a small reduction in their net disposable income. Here the point to notice is that the policy is being judged on a narrow view of what it would not manage to do for people who are poor: that is, it would not necessarily provide them with more money. Presumably the fact that many of those households previously on means-tested benefits would no longer be on them, and that every family would for the first time have a secure financial platform that would never be at risk, is not felt to be relevant, because those no longer on means-tested benefits would no longer be the objects of a problem-centred social policy discipline, and the secure financial platform would apply to everyone and not only to the poor. Dean's and Spicker's different attitudes to Citizen's Basic Income cohere closely with their views on the subject matter of the discipline that we call social policy. It is an interesting question as to whether in general people with a broader interest in individual and social wellbeing would be more likely to find Citizen's Basic Income of positive interest, and those focused on alleviating the social problems afflicting the poor might be more likely to question

Citizen's Basic Income's usefulness. What is difficult to understand is why the discussion between Spicker and Dean was framed as a conflict between two opposing views of the discipline of social policy (Dean, 2004; Spicker, 2004), when Spicker's understanding of social policy could equally well have been framed as a subset of Dean's broader view. If this view is taken, then no longer are the two views of the debate on Citizen's Basic Income in opposition to each other: they are complementary understandings, the one taking a broad view of the benefits that would accrue to individuals and to society as a whole if a Citizen's Basic Income were to be implemented, and the other a detailed exploration of the parameters within which a Citizen's Basic Income scheme would in practice generate those social and individual benefits, particularly for people currently on low incomes.

In relation to either perspective or to both, the twin disciplines of social policy and social administration will remain essential to the developing global debate on Citizen's Basic Income. Both disciplines are practice-oriented: that is, they are undertaken for a specific purpose (Spicker, 2014: 429–46), whether that be to promote the wellbeing of society, or to solve social problems. It will be by the application of the very best research methods available to these two disciplines that the Citizen's Basic Income debate will be best served.

CASE STUDY

A Consultation on Implementation

In 2016, the Institute for Chartered Accountants in England and Wales held a consultation on the implementation of Citizen's Basic Income. The consultation studied four implementation methods:

1. A citizen's income [Citizen's Basic Income] for every UK citizen, large enough to take every household off means-tested benefits (including Working Tax Credits, Child Tax Credits, and Universal Credit), and large enough to ensure that no household with low earned income would suffer a financial loss at the point of implementation. The scheme would be implemented all in one go.
2. A citizen's income for every UK citizen, funded from within the current tax and benefits system. Current means-tested benefits would be left in place, and each household's means-tested benefits would be recalculated to take into account household members' citizen's incomes in the same way as earned income is taken into account. Again, implementation all in one go.
3. This scheme would start with an increase in Child Benefit. A citizen's income would then be paid to all 16-year-olds, and they would be allowed

to keep it as they grew older, with each new cohort of 16-year-olds receiving the same citizen's income and being allowed to keep it.
4. Inviting volunteers among the pre-retired, between the age of 60 and the state pension age. (Torry, 2016c: 6)

As we have discovered during our discussion of feasibilities, if the first method were to take every household off means-tested benefits without imposing losses on low income households, then sizeable, and probably politically unsustainable, Income Tax rises would be required, or additional funding would have to be found from outside the income tax system (Torry, 2015b: 6). If such a scheme were to become possible then it would offer the advantages of increased personal freedom, and in particular release from means-tested benefits, along with their sanctions, stigma, errors, and bureaucratic intrusion. Every household previously on means-tested benefits would experience lower marginal deduction rates (total withdrawal rates on additional earned income), but if Income Tax rises were to be employed to fund the Citizen's Basic Incomes then anyone receiving earned income and not previously on means-tested benefits would suffer significant increases in marginal deduction rates. If funding from elsewhere were to be employed – for instance, from carbon taxes – then the scheme as a whole would have to ensure that increased fuel, transport, and other costs would not reduce household net disposable incomes by more than the Citizen's Basic Incomes would increase them.

A possible disadvantage might be that the sizeable Citizen's Basic Income would generate an employment disincentive. Whether this would be larger than the increased incentive due to lower marginal deduction rates for those previously on means-tested benefits would need to be tested. A further disadvantage might be connected: The effects of the scheme would be unpredictable, and it is unpredictable effects that a normal policy process is designed to prevent. This suggests that the scheme might not be able to struggle through the policy process to implementation. A scenario in which the scheme might be able to get through the policy process would be a highly mechanized society in which governments found it possible to extract a high proportion of the proceeds of production going to the owners of capital. In those circumstances, employment incentives might not be particularly relevant (Torry, 2016c: 7).

If the second option were to be chosen in the UK, then a Citizen's Basic Income scheme that paid a working age adult Citizen's Basic Income of between £65 and £70 per week, with different amounts for children, elderly people, and young adults, could be funded by reducing to zero the Income Tax Personal Allowance and the National Insurance Contributions Primary Earnings Threshold, charging the same rate of National Insurance Contributions above the Upper Earnings Limit as is currently charged below it, and raising Income Tax Rates by just three percentage points. The scheme would reduce poverty and inequality, avoid significant losses for low income households and unmanageable losses for higher income households, take a lot of households off means-tested benefits, and bring a lot more households within striking distance of coming off them: that is, they would be able to come off them by adding a few more hours of employment a week or by reducing their outgoings, whereas previously that would not have been possible. A further possibility with similar results would be a £50 per week Citizen's Basic Income for working age adults and a retained Income Tax Personal Allowance of £4,000 per annum (Torry, 2019a). All of those households able to escape from means-tested benefits would no longer experience the sanctions, stigma, errors, and bureaucratic intrusion that accompany them. A further advantage would be that the limited nature of the scheme, and the fact that it would leave in place the existing tax and benefits system, would mean that the effects might be more predictable than with the first implementation option; and because the scheme would be a minor rearrangement of the current system, it could be implemented almost overnight.

One disadvantage of this implementation option relative to the first one is that quite a lot of households would still be on means-tested benefits; and a disadvantage relative to the current system is that Income Tax rates would be higher for everyone employed and self-employed, and National Insurance Contributions would be at a higher rate for high earners. An advantage is that the scheme would be eminently financially feasible without anyone having to consider the possibility of funding from outside the tax and benefits system (Torry, 2016c: 7–8).

Because with this implementation method the whole of the revenue for the Citizen's Basic Incomes must come from the existing tax system, it might be worth asking how the tax increases might be framed in order to enhance their psychological acceptability. Mark Wadsworth has suggested that a tax specifically stated to be for funding Citizen's Basic Incomes might prove more acceptable than simply raising the rates of the existing Income Tax (Wadsworth, 2018). There are arguments both for and against hypothecated taxes (Macfarland, 2018); and a decision would have to be taken as to whether to employ 'strong' hypothecation (in which the whole of the revenue from the specific tax is used to fund the Citizen's Basic Income, and no other revenue source is required) or 'weak' hypothecation (in which one of the two conditions can be relaxed) (Macfarland, 2018: 11): but the idea is clearly worth consideration.

During our discussion of the British social policy tradition we recognized that incremental change is an important characteristic of it (Hill, 2009: 164). The first two implementation options that we have considered assume implementation of the entire scheme all in one go. This might be unwise in relation to the first option, simply because unpredictable effects might be quite large: but with the second option, with more predictable effects, implementation all at once would certainly be a possibility. However, even if the effects of the second option might be beneficial, and the transition might be manageable, there might be considerable concern that this might not be the case. This suggests that gradual implementation might be a useful approach, and the most obvious way to approach this would be by implementing Citizens' Basic Incomes for one demographic group at a time, perhaps starting with an enhanced Child Benefit, and then adding a Citizen's Basic Income for a group of young adults defined by their age: perhaps 16-year-olds, or 18-year-olds, or everyone between the ages of eighteen and twenty-one (Torry, 2013: 49–52; OECD, 2017). If a scheme that abolished rather than reduced the Income Tax Personal Allowance was to be implemented, then recipients would receive neither an Income Tax Personal Allowance nor a National Insurance Contributions Primary Earnings Threshold, because they would already be receiving a Citizen's Basic Income equal in value to the two allowances. As the initial age group grew older, they would keep their Citizen's Basic Incomes. The end result would be a Citizen's Basic Income slowly rolled out to the entire population. Additional funding would be by repeated small increases in Income Tax and National Insurance Contribution rates: increases that would be more manageable than those related to the first and second implementation options simply because they would be gradual rather than immediate (Torry, 2015b). This scheme, like implementation option 2, would not impose significant losses on low income households, would reduce both poverty and inequality, and would mean fewer households on means-tested benefits. The enhanced Child Benefit would assist with the costs of bringing up children, and would mean fewer children in poverty; and the Citizen's Basic Incomes for young adults would provide funds during the crucial years of training and education, and could reduce levels of student debt (Torry, 2016c: 8–9).

Disadvantages of the scheme relative to the first and second implementation options is that two individuals very close to each other in age might find themselves on different sides of the age dividing line at the point of implementation, meaning that throughout their lives the older individual would never experience a Citizen's Basic Income, whereas the younger would *always* have one. This might bring pressure to bear on government to extend the scheme to all age groups. Perhaps a more significant disadvantage is that it could take fifty years to implement Citizen's Basic Incomes for every member of the population, which could make the scheme vulnerable to either tampering or abolition. This would be another reason for incorporating additional demographic groups as quickly as possible. As for feasibility: the fact that the enhanced Child

Benefit would reduce child poverty could be of significant assistance to the scheme as it found its way through the policy process.

In relation to the fourth option: above the age of 60 any individual would be able to exchange their Income Tax Personal Allowance, their National Insurance Contributions Primary Earnings Threshold, and their ability to claim means-tested benefits, for a Citizen's Basic Income of the same value as the Personal Allowance and the Primary Earnings Threshold. If it was agreed that means-tested benefits would still be payable, then these would be recalculated to take into account the value of the Citizen's Basic Income. Backing out would not be possible once the pre-retirement Citizen's Basic Income was in payment. For most participants, disposable income would remain the same as before. In a couple in which one partner was not employed, the new scheme would provide additional net household income, and it is for the Citizen's Basic Incomes for non-earning partners, who currently receive no benefit from their Income Tax Personal Allowances and their National Insurance Contribution Primary Earnings Thresholds, that tax rises would be required (Torry, 2016c: 9–10).

Advantages would be that take-up would provide a measure of the scheme's popularity; those receiving Citizen's Basic Incomes would find themselves with more freedom to use their time as they wished – for family care, community work, occasional employment, and so on; and those who had been on means-tested benefits could find themselves on none at all, or on less of them, and so would be more able to escape from high marginal deduction rates and therefore to gain more net disposable income from additional earnings. This would mean that they would be more able to seek occasional employment, or to risk starting their own businesses, and they would be more able to release themselves from poverty and unemployment traps (Torry, 2016a: 3–6). As retirement age rises, there will be more people who, following a lifetime of full-time and fairly secure employment, might find themselves without that for the years leading up to retirement. To have a secure financial platform on which to build during those years would enable them to cope more easily with a period of diverse kinds of work, and to welcome the experience: a far more beneficial preparation for retirement than a period spent suffering from the work tests, means tests and sanctions related to means-tested benefits. The scheme would be feasible in all respects, and it would not be long before demand would bring about a pre-retirement Citizen's Basic Income for everyone over the age of sixty, or perhaps fifty-five.

But there are disadvantages to the voluntary approach: Granting Citizen's Basic Incomes to non-earning spouses might be unpopular among couples in which both partners are employed, unless a claw-back mechanism could be applied to high earners; employers and other institutions would have to cope with two separate tax and benefits systems for the pre-retired age group; and because means-tested benefits are calculated on the basis of the couple, it might have to be a requirement that both members of a couple would have to apply together to transfer to Citizen's Basic Incomes. This might prove problematic if the members of a couple disagreed about what to do. These disadvantages might add to pressure for the scheme to apply to every pre-retired individual.

The first implementation method would require substantial additional public funding if it were to avoid losses for low income households, so in the short term it would not be feasible. If additional funding were to be available, and if the funding method would not reduce the net disposable incomes of low income households by more than they would be increased by the net effects of their Citizen's Basic Incomes, then the scheme would be both feasible and welcome. The second implementation method would be financially feasible, and it would not impose significant losses at the point of implementation. It might, however, prove to be psychologically infeasible, as might be the first implementation method. The third implementation method could potentially satisfy all of the feasibility tests, as could the fourth method.

11. The politics of Citizen's Basic Income

Politics: The science or study of government and the state.
(Oxford English Dictionary)

INTRODUCTION

Politics, like Social Policy, and unlike economics, is an academic discipline with the same name as its subject matter. Because the subject matter of politics covers a broad range of ideas and activity, and it crosses numerous boundaries into society and the economy, the academic discipline of politics crosses boundaries into a number of disciplines tackled in the chapters of this book: in fact, it would be difficult to identify another discipline that does not relate in some way to the academic subject that we call politics. I shall therefore employ my usual constraint and concentrate on issues that might be those most closely related to politics: that is, to the study of government and the state.

I shall take as my guides to the subject *Introduction to Politics* by Robert Garner, Peter Ferdinand and Stephanie Lawson (2009) and *Political Theory: An introduction* by Andrew Heywood (1999). The sections of the first book study concepts and ideologies; such institutions as constitutions, bureaucracies, and elections; and international relations. The second book is more theme-based: human nature, the individual, society, rights, obligations, citizenship, democracy, freedom, toleration, liberation, equality, social justice, welfare, and so on. In this book, we deal with rights in Chapter 13, and with institutions in the section on the policy process in Chapter 9. Here we shall discuss political ideologies, poverty, inequality, redistribution, and citizenship. Poverty, inequality and redistribution are of course subjects frequently studied by social policy academics: but of all of the subjects that social policy academics study, these three connected topics might be the most political. In Chapters 10 and 13 we ask who should receive a Citizen's Basic Income: here we take a more detailed look at the highly political issue of citizenship. Central to politics, and to the academic discipline of politics, is the notion of political ideology – sets of ideas that issue in more or less distinctive social policies: so we shall begin this chapter by asking how a variety of political ideologies might relate to Citizen's Basic Income.

POLITICAL IDEOLOGIES

Ideologies are 'inter-related sets of ideas and values which shape the way that problems are understood and acted on' (Spicker, 2014: 190); they are significant drivers of social policy change (Botterill and Fenna, 2019: 45, 110); and they are

> action-orientated in the sense that they seek to promote a particular social and political order for which they urge people to strive ... all ideologies have different strands or schools, and sometimes there is considerable overlap between one ideology and another ... it is possible to distinguish between concepts at the core of an ideology from those which are further away from the centre and those which are at the periphery ... ideologies reflect, as well as shape, the social and historical circumstances in which they exist. (Garner et al., 2009: 115–16)

We shall study a variety of ideologies, and in particular we shall ask whether they can generate arguments for Citizen's Basic Income, whether they can generate arguments against Citizen's Basic Income, and whether they have in fact generated such arguments for and against.

Liberalism

The classical liberal tradition wanted the state to 'ensure internal and external security and to ensure that private property rights are enforced' (Garner et al., 2009: 117), and believed that the market rather than the state was the most effective way to meet human need (Spicker, 2014: 196): but the contemporary tradition recognizes that the quest for freedom that is at the heart of the liberal tradition might best be pursued in the context of a state that guarantees a broader variety of rights. State action to ensure that individuals can exercise positive freedom to pursue personal goals has become more important than a negative freedom achieved by removing external constraints. The consistent element in liberal thought is the focus on the individual and their goals (Garner et al., 2009: 117–18). 'It is individuals who feel, exult, despair and rejoice. And statements about group welfare are a shorthand way of referring to such individual effects' (Brittan, 1998: 11). Because 'there is nothing inherently right about the pattern of rewards produced by the combination of inheritance and the market', what is needed is 'a framework of rules – including, if necessary, redistributive taxation and transfers – by which a market economy can be induced to serve broader objectives' (Brittan, 1998: 42).

In the liberal context, society becomes a group of free individuals who work together to maintain the conditions for their individual liberties; and the economy is a network of free trade between nations, with regulation required where that will facilitate greater individual liberty. However, as Samuel Brittan has recognized, 'the key problem for European economic and social policy is how to obtain the benefits of a flexible US style labour market, without US poverty or US ghettoes' (Brittan and Webb, 1990: 5).

A Citizen's Basic Income would enable people more easily to choose their employment pattern, how to spend their time, and how to form households, so it would enhance individual autonomy, which is the chief aim of a liberal ideology. The 'ladder of opportunity' is often rather shaky, and a Citizen's Basic Income would ameliorate the poverty and unemployment traps and enable people to pursue their economic and occupational goals. As Brittan suggests, 'it is positively desirable that people should have a means of subsistence independent of needs' because this would 'separate the libertarian, free choice aspects of capitalism from the puritan work ethic' (Brittan and Webb, 1990: 2); and in tune with a liberal concern for property rights, Brittan sees a Citizen's Basic Income 'not as a handout, but as a property right', and as a 'return on the national capital' (Brittan and Webb, 1990: 3).

A liberal's attitude to Citizen's Basic Income will be very different from their attitude to a National Minimum Wage:

> Minimum wages represent just that kind of interference with markets which does most harm. ... Those most likely to suffer are just the people whom the proponents of minimum wages say they most want to help. They include those on the fringes of the labour market or on the borderline of disablement or other incapacity ... and all the others who face a choice between low pay and no pay. Minimum wages are a denial of the human right to sell one's labour to a willing buyer and to make one's own decision about whether or not to take paid work at going rates. (Brittan and Webb, 1990: 7)

In the UK, both the Liberal Democratic Party and elements of the Labour Party used to be broadly liberal in their outlook: but since 2015 the Labour Party has become more explicitly socialist, leaving the Liberal Democrats as the representative of the modern liberal tradition. Thirty years ago, before the Liberal Party and the Social Democratic Party joined to form the Liberal Democrats, Citizen's Basic Income became briefly Liberal Party policy, until in 1994 the party's leadership decided to drop the idea because the Chair of the party's tax and benefits working group claimed that it would be too expensive – to shouts of 'rubbish' from the conference floor (Goodwin, 1994). A more recent and more ideological objection is that Citizen's Basic Income is

> underpinned by a negative image of humankind as weak, vulnerable and isolated. The basic thrust of this sentiment is that people cannot cope within the

harsh environment of globalized capitalism without state assistance. (Richardt, 2011)

The argument from cost is a generic argument, in the sense that it does not stem from a liberal point of view, but could be made by anyone, whatever their ideological commitment, and it is easily refuted (Torry, 2017d; 2018c; 2019a). In response to Richardt's more ideological argument: The world has become more complex, and yes, we are more vulnerable. In these circumstances, a secure income base alongside existing forms of security would enhance individual freedom.

Socialism

Socialism is one of the political strands that emerged with an industrial working-class. Trades unions evolved to protect and enhance the rights of workers, and to extract the maximum possible share of the proceeds of production for labour, whereas socialism envisages the transformation of society in a co-operative and egalitarian direction. These two strands, and more (Spicker, 2014: 194–5), have frequently jostled for influence in political parties, such as the UK's Labour Party, which was founded to serve working-class interests but has often been controlled or heavily influenced by more middle-class socialists (Garner et al., 2009: 119, 123).

'Socialism' has a variety of meanings. It can mean

- an end in view: that is, a society in which all contribute according to their ability, and all consume according to their needs, in perfect harmony and without coercion;
- socialist parties gaining power democratically, nationalizing industries, and employing the profits to improve public services;
- workers managing industries;
- redistribution from rich to poor;
- local control of the means of production; and
- co-operative enterprises that distribute profits to workers.

Underlying all of these meanings lies a conviction that all human beings are fundamentally equal, and that that equality needs to be given effect in social and economic arrangements.

A particular variant of socialism is communism, which seeks

the abolition of private property ... Communism deprives no man of the power to appropriate the products of society; all that it does is to deprive him of the power to subjugate the labour of others by means of such appropriation. ... The first step in the revolution by the working-class is to raise the proletariat to the position of ruling class, to win the battle of democracy. The proletariat will use its political supremacy to wrest, by degrees, all capital from the bourgeoisie, to centralize all instruments of production in the hands of the State, i.e., of the proletariat organized as the ruling class; and to increase the total of productive forces as rapidly as possible. (Marx and Engels, [1888] 1967: 96, 99, 104)

Marx goes on to argue that workers should be drafted into industrial armies to staff state-run factories (Marx and Engels, [1888] 1967: 105). A partial realization of this policy occurs when socialist or semi-socialist governments nationalize major industries: a situation that we might call 'state capitalism'. This is a practice often plagued by the inefficiencies that result from monopoly, and by financial losses resulting from a combination of inefficiency and price controls. Employment practices can be diverse (Benn, 1974: 31).

Democracy does not always deliver socialist governments, and socialism is sometimes found in non-democratic states, so a further variant of socialism is democratic socialism: 'the supremacy of conscience over the law ... the accountability of power to the people ... the sovereignty of the people over Parliament' (Benn, 1974: 165). This is 'socialism from below', and a more idealistic and global idea of it looks to 'the power of the working-class to transform society ... The working people of the world would co-operate together, rather than being chained to warring nation-states' (Callinicos, 1983: 9, 20). More often, democratic socialism means a freely elected socialist government employing the proceeds of a free market economy to equalize net incomes and provide adequate public services (Garner et al., 2009: 123), so that 'people who cannot contribute fully to social production are still entitled to share substantially in its wealth ... in which inequalities of ability and differences of social function do not crystallize into major and persistent social inequalities of wealth and power' (Breitenbach et al., 1990: 22).

It is easy to see how socialists can understand Citizen's Basic Income as a meeting of needs that we all share in common, and as a means towards equalizing net incomes (providing, of course, that the Citizen's Basic Income scheme implemented, including the associated changes to the existing tax and benefits systems, does in fact redistribute from rich to poor). In theory, the primacy of providing for everyone's needs implies that reciprocity has to be understood as the individual responding to an income and services that are provided without conditions attached: a version of reciprocity in which rights are prior to obligation. As Pateman puts it:

> We all rely every day, to a large extent implicitly, on countless acts that look forward to other reciprocal acts that we expect in the future, or reflect actions that have assisted us in the past; we rely, that is, on the performance

of duties. Reciprocity stretches over time and space. Neither mothers nor all those engaged in caring work or education demand an immediate reciprocal contribution from, for example, young children, the sick, infirm, elderly, or pupils in return for benefits; their work is not conditional upon a contribution. Indeed, love, not expectation of reciprocity, is seen as motivating the work of wives and mothers. Providing for the welfare of citizens and the work of, and time devoted to, the social reproduction of citizens who can actively participate in a democratic polity cannot depend on immediate reciprocal contributions. (Pateman, 2005: 56)

Reciprocation would emerge if everyone were to be given a Citizen's Basic Income, because 'most people do not want to be idle' (Pateman, 2005: 52): and, in the context of a Citizen's Basic Income, reciprocation in the form of paid employment would be more likely to occur for any household that found itself removed from means-tested benefits (Pateman, 2005: 53, 54, 56). None of this means that Citizen's Basic Income would not be experienced by policymakers as a political risk in a context in which public opinion appears to favour paying benefits only to the 'deserving' and to those who are actively seeking paid employment (Sage and Diamond, 2017: 27). On the other hand, neither the UK's Child Benefit, nor its National Health Service, which is free at the point of use, are experienced as illegitimate, which rather suggests that, once in place, an unconditional and therefore universal benefit or service can be regarded as legitimate social policy by a public still concerned to restrict benefits only to those believed to be deserving of them.

An argument for Citizen's Basic Income that goes to the heart of a socialist ideology is made by Alex Callinicos:

One of the attractions of the idea that every citizen be granted as of right a basic income set, say, at a level that would allow them to meet their socially recognised subsistence needs is that it could help to emancipate workers from the dictatorship of capital. Such a basic income would radically alter the bargaining power between labour and capital, since potential workers would now be in a position, if they chose, to pursue alternatives to paid employment. Moreover, because all citizens would receive the same basic income ... , its introduction would be an important step towards establishing equality of access to advantage. (Callinicos, 2003: 134; cf. Dean, 2012c: 125–6)

Breitenbach, Burden and Coates argue that a Citizen's Basic Income would reduce inequality and end the 'dull compulsion to labour' and 'the pre-eminent place of commodity production under capitalism' (Breitenbach et al., 1990: 31), and they regard the purpose of Citizen's Basic Income to be

> to reduce the extent of reliance on wage labour as the determinant of individual and household incomes. The existence of the basic income would also reduce the proportional inequality between the highest and the lowest personal and household incomes since it would represent a higher proportional addition to the funds available to low-income recipients. The universal basic income would also perform another important function: it would allow individuals to choose whether to work or not. Initially, basic income would need to be set at a level low enough just to allow a bare existence without income from work for those who wished to live in this way. It seems to us unlikely that many people would actually choose this as a mode of life except for short periods, but the fact that it would be possible to live in this fashion would considerably reduce the monitoring, surveillance and enforcement of regulations on the duty to work that would otherwise be necessary. (Breitenbach et al., 1990: 33)

A Citizen's Basic Income would encourage self-employment and co-operatives, provide people with more of a choice between part-time and full-time paid employment (Breitenbach et al., 1990: 81–2, 78), provide an income for those caring for others, and encourage artistic activity (Breitenbach et al., 1990: 93, 108). In the longer term, it could become 'an equal dividend for all citizens from the wealth they collectively produce' (Breitenbach et al., 1990: 141).

The most significant of the arguments against Citizen's Basic Income offered by socialists is that it would be a 'subsidy to wages': 'Employers should be compelled to meet the costs of employing the labour from which they derive a benefit' (Esam et al., 1985: 53). This is a fair argument: but what Esam, Good and Middleton fail to recognize is that current in-work and out-of-work means-tested benefits function as a 'dynamic' subsidy, which rises if wages fall, and therefore imposes substantial downward pressure on wages, whereas Citizen's Basic Income would be a 'static' subsidy that would not change, whatever happened to wages; neither do they recognize that an Income Tax Personal Allowance functions as a subsidy to wages, and that replacing it with a cash payment of the same value would make no difference to wage levels. A second complaint is that to pay a Citizen's Basic Income would make 'economic planning' impossible. Esam, Good and Middleton would rather see 'selective subsidies to those jobs which met collectively determined needs for employment and for services' (Esam et al., 1985: 53): but they do not say why paying such subsidies could not work happily alongside a revenue neutral Citizen's Basic Income scheme. A third complaint is that a Citizen's Basic Income would not solve the problem of inequality. This is of course true: but it is no argument against a Citizen's Basic Income.

The clear relationship between Citizen's Basic Income – the same income for everyone of the same age – and the equality at the heart of socialism might suggest that socialists should have no difficulty supporting Citizen's Basic Income. But every socialist will experience their own bundle of ideas and motivations, not all of which will be equally informed by their socialism: so it should be no surprise that socialists can be found on all sides of the debate.

Conservatism

During our brief discussions of socialism and liberalism we have noted a certain amount of diversity among proponents of the ideologies, but in relation to conservatism we have to recognize that there has been a substantial shift. For instance, the post-war British Conservative Party was genuinely 'conservative' in that it aimed to preserve tried and tested institutions, which by then included a welfare state; but during the 1970s it was heavily influenced by the New Right and became more attached to the ideology of free markets than to the pragmatism that had characterized previous conservatism (Garner et al., 2009: 125).

For the previous conservatism, society is a complex organism that has evolved useful social structures, within which a meritocracy works to the benefit of society. Because interference in these structures can have unforeseen consequences, the state should take a pragmatic view, and policy changes should be small and careful. Free markets are generally efficient, but they too can have consequences, so society, and therefore government, has an obligation to assist people who find themselves disadvantaged. This 'one nation' conservatism was the birthplace of the rise in interest in Citizen's Basic Income in the UK during the early 1980s:

> There is a strong emphasis in policy today on the need for what in the jargon is called 'targeting' of state resources on the most needy. This is a popular approach which at first glance seems to make eminent good sense. Yet beneath the surface of this apparently attractive proposition lurks a frightening void – which we call the poverty trap. The more you relate benefits to some measure of means (and also, the lower down the income scale you take income taxation), the greater the deterrent to benefit recipients to lift their earnings. ... Here, in the impenetrably complex brew of benefits, thresholds, tax allowances, penalties and disregards, we have the makings of that strange paradox whereby unemployment and labour shortage co-exist, where saving makes you poorer, where a subculture of benefit dependency flourishes. (David Howells MP, in Rhys Williams, 1989: vii–viii)

Governments have an obligation not to interfere in people's lives, but means-tested benefits do interfere, and in particular with employment incentives (Rhys Williams, 1989: 16), the solution is 'a partial basic income payment for all' (David Howells MP, in Rhys Williams, 1989: viii), which would not make it less likely that people would seek employment because 'there is no reason to suppose that people on low incomes react differently to increased economic incentives than people who are rich' (Rhys Williams, 1989: 35–6).

One Nation Conservatives saw the emerging European institutions as helpful to the stability of the free markets that they wished to see, and therefore Citizen's Basic Income as 'the basis of a Europe-wide process of reform, underpinning the growth of the great Single Market. Above all, it [is] a *translucent* process which people would genuinely understand, as against the murky pattern of today' (David Howells MP, in Rhys Williams, 1989: viii). A Citizen's Basic Income would encourage 'small-scale capital ownership to spread and deepen, so as to create a genuine capital-owning democracy and the "share economy" – the modern version of One Nation' (David Howells MP, in Rhys Williams, 1989: viii).

> We need liberation for the millions held in dependency on state benefits to take work without committing a crime; liberation for savers to accumulate fortunes and put them to work fruitfully, without the risk of confiscatory taxation; liberation of women, so that they become wholly equal citizens whether single or married; and liberation for employers from needless, costly paperwork. (Rhys Williams, 1989: 22)

As Brandon Rhys Williams said of the UK's Child Benefit:

> It is one of the easiest benefits to administer and take-up is almost 100 per cent … it is far, far too low. … Child benefit helps all families equally. My answer to those who attack it on the grounds that rich families do not need it, is to say that child benefit does not belong either to the father or to the mother, but is the start of a life-long relationship of obligation and entitlement between the child as junior citizen and the community. (Rhys Williams, 1989: 28)

During the 1980s, the Conservative Party in the UK, along with other parties in the same tradition, turned in the direction of the 'New Right', which Anthony Giddens defines in terms of

> minimal government, autonomous civil society, market fundamentalism, moral authoritarianism (plus strong economic individuation), a labour market which clears like any other, acceptance of inequality, traditionalist nationalism, the welfare state as a safety net, linear modernization, low ecological consciousness, a realist theory of the international order … . The welfare state is seen as the source of all evils in much the same way capitalism once was by the revolutionary left. (Giddens, 1998: 8, 13)

This is not exactly conservative, in the normal sense of that word. Time-honoured institutions that stand in the way of the free market can be happily dispensed with – including society:

> There is no such thing as society. There is living tapestry of men and women and people and the beauty of that tapestry and the quality of our lives will depend upon how much each of us is prepared to take responsibility for ourselves and each of us prepared to turn round and help by our own efforts those who are unfortunate. (Thatcher, 1987)

There might not be 'society', but there are other corporate entities, such as the 'underclass':

> Britain has a growing population of working-aged healthy people who live in a different world from other Britons, who are raising their children to live in it, and whose values are now contaminating the life of entire neighbourhoods ... large numbers of young, healthy, low-income males choose not to take jobs ... A key to an underclass is ... a situation in which a very large proportion of an entire community lacks fathers. (Murray, 1996: 25, 37, 33)

Whether among individuals, nations, or organizations, relationships are understood in terms of contracts freely entered into. A minimal state that does not over-regulate markets is an obvious requirement. For this reason, and because income redistribution might be thought to interfere with the efficiency of the employment market, 'it is only a modest degree of redistribution which can be justified in the name of relieving poverty' (Joseph and Sumption, 1979: 27).

The New Right's positive interest in Citizen's Basic Income is a result both of its concern to avoid 'dependency at the bottom of society' (Mead, 1992: ix) and of its desire to reduce the extent of the welfare state, which authors like Murray regard as a cause of poverty rather than as its solution. Thus Murray would like to see much of the current welfare state *replaced* by a Citizen's Basic Income (Murray, 1984: 227, 230; 1996: 50). The mechanism that Murray proposes is a Negative Income Tax, but he could have made the same argument for a Citizen's Basic Income: that at a sufficient level it would remove the possibility of applying for means-tested cash benefits, and would therefore remove any employment market disincentive (Murray, 1996: 125). So yes, it would be possible to replace an existing means-tested benefits system with a high enough Citizen's Basic Income. However, other parts of the welfare state could not be replaced in this way. In the UK context, the National Health Service exhibits unconditional access at the point of need, whereas Child Benefit exhibits unconditional provision. The one kind of unconditionality cannot be substituted for the other. Only those welfare programmes that together cost the same for every single individual of the same age could be replaced by an unconditional income. The burden of proof lies with Charles Murray to prove that this would be the case. If this is not understood then there remains a clear danger that a Citizen's Basic Income could be used to dismantle existing welfare states. If it *is* understood, then to implement a Citizen's Basic Income scheme could enhance existing welfare states, and could contribute to creating the kinds of reinvigorated welfare states that our societies now need (Haagh, 2019a: 138–52).

From the perspective of New Right Conservatism, the strongest argument for Citizen's Basic Income is that it would not interfere with employment market decisions in the same way that means-tested benefits do, and that it would therefore make the employment market more efficient for both workers and employers. The argument against Citizen's Basic Income that comes most naturally is the 'safety net' argument: that the state's only welfare function is to prevent destitution, and not to provide everyone with an income. In the UK, this was heard most clearly at the 2010 Conservative Party Conference when the Chancellor of the Exchequer told the audience that households containing higher rate taxpayers would have their Child Benefit withdrawn. Televised members of the audience suggested that 'the money should be targeted on the poor'. (Child Benefit was not in fact means-tested in the way promised, because there is no database that connects Child Benefit recipients with higher rate taxpayers: so instead, additional Income Tax is charged to high earners in households that receive Child Benefit.) The 'safety net' argument is just one possible interpretation of the 'minimal state'. Another way to work towards a minimal state would be to get the bureaucratic state out of people's lives by paying the same unconditional income to every legal resident of the same age. No active administration would be required between birth and death. A more 'minimal state' welfare system would not be possible.

Ideological and Generic Arguments

The relationships between social policy and political ideologies are always historically determined, with every social policy being the result of a variety of ideological pressures, leading to multiple compromises and therefore complexity (Dean, 2012c: 25). Citizen's Basic Income is a somewhat different kind of social policy. It has a clear definition that cannot be influenced by ideologies. Different Citizen's Basic Income schemes – with the levels of the Citizen's Basic Income specified, and associated changes to existing tax and benefits also specified – can of course be so influenced, and will always no doubt be the result of ideological compromises.

The three political ideologies that we have studied are able to generate arguments for Citizen's Basic Income, and have in fact done so. Arguments against Citizen's Basic Income tend to exhibit little relationship to the ideologies. Arguments from cost (spurious in relation to revenue neutral Citizen's Basic Income schemes), disincentives (spurious in relation to the high marginal deduction rates associated with current means-tested benefits), subsidy effects (ditto), and minimal state (spurious in relation to the bureaucratic interference imposed by means-tested benefits) are all generic arguments that could be made by anyone, whatever their ideological preferences: and they are all easily refuted.

Perhaps what is most interesting about Citizen's Basic Income is the way in which it is both/and: both a facilitator of social cohesion and a route to individual freedom, both a means of freedom and a way to increase equality, and both a response to the problems generated by our current polity and the financial infrastructure for a new 'human development' society (Haagh, 2019a: 12–24, 36–45). It is this both/and nature of Citizen's Basic Income that is arguably unique, and that lies at the root of the arguments in its favour generated by very different political ideologies.

POVERTY

Poverty is not a simple issue, and it is certainly not entirely defined by the amount of disposable income that an individual or a family has available to them. For instance: Who is the poorest: someone with few skills and on means-tested benefits who finds it difficult to raise their disposable income however hard they work; someone on a lower earned income, but not on means-tested benefits, who can easily add to their disposable income by finding a few extra hours of employment when they need to; someone with substantial income and a high investment income but in seriously poor health; someone with two degrees and on a high salary, who is struggling to pay a mortgage and to manage substantial debts; or someone living on a small pension who has sufficient for their needs? The question reveals the difficulty of defining the word 'poverty': and the resulting lack of consensus as to what the word means can lead to it being used with problematic narrow meanings (Spicker, 2014: 90–1; Torry, 2013: 161–8). So, for instance, Brian Abel-Smith and Peter Townsend, in their *The Poor and the Poorest* (Abel-Smith and Townsend, 1965), use 'poverty' to mean simply 'income poverty', which leaves off the agenda such issues as poor housing, inadequate healthcare, and so on. On the other hand, to include every aspect of social policy in a definition of poverty – substandard housing, poor educational provision, low social security benefits, high marginal deduction rates, lack of public transport, inadequate healthcare, and so on

– can compromise the ability to take action to abolish specific difficulties. Resorting to anecdote to explore the meaning of poverty (Donnison, 1982; Seebrook, 1985) is no substitute for consensus about a definition, because without such consensus different participants in a discussion can be using the word in different ways, which means that accurate communication cannot occur, and neither can rational debate. Defining poverty in relation to a different word or phrase turns out to be no solution. For instance, defining 'poverty' as 'unmet needs' assumes that we know what the word 'needs' means, when it has just as diverse and culture-specific a meaning as 'poverty' (Dean, 2010: 24–6, 46–7). All of these problems are compounded by the difficulty of knowing how resources are shared within families, so that a family might be described as in poverty, whereas one of its members might not be, and a family might not be categorized as poor, whereas one or more of its members might be (Pahl, 1983); and are again compounded by the difficulty of knowing precisely what resources a family might have available: for instance, through the informal economy (Jordan et al., 1992).

Perhaps the most serious problem with the word 'poverty' is that it enables us to categorize people as 'in poverty', or as 'poor', when they might not wish to categorize themselves in that way. W.G. Runciman has shown that we compare our circumstances with those of people in social and geographical situations similar to ours, rather than in relation to an agreed standard of living, or to people in very different situations (Runciman, 1966: 18); similarly, Stouffer et al. (1949) have found that our feelings about hardship do not necessarily correlate with any objective measures of it; and work by Bill Jordan and his colleagues on an Exeter housing estate provides additional evidence for these findings, and shows how complex people's understandings of their economic and social situations can often be (Jordan et al., 1992). We are here in the realm of relative rather than absolute poverty: that is, poverty understood as 'exclusion from ordinary living patterns' (Townsend, 1979: 131) through having fewer resources than other people in society, rather than in relation to some objective measure (Fahey, 2010): hence the alternative term 'social exclusion' (Hills et al., 2002).

What can sometimes look like an absolute poverty standard might in fact represent a relative understanding of poverty. Lansley and Mack, in both 1983 and 2015, published the results of surveys designed to discover what resources people in the UK think are required for a decent standard of living in contemporary society (Lansley and Mack, 1983; 2015). The Poverty and Social Exclusion 2012 survey used the same method (Bailey and Bramley, 2018; Dermott, 2018; Mack, 2018); and the same approach generates the Minimum Income Standards researched at Loughborough University for the Joseph Rowntree Foundation (Davis et al., 2018).

An appearance of objectivity masks the socially constructed nature of the process. If capabilities are socially defined, then a similarly relative approach is Amartya Sen's, which asks about the resources required to enable someone to exercise capabilities (Alkire, 2007: 91; Reader, 2006). Somewhat closer to a more absolute definition of poverty lies John Rawls' definition as income below a level that, 'together with the whole family of social policies, maximizes the life prospects of the least advantaged over time' (Rawls, 2001: 129–30; cf. Barrientos, 2016: 154–6); and yet further towards the 'absolute' end of the spectrum lie approaches that start from a concept of human need, with need defined in some normative way (Maslow, 1943: 376–82; Spicker, 2014: 88–108; Townsend, 1979: 32–4): although, as we have seen, need is largely socially constructed (Dean, 2010: 46–7; Spicker, 2014: 89), which means that this approach might also be regarded as an attempt to measure relative rather than absolute poverty.

All of this suggests that poverty is 'socially constructed': that is, we create a category labelled 'poverty' and then we decide who we should put into it. One particularly intriguing consequence of creating such a category is that

> the spectre of poverty will not be eliminated as long as mechanisms for the relief or prevention of poverty remain in place, nor so long as such mechanisms make poverty an object of definition and regulation ... social policies calculated to relieve or prevent poverty in fact sustain poverty as a definable and manageable phenomenon and as a presence in the lives of everybody. (Dean and Melrose, 1999: 27, 48)

Means-tested social security benefits designed to provide for people in poverty tell claimants that they are in poverty, whereas such unconditional and therefore universal benefits as the UK's Child Benefit, and such universal services as the UK's National Health Service, dissolve the 'poverty' category because nobody feels poor if they receive Child Benefit or use the National Health Service.

But this does not mean that we should abandon the concept of poverty, as this might result in even more problems. One way to mitigate the problems of keeping the term would be to qualify the term 'poverty': 'housing poverty', 'health poverty', 'income poverty', and so on. With more restricted categories, it can be easier to develop poverty thresholds (for instance, for income poverty, 60 per cent of the median wage (Cantillon et al., 2019)), easier to find ways to ameliorate particular kinds of poverty (for instance, by increasing the National Minimum Wage), and easier to communicate trends (for instance, that increasing numbers of households are falling below the Joseph Rowntree Foundation Minimum Income Standards (Davis and Padley, 2018)). However, an umbrella term 'poverty' might still be useful as an expression of the multiple deprivations that many families suffer, in both the developing and the developed worlds. To abandon the word might suggest that such complex multiple deprivations no longer exist, when they do (Fée and Kober-Smith, 2018).

A significant characteristic of today's context is the way in which people's incomes vary from month to month (Hills, 2014; Tomlinson, 2018). This suggests that in relation to income poverty, the rather static concepts of relative and absolute poverty might not be as useful as they were, and that we might need a concept of poverty that is more dynamic. Ruth Lister's understanding of social exclusion as a process rather than as a state might be useful to us here. Lister's definition of poverty regards individuals as free agents who are able to seek and implement ways out of poverty, although they might be prevented from doing so by social structures. This means that it is the relationship between those social structures and the individual's agency that defines their poverty (Lister, 2004: 94–7, 145–6, 178–83). We might describe Lister's idea of poverty as an inability, through a combination of social structures and personal history and characteristics, to climb out of a variety of deprivations. This is intuitively correct. If we experience a variety of deprivations but are able to climb out of them, then we would be less likely to call ourselves poor than somebody who was unable to do that. We are socially excluded if we cannot find a route to social inclusion.

Citizen's Basic Income would protect against poverty by establishing virtuous feedback loops. By providing working age adults with more ability to say no to poor quality jobs, job quality would be likely to improve, wages in many less desirable and low wage jobs would have to rise to attract workers, and career progressions would improve, all of which would enable people to climb out of poverty. A Citizen's Basic Income would make it easier to take time out to improve existing skills or to retrain, either full-time or part-time, again improving workers' prospects and providing them with more ways of climbing out of poverty (Taylor-Gooby et al., 2014). The solid financial floor that every individual would have available to them would encourage more self-employment and more small businesses, providing yet more routes out of poverty.

To define poverty as an inability to climb out of deprivation is the beginning of a journey towards finding mechanisms that improve people's ability to climb out of deprivation. Unconditional benefits, and universal provisions and services generally, improve people's ability to climb out of poverty, because such provisions and services are not reduced as other resources rise, whereas means-tested benefits and services prevent people from emerging from deprivation, simply because they lose the benefits and services as other resources rise. So unconditional benefits provide people with 'process freedom', that is, more ability to make choices that can generate 'capabilities freedom': the ability to exercise our capabilities (Sen, 2009: 225–52, 370–1). Not only do universal provisions and services enable people to climb out of poverty: they also provide constant streams of provision, and constant availability of services such as healthcare, and so prevent people from falling into poverty in the first place (Burchardt and Vizard, 2007; Rosner, 2003: xiv–xv). Where provision is always made, deprivation cannot occur.

To increase the unconditional and universal layer of social security provision by implementing a Citizen's Basic Income could both keep people out of poverty, and enable them more easily to climb out of it if they found themselves in it. I say 'could' here, rather than 'would', because the effect of a Citizen's Basic Income being implemented would depend as much on the ways in which the existing tax and benefits systems were adjusted as on the characteristics and effects of the Citizen's Basic Incomes themselves. In the UK, if means-tested benefits were abolished at the same time as a small Citizen's Basic Income was implemented, then many households would find themselves in deeper poverty (Piachaud, 2016: 15; Stapenhurst, 2014; Torry, 2015b). However, Citizen's Basic Income schemes that leave means-tested benefits in place can take a lot of people off those benefits, and can provide a solid financial floor that would never be removed, and would therefore assist individuals and families to lift themselves out of poverty (Torry, 2019a). Citizen's Basic Income is not a handout. It would function as a universal right that would prevent a lot of the poverty experienced by families today (Dean and Melrose, 1999: 172; Sen, 2009; Walter, 1988).

INEQUALITY

Does inequality matter as much as poverty? The answer would appear to be: Yes. First of all, inequality results in lower economic growth rather than the opposite, and it also results in higher economic turbulence (Lansley, 2018); and second, there is empirical evidence to support a causal link between levels of inequality and poverty.

> The evidence we present suggests that for those whose primary concern is with tackling poverty, it is hard to do this in countries such as the UK without simultaneously reducing inequalities, given the strong associations we see between them empirically, and the ways in which inequality can itself act as a driver of poverty. At the same time, for those for whom both poverty and inequality are concerns, the links between them suggest that policies to tackle either can have a double dividend. (Hills et al., 2019)

Following a period between the two world wars during which wealth and income inequalities remained fairly stable, inequality started to rise during the 1960s. Wealth inequality has continued to rise, but the financial crisis of 2007 caused a temporary reduction in income inequality, meaning that levels of income inequality in the UK are now where they were during the 1990s: but the overall level of income inequality as measured by the Gini coefficient masks the fact that inequality has fallen across most of the earnings range at the same time as it has risen at the top. The share of income going to the top 1 per cent has increased from 5.7 per cent to 7.8 per cent since the 1990s (Atkinson, 2015: 105; Cribb et al., 2018: 34). Behind these trends lie globalization and technological change, which have resulted in an increase in the proportion of the proceeds of production going to capital, and a decrease in the proportion going to labour (Crocker, 2019; Piketty, 2014), and in an employment market increasingly divided between high-skilled, well-paid and fairly secure jobs, and jobs that are low-skilled, badly paid, insecure, and often pointless and soul-destroying. Globalization has resulted in globally similar wage levels for individuals with few skills; migration of labour and the ability for production facilities to move across borders have lowered low wages in previously higher-wage economies; financial services can generate high rewards for traders, which increases demand for financial services, causing even higher rewards; and unpaid internships increase inequality of opportunity, which increases income inequality. Increasing skills at the lower end of the earnings range would not address these ubiquitous processes (Turner, 2012). Trades unions' inability to organize most of today's employees, and a reduction in redistribution through the tax and benefits system, have contributed to the stagnation of disposable incomes across most of the incomes range, but not those at the top (Atkinson, 2015: 82; Evans and Williams, 2009: 313; Graeber, 2018).

In 2009, Richard Wilkinson and Kate Pickett suggested that higher income inequality causes a higher incidence of other social ills, such as mental illness and imprisonment (Wilkinson and Pickett, 2009). However, an alternative explanation is available, for which there is evidence in the statistics published by Wilkinson and Pickett: that is, that inequality can only be understood as a diverse reality, involving social class, status, power, and identities (Dean, 2012c: 84–91; Spicker, 2014: 43–50), and that deep social structures are the root of a variety of different inequalities, including income inequality (Bergh et al., 2016: 70; Dorling, 2010; Spicker, 2014: 50–7; Torry, 2010; and see the case study at the end of Chapter 7). This suggests that tackling the deep social structures underlying inequality would be the only way to reduce the different inequalities, and that reducing income inequality alone would not solve the problem. There are 'social ladders' deeply embedded in societies, and particularly in the UK, and only tackling that will enable income, health, educational and other inequalities to be reduced. The concept of a 'social ladder' might suggest that social mobility might be part of the solution. Unfortunately not. First of all, the ability of some individuals to move to higher portions of the ladder might be good for them, and might enable them to realize more of their potential, to their own benefit and to the benefit of society: but that process will not change the ladder itself; and second, the more inequality a society experiences, the less social mobility there will be: so only solving the deeper problem will make widespread social mobility possible (Dickens and McKnight, 2008; Dorling, 2012: 47–8). The ladder needs to look more like a platform; only attention to the roots of the social structure, by addressing differential educational opportunities, wealth disparities, inheritance, and so on, will begin to flatten the ladder; and only doing that will enable the widespread economic and social flourishing that is required.

It is of course true that reducing income inequality could have some useful effects, and could contribute to the reduction of other inequalities: but attempting to reduce income inequality by any available means would not necessarily achieve that. If means-tested benefits were to be increased in order to reduce income inequality – which it would – then society would become more deeply divided, not less. There would be more people deeply buried in poverty traps, more people unable to climb out of poverty, more people with constrained employment market choices, more families subject to intrusive enquiry and demotivating sanctions, more people using food-banks (Garthwaite, 2017), and so on. Employing increased means-tested benefits in an attempt to reduce inequalities would increase the social rift that is 'undermining the effectiveness, inalienability and universality of social citizenship in the UK' (Edmiston, 2017: 267), whereas implementing additional unconditional provisions would start to repair the rift (Dorling, 2010: 245) and to create an emancipatory social citizenship (Patrick, 2017a: 301). (The notion of social citizenship is discussed later in this chapter.)

Wilkinson and Pickett recommend a Citizen's Basic Income (Wilkinson and Pickett, 2009: 263–4). If implemented in conjunction with a progressive tax system, this could reduce income inequality, and by increasing income security, reducing employment disincentives, providing more employment market choices, encouraging skills acquisition, increasing social cohesion, and so on, it could tackle both other particular inequalities and also the social ladder as a whole (Lo Vuolo, 2015: 35). As the roots of inequality are likely to be deep social structures, what needs to change is not the levels of existing benefits, but rather the structure of the benefits system (White, 2007: 84, 93).

Rising inequality is more important than the fact that on average we are better off than we used to be (Evans and Williams, 2009: 315), and tackling it properly will require multiple policies (Atkinson, 2015) that attend to the roots of inequality in deep social structures (Dore, 2001: 84; Dorling, 2017). A Citizen's Basic Income would not be the answer to all of our global social and economic inequalities (Haagh, 2015; Lo Vuolo, 2015), but a Citizen's Basic Income scheme that reduced income inequality would begin to change the deeper structures of society, which would reduce both income inequality and a variety of other kinds as well.

REDISTRIBUTION

As Citizen's Basic Income is an income, we shall be discussing redistribution of income: which is not to say that the highly unequal distribution of wealth is not a problem. It is: but all that needs to be said here is that redistribution of income would contribute to the redistribution of wealth. We shall be discussing 'vertical' redistribution rather than 'horizontal' redistribution: that is, redistribution between households with different levels of income, and not redistribution between households with similar incomes; we shall be addressing redistribution from one group to another (for instance, from women to men, and from families with children to families without them), and not between different time periods in relation to the same household (Parker, 1989: 303–17; Spicker, 2014: 59–60); we shall be studying 'dynamic' redistribution, that is, the changes in existing redistributive mechanisms that policy change would achieve, rather than the redistribution that goes on constantly through the tax and benefits systems. Dynamic redistribution can be either positive or negative, depending on whether increasing or decreasing amounts are redistributed from rich to poor. In the UK, dynamic redistribution is currently negative (Corlett et al., 2018: 7): so we shall therefore be asking about Citizen's Basic Income schemes that might turn it positive.

But how much positive redistribution is desirable, and how much is feasible? (Spicker, 2014: 60–2). The amount of redistribution that is possible is likely to be less than might be desirable. If income tax rates rise, then hours of employment are worth less in monetary terms, so leisure time might be substituted for employment hours, which would cause tax revenues to fall and redistribution to be less possible. Increases in consumption taxes would cause fewer goods and services to be purchased, fewer people would be employed, income tax revenue would fall, and again it would become more difficult to redistribute income. Tax bases that would not decline if taxes were raised would be a country's population and a country's land area. The UK's attempt to impose a 'community charge' (a poll tax) on every individual was brought to an end by widespread street protests. Taxing the value of land, if carefully done, ought not to have the same result: although political pressure from large landowners might make legislation difficult to pass. It is difficult to think of a new tax that would not meet with some political counterpressure: which means that tax-raising powers will always be limited in their effectiveness, positive dynamic redistribution will always be difficult to achieve (Atkinson, 2015: 5–11), and only short-term and marginal positive dynamic redistribution will be possible, with its extent dependent on the ideological commitments of a population and its government. While socialism might suggest positive dynamic redistribution, a liberal ideology could go either way: we could argue that additional taxation would reduce the freedom of those taxed; and also that not to redistribute from rich to poor would reduce the practical economic and social freedoms of the poorest in society. Rather than see growing inequality and its causes widely discussed, wealthier members of society in the UK with control of the media and of the Conservative Party have offered the European Union as a scapegoat to poorer members of society. Those with most to lose have believed the message, have voted to leave the European Union, and have helped the wealthy to distract everyone's attention from the real causes of inequality, which lie in our society's deeper social structures (Torry, 2010). We are left with increasingly stigmatized redistribution falling to a level that foodbanks can still just about cope with.

There will always be liberals who understand that additional redistribution can increase the sum of personal freedom; socialists who would like to see redistribution bring all of us closer to income equality; 'one nation' conservatives who recognize the need to provide adequately for poorer members of society; utilitarians who understand that a poorer person's utility will increase more than a wealthier person's utility will decrease if additional redistribution takes place (Arneson, 2002); Christians for whom the doctrine of God's grace – that is, God's unconditional love – implies unconditional incomes paid in such a way as to increase redistribution (Torry, 2016b: 22–30, 36–41); adherents of other religious and ethical traditions who wish to see increased redistribution; and in particular those attracted to social policy characterized by unconditional gifts (Collard, 1978) and to such examples of it as the UK's National Health Service that invites reciprocating voluntary blood donation (Titmuss, 1970). However, the problem for the UK and many increasingly secular and pluralistic societies, is that no one of these motives will by itself shift the policy agenda (Marshall, 1981). Only if a sufficient number of individuals, with different motivations and ideologies, want to see increased redistribution, will it happen (George and Wilding, 1984: 117). As R.H. Tawney has suggested,

> those who dread a dead-level of income or wealth, which is not at the moment a very pressing danger in England, do not dread, it seems, a dead-level of law and order, and of security for life and property (Tawney, 1964: 86)

– which means that seeking greater equality of opportunity might be more productive than campaigning for greater income equality (Tawney, 1964: 42).

There are of course Citizen's Basic Income schemes that would *de*crease redistribution: for instance, those that funded Citizen's Basic Incomes by adding Value Added Tax to food and clothes. But there are also feasible schemes that would *in*crease redistribution from rich to poor without imposing significant losses on low income households and without impos-ing unsustainable losses on any households (Parker and Sutherland, 1994: 6–8; Torry, 2019a). Because poorer households exhibit a greater propen-sity to consume in the local economy than wealthier households, both the increased redistribution and the new solid financial foundation that poorer households would experience would contribute to economic growth (Ehrenfreund, 2015; Hobijn and Nussbacher, 2015; Irvin et al., 2009: 15; Van Parijs, 1990: 12). It is not inequality that drives economic growth: it is increasing equality (Rowlingson, 2011: 35–6). Increases in individual freedom and social cohesion would be welcome additional outcomes (Pressman, 2005: 97).

A Citizen's Basic Income scheme that redistributed from income-rich to income-poor would be able to gather support across the political spectrum, and would also provide some protection against falling back into negative dynamic redistribution (Harrop, 2012: 9).

REDISTRIBUTING THE ABILITY TO RAISE NET DISPOSABLE INCOME

We have already asked whether poverty should be discussed in static or dynamic terms, and we have now adopted a similar approach in relation to redistribution. A further useful distinction might be that between the redis-tribution of income and the redistribution of the opportunity to increase one's disposable income.

There are many reasons why households might find it difficult to raise their net disposable incomes. Their members' upbringings might have left them with psychological challenges, few skills, or both; they might be in ill health or living with disabilities; they might live in places in which major industries, for which they possessed skills, have disappeared; or they might be suffering from the high marginal deduction rates related to in-work or out-of-work means-tested benefits: that is, as their earned incomes rise, the withdrawal of benefits at the same time as income tax begins to be paid might mean that they keep very little of their additional earnings. In the UK, marginal deduction rates of 75 per cent or more are common, meaning that for every additional £1 of earned income, the household increases its disposable income by only 25p. This seems unjust when higher earners experience marginal deduction rates of no more than 47 per cent (Standing, 2017a: 36; Torry, 2018a: 4, 11): and even more unjust when twenty economists feel able to write to the *Financial Times* to suggest that the 50 per cent income tax rate for very high earnings, introduced in the UK after the 2008 financial crisis, should be reduced back to 45 per cent because it was inhibiting economic growth, without mentioning the far higher marginal deduction rates suffered by people on low incomes (Julius et al., 2011). It is this combination of factors that restricts the ability of people on low earned incomes to increase their net disposable incomes. There is no reason to think that it is because household members are lazy (Hills, 2014): so it is not surprising that sanctions policies that make that assumption turn out to be disincentivizing and counterproductive (Welfare Reform Team, Oxford City Council, 2016).

Just as equality of opportunity is arguably more important than equality of income (Heywood, 1999: 290–2), the inequality in people's ability to raise their disposable incomes is a more significant problem than the inequality of their current disposable incomes: because to enhance someone's ability to increase their disposable income could result in a constant ability to raise disposable income, whereas to raise someone's disposable income would not necessarily enable them to continue to raise their incomes. If additional means-tested benefits were to be used to raise disposable incomes, then it might become even more difficult for someone to raise their income themselves. A fair tax and benefits system would be one in which marginal deduction rates were at least equal across the earnings range, and arguably a fairer system would be one in which marginal deduction rates at the lower end of the earnings range were lower than those at the top. If that were to happen, then we would worry somewhat less about income inequality, because it would be easier for people to increase their disposable incomes by increasing their earned incomes.

A Citizen's Basic Income, of whatever size, would either take people off means-tested benefits, or it would increase people's ability to take themselves off them by earning additional income. Depending on the details of the Citizen's Basic Income scheme, we might also see some immediate redistribution from rich to poor (Torry, 2017d: 10; 2018c: 9; 2019a: 26–7): but whether we did or not, we would certainly see a significant number of escapes from means-testing, and therefore from the associated high marginal deduction rates, stigma, and bureaucratic intrusion associated with it.

CITIZENSHIP

A citizen is a 'legally recognized subject or national of a state, commonwealth, or other polity, either native or naturalized, having certain rights, privileges, or duties' (Oxford English Dictionary). For the purpose of this book we have called an unconditional and nonwithdrawable income for every individual a Citizen's Basic Income. We could equally well have called it a Citizen's Income. Either way, the names suggest that Citizen's Basic Income's unconditionality will be compromised to the extent that the otherwise unconditional incomes will be paid only to individuals who are 'legally recognized subjects or nationals of the state, commonwealth, or other polity' in which the Citizen's Basic Income is to be implemented.

The question of who is a citizen, and what their rights and obligations might be, is therefore central to the concerns of this book: and it is a particularly significant concern to this chapter, because politics is 'the science or study of government and the state' (Oxford English Dictionary), citizens are citizens of a state, governments govern citizens, and, in democracies, citizens elect governments. As Tony Fitzpatrick has suggested, 'the ideological debate concerning [Citizen's Basic Income] is, at its heart, a debate about citizenship' (Fitzpatrick, 1999: 15).

Citizenship is different in different places: most UK residents are subjects of a monarch rather than formal citizens, but we possess a number of evolved citizenship rights, whereas China has formal citizens, but they possess fewer democratic rights (Oliver and Heater, 1994: 5). As we have seen, citizenship is defined in relation to a 'national' of a 'nation', concepts that can have just as diverse meanings as 'citizen', because 'nation' can mean territorial boundaries, a shared history, a shared culture, a shared language, or such institutions as citizenship (Spicker, 2014: 32), and these different definitions do not necessarily place the same people in the same nation. Belgium can be understood as one nation in relation to its territory and institutions, or as two in relation to culture and language (French and Flemish), with the two nations also having somewhat distinct territories within the one territory of the one nation. The United Kingdom is even more complex, with its English, Welsh, Scottish, and (Northern) Irish identities, its diversity of languages (English, Welsh, Gaelic, and Irish), its diverse histories, and its many diverse cultures.

Equally diverse are the layers of citizenship that we experience today: local, national, regional (for instance, European), and global (Handy, 1994: 101; Oliver and Heater, 1994: 7).

> The study of citizenship has to concern itself with all those dimensions which allow or exclude the participation of people in the communities in which they live and the complex pattern of national and international relations and processes which cut across them. (Held, 1984: 203)

While each person will experience their various citizenships differently (Lewis, 2004), the nation state will generally be experienced as the foundational layer of citizenship: although, as Aneesh points out, the growth of dual and multiple citizenships is beginning to dissolve the predominance of single nation state citizenship (Aneesh, 2016: 197). More local citizenships (such as those of states in federal countries, and of the separate nations in the UK) are usually, but not always, viewed as subsidiary citizenships; and such broader citizenships, such as European and global citizenships, are generally understood as extensions of national citizenship (Purdy, 1990: 9): although the increasing fluidity of citizenships means that as single nation state citizenship weakens, both more cosmopolitan and more local citizenships might strengthen (Aneesh, 2016): a process that perhaps ought to be encouraged, and might in fact be encouraged by a Citizen's Basic Income that would reduce the prevalence of mean-tested benefits and provide time-use options that might encourage the revitalization of local social institutions (Parker, 2015: x).

Citizenship Rights

In 1950, T.H. Marshall suggested that citizenship rights have evolved through three stages: civil rights (legal rights relating to contracts), political rights (the right to participate in democratic government), and social rights (the welfare state) (Heywood, 1999: 210–13). This constitutes something of a dilemma in relation to the structure of this book. Discussion of civil rights might legitimately have been placed in Chapter 13 on law; political rights in this chapter; and social rights in Chapter 9 on social policy, Chapter 12 on political economy, or Chapter 8 on sociology. But as the different kinds of rights belong within the same evolutionary process, it is important to discuss them together, and the somewhat arbitrary decision has been taken to include the discussion in this chapter on politics.

Marshall describes social rights like this:

> By the social element I mean the whole range from the right to a modicum of economic welfare and security to the right to share to the full in the social herit-

age and to live the life of a civilized being according to the standards prevailing in the society. (Marshall, 1950: 10–11)

Martin Golding has suggested that welfare rights came first (Golding, 1972: 135–6): but in the UK it might be better to regard them as having arrived together with civil and political rights: the Charter of the Forest, which granted rights to food and fuel, was published in 1217, just two years after Magna Carta, which was more about ecclesiastical and civil rights (Standing, 2017b).

However we view the evolution of citizenship rights, we should regard none of the evolutionary stages as irreversible. Social citizenship rights (Marshall's third evolutionary stage) will always be particularly vulnerable. This is important, because without social rights it is difficult to exercise civil or political rights: so if social rights begin to fail, then both civil and political rights will be more vulnerable (Coote, 1996; Heywood, 1999: 213–15; Reynolds and Healy, 1993: 8; Roche, 1992: 4, 16, 167).

Marshall thought that economic rights were a subset of social rights (Marshall, 1950: 10–11), but they could equally well be regarded as foundational rights (Heywood, 1999: 211) because without economic resources it can be difficult to exercise any of the other rights (Melden, 1981: 276; van Gunsteren, 1978). We might therefore regard the establishment of a Citizen's Basic Income as not simply an economic or social right, but as a foundation making possible the exercise of all civil, political, social and economic rights (Barry, 1990): a foundation that means-tested benefits cannot deliver because the stigma attached to them threatens the integrity of the self that needs to exercise rights (Twine, 1994: 97), and their increasing conditionality makes it difficult to regard the claimant as having a right to them (Dwyer, 2019; Watts and Fitzpatrick, 2018). A rights-based approach is sometimes criticized for ignoring the structural roots of social problems and concentrating on enabling the individual to extract what they can from efforts to ameliorate the problems caused by unjust social structures (Dean, 2012c: 103–4). Citizen's Basic Income might be one of a relatively few social policies that would both address the unjust social structures and establish a social right that would underpin other social rights.

In 1990, the Commission on Citizenship, recommended

that a floor of adequate social entitlements should be maintained, monitored and improved when possible by central government, with the aim of enabling every citizen to live the life of a civilized human being according to the standards prevailing in society. (Commission on Citizenship, 1990: xix)

Two important criteria for the provision of social rights are administrative simplicity and lack of stigma (Commission on Citizenship, 1990: 21). It is not difficult to draw the obvious conclusion.

Citizenship Duties

Granting someone a right assumes that someone else will ensure that that right can be exercised: that is, they will provide the resources or institutions through which civil, political, social and economic rights can be exercised (Culpit, 1992; Plant, 1988: 73). A fundamental duty is to pay the taxes required to fund the institutions and services required; and a subsidiary duty has often been assumed to be the duty to seek gainful employment, and to accept employment if it is offered (Heywood, 1999: 216–18). This obligation made sense in a world of full employment: but now that the demand for labour can move at short notice from one side of the planet to the other, and the opportunity to be employed can therefore disappear; and now that new investment can result in a *loss* of employment, the duty to seek and to accept employment has become problematic (Sherman and Jenkins, 1995: 57; Standing, 2009) and in particular has been deeply compromised by the ubiquity of short-term and zero hour contracts, and by the high marginal deduction rates that severely restrict the amount of net disposable income that employment can provide (Pasma, 2010: 7–9). As Fred Twine has suggested, 'the concept of social interdependence ... provides a powerful rationale for a [Citizen's Basic] Income as a means of sharing in industrial societies where people are dependent upon selling their labour power as a means to life but where this cannot be guaranteed' (Twine, 1994: 167). To understand that 'work' can mean beneficial activity, and therefore both paid employment and unpaid caring and community work, can enable us to recognize the vast amount of 'deleted labour and hidden work' (Pettinger, 2019: 39–47), and to see unpaid work as one way of meeting citizenship duties (Reynolds and Healy, 1993: 69): but changing a mindset in this way is difficult, both for those with paid employment (who might think that those without it should have it) and for those without it (who feel a duty to provide sufficient income for their families, and the stigma of not having paid employment) (Sherman and Jenkins, 1995: 156). For every individual to receive the same unconditional income might help both groups to begin to shift their understandings of work in a way more appropriate to today's employment market; and it might help those incapable of either paid or unpaid work through old age, illness or disability to be as much members of society as those capable of them (Purdy, 1990).

Diverse Citizenship

It is entirely up to a country's government as to whom it regards as a citizen, to whom it grants various citizenship rights, and from whom it expects the fulfilment of citizenship duties, and, in particular, how it treats migrants (Carmel et al., 2011). To take the UK as an example: new acts of parliament and regulations constantly shift the boundaries in relation to who has the right to reside in the UK, and who can exercise which citizenship rights, and in particular who has the right to be gainfully employed and who has a right to receive various benefits and public services (Gardner, 1990: 63). Hartley Dean suggests a fourfold categorization of regime models, each of which has consequences for access to welfare provision:

1. A regime model based on a moral-authoritarian justification that is hostile to migrants and is reminiscent of the Poor Laws: this favours minimum welfare provision;
2. A regime model based on a social-conservative justification that is capable of compassion for migrants, but does not recognize their right to belong: this favours protective (albeit measured) welfare provision;
3. A regime model based on a form of social liberalism, which (perhaps reluctantly) concedes the rights of migrants but expects them to play a part in society if they are to enjoy such rights: this favours conditional welfare provision;
4. A regime model based on a social-democratic justification that is capable of welcoming migrants and including them as citizens: this favours universal welfare provision (Dean, 2011a: 25–6).

Dean then adds a fifth model: 'global citizenship': and it is only within this model that 'migration without borders' makes sense (Dean, 2011a: 32). This global citizenship challenges the other four models:

1. The threat it poses to the moral-authoritarian construction is that 'aliens' would compete with natives for scarce resources.
2. The threat it poses to the social-conservative construction is that too many 'guests' would place strains on social solidarity and the social order.
3. The threat it poses to the liberal construction is that unproductive 'settlers' might drag down economic competitiveness.
4. The threat it poses to the social-democratic construction is that the diversity of new 'members'' needs might challenge the principles of universality on which social provision is founded (Dean, 2011a: 33).

Such regional citizenships as European Union citizenship can also challenge regime types. For instance, a German citizen moving to France possesses citizenship rights and duties as much determined by their European citizenship as by their national citizenship or by the laws about citizenship of the country to which they are moving (Heywood, 1999: 212; Lister, 1997: 65).

The diverse citizenship that we have discovered asks some significant questions in relation to how a Citizen's Basic Income might be implemented: To whom should a Citizen's Basic Income be paid? Should it be implemented within national, more local, or regional boundaries? (A discussion of a Eurodividend – a Citizen's Basic Income for the European Union – can be found in Chapter 8). If a Citizen's Basic Income were to be implemented within national boundaries, would it act as more of a magnet to migration than existing benefits, and would public and parliamentary opinion then demand increasingly strict immigration controls? (Howard, 2006). The problem with answering such questions in an often febrile political and media context is that the ways in which questions are framed and answered can sometimes have little relationship with genuine information (Perkiö et al., 2019). For instance: when migration and social security benefits are discussed together in the UK, the debate tends to be entirely about EU migrants claiming benefits in the UK. Rarely is it mentioned that far more Britons are claiming benefits in other EU countries than there are migrants from other EU states claiming benefits in the UK (Nardelli et al., 2015).

The Effects of a Citizen's Basic Income on Citizenship

A Citizen's Basic Income 'would … institutionalize citizenship principles and the social rights of citizenship' (Roche, 1992: 185), which Roche understands to be universality, equality, and participation. It would strengthen citizenship rights, and in particular social and economic rights; and it would facilitate the fulfilment of citizenship duties, for instance, by incentivizing employment for any household that it took off means-tested benefits. A particular citizenship-enhancing aspect of Citizen's Basic Income is that it would force decisions to be made as to who should receive it, and it would therefore fix a new boundary around a citizenry, and declare to everyone within that boundary that they were in fact citizens with a set of citizenship rights.

Iris Young has expressed concern that the idea of citizenship might have a homogenizing effect because it includes everyone in a country in the same category. She would like to see a diverse citizenship that can include very different groups of people (Young, 1989: 251; cf. Dahrendorf, 1974).

This is precisely the kind of diverse citizenship that a Citizen's Basic Income would encourage, because it would never specify how the money should be spent. It would therefore contribute to social solidarity, cultural diversity, and individual freedom, all at the same time. This would be enormously helpful as our society globalizes and diversifies.

Citizenship is always 'a social creation, constituted out of symbols of one sort or another' (Goodin, 1988: 85), and a Citizen's Basic Income being paid to every individual citizen would provide a country with a symbol that would express and create a citizenship, that would enhance social cohesion, and that would provide a foundation for economic citizenship rights that would enable citizens to exercise their civil, political and social citizenship rights, and provide them with a desire and an ability to exercise the citizenship duties that a society needs its citizens to undertake (Barrientos and Pellissery, 2011: 6; Dahrendorf, 1991; 1995: vii, 86; Lister, 1996: 193; Roche, 1992: 178; Sherman and Jenkins, 1995: 159). As Pateman puts it:

> A basic income is the emblem of full citizenship, and provides the security required to maintain that political standing and individual self-government. Both the vote and a basic income can be seen as fundamental rights … . A basic income provides the life-long security that helps safeguard other rights, ensures that citizens are able – that is, have the opportunities and means – genuinely to enjoy their freedom, and helps promote respect. (Pateman, 2005: 37, 50)

CONCLUSIONS

Politics, being the study of government and the state, is a vast subject, and here we have only been able to touch on a handful of political ideologies and on just a few of the issues with which politics is concerned: poverty, inequality, redistribution, and citizenship. We could have tackled decentralization/centralization (– Citizen's Basic Income could legitimately be seen as either or both), multinational institutions (– Do they have a role in relation to Citizen's Basic Income, given the idea's potential for redistribution and social cohesion? Might we one day see a Eurodividend across the European Union?), social movements (– Is the Citizen's Basic Income debate an academic field, a social movement, or both?), and elections (– a Citizen's Basic Income could facilitate greater democratic engagement if payment were to be linked to the electoral register). We could have asked the important question: Is Citizen's Basic Income a radical vision, or a minor adjustment to a tax and benefits system? Given the size of that continuing agenda, it is clear that the discipline of politics has much to offer to the Citizen's Basic Income debate.

As for the question: What does the Citizen's Basic Income debate have to offer to politics, as a social reality and as an academic discipline? – the answer is clear: The Citizen's Basic Income debate has already had a major impact on the world of politics, and therefore on the discipline of politics. There is more impact on the way.

CASE STUDY

Three Particular UK Citizen's Basic Income Schemes' Effects on Poverty and Inequality[1]

In this case study, we study the effects of the three Citizen's Basic Income schemes that were tested for financial feasibility in Chapter 9. To repeat the parameters of the schemes:

- For a scheme that pays a Citizen's Basic Income of £65 per week to each working age adult, and reduces the Income Tax Personal Allowance to zero, Child Benefit is increased by £20 per week for each child; for a scheme that pays a Citizen's Basic Income of £70 per week to each working age adult, and reduces the Income Tax Personal Allowance to zero, Child Benefit is increased by £5 per week; and for a scheme that retains an Income Tax Personal Allowance of £4,000 p.a., and pays a working age adult Citizen's Basic Income of £50 per week, Child Benefit is increased by £10 per week.
- Citizen's Basic Income levels for the various age groups will be found in Table 9.1. In all three schemes, the existing National Insurance Basic State Pension is left in place, the National Insurance Contributions Primary Earnings Threshold is reduced to zero, and National Insurance Contributions are collected at 12 per cent on all earned income. The Education Age Citizen's Basic Income is not paid to someone still in full-time education because Child Benefit will still be in payment for them.

We found in Chapter 9 that all three schemes were financially feasible: that is, they were revenue neutral with Income Tax rates raised by 3 percentage points, and they generated a manageable number of household net income losses at the point of implementation. The schemes took significant numbers of households off means-tested benefits.

Table 11.1 shows the effects of the three schemes on poverty and inequality.

---

[1]   See the footnote at the beginning of the case study at the end of Chapter 9.

Table 11.1 Inequality and poverty indices for the three Citizen's Basic Income schemes

Inequality and poverty indices	The current tax and benefits scheme in 2018	The £65 p.w. Citizen's Basic Income scheme. ITPA is zero.	Percentage change in the indices	The £70 p.w. Citizen's Basic Income scheme. ITPA is zero	Percentage change in the indices	The £50 p.w. Citizen's Basic Income scheme. ITPA is £4,000	Percentage change in the indices
Inequality							
Disposable income Gini coefficient	0.3087	0.2756	10.73%	0.2811	8.95%	0.2776	10.09%
Poverty headcount rates							
Total population in poverty	0.16	0.11	29.57%	0.12	23.46%	0.12	26.17%
Children in poverty	0.18	0.11	42.08%	0.14	25.26%	0.13	28.36%
Working age adults in poverty	0.15	0.11	28.17%	0.12	24.78%	0.12	22.72%
Economically active working age adults in poverty	0.06	0.04	37.48%	0.04	32.01%	0.04	31.75%
Elderly people in poverty	0.14	0.12	14.80%	0.12	15.75%	0.09	35.30%

Source: Torry, 2019a. Abbreviation: ITPA: Income Tax Personal Allowance.

We can see that all three schemes would take a substantial number of people out of poverty and would reduce inequality. However, there are differences. The £65 per week Citizen's Basic Income enables us to increase Child Benefit by £20 per week for every child, whereas the other two schemes increase Child Benefit by rather less. Predictably, the £65 per week scheme takes a lot more children out of poverty than the other two schemes. Somewhat less predictably, the scheme with the lowest working age adult Citizen's Basic Income still has a significant impact on poverty and inequality levels.

We can see from Figures 11.1–11.3 that all three of the schemes would redistribute income in a thoroughly useful way, by increasing substantially the average equivalized disposable incomes of low income households, and reducing the average equivalized household net disposable income of the highest income households by manageable amounts. (Equivalized household incomes are adjusted for household composition.) This kind of redistribution pattern is a further indicator of feasibility.

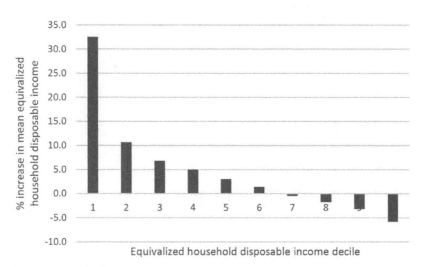

Source: Torry, 2019a.

Figure 11.1   *Increase in mean equivalized household disposable income by equivalized household disposable income decile for the £65 per week Citizen's Basic Income scheme*

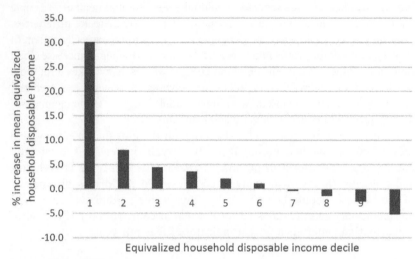

Source: Torry, 2019a.

*Figure 11.2   Increase in mean equivalized household disposable income
                by equivalized household disposable income decile for the
                £70 per week Citizen's Basic Income scheme*

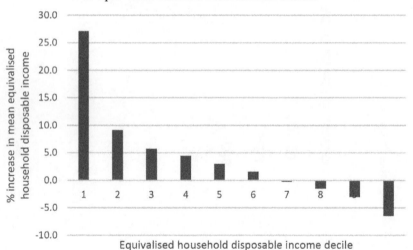

Source: Torry, 2019a.

*Figure 11.3   Increase in mean equivalized household disposable income
                by equivalized household disposable income decile for the
                £50 per week Citizen's Basic Income scheme*

12. The political economy of Citizen's Basic Income

Political economy: The branch of economics dealing with the economic problems of government.
(Oxford English Dictionary)

INTRODUCTION

Precisely what *is* political economy? The eighteenth-century Scottish lawyer James Steuart defined it as 'the science of domestic policy in free nations', and then went on to say that its aim was

> to secure a certain fund of subsistence for all the inhabitants; to obviate every circumstance which may render it precarious; to provide every thing necessary for supplying the wants of the society; and to employ the inhabitants (supposing them to be free-men) in such a manner as naturally to create reciprocal relations and dependencies between them, so as to make their several interests lead them to supply one another with their reciprocal wants. (Steuart, [1767] 1998: 21)

Nine years later, Adam Smith suggested that

> political economy, considered as a branch of the science of a statesman or legislator, proposes two distinct objects: first, to provide a plentiful revenue or subsistence for the people, or more properly to enable them to provide such a revenue or subsistence for themselves; and secondly, to supply the state or commonwealth with a revenue sufficient for the public services. It proposes to enrich both the people and the sovereign. (Smith, [1776] 2001: 557)

The meaning of the term then began to change. At the beginning of the nineteenth century, David Ricardo discussed political economy in terms of value, rent, natural and market price, wages, profits, and taxation (Ricardo, [1817] 2002); and in his essay 'On the Definition of Political Economy; and on the Method of Investigation Proper To It', John Stuart Mill defined political economy as

> a science which traces the laws of such of the phenomena of society as arise from the combined operations of mankind for the production of wealth. (Mill, 1844)

As Raworth points out (2017: 33–4), this evolution shifts political economy from being a tool for obtaining a social objective to being a method for discovering how things work: and it is on this basis that political economy became the modern social science of economics.

This leaves us with something of a dilemma. In Chapter 5 we already have a chapter on the economics of Citizen's Basic Income, so to follow the modern evolution of the term 'political economy' would make this chapter redundant. To follow Steuart and Smith (Steuart, [1767] 1998; Smith, [1776] 2001: 557) might at first sight appear to be a fruitful approach, because the implementation of a Citizen's Basic Income would partially fulfil the objectives that they describe. However, their definition of political economy could bring the whole of the content of this book into this single chapter. Dividing out a distinctively 'political economy' approach would be impossible.

If the meaning of language is its use (Wittgenstein, [1953] 2001: §1, 2), then perhaps we might be able to construct a definition of 'political economy' by studying what people mean by it today: and in particular what those who teach the subject mean by it. Take for example the descriptions of modules in political economy at the London School of Economics and the University of Sheffield:

> The course will provide students with the economic methodology and tools for the analysis of political decision making and its effect on public policy. We will consider how political institutions shape economic policy, e.g., how do institutions such as elections, legislative bargaining, political parties or non-democratic regimes shape redistributive policies, fiscal policies, and the size of government. We will also consider how in the absence of institutions, political attitudes, beliefs and norms shape policies. The course will focus on analytical models and their testable implications. (London School of Economics, 2018)

> Aim:
> • to acquaint students with the modern literature in theoretical and applied political economy; that is, the study of public policy formation as a result of the interplay between economic and political decisions; …
> • to provide an opportunity for interdisciplinary study within the undergraduate Economics degree and enrich students' knowledge of economics with insights from political science.

> Syllabus: The median voter; electoral competition; lobbying, democracy and redistribution; career concerns and political business cycles; partisan politicians and partisan cycles; electoral rules and forms of governments; globalization and institutions. (University of Sheffield, 2018)

And for a third example, take the titles of books listed under 'political economy' in the Edward Elgar economics catalogue:

- *Neoliberalism, Financialization and Welfare: The political economy of social provision in the UK*
- *All Fall Down: Debt, deregulation and financial crises*
- *Global Infrastructure Networks: The trans-national strategy and policy interface*
- *Recent Developments in Economics and Religion*
- *Handbook of Social Choice and Voting*
- *The New Global Politics of Science: Knowledge, markets and the state*
- *Features and Challenges of the EU Budget: A multidisciplinary analysis*
- *Handbook of the International Political Economy of the Corporation*
- *Regional Infrastructure Systems: The political economy of regional infrastructure* (Edward Elgar, 2018).

The conclusion that we can draw from these three examples is that the discipline of political economy straddles the boundary between the disciplines of economics, politics, and ethics, and that its subject matter is the relationship between the economy, values, and institutions, and particularly the institutions of government. This is how the mid-twentieth-century economist Wilhelm Röpke understood the subject: as both a science of quantifiable facts, and a study of practical politics; as asking how values affect economic life, and how the social cohesion on which the economy depends can be maintained; and as an exploration of the institutional settings that promote or diminish human flourishing (Gregg, 2010: 9–12); and it is how the early-twentieth-century economist Charles Devas understood both 'political economy' and 'economics' as an 'ethical science' about 'the free actions of men as bound together for the purpose of getting their subsistence and preserving their race' (Devas, 1919: 1, 634–5).

Coherent with this conclusion, but from a methodological point of view, is the definition of political economy suggested by Weingast and Wittman in their chapter at the beginning of the *Oxford Handbook of Political Economy*: political economy is 'the methodology of economics applied to the analysis of political behavior and institutions' (Weingast and Wittman, 2006: 3). This again locates us on the boundary between economics and politics, but it locates political economy's methodology within economics and its subject matter within the field of politics. We might therefore take political economy to be the application of the methods of economics to the relationship between the economy and institutions, and particularly the institutions of government. This view is reinforced if we look for guides to the boundaries around the discipline of political economy in the list of sections in the *Oxford Handbook of Political Economy* (Weingast and Wittman, 2006): methodology; micro-economics; macroeconomics and monetary economics; institutions and organizations; public policy and interventionism ... development, transition and social change; and also among the titles of chapters in Alt's and Chrystal's *Political Economics* (Alt and Chrystal, 1983): politics and economics; politics and economic policy; macroeconomic policy and economic theory; political business cycles; policy optimization and reaction functions; the economics of voting; theoretical approaches to the public sector; comparative government expenditures; and a permanent income model of government expenditure. This combination is helpful because the former source is closer to the boundary between political economy and politics, whereas the latter is closer to the boundary between political economy and economics. Taken together, the two sources suggest that subjects that we might cover in this chapter might be the behaviour of money, particularly as it relates to institutions such as banks and governments; macroeconomic policy; voting behaviour; and political institutions. The latter source would also suggest that we might have located welfare economics in this chapter, but we have already located a section on that in Chapter 5 on economics. This chapter's two case studies exemplify two very different directions in which political economy travelled during the twentieth century. The Mont Pelerin Society's aim was to embed what became known as neoliberalism in economics and institutions; and Ian Gough's political economy represents a rather different Marxist outlook.

Thomas Sheriff has suggested that the science of economics did not see the recent financial crisis coming because it had distanced itself from studying institutions. It had too easily believed that the economy could manage happily without them. 'Economists must realise that they cannot ignore the workings of governments if they are to provide useful, important work. Economics has failed us; political economy can save us' (Sheriff, 2018). We shall see if something like this might be true in relation to the two main subjects tackled in this chapter: economic growth, and the behaviour of money; and also in relation to Citizen's Basic Income.

MACROECONOMICS: ECONOMIC GROWTH

Let us suppose for the sake of argument that we wish to see economic growth. (This supposition is questioned in the section on climate change in Chapter 5, but for the purposes of this chapter we shall begin by assuming it.) By economic growth we normally mean growth in Gross Domestic Product, which is a measure of the total value of goods and services produced in the UK (Lipsey and Chrystal, 2004: 373). Economic growth matters because it is from the value of production that earned incomes are drawn, and it is the revenue from taxing both earned incomes and corporate profits that governments spend on public services, for which there is increasing need in an ageing society.

Multiple factors cause economic growth, but perhaps the two most important are the amount of money available to pay for goods and services, and the level of innovation. As we shall see, providing an unconditional income for every individual would enhance both of these mechanisms.

Secure Incomes to Pay for Goods and Services and to Incentivize Employment

Goods and services are produced if people and organizations are willing to pay for them, so economic growth will only occur if the amount of money available to purchase goods and services rises, and if people and organizations know that more income will be forthcoming in the future, because only then will they have the confidence to spend current income.

There are several ways to increase people's incomes and therefore increase demand in the economy. Raising people's wages is one of those ways. Henry Ford understood this when he doubled his workers' wages in order to cut staff turnover and absenteeism and to enable his workers to buy the cars rolling out of his factory (Huczynski and Buchanan, 2007: 424). This move is less possible in today's competitive global economy: but the lesson is still an important one.

A National Minimum/Living Wage, carefully calibrated not to increase unemployment, is currently keeping low wages more in line with prices than they might have been otherwise, but it is among the highest earners that earned incomes are increasing at the fastest rate (Office for National Statistics, 2018b), not among the low paid. The security of earned income is as important as the level, so it is not insignificant that in the UK in 2018 900,000 employees were on zero hour contracts (Office for National Statistics, 2018d), over 1.5 million were on temporary contracts (Office for National Statistics, 2018c), and in general the employment market is increasingly insecure, both in the UK and globally (Westerveld and Olivier, 2019). Whereas previously self-employment could be a route to autonomy, high status, and sufficient income, it is increasingly precarious, low status, low paid, and dependent on contracts with monopoly website management companies (Conen and Schippers, 2019). Even if someone is in fairly secure employment, they might have experienced redundancy themselves, or they might know others in precarious employment: so even if earned income is currently sufficient for a family's needs, the perceived lack of security of that income will disincentivize spending on goods and services.

We have not yet seen the major automation-induced loss of employment sometimes predicted, and we might continue to see new jobs created by automation as old jobs disappear: but we are already seeing less secure employment (Daugareilh et al., 2019: 29), and we can predict both more fragile employment experiences – particularly for those with few or non-transferable skills, and for young adults without tertiary education (OECD, 2019: 117) – and more turbulence in the employment market. As Chris Hughes puts it:

> The same forces that enabled the rise of Facebook, Google, and Amazon have undermined the stability and economic opportunity that most Americans have a right to expect (Hughes, 2018: 41)

– and not just Americans: increasing employment precarity is now a global phenomenon (Lund, 2019). Whether or not we see a net loss of employment hours, we are bound to see significant and rapid change as computerization and automation take over an increasing range of tasks (Bruun and Duka, 2018; Brynjolfsson and McAfee, 2014; Greve, 2017); and Mowshowitz might still be right to predict that

> relatively few people will be employed by the global corporations of the future. Technical innovation in the production of goods and services may increase productivity or improve quality and thus stimulate higher revenues, but it is not likely – barring radical demographic changes – to generate enough jobs to keep pace with demand from new entrants in the labor market … . On the contrary, the commoditization of information reduces labor requirements, and since no area of economic activity is immune to this labor-reducing effect, the net result, barring a decline in the workforce, must be steadily increasing unemployment.
>
> The long-term impact of virtual organization on employment and the nature of work, as well as other social consequences of this new type of organization, warrant more extensive discussion … , However, one general conclusion must be stated. Decreasing labor requirements in the global workplace will necessitate new ways of distributing wealth. Absent such social innovation, disorder will surely increase beyond our ability to control it. (Mowshowitz, 1994: 267)

A second method for increasing incomes, and therefore demand, might be to increase means-tested benefits, both in work and out of work. The problem with this is that it can bury people in poverty and unemployment traps that they find it difficult to climb out of (Torry, 2016a: 3–6). Because means-tested benefits are withdrawn as earned income rises, they can cause significant marginal deduction rates (total withdrawal rates) on additional earned income. If a working age adult has no paid employment, and they face high marginal deduction rates if they find a job, then they are in the 'unemployment trap' (Parker, 1995: 27). If someone is already in employment, and increasing their earned income would provide them with little additional disposable income, then they are in the 'poverty trap'. Whether high marginal deduction rates are a disincentive to employment is debatable, because full-time employment is relatively 'inelastic' (– that is, as the rate of withdrawal of additional earnings rises, if someone is already engaged with the employment market then that engagement might not change very much): but there can still be effects, particularly in relation to part-time employment and the employment of someone whose partner loses their job (Atkinson and Mogensen, 1993: 191; Emmerson et al., 2014: 161). If someone is in employment, then their awareness of a poverty trap might not be immediate. However, it can only take a wage rise for someone to discover how little additional disposable income they receive, and for them to realize that however much their earnings rise, their household's disposable income will rise by very little. The disincentive effect will be cumulative.

Much attention is understandably paid to the unemployment and poverty traps associated with means-tested benefits: but they are not the only traps caused by the withdrawal of means-tested benefits as other income rises. Hermione Parker lists seven such traps: the unemployment and poverty traps; the invalidity trap (in which low earnings potential allied to means-tested benefits withdrawal can trap individuals); the lone parent trap (constituted by the household basis of means-tested benefits incentivizing parents to live apart); the part-time trap (again because low earnings and benefits withdrawal can trap people in low disposable incomes: an issue discussed in Chapter 5 of this volume); the lack of skills trap (as benefits withdrawal rates can disincentivize the gaining of new skills in order to increase earned income); and the savings trap (– it might not be worth saving for retirement if savings will be taken into account when means-tested pensions are calculated) (Parker, 1995; Torry, 2013: 113–21; 2016a: 3–8).

This is as much a concern to governments as it is to individuals in the traps, because governments know that if they increase the incomes of poorer households by raising means-tested benefits then they can push disincentive effects further up the earnings range (Adam et al., 2006: 1).

A recent report from the Organisation for Economic Co-operation and Development (OECD, 2019) suggests that:

Social protection systems play a key stabilising role in the current context of heightened uncertainties about the pace and extent of labour market changes. But accessing social protection can be especially difficult for workers in less secure forms of employment. More volatile career patterns or a growing diversity of employment forms pose potential challenges for support provisions that link benefit entitlements or financing burdens to past or present employment. Existing social protection systems have many strengths and will remain viable. But they will need to adapt to changing risks. Key priorities include making protection sufficiently agile to respond to changes in people's need for support, ensuring that entitlements are portable across jobs, and adapting the scope of activation and employment support to evolving work patterns. Keeping funding levels in line with evolving demands on social protection also requires a proactive policy debate on how new or expanded initiatives can be paid for. (OECD, 2019: 20–1)

An unconditional layer of income, constituted by a Citizen's Basic Income, would clearly fit these requirements: so a third method for increasing incomes would be to pay a Citizen's Basic Income to every working age adult, possibly starting with young adults. This would take a lot of households off means-tested benefits, and a lot more households still on them would be within striking distance of coming off them, making it easier to escape into an earnings range at which high marginal deduction rates would no longer apply (Torry, 2017d; 2018c; 2019a). If in the UK the unconditional income were to be funded by raising Income Tax rates, then households not in receipt of means-tested benefits would experience a small rise in their marginal deduction rate: but low income households' increased ability to increase their disposable incomes could considerably increase their employment market incentives, and it is among poorer households that incentives really matter (Martinelli, 2017b: abstract).

Citizen's Basic Income's ability to increase economic growth does not rely on anybody receiving additional net income on average. At least initially, instead of an Income Tax Personal Allowance, Citizen's Basic Incomes would be provided, every week or every month, so that, either instead of or alongside means-tested benefits, an unconditional income would be provided: a financial floor on which every individual and family would be able to build. This would provide a layer of secure household income, the security of which would encourage spending in the economy; and at the same time household net incomes would increase. Both of these effects would stimulate economic growth.

Innovation in the Economy

As well as delivering a generalized employment incentive, providing Citizen's Basic Incomes to every working age adult would also generate a stimulus to certain important types of employment. As things stand, a household earning employment income and also on means-tested benefits risks serious disruption to their household budget if their circumstances change, because either their benefits will be stopped and then restarted at a different rate, or repayment will be demanded at the end of the year. This discourages change in household employment patterns and in the level of earned income. However, if household members were to receive Citizen's Basic Incomes, and either no means-tested benefits, or smaller amounts that could be abandoned if earned incomes rose slightly, then new options would present themselves. Because the unconditional income would provide a secure floor on which to build, part-time employment alongside building a business would become more feasible, or perhaps leaving behind employment entirely and creating a new business, either alone or with others.

The results of Citizen's Basic Income pilot projects in Namibia and India cannot be immediately transferred to more developed countries: but the fact that those projects generated significant amounts of new economic activity, particularly among the lowest paid, is not insignificant (Basic Income Grant Coalition, 2009: 13–17; Davala et al., 2015: 73, 76, 92–6, 113, 134, 153–5; Haarmann and Haarmann, 2007; Standing, 2017a: 232, 236). Because the same factor of a secure financial floor would be in play in developed countries, and also the additional factor of lower marginal deduction rates, we can logically predict that the innovation effect might be even larger in more developed countries.

The conclusion that we can draw is that if unconditional incomes were to replace all or parts of the means-tested benefits system, then we would see more new small businesses founded, more self-employment in general, more people forming co-operative enterprises, and so on, because they would have solid financial floors on which to rely. It is from such new enterprises that innovation flows. Some of those new businesses would fail: but because the household's Citizen's Basic Incomes would continue, not everything would be at risk as it is now, and entrepreneurs would be more able to pick themselves up and try again.

An Important Constraint: Redistribution in the Right Direction

No Citizen's Basic Income would ever be implemented on its own. It would always be implemented in the context of other changes to the benefits system and to various forms of taxation. The important constraint to keep in mind is that the bundle of changes to be made alongside the implementation of unconditional incomes would need to ensure that either no redistribution took place, or that a manageable amount of redistribution took place from rich to poor. Not only would this constraint ensure that social damage did not follow the implementation of unconditional incomes, but also, if a certain amount of redistribution did take place from rich to poor, then because propensity to consume is higher among poorer people – that is, they spend a higher proportion of their income into the economy – there would be more demand in the economy, and additional economic growth would be the result.

A further result of more money being spent into the economy would be that the velocity of money would increase: that is, the same portion of money would be spent more often because it would be circulating in the local economy and not circulated or stored elsewhere. The 'demand equation' is $PQ = VM$, where P is price; Q is the quantity of production; V is the velocity of money: that is, the number of times that the same money is spent each year; and M is the quantity of money. PQ is the Gross Domestic Product (GDP): so, from the equation, if the velocity of money rises, then because the rate of change of GDP is equal to the rate of change of the velocity of money (Galbraith, 1976: 221; Lipsey and Chrystal, 2004: 499), economic growth occurs.

Government Spending

It is not only individual consumer spending that generates economic growth. Governments spend in order to provide public services. Governments are constrained by the difficulty of taxing capital in a globalized economy in which any capital apart from land can move elsewhere. This is a pity, as the fact that companies would benefit from a Citizen's Basic Income (just as they benefit from publicly funded education, healthcare, and so on) suggests that they ought to help to pay for it. For the same reason that it is difficult to tax capital, imposing a meaningful tax on financial transactions could also be difficult, because anything other than a very low tax rate would drive financial transactions elsewhere. If earned incomes stagnate, then less Income Tax can be collected in real terms. All of these factors make it difficult for a government to raise additional revenue. However, a Citizen's Basic Income would enable earned incomes to rise, thus increasing the tax base; and if income tax personal allowances were to be replaced by unconditional incomes, then again the tax base would rise. A larger tax base enables a government to raise and spend additional revenue. It would also be able to tax growing corporate profits to some extent. As the government was able to spend more, additional economic growth would take place; and improved public services would mean that the economic growth created would be higher in quality as well as in quantity.

Taxing the Proceeds of Production Going to Capital

Companies invest in new production capital if they face increased demand for their goods and services, so an increase in demand from consumers means companies spending money in the economy, again enhancing economic growth.

But what to do about the rising proportion of national income going to the owners of capital (Piketty, 2014: 281), and in particular to the owners of the highly automated industries that are paying only small proportions of their turnover in taxable wages, and are also managing to pay only small amounts of corporation tax. There is a good argument for recycling a substantial proportion of this money to consumers in order to fill the gap between labour income and consumption, both to reduce the damaging levels of inequality that we now face (Wilkinson and Pickett, 2009), and to enable consumers to purchase the products produced by the companies making the profits. Henry Ford understood this, and some of those who own large proportions of today's equivalents are now beginning to do so as well (Clifford, 2017; Huczynski and Buchanan, 2007: 424). The answer is not to give money to the poor in the form of means-tested benefits, because that would generate the disincentivizing effects of means-tested benefits that we have already discussed, and it would exacerbate the deep roots of inequality in the structures of our society (Torry, 2010). The answer is to give money to everyone. If the proceeds of production going to capital were to be effectively taxed, then the tax collected could be paid as unconditional incomes to help to fill the gap between consumption and labour income. Another mechanism for enhancing economic growth would have been implemented.

Citizen's Basic Income: Towards Sustainable Economic Growth

It would be perfectly feasible to pay for an initial unconditional income by making a small number of changes to our current tax and benefits system. This would be the easiest way to start. And then additional funding methods could be employed to enable the unconditional incomes to grow and to have more substantial useful effects: first of all carbon-based fuels could be taxed, in order to ensure that economic growth remains sustainable; second, taxation of the proceeds of production going to capital could be taxed, insofar as that proved possible; and third, quantitative easing within the Gross Domestic Product (GDP) boundary, as discussed later in this chapter.

An important boundary would need to be respected. As the unconditional income grew, employment incentives in relation to less desirable jobs would begin to fall. This would first of all stimulate increasing automation in those jobs, alongside an improvement in the quality of jobs in order to attract workers: but there might come a point at which the size of the unconditional income would discourage people from undertaking the work that society still needed human beings to do; and before that happened, the size of the unconditional income might reduce the incentive to seek paid employment to an extent sufficient to reduce the benefits to individuals and to society of people being in gainful employment or self-employment. As soon as evidence of either of these two points being reached were to emerge, it would be important not to increase unconditional incomes any further, as their optimal level will have been reached. At what level that would occur would be an entirely empirical matter: it could not be determined prior to the event, and it would change as automation and globalization continued to evolve.

As well as pursuing a vision of a good society, social policy must operate within a political economy of prevention (Gough, 2015): that is, it must seek to prevent harm – to the environment, to individual wellbeing, and to social wellbeing. Therefore boundaries need to be set and then respected. In Chapter 5 on economics we discussed the vital matter of climate change, and recognized that care would need to be taken to ensure that if a Citizen's Basic Income were to be implemented then the scheme as a whole – the Citizen's Basic Income and any accompanying changes – would need to reduce carbon emissions. We have now encountered boundaries in relation to GDP and employment. Other boundaries might emerge.

Our treatment of economic growth has well illustrated the nature of political economy: a science on the boundaries between economics, politics and ethics that takes seriously both economics and political institutions. Perhaps it is within this discipline more than any other that Citizen's Basic Income sits as a field of study.

THE BEHAVIOUR OF MONEY

The institution of money has always been of interest to political economists. Money is a means of exchange, a store of value, and a unit of account. It is a human invention and a social construct: that is, it is something that we have created, and it behaves in ways that our global society decides that it should. Money has value because we say that it has; money can be exchanged for goods because we say that it can be used for this; and we can construct accounts with it because that is what we do (Galbraith, 1976: 15; Lipsey and Chrystal, 2004: 480–92; Mason, 2015: 10–15).

So who creates money? The banks create money by lending. When a bank makes a loan, it writes money to the account of an individual or an organization. It has created that money. As the loan is paid back, the newly created money is slowly dissolved until it disappears. Banks receive deposits on which they sometimes pay interest, and both the deposits and the newly created money are lent out, on the reasonable assumption that the bank will never have to pay back all of the deposits at the same time. A loss of confidence in the bank can then trigger requests for the repayment of deposits, which the bank cannot do: so the loss of confidence is what causes the bank to collapse. In principle anyone can create a currency by simply creating tokens that claim to be money. The reason that governments establish a currency and then forbid the creation of additional currencies (apart from local ones, and the global cryptocurrencies which they cannot control), is because in order to fund its own activity a government needs to collect taxes, and those need to be collected in a currency that the government can be confident that it can spend on goods and services (Mellor, 2019).

So why can't a government simply create as much money as it wants to create and then spend it? The reason is that this can create inflation: that is, the more money a government creates, the less value that money will have, so prices will rise: a phenomenon that has created economic, social and political chaos, both in the past (as in interwar Germany) and today (for instance, in Zimbabwe). So then the question is this: What is the *right* amount of money for a government to create each year? One answer that is given is that a government should ensure that residents should have enough money to buy the goods and services produced (Crocker, 2019).

The problem that we face today is that capital's share of national income is rising, and labour's share is falling (Piketty, 2014: 199, 216–20), meaning that labour income becomes insufficient to purchase the goods and services produced. As Geoff Crocker has shown (Crocker, 2019), before 1995 labour income tracked the value of goods and services produced in the UK economy, but since then the two have diverged, and consumer credit has filled the gap: an unsustainable situation that has led to one major financial collapse and is bound to lead to more of them. As Crocker suggests, there is no reason why a government should not fill the gap between labour income and the value of goods and services by creating money and handing it to consumers as Citizen's Basic Incomes, as long as the total amount of money available to the population does not exceed the value of goods and services. Recent experiences of 'quantitative easing' (– governments creating new money in order to buy back government bonds from the market) have shown that, as long as the practice is kept within certain limits, there is no inflationary effect (Crocker, 2019; Jackson and Dyson, 2013: 201–18).

A variant of this response is based on the demand equation $PQ = MV$, where P is price; Q is the quantity of production; V is the velocity of money: that is, the number of times that the same money is spent each year; and M is the quantity of money. PQ is the Gross Domestic Product (GDP): so, from the equation, if the velocity of money remains constant, then the rate of change of GDP is equal to the rate of change of the money supply (Galbraith, 1976: 221; Lipsey and Chrystal, 2004: 499).

But then the question arises: is it an increase in the money supply that increases GDP, or an increase in GDP that increases the money supply? Given that it is up to governments and the banks how much money is created, it would appear that the amount of money available drives the level of GDP. As Edward Miller (2014) points out, this view is confirmed by evidence from the Great Depression and its aftermath, when it was money borrowed by the US Federal Government and spent into the economy in the form of public works that drove an increase in GDP: and, as he suggests, the additional money could simply have been created by the government rather than borrowed from the banks. Again, as Miller suggests, demand will grow until an economy has reached the limit of the resources available to it (– where resources include both labour and raw materials), on condition that enough money is available (MV) to fund the demand (GDP = PQ). Money has historically been injected into the economy via public works: but a more efficient method might be a Citizen's Basic Income, because this would provide the money required to drive demand and therefore GDP, and at the same time it would enable households to avoid the unsustainable debt levels that currently cause such economic and social problems (Crocker, 2019; Mencinger, 2017).

Whilst things are obviously not quite so simple as the two expressions of the money-creation proposals outlined above might suggest – because national economies are open to other national economies, and because P, Q, V and M are influenced by multiple factors – there is an understandable logic to the arguments.

We cannot tell what will happen to the proportion of the proceeds of production going to individuals through labour income and government transfers from labour income, but there is no reason to suppose that the process of automation will go into reverse, so job polarization is likely to continue (Goos and Manning, 2007), causing wage depression among lower skilled workers; and at the same time both employers and employees are having to take increasing amounts out of wages to pay pension contributions (Van Reenen, 2011). It therefore looks as if the proportion of the proceeds of production going to labour will continue to fall, and the proportion going to the owners of capital will continue to rise, unless something is done to remedy the situation. This means that sooner or later new ways of organizing our economies will have to be tried if constant crises are to be avoided. Quantitative easing was found to be a possibility following the financial crisis of 2007. We might find that governments creating money in order to fund a Citizen's Basic Income could also turn out to be possible; and that the kind of discussion that we have held here might become 'orthodox' economics instead of being the 'heterodox' or 'alternative' economics that it is now often taken to be.

Whether or not we are entering a 'second machine age' (Brynjolfsson and McAfee, 2014), a third axial age (Torpey, 2017), or simply a period of employment market turbulence that will result in both insecurity and new opportunities (Cholbi and Weber, 2020), we are certainly experiencing a period of rapid change, and therefore of insecurity for millions of individuals and households. It is in such a context that a layer of completely secure income – a Citizen's Basic Income – might be helpful (Hudson, 2019).

CONCLUSION

'Political economy' has been perhaps the most difficult term to define in this book, and the academic field with that name has been the most difficult to delineate. I have chosen two issues on which to concentrate: economic growth, and the behaviour of money. Others could have been chosen.

Material on how taxation affects voting behaviour can be found in Chapter 7 on social psychology, but we could also have included a section on voting in this chapter. Our guides to the subject treat voting behaviour as an important political economy issue because an 'economic approach treats the vote decision as the outcome of an explicit cost-benefit calculation' (Alt and Chrystal, 1983: 152–3) relating to what candidates have done in the past and to what they have promised to do in the future (Alt and Chrystal, 1983: 153). However, as often happens when models come into contact with the real world, the common idea that politicians should and do attempt to capture the vote of the 'median voter', because then they will obtain a majority of the votes, will only be of practical use in the context of a single simple issue. Normally there is no *single* issue, because elections pit political parties against each other, and each will have offered in their manifestos a bewildering array of policy ideas:

> If all electors had single-peaked preferences, then the preference of the median voter on a single issue is a stable policy outcome under majority rule. More complex models may have no such policy implications. When more than one issue is considered at a time, it becomes likely that there will be no unique ordering of possible outcomes that is the preference of a majority, so no stable equilibrium can be reached. (Alt and Chrystal, 1983: 153)

But even that is to oversimplify. Not only is there not normally a single issue: where it looks as if there is one, the apparently simple issue normally represents a cluster of issues, leaving us in the same difficulty that Alt and Chrystal describe. The 'leave' and 'remain' options in the 2016 UK referendum about leaving or remaining in the European Union made the issue look simple, but of course it was not: the apparently simple choice masked the fact that a wide variety of issues was being voted on.

Such a discussion, and the discussions on the behaviour of money and on economic growth in this chapter, could equally well have been located in Chapter 5 on economics, or in Chapter 11 on politics, which suggests that they belong in political economy. Similarly, the case studies that follow could have been located in Chapter 11 on politics, in Chapter 5 on economics, or in Chapter 9 on social policy: but because the important and broad questions that they raise can be framed as questions about political economy paradigms, they are appropriately located at the end of this chapter.

We have seen that political economy is perhaps the most appropriate discipline within which to study Citizen's Basic Income. At the same time, Citizen's Basic Income has provided for political economy an important example of precisely the kind of issue that its practitioners should be studying.

CASE STUDIES

The Mont Pelerin Society

In 1938, a gathering of intellectuals in Paris coined the term 'neoliberalism':

> The figures who gathered in 1938 saw the point of ranging widely over the tradi-
> tional preserves of philosophy, politics, theology, and even the natural sciences.
> Neoliberals started to recognize the growing need 'to organize individualism' in
> order to counter what was perceived as an unfortunate but irreversible politicization
> of economics and science ... To achieve their goal of the 'Good Society', neoliberal
> agents agreed on the need to develop long-term strategies projected over a horizon
> of several decades, possibly to involve several generations of neoliberal intellectuals
> ... . (Mirowski and Plehwe, 2015: 15)

In their sights were scholars such as John Maynard Keynes, whose *General
Theory of Employment, Interest, and Money* was

> a study of the forces which determine changes in the scale of output and employ-
> ment as a whole; ... our method of analysing the economic behaviour of the present
> under the influence of changing ideas about the future is one which depends on the
> interaction of supply and demand ... . (Keynes, 1936: vii)

Keynes had found that the 'classical economics' in which 'the wage is equal
to the marginal product of labour ... [and] the utility of the wage when a given
volume of labour is employed is equal to the marginal disutility of that amount
of employment' (Keynes, 1936: 4–5), had led him to the conclusion that it
was essential for a government to establish 'certain central controls in matters
which are now left in the main to individual initiative' (Keynes, 1936: 377–8).
For Keynes, 'the requirements of practical application determined the methodology of theory development and, given the open-system nature of the subject
matter, that methodology was pluralist' (Dow, 2017: 38).

> A long-run policy towards full employment, with some redistribution of income ...
> progressive taxation, easy money, and the socialization of a number of investment
> possibilities, would be the most appropriate mix of policies to bring the economic
> system to its maximum potential by avoiding waste and poverty through a constant
> state of full employment. (Arthmar and McLure, 2017: 65–6, summarizing Keynes,
> 1936: 372–84)

The resulting 'Keynesian' economic consensus of the time assumed that governments should closely manage their countries' economies by nationalizing
what they regarded as crucial industries, managing exchange rates and capital
flows, spending on infrastructure projects during economic downturns in order

to manage demand (and permitting budget deficits in order to achieve that), and establishing substantial welfare states funded and managed by government (Barber, 1967: 242–51). Strong trades unions and government by consensus went largely unquestioned. This was a political economy paradigm: an integrated set of ideas along with associated government policy, legislation, and regulations.

And then in 1947 Friedrich von Hayek and other like-minded economists established the Mont Pelerin Society, named after the village in the Swiss Alps where the first meeting took place, to pursue the neoliberal agenda. The Mont Pelerin Society wanted to see a political economy very different from the one espoused by Keynes and his colleagues: one more based on free markets, private rather than public ownership, and the freedom and responsibility of the individual: an individualism not balanced by the 'moral sentiments' characteristic of a previous British individualism, which it displaced (Fevre, 2016): and to that end its members developed a strategy largely based on the establishment of think tanks, tasked with propagating what became known as neoliberal ideas, and with circulating their staff members into academia and governments so that eventually there would be a critical mass of influential individuals with the alternative paradigm embedded in their minds. The aim of the strategy was to ensure that whenever a crisis occurred in the prevailing paradigm, it would be possible to shift governments into a new one (Berry, 2018: 5–6).

That is how the story is often told: and the way in which the neoliberal paradigm began to take over from the previous Keynesian one during the late 1970s and the 1980s, and in which it had become *the* paradigm by the 1990s, might lead us to think that the strategy put together by the Mont Pelerin Society worked seamlessly from beginning to end. The privatization of public assets and services, the weakening of trades unions, uncontrolled exchange rates and capital movements, the individual's responsibility for their own economic and social destiny, and so on, are now the prevailing mindset (Russell and Milburn, 2018: 45, 47–8). But the transition from a discussion of ideas in 1947 to a new economic and social paradigm was not in fact as seamless as we might now think it was. As the transition between paradigms slowly took place, there appears to have been little coherent strategy among those closest to the heart of government in the UK, the USA, and elsewhere (Berry, 2018: 8). The Mont Pelerin Society's strategy was no doubt a crucial element in ensuring that directions were set and maintained, but other factors were also important: the inability of the Keynesian model to cope with rapid oil price rises during the 1970s; trades unions' irresponsible use of their power, and their frequently undemocratic behaviour; automation, computerization, and the development of powerful transnational companies able to move production anywhere in the world; and so on.

The Keynesian paradigm lasted a generation, and the neoliberal paradigm has now lasted for the same length of time. Are we due for another transition? If so, then it is not obvious to what the next transition will take us, as it is difficult to identify a coherent set of ideas that might constitute a new political economy paradigm. The neoliberal paradigm might be struggling, but the fact that the financial crisis of 2007 did not see the beginning of a shift to a new paradigm rather suggests that there is still sufficient life in neoliberalism to enable it to remain the prevailing paradigm, and that there is no new paradigm waiting to take over from it. There are those who see municipal and co-operative enterprises as a sign of things to come (Russell and Milburn, 2018: 46), but these are probably best seen as throwbacks to a Keynesian paradigm.

In one sense there was nothing new about Keynes. For centuries there had always been some state involvement in the economy (often military in character), state policy on employment (if only conscription into armies or the navy), and welfare policy (from the Elizabethan Poor Law of 1601 onwards in the UK). And governments had always controlled the issuing of money when they could. The Second World War and Keynes ushered in a new bundle of emphases, not something entirely new. This was inevitable, because anything new always has to be implemented by institutions as they are. And similarly with what we now term neoliberalism. Private firms operating without being regulated or subsidized by states was hardly new; and there had always been private sector involvement in public services (– it has always been common for hospital laundry to be done by private companies; and in the UK medical General Practices have always been private partnerships under contract to the National Health Service). Neoliberalism represented a change of emphasis: again the only option because institutions as they were had to implement the changes. Similarly, any new paradigm will need to set out from the institutions of neoliberalism and those still characterized by Keynesian traits. Because Citizen's Basic Income can be seen to belong within both of these recent significant paradigms (Crocker, 2015), its implementation is a practical possibility; and because there is something radically new about it – its unconditionality – it could possibly represent the next new paradigm. If we view Keynesianism as a Hegelian and Marxist thesis, and neoliberalism as the inevitable antithesis, then perhaps we might best view Citizen's Basic Income as a 'sublation' of the two (Burbidge, 1993: 95; Hegel, [1812] 1969: §§ 132–33; Hook, 1962: 55; Marx, [1859] 1977: preface), and as an important element in a new paradigm that would serve society and the economy in today's situation in a way similar to the ways in which the two previous paradigms served society and the economy in their own times. If that is correct, then Citizen's Basic Income is an indication that both the Keynesian and neoliberalism paradigms could be replaced by an unconditionality paradigm: that is, an entire political economy characterized by unconditionality.

How might that come about? First of all, the new paradigm has been slowly coming to birth for over half a century. The UK's National Health Service, free at the point of use, and the UK's unconditional Family Allowance/Child Benefit, have belonged to the new paradigm as well as finding a place within the old ones. Genuine Citizen's Pensions in various places have also belonged to the new paradigm. In the UK, free television licences for the over 75s, the Winter Fuel Allowance, and free bus travel for young and elderly people in London, also represent unconditionality. But there is no overall strategy related to a new paradigm. Significantly, there is no equivalent to the Mont Pelerin Society. Organizations relating to particular elements of the new paradigm, such as those organizations that either long term or short term research Citizen's Basic Income, fit the bill to some extent: but not entirely. Perhaps what is needed is a new Mont Pelerin Society with the aim of establishing the hegemony of an 'unconditionality' narrative through the establishment of think tanks, journals, and so on. An early objective would be the establishment of Citizen's Basic Incomes in a variety of developing and more developed countries. This could propel global society and its economy towards the gradual establishment of the new paradigm.

Alternatively, of course, we might find that by implementing a Citizen's Basic Income we would have rescued neoliberalism. That is a risk that would have to be taken.

A Marxist Political Economy

Published in 1979, Ian Gough's *The Political Economy of the Welfare State* (Gough, 1979) is certainly 'political economy', as it lies on the boundary between economics and politics, and it is about the economics of institutions. It is, as suggested by the title, about the political economy of the welfare state, but it is not *the* political economy of the welfare state. Rather than being a survey of a field of study, it is an explicitly Marxist political economy of the welfare state: a clear alternative to the political economy exemplified by the Mont Pelerin Society.

Gough suggests that the welfare state – such public services as education, healthcare, and income maintenance – has as its purpose

> the use of state power to modify the reproduction of labour power and to maintain the non-working population in capitalist societies. (Gough, 1979: 44–5)

He regards the welfare state as a 'constituent feature of modern *capitalist* societies' (Gough, 1979: 3: italics in the original), and he applies to the welfare state a Marxist political economy 'founded on the premises of historical materialism' (Gough, 1979: 10) in order to understand 'the relationship between the capitalist mode of production and the set of institutions and processes that we call the welfare state' (Gough, 1979: 10). As he suggests,

> some writers see the welfare state as a functional response to the needs of capital (whether its economic needs or its political needs to absorb potential unrest and threats to stability); others see the welfare state as the unqualified fruits of working-class struggle, as concessions wrested from an unwilling state. (Gough, 1979: 56–7)

Gough's own starting point is the 'elements of *control* and service *provision*' (Gough, 1979: 4: again, italics in the original) that characterize the modern welfare state, so that it

> simultaneously embodies tendencies to ensure social welfare, to develop the powers of individuals, to exert social control over the blind play of market forces; and tendencies to repress and control people, to adapt them to the requirements of the capitalist economy. (Gough, 1979: 12)

In order to reveal the inevitable nature of this contradiction, Gough offers a thought experiment about social security benefits in an ideal benevolent state:

> If the state were to provide a higher minimum income to eliminate poverty, it would very soon surpass the wages paid to low-paid workers and would act as a disincentive to people to work. It would substantially interfere with the free operation of the labour market. One solution to this might be to replace economic choice by administrative persuasion and coercion, but this would conflict with the intentions of a more welfare-oriented policy. Nor is this all. If the higher minimum income were to be provided on a selective, means-tested basis, either the 'marginal tax rate' (the rate at which benefit is reduced as income increases) would have to be very high, resulting in the 'poverty trap' and the collapse of the work effort, or the total cost would be extraordinarily high, in which case the problems of financing this would lead to higher inflation, slower economic growth, or both. If the benevolent state, perplexed by these unforeseen problems, tried to raise minimum wages directly, it would find the competitiveness of the economy eroded and/or unemployment and inflation rising. (Gough, 1979: 12–13)

Gough only mentions the UK's unconditional incomes for children (Family Allowance, and then Child Benefit) along with means-tested and social insurance benefits rather than in a category of their own. I shall take a different approach: I shall separate out for discussion the existing unconditional income provided by Child Benefit, along with the possibility of an unconditional Citizen's Basic Income, in order to ask whether unconditional incomes exemplify the contradictions that Gough finds to characterize the welfare state, or whether perhaps they function rather differently in this respect.

First of all, should we regard unconditional incomes as elements of a welfare state? In one sense yes, because they 'use ... state power to modify the reproduction of labour power and to maintain the non-working population in capitalist societies' (Gough, 1979: 44–5): but in another sense no, because they can be regarded as an alternative to such tax allowances as the UK's Income Tax Personal Allowance: and such allowances are not generally regarded as elements of the welfare state. For the sake of this exercise, we shall regard unconditional incomes as elements of the welfare state, and we shall evaluate them on that basis.

In relation to Gough's thought experiment (Gough, 1979: 12–13):

- A Citizen's Basic Income that was set too high certainly could act as a 'disincentive to people to work': but any Citizen's Basic Income that would be feasible in the short to medium term would not be high enough to do that. (See the case study in Chapter 9.) Instead, such a Citizen's Basic Income would release a substantial number of households from means-tested benefits, and would provide every one of them with lower 'marginal tax rates', would release them from the 'poverty trap', and would provide them with an immediate increase in employment incentive.
- There are of course proposals for Citizen's Basic Income schemes of which 'the total cost would be extremely high': but there are also schemes that would go some way towards 'eliminating poverty', and that would reduce inequality, and of which the net cost would be zero (again, see the case study in Chapter 9).
- Means-tested benefits 'interfere with the free operation of the employment market' because they rise as wages fall and fall as wages rise. A Citizen's Basic Income would not do that, but would instead function as a reverse lump sum tax – the most efficient kind available – and as a static wage subsidy rather than as a dynamic one, and so with less of a wage-depressing effect. (See Chapter 5.)
- With a Citizen's Basic Income, 'administrative persuasion and coercion' would be impossible, simply because by definition the income is provided unconditionally.

So in relation to those elements of Gough's thought experiment that relate to the state providing an income, a Citizen's Basic Income would not suffer from the contradictions that Gough finds to afflict means-tested benefits. In relation to the element of the thought experiment related to a government setting a minimum wage, experience with the UK's National Minimum Wage suggests that such minimum wages do not necessarily raise the level of unemployment (Torry, 2016a: 209–11), and that they can make the economy more efficient rather than less.

In relation to the broad contradiction that Gough suggests afflicts the welfare state, Citizen's Basic Income 'embodies tendencies to ensure social welfare, to develop the powers of individuals, to exert social control over the blind play of market forces'; and it exhibits no 'tendencies to repress and control people, to adapt them to the requirements of the capitalist economy' (Gough, 1979: 4, 12). Therefore it does not appear to conform to Gough's political economy of the welfare state. There are of course elements of the welfare state that do exemplify the various contradictions that Ian Gough has discovered, and mean-tested benefits are possibly the clearest example: but there are also elements that do not, such as the UK's Child Benefit; and there are elements that would not do so if they were implemented, of which a Citizen's Basic Income would be the clearest example.

As Gough suggests,

> the positive aspects of welfare policies need defending and extending, their negative aspects need exposing and attacking, (Gough, 1979: 153)

which means that we need to reduce the prevalence of means-tested benefits, and increase the coverage of unconditional incomes.

13. The law of Citizen's Basic Income

Law: That department of knowledge or study of which laws are the subject matter.
(Oxford English Dictionary)

INTRODUCTION

This chapter will discuss the discipline of law; the discipline's perspective on Citizen's Basic Income (for instance, in relation to human rights, and to legislation on a social minimum); what the discipline offers to the Citizen's Basic Income debate; and what the Citizen's Basic Income debate offers to the discipline of law. A substantial case study will be offered at the end of the chapter.

As always in this book, boundaries are crossed. Citizenship rights have been discussed in Chapter 11 on politics, and could easily have been discussed in Chapter 9 on social policy: but they have to be discussed here as well because of their relationship with human rights. Discussion of the broader subject of citizenship can be found in Chapter 2 on language, Chapter 4 on ethics, Chapter 7 on social psychology, Chapter 9 on social policy, Chapter 10 on social administration, and Chapter 11 on politics: but because coverage is at the heart of any discussion of the law of benefits provision, citizenship has to be discussed here as well.

LAW, POLITICS, AND SOCIAL POLICY

But immediately we face two problems. The first is that the discipline of law is a vast and many-faceted discipline, encompassing the histories of law-making in a wide variety of different contexts, the study of the many different legal structures that have evolved through those histories, research on the different changing relationships between the politics of law-making and the laws that result from the politics, and the laborious study of the minutiae of laws, cases and regulations in particular jurisdictions. The discipline of law cannot be simplified. We have no option but to restrict our agenda, and the obvious strategy will be to concentrate on social security law. But then we encounter our second problem. The existing literature on social security law is understandably about the minutiae of laws, cases, and regulations in particular jurisdictions. So, for instance, Frans Pennings' *Introduction to European Social Security Law* (Pennings, 2001) is a highly detailed study of the European Union's institutions, policies, laws, regulations, and legal cases relating to social security benefits, employment, migration, and much else besides, with at the end a suggestion that additional co-ordination between European member states would be useful, along with a recognition that member states will resist establishing a 'European social policy' out of concern that this might hand too much power to European Union institutions (Pennings, 2001: 319–20). In relation to the UK, Robert East's *Social Security Law* (East, 1999) defines poverty, discusses the causes of poverty, describes the UK's social security system as it was twenty years ago, recounts the system's history, describes in detail the different benefits and their regulations, and concludes with a critique of the increasing emphasis on means-testing and conditionality: a conclusion that could have been drawn today. Similarly, *The Law of Social Security*, by Ogus et al. (1995), begins with an overview of the evolution of social security benefits in Britain, and then discusses in minute detail the UK's social security legislation, regulations, and case law. John Kirkwood (1986) conducts a similar exercise for Australia, although in this case the detailed description of laws, regulations, and legal cases is followed by a heartfelt critique of the system and its detrimental effects (Kirkwood, 1986: 248–63). A somewhat different approach to social security in the UK is taken by Neville Harris in his *Social Security Law in Context* (Harris, 2000). Rather than structure the book according to the different social security benefits, he first asks about the theoretical, social, and historical contexts, and then discusses the social security system's structure in broad outline (social insurance benefits, pensions, means-tests, decision-making, and the European dimension), and then a variety of other authors explore the relationships between social security law and family, gender, unemployment, education, disability, housing, debt, and industrial injury. It is Harris' approach that we shall take as our guide as we study the relationship between law and Citizen's Basic Income.

Harris's *Social Security Law in Context* is structured as we would expect a book on social policy to be structured – that is, in relation to different policy areas: family, gender, unemployment, education, disability, housing, and so on; and as we read the first part of his book we find ourselves reading history, and in particular political history. This is no accident. We might understand the situation like this: The discipline of law might be interested in social security laws and regulations themselves, and in the legislative and legal processes by which those laws and regulations have been enacted and interpreted. The discipline of politics might study the political processes that have given rise to new laws and regulations, and how the political process copes with their consequences. And the discipline of social policy might ask how the policies that gave birth to the laws and regulations were made, and what the consequences of those policies might be. This suggests that a chapter entitled 'The law of Citizen's Basic Income' ought not to restrict itself entirely to discussion of enacted legislation, regulations that have been issued, and legal cases that have occurred, but that it should also stray into the fields of politics and social policy in order to understand the context within which those laws, regulations and cases have come about, the processes that gave rise to them, and any consequences that might have resulted from them.

Take, for instance, the question of complexity. Social security systems are complex, because means-testing and the testing of other conditionalities involve complexity; the involvement of a variety of government departments in the administration of benefits inevitably generates complexity; and governments have a tendency to amend existing legislation, which might require the amendment of other existing legislation, and so on. In the context of existing complexity, if governments wish to constrain the discretion available to street-level bureaucrats as they navigate themselves and their clients through the system, then additional regulations have to be imposed, adding yet another layer of complexity. As Harris suggests, social security might best be viewed as a complex adaptive system (see Chapter 9) in which we should expect unpredictable outcomes (Harris, 2006; 2015). An important consequence of this is that attempting to simplify the system might make the situation worse, as the UK Government has discovered in relation to its attempt to roll a number of means-tested benefits into a single means-tested Universal Credit. A further consequence of the complexity is that attempting to simplify a means-tested system might deprive some groups of claimants of previous entitlements.

Harris discusses the simplicity of the UK's Child Benefit (Harris, 2015: 218–19), but does not ask how this relates to his overall thesis that social security is a complex adaptive system. This is probably because he assumes that the social security system is a *single* system within which a balance must be struck between simplicity (to facilitate access to benefits to which people are entitled) and complexity (to recognize differing needs). If instead we were to consider social security as two *different* systems, with different aims – unconditional benefits to provide efficiently for needs that we all have in common, and means-tested benefits to provide for needs that we do not all share – then we could happily seek to maintain and manage complexity in one of those systems, and vigorously pursue simplicity in the other. If we were to take this view of the situation, and if we were to ask whether such an understanding might suggest that every age group, and not just children, would benefit from an unconditional income, then we might find a little more divergence opening up between law, politics, and social policy, because both politics and social policy would need to ask how unconditional and conditional provisions might relate to each other, whereas legislation for new unconditional benefits might be best separated from other social security legislation, while recognizing, of course, that any new provision would require existing legislation to be amended. An exercise of this kind can be found in the case study at the end of this chapter.

I shall now tackle three particular areas of law of particular relevance to the Citizen's Basic Income debate: the idea of citizenship, and its relationship to the coverage of Citizen's Basic Income; human rights law, and its relationship to the status of Citizen's Basic Income; and legislation on a social minimum, and its relationship to the rates at which Citizen's Basic Incomes would be paid to different age groups.

COVERAGE

Any law that established a Citizen's Basic Income would need to state to whom the payments would be made; or if it was decided that the legislation itself would not prescribe coverage, then a paragraph would need to state that a government minister would make regulations to enable administrators to decide who should receive Citizen's Basic Incomes. Behind any legislation or regulations there will have been policy debates, and the debate underlying legislation or regulations relating to coverage will inevitably include some discussion of the notion of citizenship (Fitzpatrick, 1999: 15). A detailed discussion of citizenship will be found in Chapter 11 on politics, and discussion of who should receive a Citizen's Basic Income will be found in Chapter 10 on social administration: and on the basis of those discussions we can conclude that paying a Citizen's Basic Income to every citizen can be fully justified simply on the basis of the nature of citizenship: so to frame legislation and regulations to ensure that every citizen of a country would receive a Citizen's Basic Income would be entirely legitimate. However, that does not necessarily tell us who should receive a Citizen's Basic Income. For instance, in the UK citizenship is a highly complex matter. Not all British passport holders have a right to reside in the UK; and in relation to those provisions that do determine who has a right to live in the UK (the Nationality Act, the Asylum Bill), the category is far from fixed or obvious. The UK's unconditional Child Benefit therefore requires regulations to enable administrators to determine who should receive it. Child Benefit is paid to parents who are physically present in the UK together with their child, who are 'ordinarily resident' in the UK, who have a 'right to reside' in the UK, and who are responsible for the child living with them. Being present and being ordinarily resident in the UK are determined by relatively short lists of criteria: but having a right to reside can depend on which country someone is from and whether or not they are employed (HM Revenue and Customs, 2018).

The complexity of the question as to who precisely would receive a Citizen's Basic Income led the Citizen's Basic Income Trust to establish a working group to propose an illustrative response. The group proposed the following:

> Anyone living in the UK with the right to do so indefinitely, and refugees with a defined number of years of legal residence, would receive Citizen's Basic Incomes if they would be defined as resident in the UK by Her Majesty's Revenue and Customs, and they have been resident in the UK for a minimum residency period. A national of another country which had implemented a Citizen's Basic Income would be entitled to receive an individual Citizen's Basic Income on arrival in the UK if their country gave the same right to UK nationals. (Citizen's Basic Income Trust, 2018a)

HUMAN RIGHTS AS THE BASIS OF CITIZEN'S BASIC INCOME LEGISLATION?

In Chapter 11 we discuss layered citizenships, with different rights and duties relating to the different layers: for instance, rights and duties related to the European Union. But what does it mean to suggest that there is a global layer to our citizenship, and related rights? Such global rights are generally termed 'human rights' in order to distinguish them from social citizenship rights granted by the governments of particular jurisdictions. Human rights are generally of the negative variety ('protection from ...') rather than positive ('will provide ...'); they are usually less ambitious than the social rights that we expect to be granted by national governments; and they are now an increasingly important aspect of social policy debate and practice because a global south human rights development studies approach has influenced a global north social rights social policy tradition (Dean, 2019).

Why do we need human rights? Dworkin suggests that global human rights are necessary to give individuals rights over the State, so that where a more utilitarian national framework does not allow people to do what they wish to do, there is still the possibility of freedom. For Dworkin, there is no metaphysical basis to rights: there are merely particular legal or political rights; although he does think that there is one privileged right: the right to 'equal concern and respect' (Dworkin, 1977: xii).

While human rights risk creating a two-tier citizenry – with some residents of a country being granted both human and social citizenship rights, and others only human rights (Stendahl and Swedrup, 2017) – they are at least an attempt to prevent governments from heading for a moral abyss. In their content, human rights, while they suggest a global layer of citizenship alongside a nation state layer, are quite different from the social citizenship rights that we expect of democratic governments. Human rights, generally defined as those enshrined in the Universal Declaration of Human Rights (United Nations

General Assembly, 1949), aim to prevent the worst oppressions, and to guarantee human dignity, whereas nation state social citizenship rights generally aim at a variety of social minima sufficiently adequate to ensure social inclusion (King, 2017; Piachaud, 2017: 2). The practical reason for the difference is that a nation state can tax the nation's population and institutions, and can enforce co-operation from members of the population, so it can be sure that citizenship rights can be exercised by people living in that state's territory: whereas there is no global government with the ability to extract resources in order to use them to ensure that the entire global population can exercise social or economic rights (Lister, 1997: 65). The United Nations, which is the nearest we have to such a global institution, has to rely on nation states' willingness to live up to treaty commitments, and to take responsibility for their citizens being able to exercise their human rights as set out in the Universal Declaration, and only a minimal and negative approach to the formulation of human rights is likely to make that a realistic expectation.

Article 25 of the Universal Declaration of Human Rights grants to an individual a right to a 'standard of living adequate for the health and wellbeing of himself and of his family' (United Nations General Assembly, 1949; cf. Copp, 1992: 231): but, as David Piachaud points out, that does not necessarily imply an unconditional income, as Articles 22 and 23 of the Declaration indicate a different way of ensuring an adequate standard of living (Piachaud, 2016: 18; 2017: 6). Those articles grant rights to work, to free choice of employment, to just and favourable conditions of work, to protection against unemployment, and to social security, with the social security mechanism undefined. Under conditions of full full-time employment, and an adequate social security system, the rights granted in Articles 22 and 23 should indeed ensure that the right granted in Article 25 can be met. However, in the context of a more precarious employment market, there is no guarantee that granting the rights contained in Articles 22 and 23 will result in individuals having a 'standard of living adequate for the health and wellbeing of himself and of his family'. This suggests that a more rights-based and universalist approach to income maintenance is now required in the global north as well as in the global south (Rogan and Alfers, 2019), and that the obligation for ensuring that the right granted in Article 25 can be experienced in practice will increasingly fall on national governments and global institutions (Torry, 2013: 198). So while the Universal Declaration of Human Rights does not offer a right to an unconditional income, and cannot itself be employed as a basis for legislation for a Citizen's Basic Income, in the context of a highly unpredictable current and future employment market, Articles 22, 23 and 25 taken together suggest that a Citizen's Basic Income would be an appropriate means by which to ensure that the right granted in Article 25 can be met, which in turn suggests that in today's circumstances the Universal Declaration of Human Rights provides at least a sound basis for legislation to implement a Citizen's Basic Income. And if a Citizen's Basic Income might increase both incentives to seek employment, and the availability of employment, then legislation to implement a Citizen's Basic Income would better enable a government to meet the requirements of both Article 25 – the right of an individual to a 'standard of living adequate for the health and wellbeing of himself and of his family' – and Article 23 – the right 'to free choice of employment, to just and favourable conditions of work and to protection against unemployment'. As Piachaud points out, the right to paid work is crucial (Piachaud, 2017: 7), which suggests that a Citizen's Basic Income tested for its ability to incentivize both the taking of employment and the provision of employment opportunities might be crucial as well.

An additional means by which the provision of a Citizen's Basic Income might be a reasonable conclusion to draw from the Universal Declaration of Human Rights and the European Convention on Human Rights is suggested by Michael Adler. He accuses the UK's current means-tested provision, and particularly the sanctions now commonly imposed on claimants, of being 'cruel, inhuman or degrading treatment', and therefore contrary to Article 5 of the Universal Declaration of Human Rights, and also of being 'inhuman or degrading treatment or punishment', and therefore contrary to Article 3 of the European Convention on Human Rights (ECHR), which in 1998 was incorporated into UK law. The right granted by Article 3 of the ECHR is 'absolute', and so cannot be qualified by any other right; it refers to 'treatment' as well as to 'punishment'; and the 'or' between 'inhuman' and 'degrading' implies a low threshold. The European Court of Human Rights has not yet been asked whether the UK's benefit sanctions constitute 'inhuman or degrading treatment', but they clearly are. Not only are social and economic rights being denied to claimants by sanctions that are both punitive and ineffective, and by hardship payments that are inadequate, but civil rights are being denied as well, because the balance between rights and responsibilities has swung too far in the direction of responsibilities, the sanctions regime lacks many of the requirements for due process, and a juridical model of administrative justice has been replaced by a bureaucratic model.

> Violations of economic and social rights – including the right to social security – are widespread and are not currently subject to any effective remedies in the UK … it would appear that justice was not the primary consideration for those who were responsible for the design or implementation of benefit sanctions. (Adler, 2018: 112)

Benefit sanctions compare badly with court fines because they do not comply with a number of principles of the rule of law and 'they are disproportionate to the seriousness of the offence and they cannot be adjusted to take account of claimants' changing circumstances' (Adler, 2018: 127). In the Netherlands a similar sanctions regime has been found by the courts to constitute fines, and on that basis a challenge to the levels at which sanctions have been set has been upheld (Pennings, 2017). Adler concludes that 'in terms of justice, the UK benefit sanctions regime undoubtedly fails the [human rights] test' (Adler, 2018: 151).

A Citizen's Basic Income would, of course, behave very differently from sanctions-infested means-tested benefits, because a Citizen's Basic Income would function as a civil, political, and social right, and it would shift the balance towards rights functioning as an invitation to responsibility.

While it is true that there is no difference in logic between our national and global citizenships, as both are socially constructed realities, and that in relation to an aim to assist the poor there is no reason in logic for restricting our attention to the territory within our own national boundaries (Cowen, 2002: 53; Dean, 2011b), there is no realistic possibility that any global institution will be in a position in anything like the near future to establish a global Citizen's Basic Income. We are therefore left with national and regional possibilities. In a context of multi-layered citizenships, it must be an open question as to whether we should seek the implementation of a Citizen's Basic Income on a regional basis or on a one-country basis, and, in the UK, whether we should seek a Citizen's Basic Income for the UK or a separate Citizen's Basic Income for each country in the United Kingdom. Europe is probably the most likely region in which to establish a regional Citizen's Basic Income in the medium term, both because it would not be difficult to construct the necessary institutions if member state governments were to give permission for that, and because an agreed level of Citizen's Basic Income would not be impossible (Goedemé et al., 2017). But however unlikely a global Citizen's Basic Income (Bannister and Harnett, 2019) might look at the moment, we might still wish to keep the idea on the agenda:

> If global social citizenship is predicated on the idea of recognising the value of each individual, then social cash transfers could be an avenue of materialising that recognition, by global standard setting and institution building in the field of social security. (Dean, 2011b)

A global Citizen's Basic Income would be a recognition of our global citizenship, and of that citizenship defined as a global social solidarity in search of global wellbeing; and it would significantly contribute to the formation of a global citizenship. If a global carbon fee and dividend scheme were ever to be possible, then that would provide a basis for a small global Citizen's Basic Income (Bannister and Harnett, 2019): well worth doing, because even a small global Citizen's Basic Income would bind us together into a global community in a new way.

It is perhaps unfortunate that the rights listed in the European Convention on Human Rights, rather than those in the Universal Declaration of Human Rights, were written into English law in the Human Rights Act 1998, because it is the Universal Declaration that declares a right to a 'standard of living adequate for the health and wellbeing of himself and his family', not the European Convention, which contains no such provision (Equality and Human Rights Commission): but that does not mean that the Universal Declaration is irrelevant to legislation in states that belong to the United Nations, and in particular to the UK. Although Article 25 of the Universal Declaration is no closer to granting an explicit right to an unconditional income than is the Convention, we have seen that in the context of Articles 22 and 23 of the Declaration, and of an unpredictable future employment market, Articles 22, 23 and 25 of the Universal Declaration might one day be seen to be a sound basis for Citizen's Basic Income legislation.

LESSONS FROM LEGISLATING FOR A SOCIAL MINIMUM

A seminar held in Oñati in Spain in June 2017 tackled the subject 'Specifying and securing a social minimum', from legal, sociological, and social policy perspectives. The question that we need to address here is whether the papers presented, and the discussions held, throw any light on how legislation for a Citizen's Basic Income might be created and then applied.

Papers presented at the seminar come to a number of conclusions: Stendahl and Swedrup (2017) find that legislation on the provision of a social minimum reveals social norms; Boyle (2017) suggests that it is possible to write an obligation to provide a social minimum into a country's constitution; Pillay (2017) recounts South African experience of including economic and social rights in its constitution; and Kotkas (2017) finds that in Finland legislation deals with social minima directly, whereas the constitutional court, in order not to conflict with the legislative process, tends to tackle questions related to social minima indirectly, and in relation to general values and guidelines rather than close definitions of social minima. O'Cinneide's paper finds that although governments frequently state commitments to socio-economic rights, the feeling that they are somewhat indeterminate means that governments are hesitant to legislate (O'Cinneide, 2017); and Leijten (2017) finds the European Court of Human Rights to be cautious about ruling on matters related to a social minimum, instead preferring to review the procedures whereby decisions have been made. Pennings (2017) suggests that sanctions regimes compromise the legal position of social security recipients, and that loss of benefits constitutes a fine; and Warwick (2017) asks how appropriate a 'minimum core' obligation might be as political realities and resource levels change.

If we might be able to generalize from these findings and then apply them to the possibility of legislation to implement a Citizen's Basic Income, then we might find the following:

- That the legislation might reflect social norms – for instance, by calling the Citizen's Basic Income a 'fair allowance', which would reflect a social norm of fairness, and also the stigma attached to the concept of a benefit. The very existence of the legislation would reveal that unconditional provision had either achieved acceptability as a social norm, or that it was at least seen as a least bad option.
- For countries with written constitutions, it might be both possible and wise to write Citizen's Basic Incomes into them, even if constitutional courts might then not resist a Citizen's Basic Income falling in value.
- There would be nothing indeterminate about a Citizen's Basic Income, suggesting that legislation would be easy to achieve if political will were present. The risk would be that as the legislation navigated the policy process, conditionalities would be added, and what was implemented would no longer be a Citizen's Basic Income.
- In relation to Citizen's Basic Income, the only matter on which the European Court of Human Rights would be asked to rule would be the regulations about who should receive the Citizen's Basic Incomes. For instance, if legislation determined that every individual citizen, somehow defined, should receive the Citizen's Basic Income, but also added a residence requirement, then there might be occasional difficult cases to be adjudicated.
- The Citizen's Basic Income would never be removed, and there would be no sanctions, so no court would ever need to find against the characteristics or level of a sanction. The only possible challenge of this kind might relate to whether prisoners should continue to receive their Citizen's Basic Income. If a government were to decide that convicted criminals should not receive their Citizen's Basic Income during their imprisonment, then presumably the deprivation would need to be stated as part of the sentence.
- It would be appropriate for legislation to require a government to provide a Citizen's Basic Income, rather than to provide it with the ability to do so if it wished, although governments would be wise not to permit high levels of Citizen's Basic Income in the short to medium term, because a high Citizen's Basic Income might not be sustainable if it became difficult to fund it for reasons of resource constraints or political pressures. Given that the level of Citizen's Basic Income might not on its own provide sufficient income, governments would be wise not to stipulate that means-tested

benefits should be abolished on the implementation of a Citizen's Basic Income.

CONCLUSIONS

We have studied the relationship between law, citizenship, and Citizen's Basic Income; between law, human rights, and Citizen's Basic Income; and between law, a social minimum, and Citizen's Basic Income. In one sense we have not come to clear decisions, but at the same time we have discovered no absolute hindrances to the possibility of legislating to implement a Citizen's Basic Income scheme: that is, a Citizen's Basic Income along with the changes that would need to be made to taxation policy and to the existing social security structure. Throughout, we have found ourselves discussing both social policy and politics, and particularly political institutions. This is as we would expect.

One issue that we have not had occasion to discuss is how legal disputes relating to Citizen's Basic Income would be settled. This would appear to be a natural subject for a chapter on the law of a social security benefit to tackle. The ways in which individuals and groups of individuals are able to obtain their rights to benefits when their claims have been disallowed or their benefits reduced is an important subject for social policy academics to study (Spicker, 2014: 342–51). The reason that there has been no section on that in this chapter is obvious: every legal resident of a country would receive a Citizen's Basic Income of the same amount. Apart from the occasional legal case relating to whether someone was or was not a legal resident – which would in any case tend to be a case only partially related to whether or not they were receiving a Citizen's Basic Income – there would be no requirement for tribunals or other legal processes relating to Citizen's Basic Incomes.

Law is always particular: that is, a country's laws are always particular laws. It is therefore appropriate to give a proportion of this chapter to some illustrative legislation so that we can see what legislation to implement a Citizen's Basic Income might look like and begin to think about some of the consequences.

CASE STUDY

An Illustrative Act of Parliament to Implement a Citizen's Basic Income for the United Kingdom

As an educational exercise, a working group established by the Citizen's Basic Income Trust has constructed draft illustrative legislation to show what an Act of Parliament to establish a Citizen's Basic Income might look like (Citizen's

Basic Income Trust, 2018c). For the sake of this exercise, a Citizen's Basic Income is called a Fair Allowance.

The Fair Allowance Act 20xx

An Act to make provision for Fair Allowance.

Be it enacted by the Queen's most Excellent Majesty, by and with the advice and consent of the Lords Spiritual and Temporal, and Commons, in this present Parliament assembled, and by the authority of the same, as follows:

Part 1
Fair Allowance
Chapter 1: Entitlement and awards

Introductory

1. **Fair allowance**
   (1) A benefit known as Fair Allowance is payable in accordance with this Part.
   (2) Fair Allowance may, subject as follows, be awarded to an individual.
   (3) An award of Fair Allowance is, subject as follows, calculated by reference to—
       (a) a standard allowance related to the individual's age.

2. **Receipt**
   (1) Fair Allowance shall be paid to an individual.

Entitlement

3. **Entitlement**
   (1) Fair Allowance shall be paid to an individual if the individual meets the basic conditions.

4. **Basic conditions**
   (1) For the purposes of section 3, a person meets the basic conditions who—
       (a) is at least 16 years old,
       (b) is in Great Britain,
       (c) is not a person for whom Child Benefit is in payment.
   (2) Regulations may provide for exceptions to the requirement to meet any of the basic conditions.
   (3) For the basic condition in subsection (1)(b) regulations may—
       (a) specify circumstances in which a person is to be treated as being or not being in Great Britain;

(b) specify circumstances in which temporary absence from Great Britain is disregarded.

(4) Except to the extent that regulations provide otherwise, no amount in respect of Fair Allowance is payable in respect of a person for a period during which the person is undergoing imprisonment or detention in legal custody.

Awards

5. Basis of awards

(1) Fair Allowance is payable from a prescribed date.

(2) Regulations may make provision—
   (a) for a prescribed date,
   (b) for different prescribed dates for individuals of different ages.

6. Calculation of awards

(1) The amount of an award of Fair Allowance is to be the standard allowance related to the individual's age.

(2) No amount may be deducted in respect of earned income or unearned income.

Elements of an award

7. Standard allowance

(1) The calculation of an award of Fair Allowance is to include an amount by way of a standard allowance for an individual.

(2) Regulations are to specify the amount to be included under subsection (1).

(3) Regulations may specify different amounts to be included under subsection (1) in relation to an individual's age.

(4) The Secretary of State shall establish a Fair Allowance Commission which may report to the Secretary of State on all matters relating to the Fair Allowance.

(5) The Secretary of State may make regulations for the establishment and operation of the Fair Allowance Commission.

Application of work-related requirements

8. Individuals subject to no work-related requirements

(1) The Secretary of State may not impose any work-related requirement on any individual as a condition of receiving Fair Allowance.

(2) In subsection (1), 'work', in relation to 'any work-related requirement', shall include work that is either paid or unpaid.

Chapter 2: Supplementary and general

Supplementary and consequential

9. Power to make supplementary and consequential provision etc.
  (1) The appropriate authority may by regulations make such consequential, supplementary, incidental or transitional provision in relation to any provision.
  (2) The appropriate authority is the Secretary of State, subject to subsection (3)
  (3) The appropriate authority is the Welsh Ministers for—
      (a) provision which would be within the legislative competence of the National Assembly for Wales were it contained in an Act of the Assembly;
      (b) provision which could be made by the Welsh Ministers under any other power conferred on them.
  (4) Regulations under this section may amend, repeal or revoke any primary or secondary legislation (whenever passed or made).

Fair Allowance and other benefits

10. Abolition and adjustment of benefits
  (1) No benefits are abolished.
  (2) Any power to make—
      (a) regulations under this Part,
      (b) regulations under the Social Security Administration Act 1992 relating to Fair Allowance, or
      (c) regulations under the Social Security Act 1998 relating to Fair Allowance
    may be exercised so as to make provision for Fair Allowance to be included in the means to be taken into account in the calculation of awards of other benefits.

Recovery of benefit payments

11. Recovery of Benefit Payments
  (1) The Secretary of State may recover any amount of the Fair Allowance paid in excess of entitlement.
  (2) An amount recoverable under this section is recoverable from—
      (a) the person to whom it was paid, or
      (b) such other person (in addition to or instead of the person to whom it was paid) as may be prescribed.

(3) An amount paid in pursuance of a determination is not recoverable under this section unless the determination has been—
  (a) reversed or varied on an appeal, or
  (b) revised or superseded under section 9 or section 10 of the Social Security Act 1998, except where regulations otherwise provide.

(4) Regulations may provide that amounts recoverable under this section are to be calculated or estimated in a prescribed manner.

(5) An amount recoverable under this section may (without prejudice to any other means of recovery) be recovered—
  (a) by deduction from earnings (in accordance with the Social Security Administration Act 1992, section 71ZD);
  (b) through the courts etc. (Section 71ZE)
  (c) by adjustment of benefit (Section 71ZF).

(6) Recovering benefits by deduction from the Fair Allowance is not permitted.

Regulations

12. Pilot schemes

(1) Any power to make—
  (a) regulations under this Part,
  (b) regulations under the Social Security Administration Act 1992 relating to Fair Allowance, or
  (c) regulations under the Social Security Act 1998 relating to Fair Allowance,
  may be exercised so as to make provision for piloting purposes.

(2) In subsection (1), 'piloting purposes', in relation to any provision, means the purposes of testing—
  (a) the extent to which the provision is likely to make Fair Allowance simpler to understand,
  (b) the extent to which the provision is likely to promote—
    (i) people remaining in work, or
    (ii) people obtaining or being able to obtain work (or more work or better-paid work), or
  (c) the extent to which, and how, the provision is likely to affect the conduct of recipients of Fair Allowance or other people in any other way.

(3) Regulations made by virtue of this section are in the remainder of this section referred to as a 'pilot scheme'.

(4) A pilot scheme may be limited in its application to—
  (a) one or more areas;
  (b) persons selected by reference to their age.

(5) A pilot scheme may not have effect for a period exceeding three years, but—

    (a) the Secretary of State may by order made by statutory instrument provide that the pilot scheme is to continue to have effect after the time when it would otherwise expire for a period not exceeding twelve months (and may make more than one such order);

    (b) a pilot scheme may be replaced by a further pilot scheme making the same or similar provision.

(6) A pilot scheme may include consequential or transitional provision in relation to its expiry.

13. Regulations: general

(1) Regulations under this Part are to be made by the Secretary of State, unless otherwise provided.

(2) A power to make regulations under this Part may not be exercised so as to make different provision for different cases or purposes except as provided in sections (12)(3) and (12)(4).

(3) A power to make regulations under this Part may be exercised so as to make different provision in relation to the age of the person.

(4) A power to make regulations under this Part may be exercised so as to make provision for Fair Allowance to be payable in respect of a person for a period during which the person is undergoing imprisonment or detention in legal custody.

(5) Where regulations under this Part provide for an amount, the amount may not be zero.

(6) Each power conferred by this Part is without prejudice to the others.

(7) Where regulations under this Part provide for an amount for the purposes of an award, the amount may be different in relation to the age of the person.

(8) No regulation or regulations shall be made that will cause the amount of the net income of a household to be reduced below the amount of the net income of the household before the regulation or regulations had been made.

14. Regulations: procedure

(1) Regulations under this Part are to be made by statutory instrument.

(2) A statutory instrument containing regulations made by the Secretary of State under this Part is subject to the affirmative resolution procedure.

(3) A statutory instrument containing regulations made by the Welsh Ministers under section 9 may not be made unless a draft of the instrument has been laid before, and approved by resolution of, the National Assembly for Wales.

Final

15. Financial provision

(1) There shall be paid out of money provided by Parliament—

    (a) sums paid by the Secretary of State by way of Fair Allowance;

    (b) any other expenditure incurred in consequence of this Act by a Minister of the Crown or the Commissioners for Her Majesty's Revenue and Customs;

    (c) any increase attributable to this Act in the sums payable under any other Act out of money so provided.

(2) The Secretary of State shall report to Parliament on the net cost of Fair Allowance during the first full financial year of its operation.

(3) 'Net cost' in section (14)(2) shall be understood to be the total of—

    (a) the cost of Fair Allowance awards, and

    (b) the administrative cost of Fair Allowance

less the total of—

    (a) additional Income Tax and National Insurance Contribution payments in respect of the reductions in the Income Tax Personal Allowances and National Insurance Contribution Primary Earnings Threshold consequent on regulations made in relation to this Act,

    (b) additional Income Tax and National Insurance Contribution payments in respect of the increases in the rates of Income Tax and National Insurance Contributions consequent on regulations made in relation to this Act,

    (c) reductions in the cost of awards of other benefits consequent on their recalculation consequent on regulations made in relation to this Act.

Paragraphs will follow on extent, commencement, and short title.

Additional paragraphs will be required in relation to:

- electronic communications
- amendments to other Acts required to enable Fair Allowance to be taken into account when other benefits are calculated. A paragraph similar to paragraph (13)(8) above will need to be included to ensure that no amendments to other Acts leave households worse off.
- the Scottish Parliament, the Northern Ireland Assembly, and Scottish and Northern Ireland ministers. The relevant parts of the Universal Credit Act on which this illustrative draft legislation is based contain the references

to the Welsh Assembly and Welsh ministers to be found here. Further references to the Welsh Assembly and Welsh ministers might be required.

Issues not required to be included in this Act:

- Increases in Child Benefit can be dealt with in the usual way;
- Reductions in Income Tax Personal Allowances and the National Insurance Contribution Primary Earnings Threshold, and increases in Income Tax rates, can be dealt with in the usual way.

14. Conclusions

It has been both a pleasure and a challenge to write this book. In particular, it has been both a pleasure and a challenge to have to study a number of disciplines with which previously I had only a passing acquaintance. But it has also been a challenge to fit everything into the word limit. I have constantly had to cut material. This is why what might have been chapters on complexity studies, gender studies, and climate change – all now recognized as important academic disciplines in their own rights – have been cut, and essential material on those subjects has been placed in other chapters. One conclusion to draw from the experience of writing this book is that there are now so many actual and potential aspects to the Citizen's Basic Income debate that it is impossible to encompass all of them in a single volume.

At the end of each chapter I have indicated how the discipline being discussed might increase our understanding of Citizen's Basic Income, and, in some of the chapters, how the Citizen's Basic Income debate might inform the academic disciplines under review. We have sometimes found influence in both directions: although because the chapters have turned out so differently from each other, it would be difficult to discover any kind of consensus between them. I shall therefore not attempt to provide an overview of the conclusions drawn in relation to each of the academic disciplines, except to say that many of the chapters have discovered significant complexity: not, of course, in the definition or operation of a Citizen's Basic Income itself, but in relation to how our complex societies, economies, and tax and benefits systems would relate to a Citizen's Basic Income.

In 1984, a small group of people gathered in a room in Bedford Square in London to discuss the possibility of an unconditional income for every individual, and to give birth to the Basic Income Research Group: now the Citizen's Basic Income Trust; and in 1986, a larger group gathered at the University of Louvain in Belgium to give birth to BIEN, the Basic Income European Network: now the Basic Income Earth Network. For the following thirty years or so, Citizen's Basic Income remained a debate on the fringes of academic discussion of tax and benefits systems. Then things started to change. Until six or seven years ago I could legitimately claim to have read everything written on the subject in English, and some other material as well. Nobody could make that claim now. Interesting symptoms of how things have changed is that a substantial international handbook has now been published on the subject (Torry, 2019b), and in 2018 the new edition of Millar's and Sainsbury's *Understanding Social Security* contained a chapter on Citizen's Basic Income (Martinelli, 2018).

The Citizen's Basic Income debate is now global, and it continues to increase in both extent and depth. The literature is now immense. One of the very few gaps remaining was a multidisciplinary approach to the subject. In one sense, that gap is now filled. However, there is no sense in which this book has provided a complete multidisciplinary treatment of the subject. What is now required is further research on the relationships between Citizen's Basic Income and the disciplines described in this book, and also research on the relationships between Citizen's Basic Income and an even broader variety of disciplines.

One of the reasons for the intelligence with which Citizen's Basic Income is often debated is the extent and quality of the multidisciplinary research that has already taken place. The more high quality multidisciplinary research that can be achieved in the future, the more intelligent will be the global Citizen's Basic Income debate as it continues to evolve.

Bibliography

Note: Basic Income Research Group, Citizen's Income Trust, and Citizen's Basic Income Trust publications – including the *BIRG Bulletin*, the *Citizen's Income Bulletin*, and the *Citizen's Income Newsletter* – are all available to download via the Trust's website at https://citizensincome.org/publications/ if no alternative website address is given.

6, Perri (2018), 'Frames and framing in policymaking', in Hal K. Colebatch and Robert Hoppe (eds), *Handbook on Policy, Process and Governing*, Cheltenham, UK and Northampton, MA, USA: Edward Elgar Publishing, pp. 275–94.

Abdukadirov, Sherzod (2016), 'Introduction: Regulation versus technology as tools of behavior change', in Sherzod Abdukadirov (ed.), *Nudge Theory in Action: Behavioral Design in Policy and Markets*, Basingstoke: Palgrave Macmillan, pp. 1–11.

Abel-Smith, Brian and Peter Townsend (1965), *The Poor and the Poorest*, London: G. Bell and Sons.

Abelson, Donald E. (2002), *Do Think Tanks Matter? Assessing the impact of public policy institutes*, Montreal and Kingston: McGill-Queen's University Press.

Adam, Stuart, Timothy Besley, Richard Blundell, Stephen Bond, Robert Chote, Malcolm Gammie, Paul Johnson, Gareth Myles and James Poterba (eds) (2010), *Dimensions of Tax Design: The Mirrlees Review*, Oxford: Oxford University Press for the Institute for Fiscal Studies.

Adam, Stuart, Timothy Besley, Richard Blundell, Stephen Bond, Robert Chote, Malcolm Gammie, Paul Johnson, Gareth Myles and James Poterba (eds) (2011), *Tax by Design: The Mirrlees Review*, Oxford: Oxford University Press.

Adam, Stuart, Mike Brewer and Andrew Shephard (2006), *The Poverty Trade-off: Work incentives and income redistribution in Britain*, Bristol: Policy Press / York: Joseph Rowntree Foundation.

Addabbo, Tindara, Marie-Pierre Arrizabalaga, Cristina Borderias and Alastair Owens (eds) (2010), *Gender Inequalities, Households and the Production of Well-being in Modern Europe*, Aldershot: Ashgate.

Adelman, Laura, Sue Middleton and Karl Ashworth (1999), *Intra-household Distribution of Poverty and Social Exclusion: Evidence from the 1999 PSE Survey of Britain*, Working Paper no. 23, Loughborough: Centre for Research in Social Policy.

Adler, Michael (2018), *Cruel, Inhuman or Degrading Treatment? Benefit sanctions in the UK*, Cham: Palgrave Macmillan.

Alkire, Sabina (2007), 'Choosing dimensions: The capability approach and multidimensional poverty', in Nanak Kakwani and Jacques Silber (eds), *The Many Dimensions of Poverty*, Basingstoke: Palgrave Macmillan, pp. 89–119.

Alstott, Anne L. (2001), 'Good for women', in Joshua Cohen and Joel Rogers (eds), *What's Wrong with a Free Lunch?*, Boston, MA: Beacon Press, pp. 75–9.

Alt, James E. and K. Alec Chrystal (1983), *Political Economics*, Berkeley, CA: University of California Press.

Amabile, Teresa M. (1996), *Creativity in Context*, Boulder, CO: Westview.

Aneesh, A. (2016), 'Differentiating citizenship', in Kennan Ferguson and Patrice Petro (eds), *After Capitalism: Horizons of finance, culture, and citizenship*, New Brunswick, NJ: Rutgers University Press, pp. 196–214.

Anglund, Sandra M. (1999), 'American core values and policy problem definition', in Stuart S. Nagel (ed.), *The Policy Process*, New York: Nova Science Publishers, pp. 147–63.

Aristotle (1987), *Nichomachean Ethics*, selected chapters, in J.L. Ackrill (ed.), *A New Aristotle Reader*, Oxford: Clarendon Press, pp. 363–478. (References are given as book number followed by paragraph numbers.)

Arneson, Richard J. (2002), 'Why justice requires transfers to offset income and wealth inequalities', in Ellen Frankel Paul, Fred D. Miller Jr. and Jeffrey Paul (eds), *Should Differences in Income and Wealth Matter?*, Cambridge: Cambridge University Press, pp. 172–200.

Arthmar, Rogério and Michael McLure (2017), 'Cambridge theories of welfare economics', in Robert A. Cord (ed.), *The Palgrave Companion to Cambridge Economics*, volume 1, London: Palgrave Macmillan, pp. 51–92.

Atkinson, A.B. (1985), *Income Maintenance and Social Insurance: A survey*, Welfare State Programme, paper no. 5, London: London School of Economics.

Atkinson, A.B. (1989), *Basic Income Schemes and the Lessons from Public Economics*, Tax, Incentives and the Distribution of Income paper no. 136, London: London School of Economics.

Atkinson, A.B (1993), 'Participation Income', *Citizen's Income Bulletin*, no. 16, July 1993, pp. 7–11.

Atkinson, A.B. (1995), *Public Economics in Action: The Basic Income / Flat Tax proposal*, Oxford: Clarendon Press.

Atkinson, A.B. (1996), 'The case for a Participation Income', *The Political Quarterly*, **67** (1), 67–70.

Atkinson, A.B. (2015), *Inequality: What can be done?*, Cambridge, MA: Harvard University Press.

Atkinson, A.B. and J.S. Flemming (1978), 'Unemployment, social security and incentives', *Midland Bank Review*, Autumn 1978, pp. 6–16.

Atkinson, A.B. and G.V. Mogensen (eds) (1993), *Welfare and Work Incentives*, Oxford: Oxford University Press.

Avram, Silvia (2015), *Benefit Losses Loom Larger than Taxes: The effects of framing and loss aversion on behavioural responses to taxes and benefits*, Colchester: Institute for Social and Economic Research, accessed 13 August 2018 at www.iser .essex.ac.uk/research/publications/working-papers/iser/2015-17.pdf.

Badenes-Plá, Nuria, Borja Gambau-Suelves and María Navas Román (2019), *Distributional and Welfare Effects of Replacing Monetary Benefits with Universal Basic Income in Spain*, EUROMOD Working Paper EM8/19, Colchester: Institute for Social and Economic Research, accessed 25 April 2019 at https://www.iser.essex .ac.uk/research/publications/working-papers/euromod/em8-19.

Baggott, Rob (2000), *Pressure Groups and the Policy Process*, Sheffield: Sheffield Hallam University.

Bailey, Nick and Glen Bramley (2018), 'Introduction', in Glen Bramley and Nick Bailey (eds), *Poverty and Social Exclusion in the UK*: *Volume 2 – The dimensions of disadvantage*, Bristol: Policy Press, pp. 1–23.

Baillie, Richard (2011), 'An examination of the public discourse on benefit claimants in the media', *Journal of Poverty and Social Justice*, **19** (1), 67–70.

Bambrick, Laura (2006), 'Wollstonecraft's Dilemma: Is a Citizen's Income the answer?', *Citizen's Income Newsletter*, issue 2 for 2006, pp. 3–10.

Bambrough, Renford (1969), *Reason, Truth and God*, London: Methuen.

Bannister, Laura and Paul Harnett (2019), 'Basic Income and a global commons', *The Ecologist*, 6 August 2019, accessed 4 October 2019 at https://theecologist.org/2019/aug/06/basic-income-and-global-commons.

Barber, William J. (1967), *A History of Economic Thought*, Harmondsworth: Penguin.

Barclay, Coryn, Julie McLachlan and Mhairi Paterson (2019), *Exploring the Practicalities of a Basic Income Pilot*, Dunfermline: Carnegie UK Trust.

Barkai, Haim (1998), *The Evolution of Israel's Social Security System*, Aldershot: Ashgate.

Barrientos, Armando (2016), 'Justice-based social assistance', *Global Social Policy*, **16** (2), 151–65.

Barrientos, Armando and Sony Pellissery (2011), 'The road to global citizenship?', in Armando Barrientos, Benjamin Davy, Ulrike Davy, Hartley Dean, Harvey M. Jacobs, Lutz Leisering and Sony Pellissery, *A Road to Global Social Citizenship?*, Financial Assistance, Land Policy, and Global Social Rights Working Paper No. 10, pp. 6–14, accessed 2 June 2019 at www.tinyurl.com/3n9jh5h.

Barry, Brian (1990), 'The welfare state versus the relief of poverty', *Ethics*, **100** (3), 503–29.

Bartels, Koen P.R. (2018), 'Policy as practice', in Hal K. Colebatch and Robert Hoppe (eds), *Handbook on Policy, Process and Governing*, Cheltenham, UK and Northampton, MA, USA: Edward Elgar Publishing, pp. 68–88.

Basic Income Earth Network, accessed 31 May 2019 at www.basicincome.org.

Basic Income Grant Coalition (2009), *Making the Difference: The BIG in Namibia: Basic Income Grant Pilot Project, Assessment Report*, Namibia: Namibia NGO Forum, accessed 20 November 2018 at www.bignam.org/Publications/BIG_Assessment_report_08b.pdf.

Basic Income Research Group (1988), 'Implications of Basic Income for people with disabilities', *BIRG Bulletin*, no. 7, Spring 1988, pp. 10–19.

Basu, Kaushik (1980), *Revealed Preference of Government*, Cambridge: Cambridge University Press.

Baumberg, Ben (2016), 'The stigma of claiming benefits: A quantitative study', *Journal of Social Policy*, **45** (2), 181–99.

Baumberg, Ben, Kate Bell and Declan Gaffney (2012), *Benefits Stigma in Britain*, London: Turn2Us/Elizabeth Finn Care, accessed 9 August 2018 at https://wwwturn2us-2938.cdn.hybridcloudspan.com/T2UWebsite/media/Documents/Benefits-Stigma-in-Britain.pdf.

Beaumont, Jen (2011), *Households and Families: Social trends 41*, London: Office for National Statistics, accessed 12 November 2018 at www.ons.gov.uk/ons/rel/social-trends-rd/social-trends/social-trends-41/social-trends-41---household-and-families.pdf.

Bekker, M.H., P.F. De Jong, F.R. Zijlstra and B.A. van Landeghem (2000), Combining care and work: Health and stress effects in male and female academics', *International Journal of Behavioral Medicine*, **7** (1), 28–43.

Benavides, F.G., J. Benach, A.V. Diez-Roux and C. Roman (2000), 'How do types of employment relate to health indicators? Findings from the Second European Survey on Working Conditions', *Journal of Epidemiology and Community Health*, **54** (7), 494–501.

Benedict, Ruth (1935), *Patterns of Culture*, London: Routledge and Kegan Paul.

Benn, Tony (1974), *Speeches by Tony Benn*, Nottingham: Spokesman Books.

Benn, Tony (1988), *Fighting Back: Speaking out for socialism in the eighties*, London: Hutchinson.

Berg, Linda (2007), 'Multi-level Europeans: The influence of territorial attachments on political trust and welfare attitudes', Göteborg: Department of Political Science, Göteborg University.

Berger, John (1972), *G*, London: Bloomsbury.

Berger, Peter (1966), *Invitation to Sociology: A humanistic perspective,* Harmondsworth: Penguin.

Bergh, Andreas, Therese Bilsson and Daniel Waldenström (2016), *Sick of Inequality? An introduction to the relationship between inequality and health*, Cheltenham, UK and Northampton, MA, USA: Edward Elgar Publishing.

Berry, Christine (2018), 'Beyond Mont Pelerin: How does a movement prepare for power?', *Renewal*, **26** (4), 5–11.

Beveridge, Sir William (1942), *Social Insurance and Allied Services*, Cmd 6404, London: Her Majesty's Stationery Office.

BIEN Nordic Day (2018), Presentations by Gerður Pálmadótir, Øyrind Steenson and Jan Otto Andersson, at the BIEN Nordic Day held in Tampere, Finland, on 23 August 2018.

Birkland, Thomas A. (2005), *An Introduction to the Policy Process: Theories, concepts, and models of public policy making*, 2nd edition, Armonk, NY: M.E. Sharpe.

Birnbaum, Simon (2008), *Just Distribution: Rawlsian liberalism and the politics of Basic Income*, Stockholm Studies in Politics 122, Stockholm: Stockholm University.

Birnbaum, Simon (2012), *Basic Income Reconsidered: Social justice, liberalism, and the demands of equality*, New York: Palgrave Macmillan.

Birnbaum, Simon (2019), 'The ethics of Basic Income', in Malcolm Torry (ed.), *The Palgrave International Handbook of Basic Income*, Cham: Palgrave Macmillan, pp. 507–22.

Birnbaum, Simon and Jurgen De Wispelaere (2016), 'Basic Income in the capitalist economy: The mirage of "exit" from employment', *Basic Income Studies*, **11** (1), 61–74.

Bittman, Michael and Jocelyn Pixley (1997), *The Double Life of the Family: Myth, hope and experience*, St. Leonards, Australia: Allen and Unwin.

Blomberg, Helena, Johanna Kallio, Olli Kangas, Christian Kroll and Mikko Niemelä (2012), 'Attitudes among high risk groups', in Stefan Svallfors (ed.), *Contested Welfare States: Welfare attitudes in Europe and beyond*, Stanford, CA: Stanford University Press, pp. 58–80.

Blomquist, William (2018), 'Policy and socioeconomic characteristics', in Hal K. Colebatch and Robert Hoppe (eds), *Handbook on Policy, Process and Governing*, Cheltenham, UK and Northampton, MA, USA: Edward Elgar Publishing, pp. 438–56.

Blumer, Herbert (1969), *Symbolic Interactionism*, New Jersey: Prentice Hall.

Botterill, Linda Courtenay and Alan Fenna (2019), *Interrogating Public Policy Theory: A political values perspective*, Cheltenham, UK and Northampton, MA, USA: Edward Elgar Publishing.

Bowlby, John (1988), *A Secure Base: Clinical applications of attachment theory*, London: Routledge.

Boyle, Katie (2017), 'Constitutionalising a Social Minimum', paper presented at the seminar 'Specifying and Securing a Social Minimum', held at the International Institute for the Sociology of Law, Oñati, Spain, 29–30 June 2017.

Boys Smith, John (2003), 'Do men gather grapes of thorns, or figs of thistles? Matthew 7:6', in Malcolm Torry (ed.), *The Sermons of John Boys Smith*, Cambridge: St. John's College, Cambridge/Aquila Books, pp. 276–9.

Brandt, Richard B. (1979), *A Theory of the Good and the Right*, Oxford: Clarendon Press.

Bregman, Rutger (2017), *Utopia for Realists: And how we can get there*, London: Bloomsbury.

Bregman, Rutger (2018), Lecture at the BIEN Nordic Day held at Tampere, Finland, 23 August 2018.

Brehm, Jack W. and Elizabeth A. Self (1989), 'The intensity of motivation', *Annual Review of Psychology*, **40** (1), 109–31.

Brehm, Sharon, Saul M. Kassin and Steven Fein (1999), *Social Psychology*, 4th edition, Boston, MA: Houghton Mifflin Company.

Breitenbach, Hans, Tom Burden and David Coates (1990), *Features of a Viable Socialism*, Hemel Hempstead: Harvester Wheatsheaf.

British Medical Association, accessed 2 June 2019 at www.bma.org.uk.

Brittan, Samuel (1995), 'Basic Income and the welfare state', in Samuel Brittan, *Capitalism with a Human Face*, Aldershot, UK and Brookfield, VT, USA: Edward Elgar Publishing, reprinted in Karl Widerquist, José A. Noguera, Yannick Vanderborght and Jürgen De Wispelaere (eds) (2013), *Basic Income: An anthology of contemporary research*, Chichester: Wiley Blackwell, pp. 339–45.

Brittan, Samuel (1998), *Towards a Humane Individualism*, London: John Stuart Mill Institute.

Brittan, Samuel and Steven Webb (1990), *Beyond the Welfare State: An examination of Basic Incomes in a market economy*, Aberdeen: Aberdeen University Press.

Britton, Joanne (2007), 'Categorising and policy making', in Susan M. Hodgson and Zoe Irving (eds), *Policy Reconsidered*, Bristol: Policy Press, pp. 61–76.

Broadie, Sarah (1991), *Ethics with Aristotle*, New York: Oxford University Press.

Brown, C.V. and E. Levin (1974), 'The effects of income taxation on overtime: The results of a national survey', *Economic Journal*, **84** (336), 833–48.

Brown, Steve D. and Paul Stenner (2009), *Psychology without Foundations: History, philosophy and psychosocial theory*, Thousand Oaks, CA: Sage.

Bruun, Edvard P.G. and Alban Duka (2018), 'Artificial intelligence, jobs and the future or work: Racing with the machines', *Basic Income Studies*, **13** (2), accessed 25 April 2019 at https://doi.org/10.1515/bis-2018-0018.

Bryan, James B. (2005), 'Targeted programs v. the Basic Income Guarantee: An examination of the efficiency costs of different forms of redistribution', *The Journal of Socioeconomics*, **34** (1), 39–47.

Brynjolfsson, Eirk and Andrew McAfee (2014), *The Second Machine Age: Work, progress, and prosperity in a time of brilliant technologies*, New York: W.W. Norton and Co.

Bryson, Alex and George MacKerron (2013), *Are you Happy while you Work?*, CEP Discussion Paper No 1187, London: Centre for Economic Performance, London School of Economics, accessed 11 August 2018 at http://cep.lse.ac.uk/pubs/download/dp1187.pdf.

Buchanan, James M. (1965), 'An economic theory of clubs', *Economica*, **32** (125), 1–14.

Burbidge, John W. (1993), 'Hegel's conception of logic', in Frederick C. Beiser (ed.), *The Cambridge Companion to Hegel*, Cambridge: Cambridge University Press, pp. 86–101.

Burchardt, Tania and Julian Le Grand (2002), *Constraint and Opportunity: Identifying voluntary non-employment*, CASE paper 55, London: Centre for Analysis of Social Exclusion, London School of Economics.

Burchardt, Tania and Polly Vizard (2007), *Developing a Capabilities List: Final recommendations of the Equalities Review Steering Group on Measurement*, CASE paper no. 121, London: Centre for Analysis of Social Exclusion, London School of Economics.

Burkeman, Oliver (2014), 'It's hard not to wonder whether there isn't another reason simple solutions get overlooked. They seem too obvious', *The Guardian*, 7 March 2014, p. 45.

Butterworth, P.I., L.S. Leach, L. Strazdins, S.C. Olesen, B. Rodgers and D.H. Broom (2011), 'The psychosocial quality of work determines whether employment has benefits for mental health: Results from a longitudinal national household panel survey', *Occupational and Environmental Medicine*, **68** (11), 806–12.

Callinicos, Alex (1983), *The Revolutionary Road to Socialism: What the Socialist Workers Party stands for*, London: Socialist Worker's Party.

Callinicos, Alex (2001), *Against the Third Way: An anti-capitalist criticism*, Cambridge: Polity Press.

Callinicos, Alex (2003), *An Anti-Capitalist Manifesto*, Cambridge: Polity Press.

Calnitsky, D. (2016), '"More normal than welfare": The Mincome experiment, stigma, and community experience', *Canadian Review of Sociology/Revue Canadienne de Sociologie*, **53** (1), 26–71.

Cambridge Essential American English Dictionary, accessed 2 June 2019 at https://dictionary.cambridge.org/dictionary/essential-american-english.

Cameron, Judy and W. David Pierce (1994), 'Reinforcement, reward, and intrinsic motivation: A meta-analysis', *Review of Educational Research*, **64** (3), 363–423.

Campbell, Jim and Morag Gillespie (eds) (2016), *Feminist Economics and Public Policy*, London: Routledge.

Campbell, Mary (2010), *White Paper on Universal Credit: Evidence submitted by Mary Campbell*, London: House of Commons Work and Pensions Committee, accessed 5 December 2018 at www.publications.parliament.uk/pa/cm201011/cmselect/cmworpen/writev/whitepap/uc52.htm.

Cantillon, Bea, Tim Goedemé and John Hills (eds) (2019), *Decent Incomes for All: Improving policies in Europe*, Oxford: Oxford University Press.

Capano, Giliberto, Michael Howlett, M. Ramesh and Altaf Virani (eds) (2019), *Making Policies Work: First- and second-order mechanisms in policy design*, Cheltenham, UK and Northampton, MA, USA: Edward Elgar Publishing.

Carmel, Emma, Alfio Cerami and Theodoros Papadopoulos (eds) (2011), *Migration and Welfare in the New Europe: Social protection and the challenges of integration*, Bristol: Policy Press.

Carmen, Raff (2000), 'The crisis of work and the welfare reform plans in Western countries', in Raff Carmen and Miguel Sobrado, *A Future for the Excluded: Job creation and income generation by the poor: Clodomir Santos de Morais and the Organization Workshop*, London: Zed Books, pp. 162–71.

Carpenter, Mick, Belinda Freda and Stuart Speeden (eds) (2007), *Beyond the Workfare State*, Bristol: Policy Press.

Carr, E. and H. Chung (2014), 'Employment insecurity and life satisfaction: The moderating influence of labour market policies across Europe', *Journal of European Social Policy*, **24** (4), 383–99.

Casassas, David (2016), 'Economic sovereignty as the democratization of work: The role of Basic Income', *Basic Income Studies*, **11** (1), 1–15.

Cato, Molly Scott (2010), *Green Economics: An introduction to theory, policy and practice*, Abingdon: Earthscan.

Centre for Economic Studies/Ifo Institute (2008), *Bismarck Versus Beveridge: Social insurance systems in Europe*, Munich: Ifo Institute for Economic Research/Centre for Economic Studies, accessed 4 December 2018 at https://www.cesifo-group.de/DocDL/dicereport408-db6.pdf.

Centre for the Modern Family (2011), *Family: Helping to understand the modern British family*, Edinburgh: Scottish Widows, Centre for the Modern Family.

Centre for Social Justice (2009), *Dynamic Benefits: Towards welfare that works*, London: Centre for Social Justice.

Centre for Social Justice (2018), *Universal Basic Income: An effective policy for poverty reduction?*, London: Centre for Social Justice.

Choi, I. and R.E. Nisbett (1998), 'Situational salience and cultural differences in the correspondence bias and actor-observer bias', *Personality and Social Psychology Bulletin*, **24** (9), 949–60.

Cholbi, Michael and Michael Weber (eds) (2020), *The Future of Work, Technology, and Basic Income*, New York and Abingdon: Routledge.

Chrisp, Joe (2018), 'Snowballing or wilting? Identifying public support for basic income', paper presented at the BIEN Congress in Tampere, Finland, 25 August 2018.

Citizen's Basic Income Trust (2015), 'Book review: *Inequality*, by Anthony B. Atkinson', accessed 5 December 2018 at https://citizensincome.org/book-reviews/inequality-by-anthony-b-atkinson.

Citizen's Basic Income Trust (2018a), *Citizen's Basic Income: A brief introduction*, London: Citizen's Basic Income Trust.

Citizen's Basic Income Trust (2018b), 'Book review: Peter John, *How Far to Nudge?*', London: Citizen's Basic Income Trust, accessed 2 June 2019 at https://citizensincome.org/book-reviews/peter-john-how-far-to-nudge.

Citizen's Basic Income Trust (2018c), 'Illustrative draft legislation for a Citizen's Basic Income', London: Citizen's Basic Income Trust, accessed 4 October 2019 at https://citizensincome.org/news/illustrative-draft-legislation-for-a-citizens-basic-income/.

Citizen's Basic Income Trust (2019a), 'Book review: Isabel Ortiz, Christina Behrendt, Andrés Acuña-Ulate and Quynh Anh Nguyen, *Universal Basic Income Proposals in Light of ILO standards*', London: Citizen's Basic Income Trust, accessed 22 September 2019 at https://citizensincome.org/news/ilo-paper-on-citizens-basic-income-and-ilo-social-protection-floors/.

Citizen's Basic Income Trust (2019b), 'Book review: Disabled People Against Cuts, *UBI: Solution or Illusion?*', accessed 23 September 2019 at https://citizensincome.org/news/disabled-people-against-cuts-ubi-solution-or-illusion/.

Clifford, Catherine (2017), 'What billionaires and business titans say about cash hand-outs in 2017 (Hint: lots!)', accessed 21 November 2018 at https://www.cnbc.com/2017/12/27/what-billionaires-say-about-universal-basic-income-in-2017.html.

Cogolati, Samuel and Jan Wouters (eds) (2018), *The Commons and New Global Governance*, Cheltenham, UK and Northampton, MA, USA: Edward Elgar Publishing.

Cohen, Sheldon and Jeffrey R. Edwards (1989), 'Personality characteristics as moderators of the relationship between stress and disorder', in Richard W.J. Neufeld (ed.), *Advances in the Investigation of Psychological Stress*, New York: John Wiley and Sons, pp. 235–83.

Cohen, Sheldon and Gail M. Williamson (1991), 'Stress and infectious disease in humans', *Psychological Bulletin*, **109** (1), 5–24.

Colebatch, H.K. (2018a), 'Design as a window on the policy process', in Hal K. Colebatch and Robert Hoppe (eds), *Handbook on Policy, Process and Governing*, Cheltenham, UK and Northampton, MA, USA: Edward Elgar Publishing, pp. 131–46.

Colebatch, H.K. (2018b), 'Linkage and the policy process', in Hal K. Colebatch and Robert Hoppe (eds), *Handbook on Policy, Process and Governing*, Cheltenham, UK and Northampton, MA, USA: Edward Elgar Publishing, pp. 204–19.

Collard, David (1978), *Altruism and Economy: A study in non-selfish economics*, Oxford: Martin Robertson.

Commission on Citizenship (1990), *Encouraging Citizenship*, Report of the Commission on Citizenship, London: Her Majesty's Stationery Office.

Conen, Wieteke and Joop Schippers (eds) (2019), *Self-Employment as Precarious Work: A European perspective*, Cheltenham, UK and Northampton, MA, USA: Edward Elgar Publishing.

Coote, Anna (1996), 'Social rights and responsibilities', *Soundings*, issue 2, pp. 203–12.

Coote, Anna, Jane Franklin and Andrew Simms (2010), *21 Hours: Why a shorter working week can help us all to flourish in the 21st century*, London: New Economics Foundation.

Copp, David (1992), 'The right to an adequate standard of living: Justice, autonomy, and the basic needs', in Ellen Frankel Paul, Fred D. Miller and Jeffrey Paul (eds), *Economic Rights*, Cambridge: Cambridge University Press, pp. 231–61.

Corlett, Adam, Stephen Clarke, Conor D'Arcy and John Wood (2018), *The Living Standards Audit 2018*, London: The Resolution Foundation.

Cornes, Richard and Todd Sandler (1986), *The Theory of Externalities, Public Goods and Club Goods*, Cambridge: Cambridge University Press.

Cory, Giselle (2013), *All Work and No Pay: Second earners' work incentives and childcare costs under Universal Credit*, London: Resolution Foundation.

Costabile, Lilia (ed.) (2008), *Institutions for Social Well-Being: Alternatives for Europe*, Basingstoke: Palgrave Macmillan.

Coughlin, Richard M. (1980), *Ideology, Public Opinion and Welfare Policy: Attitudes towards taxes and spending in industrialized societies*, Berkeley, CA: Institute of International Studies, University of California.

Cowen, Tyler (2002), 'Does the welfare state help the poor?', in Ellen Frankel Paul, Fred D. Miller Jr. and Jeffrey Paul (eds), *Should Differences in Income and Wealth Matter?*, Cambridge: Cambridge University Press, pp. 36–54.

Craig, David with Richard Brooks (2006), *Plundering the Public Sector*, London: Constable.

Cribb, Jonathan, Agnes Norris Keiller and Tom Waters (2018), *Living Standards, Poverty and Inequality in the UK: 2018*, London: Institute for Fiscal Studies, accessed 22 December 2018 at https://www.ifs.org.uk/uploads/R145%20for%20web.pdf.

Crocker, Geoff (2012), 'Why austerity is the wrong answer to debt: A call for a new paradigm', *Citizen's Income Newsletter*, issue 3 for 2012, pp. 13–16.

Crocker, Geoff (2015), 'Keynes, Piketty, and Basic Income', *Basic Income Studies*, **10** (1), 91–113.

Crocker, Geoff (2019), 'Funding Basic Income by money creation', in Malcolm Torry (ed.), *The Palgrave International Handbook of Basic Income*, Cham: Palgrave Macmillan, pp. 180–5.

Cuff, E.C., W.W. Sharrock and D.W. Francis (1998), *Perspectives in Sociology*, 4th edition, London: Routledge.

Culpit, Ian (1992), *Welfare and Citizenship: Beyond the crisis of the welfare state*, Beverly Hills: Sage.

Cusworth, Linda (2009), *The Impact of Parental Employment: Young people, well-being and educational achievement*, Aldershot: Ashgate.

Dahrendorf, Ralf (1974), 'Citizenship and beyond: The social dynamics of an idea', *Social Research,* **41** (4), 673–701.

Dahrendorf, Ralf (1991), 'Can it happen?', An interview with Susan Raven, *BIRG Bulletin*, no. 13, August 1991, pp. 12–13.

Dahrendorf, Ralf (1995), *Report on Wealth Creation and Social Cohesion in a Free Society* (The Dahrendorf Report), London: The Commission on Wealth Creation and Social Cohesion.

Dalziel, Paul, Caroline Saunders and Joe Saunders (2018), *Wellbeing Economics: The capabilities approach to prosperity*, Basingstoke: Palgrave Macmillan.

Darley, John M. and Paget H. Gross (1983), 'A hypothesis-confirming bias in labelling effects', *Journal of Personality and Social Psychology*, **44** (1), 20–33.

Darton, David, Donald Hirsch and Jason Strelitz (2003), *Tackling Disadvantage: A 20-year enterprise: A working paper for the Joseph Rowntree Foundation's Centenary Conference, December 2004*, York: Joseph Rowntree Foundation.

Daugareilh, Isabelle, Christophe Degryse and Philippe Pochet (2019), *The Platform Economy and Social Law: Key issues in comparative perspective*, Brussels: European Trade Union Institute, accessed 18 July 2019 at https://www.etui.org/Publications2/Working-Papers/The-platform-economy-and-social-law-Key-issues-in-comparative-perspective.

Davala, Sarath (2019), 'Pilots, evidence and politics: The Basic Income debate in India', in Malcolm Torry (ed.), *The Palgrave International Handbook of Basic Income*, Cham: Palgrave Macmillan, pp. 373–87.

Davala, Sarath, Renana Jhabvala, Soumya Kapoor Mehta and Guy Standing (2015), *Basic Income: A transformative policy for India*, London: Bloomsbury.

Davies, Paul (1989), in Paul Davies (ed.), *The New Physics*, Cambridge: Cambridge University Press, p. 4.

Davis, Abigail, Donald Hirsch, Matt Padley and Claire Shepherd (2018), *A Minimum Income Standard for the UK 2008–2018: Continuity and change*, York: Joseph Rowntree Foundation, accessed 21 December 2018 at https://www.jrf.org.uk/report/minimum-income-standard-uk-2018.

Davis, Abigail and Matt Padley (2018), 'What the Minimum Income Standard tells us about living standards in the United Kingdom', in David Fée and Anémone Kober-Smith (eds), *Inequalities in the UK: New discourse, evolutions and actions*, Bingley: Emerald Publishing, pp. 101–17.

Day, Alan J. (2000), 'Think tanks in Western Europe', in James McGann and R. Kent Weaver (eds), *Think Tanks and Civil Societies: Catalysts for ideas and action*, New Brunswick: Transaction Publishers, pp. 103–38.

De Wispelaere, Jurgen (undated), *Universal Basic Income: Reciprocity and the right to non-exclusion*, London: Citizen's Income Trust.

De Wispelaere, Jurgen, Antti Halmetoja and Ville-Veikko Pulkka (2019), 'The Finnish Basic Income Experiment: A primer', in Malcolm Torry (ed.), *The Palgrave International Handbook of Basic Income*, Cham: Palgrave Macmillan, pp. 389–406.

De Wispelaere, Jurgen and José Antonio Noguera (2012), 'On the political feasibility of Universal Basic Income: An analytic framework', in Richard Caputo (ed.), *Basic Income Guarantee and Politics: International experiences and perspectives on the viability of income guarantee*, New York: Palgrave Macmillan, pp. 17–38.

De Wispelaere, Jurgen and Lindsay Stirton (2008), 'Why Participation Income might not be such a great idea after all', *Citizen's Income Newsletter*, issue 3 for 2008, pp. 3–8.

De Wispelaere, Jurgen and Lindsay Stirton (2011), 'The administrative efficiency of Basic Income', *Policy and Politics*, **39** (1), 115–32.

Dean, Hartley (1998), 'Popular paradigms and welfare values', *Critical Social Policy*, **18** (55), 131–56.

Dean, Hartley (2004), 'Where next for social policy?', accessed 19 December 2018 at https://www.jiscmail.ac.uk/cgi-bin/webadmin?A2=social-policy;3328cad7.0412.

Dean, Hartley (2010), *Understanding Human Need*, Bristol: Policy Press.

Dean, Hartley (2011a), 'The ethics of migrant welfare', *Ethics and Social Welfare*, **5** (1), 18–35.

Dean, Hartley (2011b), 'What role for social solidarity?', in Armando Barrientos, Benjamin Davy, Ulrike Davy, Hartley Dean, Harvey M. Jacobs, Lutz Leisering and Sony Pellissery (eds), *A Road to Global Social Citizenship?*, Financial Assistance, Land Policy, and Global Social Rights Working Paper no. 10, p. 16, accessed 2 June 2019 at www.tinyurl.com/3n9jh5h.

Dean, Hartley (2012a), 'The ethical deficit of the UK's proposed Universal Credit: Pimping the precariat?' *Political Quarterly*, **83** (2), 353–9.

Dean, Hartley (2012b), 'Re-conceptualising Welfare-to-Work for people with multiple problems and needs', *Journal of Social Policy*, **32** (3), 441–59.

Dean, Hartley (2012c), *Social Policy*, 2nd edition, Cambridge: Polity Press.

Dean, Hartley (2016), 'Poverty and social exclusion', in Hartley Dean and Lucinda Platt (eds), *Social Advantage and Disadvantage*, Oxford: Oxford University Press, pp. 3–24.

Dean, Hartley (2019), 'Social and human rights', in James Midgley, Rebecca Surender and Laura Alfers (eds), *Handbook of Social Policy and Development*, Cheltenham, UK and Northampton, MA, USA: Edward Elgar Publishing, pp. 130–46.

Dean, Hartley (forthcoming, 2020), *Understanding Human Need*, 2nd edition, Bristol: Policy Press.

Dean, Hartley and Margaret Melrose (1999), *Poverty, Riches and Social Citizenship*, Basingstoke: Macmillan.

Dean, Hartley and Lucinda Platt (eds) (2016), *Social Advantage and Disadvantage*, Oxford: Oxford University Press.

Deaton, Angus (1992), *Understanding Consumption*, Oxford: Clarendon Press.

Deaton, Angus and John Muellbauer (1980), *Economics and Consumer Behaviour*, Cambridge: Cambridge University Press.

Deci, Edward L. and Richard M. Ryan (1985), *Intrinsic Motivation and Self-determination in Human Behaviour*, New York: Plenum.

Deeming, Christopher and Paul Smyth (eds) (2017), *Reframing Global Social Policy: Social investment for sustainable and inclusive growth*, Bristol: Policy Press.

Dekker, S.W. and W.B. Schaufeli (1995), 'The effects of job insecurity on psychological health and withdrawal: A longitudinal study', *Australian Psychologist*, **30** (1), 57–63.

Denham, Andrew and Mark Garnett (1998), *British Think-tanks and the Climate of Opinion*, London: UCL Press.

Department for Work and Pensions (2012), *Digital Strategy*, London: Department for Work and Pensions, accessed 5 December 2018 at https://assets.publishing .service.gov.uk/government/uploads/system/uploads/attachment_data/file/193901/ dwp-digital-strategy.pdf.

Department for Work and Pensions (2018a), *Family Resources Survey: Financial year 2016–17*, London: Department for Work and Pensions, accessed 30 November 2018 at https://www.gov.uk/government/statistics/family-resources-survey-financial-year -201617.

Department for Work and Pensions (2018b), *Fraud and Error in the Benefits System*, London: Department for Work and Pensions, accessed 5 December 2018 at https:// assets.publishing.service.gov.uk/government/uploads/system/uploads/attachment _data/file/707831/fraud-and-error-preliminary-estimates-2017-2018.pdf.

DePaulo, Bella M. (1992), 'Nonverbal behaviors and self-presentation', *Psychological Bulletin*, **111** (2), 203–43.

Dermott, Esther (2018), 'Introduction: Poverty and social exclusion in the UK', in Esther Dermott and Gill Main (eds), *Poverty and Social Exclusion in the UK: Volume 1 – the nature and extent of the problem*, Bristol: Policy Press, pp. 1–15.

Dermott, Esther and Christina Pantazis (2018), 'Which men and women are poor? Gender, poverty and social exclusion', in Esther Dermott and Gill Main (eds), *Poverty and Social Exclusion in the UK: Volume 1 – the nature and extent of the problem*, Bristol: Policy Press, pp. 95–114.

Desai, Meghnad and Ana Helena Palermo (2019), 'Some effects of Basic Income on economic variables', in Malcolm Torry (ed.), *The Palgrave International Handbook of Basic Income*, Cham: Palgrave Macmillan, pp. 91–110.

Devas, Charles S. (1919), *Political Economy*, London: Longmans, Green and Co.

Di Domenico, S.I. and M.A. Fournier (2014), 'Socioeconomic status, income inequality, and health complaints: A basic psychological needs perspective', *Social Indicators Research*, **119** (3), 1679–97.

Diamond, Patrick (2018), *The End of Whitehall*, Basingstoke: Palgrave Macmillan.

Dickens, Richard and Abigail McKnight (2008), *Changes in Earnings Inequality and Mobility in Great Britain 1978/9 – 2005/6*, CASE paper no. 132, London: Centre for Analysis of Social Exclusion, London School of Economics.

DiMaggio, Paul and W. Powell (1983), 'The iron cage revisited: Conformity and diversity in organisational fields', *American Sociological Review*, **48** (2), 147–60.

Disabled People Against Cuts (2019), 'UBI: Solution or illusion?', accessed 23 September 2019 at https://dpac.uk.net/2019/01/universal-basic-income/.

Dolton, Peter, Chiara Rosazza Bondibene and Jonathan Wadsworth (2010), 'The UK National Minimum Wage in retrospect', *Fiscal Studies*, **31** (4), 510–32.

Donagan, Alan (1977), *The Theory of Morality*, Chicago: University of Chicago Press.

Donnison, David (1982), *The Politics of Poverty*, Oxford: Martin Robertson.

Dooley, D. (2003), 'Unemployment, underemployment, and mental health: Conceptualizing employment status as a continuum', *American Journal of Community Psychology*, **32** (1–2), 9–20.

Dore, Ronald (2001), 'Dignity and deprivation', in Joshua Cohen and Joel Rogers (eds), *What's Wrong with a Free Lunch?*, Boston: Beacon Press, pp. 80–4.

Dorling, Daniel (2010), *Injustice: Why social inequality persists*, Bristol: Policy Press.

Dorling, Danny (2012), *The No-nonsense Guide to Equality*, London: New Internationalist.

Dorling, Danny (2017), *The Equality Effect: Improving life for everyone*, Oxford: New Internationalist Publications.

Douillard, Austin (2017), 'New study published on results of Basic Income pilot in Kenya', *Basic Income News*, BIEN, accessed 17 May 2017 at http://basicincome.org/news/2017/03/us-kenya-new-study-published-results-basic-income-pilot-kenya/.

Dow, Sheila C. (2017), 'Cambridge's contribution to methodology of economics', in Robert A. Cord (ed.), *The Palgrave Companion to Cambridge Economics*, volume 1, London: Palgrave Macmillan, pp. 27–49.

Dowding, Keith (2018), 'The advocacy coalition framework', in Hal K. Colebatch and Robert Hoppe (eds), *Handbook on Policy, Process and Governing*, Cheltenham, UK and Northampton, MA, USA: Edward Elgar Publishing, pp. 220–31.

Drew, Joseph and Glenn Fahey (2018), 'Framing unpopular policies and creating policy winners: The role of heresthetics', *Policy and Politics*, **46** (4), 627–43.

Dunlop, Claire A., Claudio M. Radaelli and Philipp Trein (eds) (2018), *Learning in Public Policy: Analysis, modes and outcomes*, Cham: Palgrave Macmillan.

Dunn, William N. (2018), '"Stage" theories of the policy process', in Hal K. Colebatch and Robert Hoppe (eds), *Handbook on Policy, Process and Governing*, Cheltenham, UK and Northampton, MA, USA: Edward Elgar Publishing, pp. 112–30.

Durkheim, Emile (1938), *The Rules of Sociological Method*, Chicago: University of Chicago Press.

Durkheim, Emile (1952), *Suicide*, London: Routledge.

Durkheim, Emile (1961), *Moral Education*, New York: The Free Press. Originally published in French in 1925.

Durkheim, Emile (1984), *The Division of Labour in Society*, Basingstoke: Macmillan.

Duverger, Timothée (2018), *L'Invention du Revenu de Base: La fabrique d'une utopie démocratique*, Lormont: Le Bord de L'Eau.

Dworkin, Ronald (1977), *Taking Rights Seriously*, London: Duckworth.

Dwyer, Peter (2004), *Understanding Social Citizenship*, Bristol: Policy Press.

Dwyer, Peter (ed.) (2019), *Dealing with Welfare Conditionality: Implementation and effects*, Bristol: Policy Press.

East, Robert (1999), *Social Security Law*, Basingstoke: Macmillan.

Edmiston, Daniel (2017), 'Review article: Welfare, austerity and social citizenship in the UK', *Social Policy and Society*, **16** (2), 261–70.

Edmiston, Daniel, Ruth Patrick and Kayleigh Garthwaite (2017), 'Introduction: Austerity, welfare and social citizenship', *Social Policy and Society*, **16** (2), 253–9.

Edward Elgar (2018), *2019 New Titles and Selected Backlist: Economics*, Cheltenham, UK and Northampton, MA, USA: Edward Elgar Publishing,

Egan, Mark (2017), *A Macat Analysis: Richard H. Thaler and Cass R. Sunstein's Nudge: Improving decisions about health, wealth and happiness*, London: Macat.

Ehrenfreund, Ernst (2015), 'Where the poor and rich really spend their money', *The Washington Post*, 14 April 2015, accessed 27 December 2018 at https://www.washingtonpost.com/news/wonk/wp/2015/04/14/where-the-poor-and-rich-spend-really-spend-their-money.

Eisenberger, Robert and Judy Cameron (1996), 'Detrimental effects of reward: Reality or myth?', *American Psychologist*, **51** (11), 1153–66.

Electoral Commission (2017), *Analysis of the December 2016 Electoral Registers in the United Kingdom*, London: Electoral Commission, accessed 29 November 2018 at https://www.electoralcommission.org.uk/__data/assets/pdf_file/0010/222877/ Analysis-of-the-December-2016-electoral-registers-in-the-United-Kingdom.pdf.

Elgarte, Julieta M. (2008), 'Basic Income and the gendered division of labour', *Basic Income Studies*, **3** (3), 1–7.

Emmerson, Carl, Paul Johnson and Helen Miller (2013), *The IFS Green Budget: February 2013*, London: Institute for Fiscal Studies, accessed 20 November 2018 at www.ifs.org.uk/publications/6562.

Emmerson, Carl, Paul Johnson and Helen Miller (2014), *The IFS Green Budget: February 2014*, London: Institute for Fiscal Studies, accessed 13 August 2018 at www.ifs.org.uk/budgets/gb2014/gb2014.pdf.

Enríquez, Corina Rodríguez (2016), 'Basic Income and time use democratization', *Basic Income Studies*, **11** (1), 39–48.

Enzle, Michael E. and Sharon C. Anderson (1993), 'Surveillant intentions and intrinsic motivation', *Journal of Personality and Social Psychology*, **64** (2), 257–66.

Epstein, Seymour and Lori Katz (1992), 'Coping ability, stress, productive load, and symptoms', *Journal of Personality and Social Psychology*, **62** (5), 813–25.

Equality and Human Rights Commission, accessed 2 June 2019 at https://www .equalityhumanrights.com/en/human-rights/human-rights-act.

Esam, Peter and Richard Berthoud (1991), *Independent Benefits for Men and Women*, London: Policy Studies Institute.

Esam, Peter, Robert Good and Rick Middleton (1985), *Who's to Benefit? A radical review of the social security system*, London: Verso.

Esping-Andersen, Gøsta (1990), *The Three Worlds of Welfare Capitalism*, Cambridge: Polity Press.

European Social Survey (2017), 'Assessing support for universal basic income', accessed 20 May 2019 at https://www.europeansocialsurvey.org/findings/singleblog .html?a=/findings/blog/essblog0010.html.

European Union (2018), 'EU citizenship', accessed 29 November 2018 at https:// europa.eu/european-union/topics/eu-citizenship_en.

Evans, Martin and Lewis Williams (2009), *A Generation of Change, a Lifetime of Difference? Social policy in Britain since 1979*, Bristol: Policy Press.

Exley, Sonia (2014), 'Think tanks and policy networks in English education', in Michael Hill (ed.), *Studying Public Policy: An international approach*, Bristol: Policy Press, pp. 180–9.

Fahey, Tony (2010), *Poverty and the Two Concepts of Relative Deprivation*, University College Dublin Working Paper, WP10/1, Dublin: University College Dublin, accessed 21 December 2018 at https://www.ucd.ie/t4cms/Poverty%20Seminar %20Tony%20Fahey,%2019%20May%202011.pdf.

Federici, Silvia (1975), *Wages Against Housework*, Bristol: Falling Wall Press.

Fée, David and Anémone Kober-Smith (eds) (2018), *Inequalities in the UK: New discourse, evolutions and actions*, Bingley: Emerald Publishing.

Fenger, Menno, John Hudson and Catherine Needham (2016), *Social Policy Review 28: Analysis and debate in social policy, 2016*, Bristol: Policy Press.

Ferguson, Iain, Michael Lavalette and Gerry Mooney (2002), *Rethinking Welfare: A critical perspective*, London: Sage.

Festinger, L., A. Pepitoni and T. Newcomb (1952), 'Some consequences of deindividuation in a group', *Journal of Abnormal and Social Psychology*, **47** (S2), 382–9.

Fevre, Ralph (2016), *Individualism and Inequality: The future of work and politics*, Cheltenham, UK and Northampton, MA, USA: Edward Elgar Publishing.

Fitzpatrick, Tony (1999), *Freedom and Security: An introduction to the Basic Income debate*, Basingstoke: Macmillan.

Foldvary, Fred (1994), *Public Goods and Private Communities: The market provision of social services*, Aldershot, UK and Brookfield, VT, USA: Edward Elgar Publishing.

Folkman, Susan and Richard S. Lazarus (1988), 'Coping as a mediator of emotion', *Journal of Personality and Social Psychology*, **54** (3), 466–75.

Foot, Philippa (1988), 'Utilitarianism and the virtues', in Samuel Scheffler (ed.), *Consequentialism and its Critics*, Oxford: Oxford University Press, pp. 224–42.

Forget, Evelyn (2011), 'The town with no poverty: The health effects of a Canadian guaranteed annual income field experiment', *Canadian Public Policy/Politiques Canadienne*, **37** (3), 283–305.

French, J.R.P. Jr. and B.H. Raven (1959), 'The bases of social power', in D. Cartwright (ed.), *Studies in Social Power*, Ann Arbor, MI: Institute for Social Research, reprinted in D.S. Pugh (ed.) (1984), *Organization Theory: Selected readings*, 2nd edition, Harmondsworth: Penguin, pp. 150–67.

Friedli, L. and R. Stearn (2015), 'Positive affect as coercive strategy: Conditionality, activation and the role of psychology in UK government workfare programmes', *Medical Humanities*, **41** (1), 40–7.

Fryer, D. and R. Fagan (2003), 'Towards a critical community psychological perspective on unemployment and mental health', *American Journal of Community Psychology*, **32** (1–2), 89–96.

Fryers, T., D. Melzer and R. Jenkins (2003), 'Social inequalities and the common mental disorders', *Social Psychiatry and Psychiatric Epidemiology*, **38** (5), 229–37.

Fukuma, Satoshi (2017), 'Meaningful work, worthwhile life, and self-respect: Reexamination of the Rawlsian perspective on Basic Income in a property-owning democracy', *Basic Income Studies*, **12** (1), accessed 25 April 2017 at https://doi.org/10.1515/bis-2017-0011.

Galbraith, J.K. (1969), *The Affluent Society*, 2nd edition, London: Hamish Hamilton.

Galbraith, J.K. (1976), *Money: Whence it came, where it went*, Harmondsworth: Penguin.

Galbraith, J.K. (2002), 'The importance of being sufficiently equal', in Ellen Frankel Paul, Fred D. Miller, Jr. and Jeffrey Paul (eds), *Should Differences in Income and Wealth Matter?*, Cambridge: Cambridge University Press, pp. 201–24.

Gamble, Andrew (2016), *Can the Welfare State Survive?*, Cambridge: Polity Press.

Gardner, J.P. (1990), *Encouraging Citizenship: Report of the Commission on Citizenship*, London: Her Majesty's Stationery Office.

Garner, Robert, Peter Ferdinand and Stephanie Lawson (2009), *Introduction to Politics*, Oxford: Oxford University Press.

Garthwaite, Kayleigh (2017), '"I feel I'm giving something back to society": Constructing the "active citizen" and responsibilising foodbank use', *Social Policy and Society*, **16** (2), 283–92.

George, Vic and Paul Wilding (1984), *The Impact of Social Policy*, London: Routledge and Kegan Paul.

Gheaus, Anca (2008), 'Basic Income, gender justice and the costs of gender-symmetrical lifestyles', *Basic Income Studies*, **3** (3), 1–8.

Giddens, Anthony (1998), *The Third Way: The renewal of social democracy*, Cambridge: Polity Press.

Giddens, Anthony (2001), *Sociology*, 4th edition, Cambridge: Polity.

Gilbert, Richard, Ursula Huws and Gunmin Yi (2019), 'Employment market effects of Basic Income', in Malcolm Torry (ed.), *The Palgrave International Handbook of Basic Income*, Cham: Palgrave Macmillan, pp. 47–72.

Gilbert, Richard, Nora A. Murphy, Allison Stepka, Mark Barrett and Dianne Worku (2018), 'Would a Basic Income Guarantee reduce the motivation to work? An analysis of labor responses in 16 trial programs', *Basic Income Studies*, **13** (2), accessed 25 April 2019 at https://doi.org/10.1515/bis-2018-0011.

Gingrich, Jane (2014), 'Structuring the vote: Welfare institutions and value-based vote choices', in Staffan Kumlin and Isbele Stadelmann-Steffen (eds), *How Welfare States Shape the Democratic Public: Policy feedback, participation, voting and attitudes*, Cheltenham, UK and Northampton, MA, USA: Edward Elgar Publishing, pp. 93–112.

Ginn, Jay (1993), 'Pension penalties: The gendered division of occupational welfare', *Work, Employment & Society*, **7** (1), 47–70.

Ginn, Jay (2003), *Gender, Pensions and the Lifecourse*, Bristol: Policy Press.

Glaeser, Edward L., Bruce I. Sacerdote and Jose A. Scheinkman (2002), *The Social Multiplier*, Cambridge, MA: National Bureau of Economic Research, accessed 9 August 2018 at http://www.nber.org/papers/w9153.pdf.

Goedemé, Tim, Bérénice Storms, Karel Van den Bosch and Tess Penne (2017), 'Is there common ground for defining a decent social minimum in Europe?', Paper presented at the seminar 'Specifying and Securing a Social Minimum', held at the International Institute for the Sociology of Law, Oñati, Spain, 29–30 June 2017.

Goffman, Erving (1968), *Asylums: Essays on the social situation of mental patients and other inmates*, Harmondsworth: Penguin.

Goffman, Erving (1969), *The Presentation of the Self in Everyday Life*, London: Allen Lane.

Goffman, Erving (1990), *Stigma: Notes on the management of spoiled identity*, London: Penguin.

Golding, Martin P. (1972), 'The primacy of welfare rights', *Social Philosophy and Policy*, **1** (2), 119–136.

Golding, Peter and Sue Middleton (1982), *Images of Welfare: Press and public attitudes to poverty*, Oxford: Basil Blackwell.

Goldsmith, Scott (2012), 'The economic and social impacts of the Permanent Fund Dividend on Alaska', in Karl Widerquist and Michael W. Howard (eds), *Alaska's Permanent Fund Dividend: Examining its suitability as a model*, New York: Palgrave Macmillan, pp. 49–63.

Goodin, Robert E. (1988), *Reasons for Welfare: The political theory of the welfare state*, Princeton, NJ: Princeton University Press.

Goodwin, Stephen (1994), 'Liberal Democrats' Conference: Citizen's income plan dropped', *The Independent*, Thursday 22 September 1994, accessed 12 January 2019 at www.independent.co.uk/news/uk/liberal-democrats-conference-citizens-income-plan-dropped-1450315.html.

Goos, Maarten and Alan Manning (2007), 'Lousy and lovely jobs: The rising polarization of work in Britain', *Review of Economics and Statistics*, **89** (1), 118–33.

Gordon, Ian, Janet Lewis and Ken Young (1997), 'Perspectives on policy analysis', in Michael Hill (ed.), *The Policy Process: A reader*, London and New York: Prentice Hall/Harvester Wheatsheaf, pp. 5–9.

Gosling, R. and S. Taylor (eds) (2005), *Principles of Sociology*, London: London School of Economics and Political Science.

Gough, Ian (1979), *The Political Economy of the Welfare State*, London: Macmillan.

Gough, Ian (2015), 'The political economy of prevention', *British Journal of Political Science*, **45** (2), 307–27.

Gough, Ian (2017), *Heat, Greed and Human Need: Climate change, capitalism and sustainable wellbeing*, Cheltenham, UK and Northampton, MA, USA: Edward Elgar Publishing.

Gourevitch, Alex (2016), 'The limits of a Basic Income: Means and ends of workplace democracy', *Basic Income Studies*, **11** (1), 17–28.

Government of Canada (2018), 'Government of Canada fighting climate change with price on pollution', accessed 5 April 2019 at https://pm.gc.ca/eng/news/2018/10/23/government-canada-fighting-climate-change-price-pollution.

Graeber, David (2018), *Bullshit Jobs: A theory*, London: Allen Lane.

Gramsci, Antonio (1971), *Selections from Prison Notebooks*, London: Lawrence and Wishart.

Gray, John (2007), 'On top of the world', a review of Will Hutton's *The Writing on the Wall: China and the West in the 21st century*, *The Guardian Weekly*, 2–8 February 2007, p. 23.

Grayling, A.C. (1988), *Wittgenstein*, Oxford: Oxford University Press.

Greener, Ian (2018), *Social Policy after the Financial Crisis*, Cheltenham, UK and Northampton, MA, USA: Edward Elgar Publishing.

Gregg, Paul (2009), 'Job guarantees – easing the pain of long-term unemployment', *Public Policy Research*, **16** (3), 174–9.

Gregg, Samuel (2010), *Wilhelm Röpke's Political Economy*, Cheltenham, UK and Northampton, MA, USA: Edward Elgar Publishing.

Gregory, Lee (2018), *Exploring Welfare Debates: Key concepts and questions*, Bristol: Policy Press.

Gregory, Robert (1997), 'Political rationality or incrementalism?', in Michael Hill (ed.), *The Policy Process: A reader*, London and New York: Prentice Hall/Harvester Wheatsheaf, pp. 175–91.

Greve, Bent (2017), *Technology and the Future of Work: The impact on labour markets and welfare states*, Cheltenham, UK and Northampton, MA, USA: Edward Elgar Publishing.

Griffiths, Rita (2017), 'No love on the dole: The influence of the UK means-tested welfare system on partnering and family structure', *Journal of Social Policy*, **46** (3), 543–61.

Grin, John (2018), 'Stasis and change', in Hal K. Colebatch and Robert Hoppe (eds), *Handbook on Policy, Process and Governing*, Cheltenham, UK and Northampton, MA, USA: Edward Elgar Publishing, pp. 418–37.

Groenewegen, Peter (1987), 'Political economy', in Palgrave Macmillan (eds), *The New Palgrave Dictionary of Economics*, Basingstoke: Palgrave Macmillan, accessed 2 June 2019 at https://link.springer.com/referenceworkentry/10.1057/978-1-349-95121-5_1365-2.

Groot, Loek, Ruud Muffels and Timo Verlaat (2019), 'Welfare states' social investment strategies and the emergence of Dutch experiments on a Minimum Income Guarantee', *Social Policy and Society*, **18** (2), 277–87.

Groves, Peter (2012), *Grace*, Norwich: Canterbury Press.

Haagh, Louise (2015), 'Alternative social states and the Basic Income debate: Institutions, inequality and human development', *Basic Income Studies*, **10** (1), 45–81.

Haagh, Louise (2019a), *The Case for Universal Basic Income*, Cambridge: Polity Press.

Haagh, Louise (2019b), 'Review article: The political economy of governance capacity and institutional change: The case of Basic Income security reform in European welfare states', *Social Policy and Society*, **18** (2), 243–63.

Haarmann, Claudia and Dirk Haarmann (2007), 'From survival to decent employment: Basic Income security in Namibia', *Basic Income Studies*, **2** (1), 1–7.

Haarmann, Claudia and Dirk Haarmann (2012), 'Namibia: Seeing the sun rise – The realities and hopes of the Basic Income Grant Pilot Project', in Matthew C. Murray and Carole Pateman (eds), *Basic Income Worldwide: Horizons of reform*, New York: Palgrave Macmillan, pp. 33–58.

Haarmann, Claudia, Dirk Haarmann and Nicoli Nattrass (2019), 'The Namibian Basic Income Grant pilot', in Malcolm Torry (ed.), *The Palgrave International Handbook of Basic Income*, Cham: Palgrave Macmillan, pp. 357–72.

Hakim, Catherine (2003), *Models of the Family in Modern Society: Ideals and realities*, Aldershot: Ashgate.

Halmetoja, Antti, Jurgen De Wispelaere and Johanna Periö (2019), 'A policy comet in Moominland? Basic Income in the Finnish welfare state', *Social Policy and Society*, **18** (2), 309–30.

Ham, Christopher and Michael Hill (1984), *The Policy Process in the Modern Capitalist State*, Brighton: Wheatsheaf Books.

Hamilton, Peter (1992), 'The Enlightenment and the birth of social science', in Stuart Hall and Bram Gieben (eds), *Formations of Modernity*, Milton Keynes: Open University, pp. 17–70.

Handler, Joel. F. (2005), 'Myth and ceremony in workfare: Rights, contracts, and client satisfaction', *The Journal of Socioeconomics*, **34** (1), 101–24.

Handy, Charles (1994), *The Empty Raincoat: Making sense of the future*, London: Hutchinson.

Harari, Daniel (2018), *Household Debt: Statistics and impact on economy*, London: House of Commons Library, accessed 2 June 2019 at https://researchbriefings .parliament.uk/ResearchBriefing/Summary/CBP-7584.

Hare, R.M. (1963), *Freedom and Reason*, Oxford: Oxford University Press.

Hare, R.M. (1981), *Moral Thinking: Its levels, method, and point*, Oxford: Clarendon Press.

Harris, José (1977), *William Beveridge: A biography*, Oxford: Clarendon Press.

Harris, Neville (2000), *Social Security Law in Context*, Oxford: Oxford University Press.

Harris, Neville (2006), 'Complexity, law and social security in the United Kingdom', *European Journal of Social Security*, **8** (2), 145–78.

Harris, Neville (2015), 'Complexity in the law and administration of social security: Is it really a problem?', *Journal of Social Welfare and Family Law*, **37** (2), 209–27.

Harrison, Robert, Aled Jones and Peter Lambert (2004a), 'The institutionalisation and organisation of history', in Peter Lambert and Philipp Schofield (eds), *Making History: An introduction to the history and practices of a discipline*, Abingdon: Routledge, pp. 9–25.

Harrison, Robert, Aled Jones and Peter Lambert (2004b), 'Methodology: "Scientific" history and the problem of objectivity', in Peter Lambert and Philipp Schofield (eds), *Making History: An introduction to the history and practices of a discipline*, Abingdon: Routledge, pp. 26–37.

Harrison, Robert, Aled Jones and Peter Lambert (2004c), 'The primacy of political history', in Peter Lambert and Philipp Schofield (eds), *Making History: An introduction to the history and practices of a discipline*, Abingdon: Routledge, pp. 38–54.

Harrop, Andrew (2012), *The Coalition and Universalism*, London: The Fabian Society.

Harrop, Andrew and Cameron Tait (2017), *Universal Basic Income and the Future of Work*, London: Fabian Society, accessed 26 April 2019 at https://www.tuc.org.uk/sites/default/files/UBI.pdf.

Haslam, S.A. and S.D. Reicher (2012), 'When prisoners take over the prison: A social psychology of resistance', *Personal and Social Psychology Review*, **16** (2), 154–79.

Haushofer, J. and J. Shapiro (2016), 'The short-term impact of unconditional cash transfers to the poor: Experimental evidence from Kenya', accessed 28 July 2018 at https://www.princeton.edu/~joha/publications/Haushofer_Shapiro_UCT_2016.04.25.pdf.

Hegel, G.W.F. (1969), *Hegel's Science of Logic*, translated by A.V. Miller from *Wissenschaft der Logik* (1812), London: George Allen & Unwin, accessed 2 June 2019 at Project Gutenberg, http://projekt.gutenberg.de/buch/wissenschaft-der-logik-1653/1.

Held, David (1984), *Political Theory and the Modern State*, Cambridge: Polity Press.

Henderson, Troy (2017), *'Real Freedom for All* revisited: Normative justifications of Basic Income', *Basic Income Studies*, **12** (1), accessed 25 April 2019 at https://doi.org/10.1515/bis-2016-0022.

Heydorn, M. Oliver (2016), 'A National Dividend vs. a Basic Income: Similarities and differences', *Basic Income Studies*, **11** (2), 133–7.

Heyman, Philip B. (2008), *Living the Policy Process*, New York: Oxford University Press.

Heywood, Andrew (1999), *Political Theory: An introduction*, 2nd edition, Basingstoke: Palgrave.

Hill, Michael (1990), *Social Security Policy in Britain*, Aldershot, UK and Brookfield, VT, USA: Edward Elgar Publishing.

Hill, Michael (2009), *The Public Policy Process*, 5th edition, Harlow: Pearson/Longman.

Hills, John (2014), *Good Times, Bad Times: The welfare myth of them and us*, Bristol: Policy Press.

Hills, John, Julian Le Grand and David Piachaud (eds) (2002), *Understanding Social Exclusion*, Oxford: Oxford University Press.

Hills, John, Abigail McKnight, Irene Bucelli, Eleni Karagiannaki, Polly Vizard and Lin Yang, with Magali Duque and Mark Rucci (2019), *Understanding the Relationship between Poverty and Inequality: Overview report*, London: International Inequality Institute, London School of Economics, accessed 31 January 2019 at http://sticerd.lse.ac.uk/dps/case/cr/casereport119.pdf.

Hilton, Anthony (2014), 'Flexible labour is impoverishing for all', *Evening Standard*, 3 June 2014, p. 44.

Hindriks, Jean and Gareth D. Myles (2006), *Intermediate Public Economics*, Cambridge, MA: The MIT Press.

Hirsch, Donald (2015), *Could a 'Citizen's Income' work?*, York: Joseph Rowntree Foundation, accessed 2 June 2019 at www.jrf.org.uk/publications/could-citizens-income-work.

HM Revenue and Customs (2018), 'Child Benefit', accessed 29 December 2018 at https://www.gov.uk/browse/benefits/child.

Hobijn, Bart and Alexander Nussbacher (2015), *The Stimulative Effect of Redistribution*, San Francisco: Federal Reserve Bank of San Francisco, accessed 27 December 2018 at https://www.frbsf.org/economic-research/files/el2015-21.pdf.

Hodge, John and Stuart Lowe (2009), *Understanding the Policy Process: Analysing welfare policy and practice*, 2nd edition, Bristol: Policy Press.

Hodgson, Geoffrey M. (1999), *Evolution and Institutions: On evolutionary economics and the evolution of economics*, Cheltenham, UK and Northampton, MA, USA: Edward Elgar Publishing.

Hofstede, Geert (1980), *Culture's Consequences: International differences in work-related values*, Beverly Hills: Sage.

Hofstede, Geert (1997), *Culture and Organizations: Software of the mind: Intercultural co-operation and its importance for survival*, New York: McGraw-Hill.

Hofstede, G.H. (2001), *Culture's Consequences: Comparing values, behaviors, institutions and organizations across nations*, 2nd edition, Thousand Oaks: Sage.

Hogg, Michael A. and Graham M. Vaughan (2014), *Social Psychology*, 7th edition, Harlow: Pearson.

Hogwood, Brian and Lewis Gunn (1997), 'Why "perfect" implementation is unattainable', in Michael Hill (ed.), *The Policy Process: A reader*, London and New York: Prentice Hall/Harvester Wheatsheaf, pp. 217–25.

Holt-Lunstad, Julianne (2018), 'Why social relationships are important for physical health: A systems approach to understanding and modifying risk and protection', *Annual Review of Psychology*, **69**, 437–58.

Honkanen, Pertti (2014), 'Basic Income and Negative Income Tax: A comparison with a simulation model', *Basic Income Studies*, **9** (1–2), 119–35.

Hook, Sidney (1962), *From Hegel to Marx*, Ann Arbor: University of Michigan Press.

Hoppe, Robert (2018), 'Choice v. incrementalism', in Hal K. Colebatch and Robert Hoppe (eds), *Handbook on Policy, Process and Governing*, Cheltenham, UK and Northampton, MA, USA: Edward Elgar Publishing, pp. 398–417.

Horton, Tim and James Gregory (2009), *The Solidarity Society: Why we can afford to end poverty, and how to do it with public support*, London: The Fabian Society.

House of Commons Treasury and Civil Service Committee (1983), *Enquiry into the Structure of Personal Income Taxation and Income Support*, Third Special Report, Session 1982–3, London: Her Majesty's Stationery Office.

House of Commons Treasury and Civil Service Committee Sub-Committee (1982), *The Structure of Personal Income Taxation and Income Support: Minutes of Evidence*, HC 331–ix, London: Her Majesty's Stationery Office.

House of Commons Work and Pensions Committee (2010), *Decision Making and Appeals in the Benefits System*, HC313, accessed 4 December 2018 at www.publications.parliament.uk/pa/cm200910/cmselect/cmworpen/313/313.pdf.

Hout, M. (2016), 'Money and morale: Growing inequality affects how Americans view themselves and others', *The Annals of the American Academy of Political and Social Science*, **663** (1), 204–28.

Howard, Marilyn and Tim Lawrence (1996), 'Private provision – public concern: Meeting the needs of people with disabilities', *Citizen's Income Bulletin*, no. 22, July 1996, pp. 9–11.

Howard, Michael W. (2006), 'Basic Income and migration policy: A moral dilemma?', *Basic Income Studies*, **1** (1), 1–22.

Howard, Michael W., Jorge Pinto and Ulrich Schachtschneider (2019), 'Ecological effects of Basic Income', in Malcolm Torry (ed.), *The Palgrave International Handbook of Basic Income*, Cham: Palgrave Macmillan, pp. 111–32.

Huczynski, Andrzej A. and David A. Buchanan (2007), *Organizational Behaviour*, 6th edition, Harlow: Pearson Education.

Hudson, John (2019), *The Robot Revolution: Understanding the social and economic impact*, Cheltenham, UK and Northampton, MA, USA: Edward Elgar Publishing.

Hughes, Chris (2018), *Fair Shot: Rethinking inequality and how we earn*, London: Bloomsbury.

Hughes, Matthew (ed.) (2010), *Social Trends*, no. 40, London: Palgrave Macmillan, for the Office for National Statistics, accessed 12 November 2018 at www.ons.gov.uk/ons/rel/social-trends-rd/social-trends/social-trends-40/index.html.

Humpage, Louise (2015), *Policy Change, Public Attitudes and Social Citizenship: Does Neoliberalism matter?*, Bristol: Policy Press.

Hupe, Peter (2018), 'Implementation', in Hal K. Colebatch and Robert Hoppe (eds), *Handbook on Policy, Process and Governing*, Cheltenham, UK and Northampton, MA, USA: Edward Elgar Publishing, pp. 169–85.

Hyggen, Christer (2006), 'Risks and resources: Social capital among social assistance recipients in Norway', *Social Policy and Administration*, **40** (5), 493–508.

International Labour Organization (2010), *Effects of Non-contributory Social Transfers in Developing Countries: A compendium*, Geneva: International Labour Organization, accessed 16 May 2019 at https://www.research.manchester.ac.uk/portal/files/32800126/FULL_TEXT.pdf.

Irvin, George, Dave Byrne, Richard Murphy, Howard Reed and Sally Ruane (2009), *In Place of Cuts: Tax reform to build a fairer society*, London: Compass, accessed 27 December 2018 at http://www.compassonline.org.uk/publications/in-place-of-cuts-tax-reform-to-build-a-fairer-society.

Jackson, Andrew and Ben Dyson (2013), *Modernising Money: Why our monetary system is broken and how it can be fixed*, London: Positive Money.

Jacobs, Lawrence R. and Robert Y. Shapiro (1999), 'The media reporting and distorting of public opinion towards entitlements', in Stuart S. Nagel (ed.), *The Policy Process*, New York: Nova Science Publishers, pp. 135–45.

James, Estelle, Alejandra Cox Edwards and Rebecca Wong (2008), *The Gender Impact of Social Security Reform*, Chicago: University of Chicago Press.

James, William (1902), *The Varieties of Religious Experience: A study in human nature*, reprinted in 2012, Oxford: Oxford University Press.

Janky, Béla (2012), 'Social solidarity and preferences on welfare institutions across Europe', in Marion Ellison (ed.), *Reinventing Social Solidarity Across Europe*, Bristol: Policy Press, pp. 209–49.

Jenkins, Stephen (2017), 'Anthony B. Atkinson', in Robert A. Cord (ed.), *The Palgrave Companion to Cambridge Economics*, volume 1, London: Palgrave Macmillan, pp. 1151–74.

John, Peter (2018a), *How Far to Nudge? Assessing behavioural public policy*, Cheltenham, UK and Northampton, MA, USA: Edward Elgar Publishing.

John, Peter (2018b), 'Agenda formation and change', in Hal K. Colebatch and Robert Hoppe (eds), *Handbook on Policy, Process and Governing*, Cheltenham, UK and Northampton, MA, USA: Edward Elgar Publishing, pp. 295–308.

Johnson, Mark (1993), *Moral Imagination: Implications of cognitive science for ethics*, Chicago: Chicago University Press.

Jones, Alasdair, Jonathan Rowson and Steve Broome (2010), *Connected Communities: How social networks power and sustain the Big Society*, London: Royal Society for the Arts, accessed 8 August 2018 at https://www.thersa.org/discover/publications-and-articles/reports/connected-communities-how-social-networks-power-and-sustain-the-big-society.

Jones, Elizabeth, Leslie Gutman and Lucinda Platt (2013), *Family Stressors and Children's Outcomes*, London: Department of Education, accessed 8 August 2018 at http://dera.ioe.ac.uk/16415/1/DFE-RR254.pdf.

Jordan, Bill (1996), *A Theory of Poverty and Social Exclusion*, Cambridge: Polity.

Jordan, Bill (2008), *Welfare and Well-being: Social value in public policy*, Bristol: Policy Press.

Jordan, Bill (2010), 'Basic Income and social value', *Basic Income Studies*, **5** (2), 1–19.

Jordan, Bill, Simon James, Helen Kay and Marcus Redley (1992), *Trapped in Poverty? Labour-market decisions in low-income households*, London: Routledge.

Joseph, Keith and Jonathan Sumption (1979), *Equality*, London: John Murray.

Julius, DeAnne et al. (2011), 'Coalition must ditch 50p tax rate for growth', *Financial Times*, 7 September 2011, accessed 27 December 2018 at https://www.ft.com/content/d92b0bc4-d7e9-11e0-a5d9-00144feabdc0.

Kahneman, Daniel and Angus Deaton (2010), 'High income improves evaluation of life but not emotional wellbeing', *Proceedings of the National Academy of Sciences of the United States of America*, **107** (38), 16489–93.

Kangas, Olli (2016), 'The Finnish Basic Income experiment – "a foolish and outrageously expensive travesty"?', *Tutkimusblogi*, Helsinki: Kela, accessed 20 November 2018 at http://blogi.kansanelakelaitos.fi/arkisto/3316.

Kant, Immanuel (1785), *Groundwork for the Metaphysics of Morals*, translated by Arnulf Zweig and reprinted in 2002, Oxford: Oxford University Press.

Karasek, Robert A. (1979), 'Job demands, job decision latitude, and mental strain: Implications for job redesign', *Administrative Science Quarterly*, **24** (2), 285–308.

Kasser, Tim (2016), 'Materialistic values and goals', *Annual Review of Psychology*, **67**, 489–514.

Kasser, Tim, Katherine L. Rosenblum, Arnold J. Sameroff, Edward L. Deci, Christopher P. Niemiec, Osp Árnadóttir, Rod Bond, Helga Dittmar, Nathan Dungan and Susan Hawks (2014), 'Changes in materialism, changes in psychological well-being: Evidence from three longitudinal studies and an intervention experiment', *Motivation and Emotion*, **38** (1), 1–22.

Kasser, Tim, Richard M. Ryan, M. Zax and Arnold J. Sameroff (1995), 'The relations of maternal and social environments to late adolescents' materialistic and prosocial values', *Developmental Psychology*, **31** (6), 907–14.

Kauffman, Stuart A. (1993), *The Origins of Order: Self-organisation and selection in evolution*, Oxford: Oxford University Press.

Kay, John (2017), 'The basics of Basic Income', *Intereconomics*, **52** (2), 69–74.

Kellow, Aynsley (2018), 'From policy typologies to policy feedback', in Hal K. Colebatch and Robert Hoppe (eds), *Handbook on Policy, Process and Governing*, Cheltenham, UK and Northampton, MA, USA: Edward Elgar Publishing, pp. 457–72.

Kenis, Patrick and Volker Schneider (1991), 'Policy networks and policy analysis', in Bernd Marin and Renate Mayntz (eds), *Policy Networks*, Frankfurt am Main: Campus Verlag, pp. 25–59.

Keynes, John Maynard (1936), *The General Theory of Employment, Interest, and Money*, London: Macmillan and Co.

King, Jeff (2017), 'Social rights, the social minimum and social citizenship rights', paper presented at the seminar 'Specifying and Securing a Social Minimum', held at the International Institute for the Sociology of Law, Oñati, Spain, 29–30 June 2017.

King, J.E. and J. Marangos (2006), 'Two arguments for Basic Income: Thomas Paine (1737–1809) and Thomas Spence (1750–1814)', *History of Economic Ideas*, **14** (1), 55–71.

Kirkwood, John (1986), *Social Security Law and Policy*, North Ryde: The Law Book Company.

Knight, Barry (2013), 'Reframing poverty', *Poverty*, **146**, 14–17.

Knight, Barry (2017), *Rethinking Poverty: What makes a good society?*, Bristol: Policy Press.

Kohn, Paul M., Kathryn Lanfreniere and Maria Guervich (1991), 'Hassles, health and personality', *Journal of Personality and Social Psychology*, **61** (3), 478–82.

Kotkas, Toomas (2017), 'How courts deal with the question of social minimum? A systems-theoretical approach', paper presented at the seminar 'Specifying and Securing a Social Minimum', held at the International Institute for the Sociology of Law, Oñati, Spain, 29–30 June 2017.

Kuhn, Thomas (1962), *The Structure of Scientific Revolutions*, Chicago: Chicago University Press.

Lambert, Peter and Philipp Schofield (eds) (2004), *Making History: An introduction to the history and practices of a discipline*, Abingdon: Routledge.

Lansley, Stewart (2011a), 'From inequality to instability: Why sustainable capitalism depends on a more equal society', *Fabian Review*, London: The Fabian Society, Winter 2011: 12–14.

Lansley, Stewart (2011b), *The Cost of Inequality: Three decades of the super-rich and the economy*, London: Gibson Square.

Lansley, Stewart (2016), *A Sharing Economy: How social wealth funds can reduce inequality and help balance the books*, Bristol: Policy Press.

Lansley, Stewart (2018), 'Tackling inequality is an economic imperative', in David Fée and Anémone Kober-Smith (eds), *Inequalities in the UK: New discourse, evolutions and actions*, Bingley: Emerald Publishing, pp. 39–57.

Lansley, Stewart and Joanna Mack (1983), *Breadline Britain*, London: London Weekend Television.

Lansley, Stewart and Joanna Mack (2015), *Breadline Britain*, London: Oneworld.

Lansley, Stewart, Duncan McCann and Steve Schifferes (2018), *Remodelling Capitalism: How social wealth funds could transform Britain*, London: Friends Provident, accessed 26 April 2019 at https://www.friendsprovidentfoundation.org/news/creating-britains-first-citizens-wealth-fund-powerful-new-economic-social-instrument/.

Lansley, Stewart and Howard Reed (2019), *Basic Income for All: From desirability to feasibility*, London: Compass, accessed 26 April 2019 at http://www.compassonline.org.uk/basic-income-for-all/.

Larsen, Christian Albrekt (2006), *The Institutional Logic of Welfare Attitudes: How welfare regimes influence public support*, Aldershot: Ashgate.

Lawrence, Jon (2003), 'Political history', in Stefan Berger, Heiko Feldner and Kevin Passmore (eds), *Writing History: Theory and practice*, London: Hodder Arnold, pp. 183–202.

Leaper, R.A.B. (1986), 'Cash and caring', *BIRG Bulletin*, no. 5, Spring 1986: 20–2.

Lee, Soomi (2018), 'Attitudes toward Universal Basic Income and welfare state in Europe: A research note', *Basic Income Studies*, **13** (1), accessed 25 April 2019 at https://doi.org/10.1515/bis-2018-0002.

Legein, Thomas, Audrey Vandeleene, François Randour, Pauline Heyvaert, Julien Perrez and Min Reuchamps (2018), 'Framing the Basic Income: An experimental study of how arguments and metaphors influence individuals' opinion formation', *Basic Income Studies*, **13** (2), accessed 26 April 2019 at https://doi.org/10.1515/bis-2018-0010.

Leijten, Ingrid (2017), 'Potential and pitfalls of indivisible judicial protection of a social minimum: From inflation to procedural protection?', paper presented at the seminar 'Specifying and Securing a Social Minimum', held at the International Institute for the Sociology of Law, Oñati, Spain, 29–30 June 2017.

Lejano, Raul, Mrill Ingram and Helen Ingram (2018), 'Narrative in the policy process', in Hal K. Colebatch and Robert Hoppe (eds), *Handbook on Policy, Process and Governing*, Cheltenham, UK and Northampton, MA, USA: Edward Elgar Publishing, pp. 309–26.

Lepper, Mark R. and David Greene (eds) (1978), *The Hidden Costs of Reward: New perspectives on the psychology of human motivation*, Hillsdale, NJ: Lawrence Erlbaum Associates.

Levasseur, Karine, Stephanie Paterson and Nathalia Carvalho Moreira (2018), 'Conditional and unconditional cash transfers: Implications for gender', *Basic Income Studies*, **13** (1), accessed 25 April 2019 at https://doi.org/10.1515/bis-2018-0005.

Lévinas, Emmanuel (2000), *Entre Nous: Essays on thinking-of-the-other*, first published in French in 1991, New York: Columbia University Press.

Levitas, Ruth (2012), 'Utopia calling: Eradicating child poverty in the United Kingdom and beyond', in Alberto Minujin and Shailen Nandy (eds), *Global Child Poverty and Well-Being: Measurement, concepts, policy and action*, Bristol: Policy Press, pp. 449–73.

Levy, Horacio, Manos Matsaganis and Holly Sutherland (2014), *Simulating the Costs and Benefits of a Europe-wide Basic Income Scheme for Children*, New York: UNICEF, accessed 11 August 2018 at https://www.unicef.org/socialpolicy/files/CPI_Manos_January_2014.pdf.

Lewis, Gail (2004), *Citizenship: Personal lives and social policy*, Bristol: Policy Press.

Lipsey, Richard G. and K. Alec Chrystal (2004), *Economics*, 10th edition, Oxford: Oxford University Press.

Lipsky, Michael (1980), *Street-level Bureaucracy: Dilemmas of the individual in public services*, New York: Russell Sage Foundation.

Lister, Ruth (1996), 'One step nearer to genuine citizenship: Reflections on the Commission on Social Justice Report', *Soundings*, issue 2, Spring 1996, p. 193.

Lister, Ruth (1997), *Citizenship: Feminist perspectives*, Basingstoke: Macmillan.

Lister, Ruth (2004), *Poverty*, Cambridge: Polity Press.

Lister, Ruth (2017), 'Unequal recognition: Othering "the poor"', *Citizen's Income Newsletter*, issue 3 for 2017, pp. 3–5.

Lo Vuolo, Rubén M. (2015), 'Piketty's *Capital*, his critics and Basic Income', *Basic Income Studies*, **10** (1), 29–43.

London School of Economics (2018), *Political Economy for Research Students*, accessed 9 January 2019 at http://www.lse.ac.uk/resources/calendar/courseGuides/EC/2018_EC540.htm.

Lott, Yvonne (2017), 'When my money becomes our money: Changes in couples' money management', *Social Policy and Society*, **16** (2), 199–218.

Lund, Francie (2019), 'The informal economy and informal employment', in James Midgley, Rebecca Surender and Laura Alfers (eds), *Handbook of Social Policy and Development*, Cheltenham, UK and Northampton, MA, USA: Edward Elgar Publishing, pp. 246–64.

Lundberg, Ulf and Marianne Frankenhaeuser (1999), 'Stress and workload of men and women in high-ranking positions', *Journal of Occupational Health Psychology*, **4** (2), 142–51.

Lundvall, Bengt-Åke and Edward Lorenz (2012), 'From the Lisbon Strategy to EUROPE 2020', in Nathalie Morel, Bruno Palier and Joakim Palme (eds), *Towards a Social Investment Welfare State? Ideas, policies and challenges*, Bristol: Policy Press, pp. 333–51.

Macfarland, Caroline (2018), *Follow the Money: Is the time right for (more) tax hypothecation*, London: Responsible Tax Lab, accessed 30 April 2019 at http://www.covi.org.uk/is-the-time-right-for-more-tax-hypothecation/.

Mack, Joanna (2018), 'Fifty years of poverty in the UK', in Glen Bramley and Nick Bailey (eds), *Poverty and Social Exclusion in the UK: Volume 2 – The dimensions of disadvantage*, Bristol: Policy Press, pp. 27–55.

Mackenzie, Mhairi, Annette Hastings, Breannon Babbel, Sarah Simpson and Graham Watt (2018), 'Proportionate universalism as a route to mitigating health inequalities: Exploring political, policy and practice uncertainties in times of austerity', in David Fée and Anémone Kober-Smith (eds), *Inequalities in the UK: New discourse, evolutions and actions*, Bingley: Emerald Publishing, pp. 217–31.

Majone, Gian Domenico (1989), *Evidence, Argument, and Persuasion in the Policy Process*, New Haven: Yale University Press.

Major, Aaron (2016), 'Affording Utopia: The economic viability of "a capitalist road to communism"', *Basic Income Studies*, **11** (2), 75–95.

Mani, Anandi, Sendhil Mullainathan, Eldar Shafir and Jiyaing Zhao (2013), 'Poverty impedes cognitive function', *Science*, **341** (6149), 976–80.

Mappes, Thomas A. and Jane S. Zembaty (1997), *Social Ethics: Morality and social policy*, New York: McGraw-Hill.

Marin, Bernd and Renate Mayntz (eds) (1991), *Policy Networks*, Frankfurt am Main: Campus Verlag.

Marinetto, Michael (1999), *Studies of the Policy Process: A case analysis*, London: Prentice Hall Europe.

Marion, Jean-Luc (1997), *Étant Donné: Essai d'une phénoménologie de la donation*, Paris: Presses Universitaires de France. English translation: Jean-Luc Marion (2002), *Being Given: Toward a phenomenology of givenness*, Stanford, CA: Stanford University Press.

Markus, Hazel Rose and Shinobu Kitayama (1991), 'Culture and the self: Implications for cognition, emotion, and motivation', *Psychological Review*, **98** (2), 224–53.

Marmot, Michael G. (2003), 'Understanding social inequalities in health', *Perspectives in Biology and Medicine*, **46** (3), S9–S23.

Marmot, Michael (2013), *Fair Society, Healthy Lives*, Firenze: Leo S. Oslchlei.

Marshall, T.H. (1950), *Citizenship and Social Class and Other Essays*, Cambridge: Cambridge University Press.

Marshall, T.H. (1981), *The Right to Welfare and Other Essays*, London: Heinemann.

Martin, Josh (2016), 'Universal Credit to Basic Income: A politically feasible transition?', *Basic Income Studies*, **11** (2), 97–131.

Martinelli, Luke (2017a), *The Fiscal and Distributional Implications of Alternative Universal Basic Income Schemes in the UK*, Bath: Institute for Policy Research, accessed 5 December 2018 at www.bath.ac.uk/ipr/policy-briefs/working-papers/the-fiscal-and-distributional-implications-of-alternative-universal-basic-income-schemes-in-the-uk.html.

Martinelli, Luke (2017b), *Exploring the Distributional and Work Incentive Effects of Plausible Illustrative Basic Income Schemes*, Bath: Institute for Policy Research, accessed 20 November 2018 at www.bath.ac.uk/ipr/publications/reports/work-incentive-effects-on-basic-income.html.

Martinelli, Luke (2017c), *Assessing the Case for a Universal Basic Income in the UK*, Bath: Institute for Policy Research, accessed 26 April 2019 at www.bath.ac.uk/publications/assessing-the-case-for-a-universal-basic-income-in-the-uk/.

Martinelli, Luke (2018), 'Making it simple? Universal Basic Income', in Jane Millar and Roy Sainsbury (eds), *Understanding Social Security*, 3rd edition, Bristol: Policy Press, pp. 235–52.

Martinelli, Luke and Nick Pearce (2019), 'Basic Income in the UK: Assessing prospects for reform in an age of austerity', *Social Policy and Society*, **18** (2), 265–75.

Marx, Karl (1977), *A Contribution to the Critique of Political Economy*, Moscow: Progress Publishers, accessed 4 June 2019 at https://www.marxists.org/archive/marx/works/1859/critique-pol-economy/preface.htm, translated by S.W. Ryazanskaya from Karl Marx (1859), *Zur Kritik der Politischen Ökonomie*, Berlin: Franz Duncker, accessed 4 June 2019 at http://www.mlwerke.de/me/me13/me13_007.htm.

Marx, Karl and Friedrich Engels (1888), *The Communist Manifesto*, translated by Samuel Moore, reprinted 1967, Harmondsworth: Penguin.

Maslow, Abraham (1943), 'A theory of human motivation', *Psychological Review*, **50** (4), 370–96.

Mason, Paul (2015), *PostCapitalism: A guide to our future*, London: Allen Lane/Penguin Random House.

Mau, Steffen (2003), *The Moral Economy of Welfare States: Britain and Germany compared*, Abingdon: Routledge.

Mays, Jennifer, Greg Marston and John Tomlinson (eds) (2016), *Basic Income in Australia and New Zealand: Perspectives from the neoliberal frontier*, New York: Palgrave Macmillan.

McCain, Roger A. (2017), *Approaching Equality: What can be done about wealth inequality*, Cheltenham, UK and Northampton, MA, USA: Edward Elgar Publishing.

McFarland, Kate (2017), 'US/Kenya: GiveDirectly officially launches UBI experiment', accessed 4 June 2019 at http://basicincome.org/news/2017/11/uskenya-givedirectly-officially-launches-ubi-experiment/.

McKenzie, Lisa (2015), *Getting By: Estates, class and culture in austerity Britain*, Bristol: Policy Press.

McKnight, Abigail, Magali Duque and Mark Rucci (2016), *Creating More Equal Societies: What works? Evidence review*, Brussels: European Commission, accessed 11 August 2018 at http://ec.europa.eu/social/main.jsp?catId=738&langId=en&pubId=7903&type=2&furtherPubs=yes.

McLaughlin, Eithne (1990), *Social Security and Community Care: The case of the Invalid Care Allowance*, Department of Social Security Research Report no. 4, London: Her Majesty's Stationery Office.

McLaughlin, Eithne (1994), *Flexibility in Work and Benefits*, London: IPPR/Commission on Social Justice.

Mead, Lawrence (1992), *The New Politics of Poverty: The non-working poor in America*, New York: Harper Collins.

Meichenbaum, Donald (1985), *Stress Inoculation Training*, New York: Pergamon Press.

Melden, A.I. (1981), 'Are there welfare rights?' in Peter G. Brown, Conrad Johnson and Paul Vernier (eds), *Income Support: Conceptual and policy issues*, New Jersey: Rowman and Littlefield, pp. 259–78.

Mellor, Mary (2019), *Money: Myths, truth and alternatives*, Bristol: Policy Press.

Meltzer, H., P. Bebbington, T. Brugha, R. Jenkins, S. McManus and S. Stansfeld (2010), 'Job insecurity, socioeconomic circumstances and depression', *Psychological Medicine*, **40** (8), 1401–7.

Mencinger, Jože (2017), 'Universal Basic Income and helicopter money', *Basic Income Studies*, **12** (2), accessed 25 April 2019 at https://doi.org/10.1515/bis-2016-0021.

Mewes, Jan and Steffen Mau (2012), 'Unravelling working-class welfare chauvinism', in Stefan Svallfors (ed.), *Contested Welfare States: Welfare attitudes in Europe and beyond*, Stanford, CA: Stanford University Press, pp. 119–57.

Michaelsen, Martin (2018), paper presented at the Nordic Day at the 2018 BIEN Congress in Finland, 23 August 2018.

Mideros, Andrés and Cathal O'Donoghue (2015), 'The effect of unconditional cash transfers on adult labour supply: A unitary discrete choice model for the case of Ecuador', *Basic Income Studies*, **10** (2), 225–55.

Migny, Gabriel (1982), *The Power of Minorities*, London: Academic Press.

Mill, John Stuart (1844), 'On the definition of political economy', in Essay V, 'On the definition of political economy; and on the method of investigation proper to it', in *Essays on Some Unsettled Questions of Political Economy*, accessed 16 November 2018 at http://www.econlib.org/library/Mill/mlUQP5.html.

Mill, John Stuart (1861), *Utilitarianism*, reprinted in 1993, London: Everyman/Dent.

Millar, Murray G. and Karen U. Millar (1990), 'Attitude change as a function of attitude type and argument type', *Journal of Personality and Social Psychology*, **59** (2), 217–27.

Miller, Anne (2009), 'Citizen's Income and administration', *Citizen's Income Newsletter*, issue 2 for 2009, pp. 6–8.

Miller, Anne (2012), 'Passported benefits and a Citizen's Income', *Citizen's Income Newsletter*, issue 1 for 2012, pp. 1–4.

Miller, Annie (2016), 'A Citizen's Basic Income and its implications', in Jim Campbell and Morag Gillespie (eds), *Feminist Economics and Public Policy*, Abingdon: Routledge, pp. 164–76.

Miller, Annie (2017), *A Basic Income Handbook*, Edinburgh: Luath Press.

Miller, Annie, Toru Yamamori and Almaz Zelleke (2019), 'The gender effects of a Basic Income', in Malcolm Torry (ed.), *The Palgrave International Handbook of Basic Income*, Cham: Palgrave Macmillan, pp. 133–53.

Miller, Edward J. (2014), 'Demand side economics and its consequence: The national dividend', paper presented at the 2014 BIEN Congress, Montreal, 26–29 June 2014, accessed 9 November 2018 at https://basicincome.org/bien/pdf/montreal2014/BIEN2014_Miller.pdf.

Minogue, Martin (1997), 'Theory and practice in public policy and administration', in Michael Hill (ed), *The Policy Process: A reader*, London and New York: Prentice Hall/Harvester Wheatsheaf, pp. 10–29.

Mirowski, Philip and Dieter Plehwe (2015), *The Road from Mont Pelerin: The making of the neoliberal thought collective*, Cambridge, MA: Harvard University Press.

Morçöl, Göktuğ (2012), *A Complexity Theory for Public Policy*, New York: Routledge.

Morgan, Patricia (1995), *Farewell to the Family? Public policy and family breakdown in Britain and the USA*, London: Institute of Economic Affairs.

Morris, C.N. (1982), 'The structure of personal income taxation and income support', *Fiscal Studies*, **3** (3), 210–18.

Moscovici, Serge (1976), *Influence and Social Change*, London: Academic Press.

Moscovici, Serge (1980), 'Toward a theory of conversion behavior', in Leonard Berkowitz (ed.), *Advances in Experimental Social Psychology*, vol. 13, New York: Academic Press, pp. 209–39.

Moscovici, Serge (1985), 'Social influence and conformity', in Gardner Lindzey and Elliot Aronson (eds), *Handbook of Social Psychology*, volume II, 3rd edition, New York: Random House, pp. 347–412.

Mowshowitz, Abbe (1994), 'Virtual organization: A vision of management in the information age', *The Information Society*, **10** (4), 267–88.

Muijsson, Hendrik and Sascha Liebermann (2018), 'Family and childhood under pressure. Interpretive patterns of family and childhood in times of activation policies. The case of Germany', paper given at the conference 'Basic Income and the Eurodividend as social political pillar of the EU and its member countries' in Freiburg, 11/12 October 2018.

Mullainathan, Sendhil and Eldar Shafir (2013), *Scarcity: Why having too little means so much*, London: Macmillan.

Mullarney, Maire (1999), 'The rights of children – a justification of Basic Income, hitherto unremarked', *BIRG Bulletin*, no. 12, February 1991, 30–2.

Mullen, Brian (1986), 'Atrocity as a function of lynch mob composition: A self-attention perspective', *Personality and Social Psychology Bulletin*, **12** (2), 187–97.

Mulligan, Roisin (2013), 'Universal Basic Income and recognition theory – A tangible step towards an ideal', *Basic Income Studies*, **8** (2), 153–72.

Murali, Vijaya and Femi Oyebode (2004), 'Poverty, social inequality and mental health', *Advances in Psychiatric Treatment*, **10** (3), 216–24.

Murdock-Perriera, Lisel Alice and Quentin Charles Sedlacek (2018), 'Questioning Pygmalion in the twenty-first century: The formation, transmission, and attributional influence of teacher expectancies', *Social Psychology of Education*, **21** (3), 691–707.

Murphy, Gregory C. and James A. Athanasou (1999), 'The effect of unemployment on mental health', *Journal of Occupational and Organizational Psychology*, **72** (1), 83–99.

Murray, Charles (1984), *Losing Ground: American social policy, 1950–1980*, New York: Basic Books.

Murray, Charles (1996), *Charles Murray and the Underclass: The developing debate*, London: Institute of Economic Affairs.

Murray, Michael J. and Mathew Forstater (eds) (2018), *Full Employment and Social Justice: Solidarity and sustainability*, Cham: Palgrave Macmillan.

Nagel, Thomas (1977), *The Possibility of Altruism*, Oxford: Clarendon Press.

Nardelli, Alberto, Ian Traynor and Leila Haddou (2015), 'Revealed: Thousands of Britons on benefits across EU', *The Guardian*, 19 January 2015, accessed 11 April 2019 at https://www.theguardian.com/uk-news/2015/jan/19/-sp-thousands-britons-claim-benefits-eu.

Natili, Marcello (2019), *The Politics of Minimum Income: Explaining path departure and policy departure in the age of austerity*, Cham: Palgrave Macmillan.

National Audit Office (2011), *Means Testing*, Report by the Comptroller General, HC 1464, Session 2010–2012, London: The Stationery Office, accessed 5 December 2018 at https://www.nao.org.uk/wp-content/uploads/2011/09/10121464.pdf.

National Audit Office (2016a), *HM Revenue & Customs 2015–16 accounts*, Report by the Comptroller and Auditor General, London: National Audit Office, accessed 5 December 2018 at www.nao.org.uk/wp-content/uploads/2016/07/HMRC-Annual-Report-and-Accounts-2015-16.pdf.

National Audit Office (2016b), *Department for Work and Pensions 2015–16 Accounts: Report by the Comptroller and Auditor General: Fraud and error in benefit expenditure*, London: National Audit Office, accessed 5 December 2018 at www.nao.org .uk/wp-content/uploads/2016/07/DWP-CAG-Report-2015-16.pdf.

National Audit Office (2017), *Her Majesty's Revenue & Customs Annual Accounts 2016–17*, London: National Audit Office, accessed 29 November 2018 at https:// www.nao.org.uk/report/her-majestys-revenue-customs-annual-report-and-accounts -2016-17/.

National Audit Office (2018a), *Rolling Out Universal Credit*, London: National Audit Office, accessed 4 December 2018 at https://www.nao.org.uk/wp-content/uploads/ 2018/06/Rolling-out-Universal-Credit.pdf.

National Audit Office (2018b), *Her Majesty's Revenue and Customs Annual Accounts 2017–18*, London: National Audit Office, accessed 5 December 2018 at https://www .nao.org.uk/report/her-majestys-revenue-customs-annual-accounts-2017-18/.

National MWIA Collaborative (2011), *Mental Well-being Impact Assessment. A toolkit for well-being*, accessed 9 August 2018 at http://webarchive.nationalarchives.gov .uk/20170106084723/http:// www.apho.org.uk/resource/item.aspx?RID=95836.

Nemeth, Charlan, Ofra Mayseless, Jeffrey Sherman and Yvonne Brown (1990), 'Exposure to dissent and recall of information', *Journal of Personality and Social Psychology*, **58** (3), 429–37.

Nemeth, Charlan, Mark Swedlund and Barbara Kanki (1974), 'Patterning of the minority's responses and their influence on the majority', *European Journal of Social Psychology*, **4** (1), 53–64.

Neufeld, Richard W.J. and Randolph J. Paterson (1989), 'Issues concerning control and its implementation', in Richard W.J. Neufeld (ed.), *Advances in the Investigation of Psychological Stress*, New York: John Wiley and Sons, pp. 43–67.

New York State (2018), 'Stock transfer taxes', New York: Department of Taxation and Finance, accessed 4 December 2018 at www.tax.ny.gov/bus/stock/stktridx.htm.

Newcomb, Theodore M. (1963), 'Persistence and regression of changed attitudes: Long-range studies', *Journal of Social Issues*, **19** (4), 3–14.

Nicolis, Gregoire (1989), 'Physics of far-from-equilibrium systems and self-organisation', in Paul Davies (ed.), *The New Physics*, Cambridge: Cambridge University Press, pp. 316–47.

Nisbett, Richard E. and Takahiko Masuda (2003), 'Culture and point of view', *Proceedings of the National Academy of Sciences*, **100** (19), 11163–70.

Noteboom, Bart (1987), 'Basic Income as a basis for small business', *International Small Business Journal*, **5** (3), 10–18, reprinted in Karl Widerquist, José A. Noguera, Yannick Vanderborght and Jürgen De Wispelaere (eds) (2013), *Basic Income: An anthology of contemporary research*, Chichester: Wiley Blackwell, pp. 211–15.

O'Brien, J. Patrick and Dennis O. Olson (1991), 'The Alaska Permanent Fund and Dividend Distribution Program', *BIRG Bulletin*, no. 12, February 1991, 3–6.

O'Cinneide, Colm (2017), 'Giving legal substance to the social minimum', paper presented at the seminar 'Specifying and Securing a Social Minimum', held at the International Institute for the Sociology of Law, Oñati, Spain, 29–30 June 2017.

O'Hara, Mary (2014), *Austerity Bites: A journey to the sharp end of cuts in the UK*, Bristol: Policy Press.

O'Reilly, Jacqueline (2008), 'Can a Basic Income lead to a more gender equal society?', *Basic Income Studies*, **3** (3), 1–7.

OECD (2017), *Basic Income as a Policy Option: Can it add up?*, Paris: OECD Publishing, accessed 26 April 2019 at http://www.oecd.org/employment/emp/Basic -Income-Policy-Option-2017.pdf.

OECD (2019), *OECD Employment Outlook 2019: The future of work*, Paris: OECD Publishing, accessed 30 April 2019 at https://doi.org/10.1787/9ee00155-en.

Office for National Statistics (2014), *Households and Household Composition in England and Wales: 2001–2011*, London: Office for National Statistics, accessed 12 November 2018 at https://www.ons.gov.uk/peoplepopulationandcommunity/ birthsdeathsandmarriages/families/articles/householdsandhouseholdco mpositioninenglandandwales/2014-05-29.

Office for National Statistics (2015), *Births by Parents' Characteristics in England and Wales: 2014*, London: Office for National Statistics, accessed 12 November 2018 at https://www.ons.gov.uk/peoplepopulationandcommunity/ birthsdeathsandmarriages/livebirths/bulletins/birthsbyparentscharact eristicsinenglandandwales/2014.

Office for National Statistics (2016), *Births by Parents' Characteristics in England and Wales: 2015*, London: Office for National Statistics, accessed 12 November 2018 at https://www.ons.gov.uk/peoplepopulationandcommunity/ birthsdeathsandmarriages/livebirths/bulletins/birthsbyparentscharact eristicsinenglandandwales/2015.

Office for National Statistics (2017a), *Families and Households: 2017*, London: Office for National Statistics, accessed 12 November 2018 at https://www.ons.gov .uk/peoplepopulationandcommunity/birthsdeathsandmarriages/families/bulletins/ familiesandhouseholds/2017.

Office for National Statistics (2017b), *Statistical Bulletin: Marriages in England and Wales, 2014*, London: Office for National Statistics, accessed 12 November 2018 at www.ons.gov.uk/peoplepopulationandcommunity/birthsdeathsandmarriages/ marriagecohabitationandcivilpartnerships/bulletins/marriagesin englandandwalesprovisional/2014.

Office for National Statistics (2018a), *Divorces in England and Wales: 2017*, London: Office for National Statistics, accessed 12 November 2018 at https://www.ons.gov .uk/peoplepopulationandcommunity/birthsdeathsandmarriages/divorce/bulletins/ divorcesinenglandandwales/2017.

Office for National Statistics (2018b), *Employee Earnings in the UK: 2018*, London: Office for National Statistics, accessed 12 November 2018 at https://www.ons .gov.uk/employmentandlabourmarket/peopleinwork/earningsandworkinghours/ bulletins/lowandhighpayuk/2018.

Office for National Statistics (2018c), *Temporary Employees*, London: Office for National Statistics, accessed 20 November 2018 at https://www.ons.gov.uk/ employmentandlabourmarket/peopleinwork/employmentandemployeetypes/ datasets/temporaryemployeesemp07.

Office for National Statistics (2018d), *Contracts that do not Guarantee a Minimum Number of Hours: April 2018*, London: Office for National Statistics, accessed 4 December 2018 at https://www.ons.gov.uk/employmentandlabourmarket/ peopleinwork/earningsandworkinghours/articles/contractsthatdonotguaran teeaminimumnumberofhours/april2018#how-many-no-guaranteed-hours-contracts -nghcs-are-there.

Ogus, A.I., N.J. Wikeley, M. Davey, S.F. Deakin, R.K. Lewis and L. Luckhaus (1995), *The Law of Social Security*, London: Butterworths.

Olafsen, Anja H., Hallgeir Halvari, Jacques Forest and Edward L. Deci (2015), 'Show them the money? The role of pay, managerial need support, and justice in a self-determination theory model of intrinsic work motivation', *Scandinavian Journal of Psychology*, **56** (4), 447–57.

Oliver, Dawn and Derek Heater (1994), *The Foundations of Citizenship*, New York: Harvester Wheatsheaf.

Ontario (no date), 'Ontario's Basic Income Pilot: Studying the impact of a basic income', accessed 4 June 2019 at https://files.ontario.ca/170508_bi_brochure_eng _pg_by_pg_proof.pdf.

Ortiz, Isabel, Christina Behrendt, Andrés Acuña-Ulate and Quynh Anh Nguyen (2018), *Universal Basic Income Proposals in Light of ILO standards: Key issues and global costing*, Geneva: Social Protection Department, International Labour Organization, accessed 26 April 2019 at https://www.social-protection.org/gimi/RessourcePDF .action?id=55171.

Osterkamp, Rigmar (2013), 'The Basic Income Grant Pilot Project in Namibia: A critical assessment', *Basic Income Studies*, **8** (1), 71–90.

Oxford English Dictionary, www.oed.com.

Page, Edward (2018), '"Whatever governments choose to do or not to do"', in Hal K. Colebatch and Robert Hoppe (eds), *Handbook on Policy, Process and Governing*, Cheltenham, UK and Northampton, MA, USA: Edward Elgar Publishing, pp. 16–31.

Pahl, Jan (1983), 'The allocation of money and structuring of inequality within marriage', *Sociological Review*, **31** (2), 237–62.

Pahl, Jan (1986), 'Social security, taxation and family financial arrangements', *BIRG Bulletin*, no. 5, Spring 1986, 2–4.

Paine, Thomas (1796), 'Agrarian justice', reprinted in John Cunliffe and Guido Erreygers (eds) (2004), *The Origins of Universal Grants: An anthology of historical writings on Basic Capital and Basic Income*, Basingstoke: Palgrave Macmillan, pp. 3–16.

Painter, Anthony and Chris Thoung (2015), *Creative Citizen, Creative State: The principled and pragmatic case for a Universal Basic Income,* London: Royal Society of Arts.

Palermo Kuss, Ana Helena and K.J. Bernhard Neumärker (2018), 'Modelling the time allocation effects of Basic Income', *Basic Income Studies*, **13** (2), accessed 25 April 2019 at https://doi.org/10.1515/bis-2018-0006.

Parker, Hermione (1988), 'Are Basic Incomes feasible?', *BIRG Bulletin*, no. 7, Spring 1988, 5–7.

Parker, Hermione (1989), *Instead of the Dole: An enquiry into integration of the tax and benefit systems*, London: Routledge.

Parker, Hermione (ed.) (1993), *Citizen's Income and Women*, London: Citizen's Income Trust.

Parker, Hermione (1994), 'Citizen's Income', *Citizen's Income Bulletin*, no. 17, January 1994, 4–12.

Parker, Hermione (1995), *Taxes, Benefits and Family Life: The seven deadly traps*, London: Institute of Economic Affairs.

Parker, Hermione and Andrew Dilnot (1988), 'Administration of integrated tax/benefit systems', *BIRG Bulletin*, no. 8, Autumn 1988, 6–10.

Parker, Hermione and Holly Sutherland (1994), 'Basic Income 1994: Redistributive effects of Transitional BIs', *Citizen's Income Bulletin*, no. 18, July 1994, 3–8.

Parker, Hermione and Holly Sutherland (1995), 'Why a £20 CI is better than lowering Income Tax to 20%', *Citizen's Income Bulletin*, no. 19, February 1995, 15–18.

Parker, Hermione and Holly Sutherland (1996), 'Earnings top-up or Basic Income and a minimum wage', *Citizen's Income Bulletin*, no. 21, February 1996, 5–8.

Parker, Simon (2015), *Taking Back Power: Putting people in charge of politics*, Bristol: Policy Press.

Parsfield, Matthew (2015), *Community Capital: The value of connected communities*, London: Royal Society of Arts, accessed 9 August 2018 at https://www.thersa .org/discover/publications-and-articles/reports/community-capital-the-value-of -connected-communities.

Partners in Salford (2014), *DWP Conditionality and Sanctions*, London: Child Poverty Action Group, accessed 9 August 2018 at http://www.cpag.org.uk/sites/default/files/ uploads/Salford-Conditionality-Sanctions-Interim-Report_0.pdf.

Pasma, Chandra (2010), 'Working through the work disincentive', *Basic Income Studies*, **5** (2), 1–20.

Pateman, Carole (2005), 'Another way forward: Welfare, social reproduction, and a Basic Income', in Lawrence Mead and Christopher Beem (eds), *Welfare Reform and Political Theory*, New York: Russell Sage Foundation, pp. 34–64.

Paterson, Randolph J. and Richard W.J. Neufeld (1989), 'The stress response and parameters of stressful situations', in Richard W.J. Neufeld (ed.), *Advances in the Investigation of Psychological Stress*, New York: John Wiley and Sons, pp. 7–42.

Patrick, Ruth (2017a), 'Wither social citizenship? Lived experiences of citizenship in/ exclusion for recipients of out-of-work benefits', *Social Policy and Society*, **16** (2), 293–304.

Patrick, Ruth (2017b), *For Whose Benefit? The everyday realities of welfare reform*, Bristol: Policy Press.

Pech, Wesley J. (2010), 'Behavioral economics and the Basic Income Guarantee', *Basic Income Studies*, **5** (2), 1–17.

Pennings, Frans (2001), *Introduction to European Social Security Law*, 3rd edition, The Hague: Kluwer Law International.

Pennings, Frans (2017), 'The legal position of social assistance recipients: Old and new threats', paper presented at the seminar 'Specifying and Securing a Social Minimum', held at the International Institute for the Sociology of Law, Oñati, Spain, 29–30 June 2017.

Pereira, Richard (ed.) (2017), *Financing Basic Income: Addressing the cost objection*, Cham: Palgrave Macmillan.

Perkiö, Johanna (2012), 'The struggle over interpretation: Basic Income in the Finnish public discussion in 2006–2012', paper presented at the 2012 BIEN Congress in Munich, accessed 11 August 2018 at https://basicincome.org/bien/pdf/munich2012/ perkio.pdf.

Perkiö, Johanna, Leire Rincon and Jenna van Draanen (2019), 'Framing Basic Income: Comparing media framing of Basic Income in Canada, Finland, and Spain', in Malcolm Torry (ed.), *The Palgrave International Handbook of Basic Income*, Cham: Palgrave Macmillan, pp. 233–51.

Peters, B. Guy (2018), *Policy Problems and Policy Design*, Cheltenham, UK and Northampton, MA, USA: Edward Elgar Publishing.

Pettinger, Lynne (2019), *What's Wrong with Work?*, Bristol: Policy Press.

Petty, Richard E. and John T. Cacioppo (1986), *Communication and Persuasion: Central and peripheral routes to attitude change*, New York: Springer-Verlag.

Phillips, Anthony (2018), *God B.C.: God's grace in the Old Testament*, Durham, NC: Sacristy Press.

Piachaud, David (2016), *Citizen's Income: Rights and wrongs*, London: Centre for Analysis of Social Exclusion, London School of Economics.

Piachaud, David (2017), 'Social rights, social responsibilities and a social minimum', paper presented at the seminar 'Specifying and Securing a Social Minimum', held at the International Institute for the Sociology of Law, Oñati, Spain, 29–30 June 2017.

Piketty, Thomas (2014), *Capital in the Twenty-First Century*, Cambridge, MA: The Belknap Press of Harvard University Press.

Pillay, Anashri (2017), 'Economic and social rights adjudication: What is it good for?', paper presented at the seminar 'Specifying and Securing a Social Minimum', held at the International Institute for the Sociology of Law, Oñati, Spain, 29–30 June 2017.

Pittman, Thane S. and Jack F. Heller (1987), 'Social motivation', *Annual Review of Psychology*, **38**, 461–89.

Pitts, Frederick Harry, Lorena Lomardozzi and Neil Warner (2017), 'Speenhamland, automation and the Basic Income: A warning from history?', *Renewal*, **25** (3–4), 145–55.

Plant, Raymond (1988), 'Needs, agency, and welfare rights', in T. Donald Moon (ed.), *Rights and Welfare: The theory of the welfare state*, Boulder, CO: Westview Press, pp. 55–74.

Plato, *Republic*, in John Burnet (ed.) (1903), *Platonis Opera*, Oxford: Oxford University Press. English translation by Paul Shorey (1969), *Plato in Twelve Volumes*, vols. 5 & 6, Cambridge, MA: Harvard University Press, and London: William Heinemann Ltd., accessed 27 November 2018 at www.perseus.tufts.edu/Texts/chunk_TOC.grk .html. (References given as book and section numbers.)

Prabhakar, Rajiv (2018), 'Are Basic Capital versus Basic Income debates too narrow?', *Basic Income Studies*, **13** (1), accessed 25 April 2019 at https://doi.org/10.1515/bis -2018-0015.

Prentice-Dunn, Steven and Ronald W. Rogers (1982), 'Effects of public and private self-awareness on deindividuation and aggression', *Journal of Personality and Social Psychology*, **43** (3), 503–13.

Pressman, Steven (2005), 'Income guarantee and the equity-efficiency trade-off', *The Journal of Socioeconomics*, **34** (1), 83–100.

Presthus, Robert (1974), *Elites in the Policy Process*, London: Cambridge University Press.

Preston, Ronald (1992), 'A Christian slant on Basic Income', *BIRG Bulletin*, no. 15, 8–9.

Prigogine, Ilya and Isabelle Stengers (1984), *Order out of Chaos: Man's new dialogue with nature*, London: Heinemann.

Psychologists for Social Change (2017), *Universal Basic Income: A psychological impact assessment*, London: Psychologists Against Austerity, accessed 4 June 2019 at http://www.psychchange.org/basic-income-psychological-impact-assessment .html.

Pulkka, Ville-Veikko (2018), 'Methodological pitfalls of Basic Income surveys: The Finnish case', paper presented at the BIEN Congress in Tampere, Finland, 25 August 2018.

Purdy, David (1990), 'Citizenship, Basic Income and democracy', *BIRG Bulletin*, no. 10, Autumn/Winter 1990, 9–13.

Quinlan, Michael, Claire Mayhew and Philip Bohle (2001), 'The global expansion of precarious employment, work disorganization, and consequences for occupational health: A review of recent research', *International Journal of Health Services*, **31** (2), 335–414.

Rathbone, Eleanor (1930), 'Utopia calling! A plea for family allowances', from an address broadcast by Eleanor Rathbone MP, 11 February 1930, Family Endowment Society archives, quoted in Ruth Levitas (2012) 'Utopia calling: Eradicating child poverty in the United Kingdom and beyond', in Alberto Minujin and Shailen Nandy (eds), *Global Child Poverty and Well-Being: Measurement, concepts, policy and action*, Bristol: Policy Press, pp. 449–73.

Rawls, John (1971), *A Theory of Justice*, Cambridge, MA: Harvard University Press.

Rawls, John (2001), *Justice as Fairness: A restatement*, London: The Belknap Press of Harvard University Press.

Raworth, Kate (2017), *Doughnut Economics: Seven ways to think like a 21st century economist*, London: Penguin Random House.

Reader, Soren (2006), 'Does a Basic Needs Approach need capabilities?', *The Journal of Political Philosophy*, **14** (3), 337–50.

Reed, Howard (2019), 'Book review: Annie Miller, *A Basic Income Handbook*', London: Citizen's Basic Income Trust, accessed 23 September 2019 at https://citizensincome.org/book-reviews/annie-miller-a-basic-income-handbook/

Reed, Howard and Stewart Lansley (2016), *Universal Basic Income: An idea whose time has come?*, London: Compass, accessed 26 April 2019 at http://www.compassonline.org.uk/publications/universal-basic-income-an-idea-whose-time-has-come/.

Reeve, Andrew and Andrew Williams (eds) (2002), *Real Libertarianism Assessed: Political theory after Van Parijs*, London: Palgrave Macmillan.

Reeve, John Marshall and Edward L. Deci (1996), 'Elements of the competitive situation that affect intrinsic motivation', *Personality and Social Psychology Bulletin*, **22** (1), 24–33.

Rein, Martin and Winfried Schmähl (2004), *Rethinking the Welfare State*, Cheltenham, UK and Northampton, MA, USA: Edward Elgar Publishing.

Reynolds, Brigid, SM and Sean Healy, SMA (eds) (1993), *New Frontiers for Full Citizenship*, Dublin: Conference of Major Religious Superiors of Ireland.

Rhee, Eun, James S. Uleman, Hoon K. Lee and Robert J. Roman (1995), 'Spontaneous self-descriptions and ethnic identities in individualist and collectivistic cultures', *Journal of Personality and Social Psychology*, **69** (1), 142–52.

Rhys Williams, Brandon (1989), *Stepping Stones to Independence*, edited by Hermione Parker, foreword by David Howells MP, Aberdeen: Aberdeen University Press, for the One Nation Group of Conservative MPs.

Rhys Williams, Juliet (1943), *Something to Look Forward To*, London: MacDonald and Co.

Ricardo, David (1817), *The Principles of Political Economy and Taxation*, reprinted 2002, London: Empiricus Books.

Richardson, J.J. (1969), *The Policy-Making Process*, London: Routledge and Kegan Paul.

Richardson, J. (1999), 'Interest group, multi-arena politics and policy change', in Stuart S. Nagel (ed.), *The Policy Process*, New York: Nova Science Publishers, pp. 65–99.

Richardson, J.J. and A.G. Jordan (1979), *Governing Under Pressure: The policy process in a post-parliamentary democracy*, Oxford: Basil Blackwell.

Richardt, Johannes (2011), 'Basic Income, low aspiration', *The Sp!ked Review of Books*, issue 41, January 2011, accessed 13 January 2019 at https://www.spiked-online.com/2011/01/28/basic-income-low-aspiration/.

Rincón García, Leire (2018), 'Multidimensional support for Basic Income: A conjoint analysis', paper presented at the BIEN Congress in Tampere, Finland, 25 August 2018.

Ritter, Alison and Kari Lancaster (2018), 'Multiple streams', in Hal K. Colebatch and Robert Hoppe (eds), *Handbook on Policy, Process and Governing*, Cheltenham, UK and Northampton, MA, USA: Edward Elgar Publishing, pp. 232–52.

Rizzo, Mario J. (2016), 'The four pillars of behavioral paternalism', in Sherzod Abdukadirov (ed.), *Nudge Theory in Action: Behavioral design in policy and markets*, Basingstoke: Palgrave Macmillan, pp. 37–63.

Roche, Maurice (1992), *Rethinking Citizenship: Welfare ideology and change in modern society*, Cambridge: Polity Press.

Rogan, Michael and Laura Alfers (2019), 'Employment-based social protection: "Productivism", universalism and social citizenship', in James Midgley, Rebecca Surender and Laura Alfers (eds), *Handbook of Social Policy and Development*, Cheltenham, UK and Northampton, MA, USA: Edward Elgar Publishing, pp. 265–81.

Room, Graham (2011), *Complexity, Institutions and Public Policy: Agile decision-making in a turbulent world*, Cheltenham, UK and Northampton, MA, USA: Edward Elgar Publishing.

Rosch, Eleanor (1999), 'Reclaiming concepts', in Walter J. Freeman and Rafael Núñez, (eds), 'Reclaiming cognition', *Journal of Consciousness Studies*, **6** (11–12), 61–77.

Rosch, Eleanor and Barbara B. Lloyd (1978), *Cognition and Categorization*, Mahwah, NJ: Lawrence Erlbaum.

Rose, Richard (2006), 'Inheritance before choice in public policy', in Leslie Budd, Julie Charlesworth and Rob Paton (eds), *Making Policy Happen*, London: Routledge, pp. 51–64.

Rosenthal, Robert and Lenore Jacobson (1992), *Pygmalion in the Classroom: Teacher expectations and pupils' intellectual development*, Williston, VT: Crown House Publishing Ltd.

Rosner, Peter G. (2003), *The Economics of Social Policy*, Cheltenham, UK and Northampton, MA, USA: Edward Elgar Publishing.

Rothstein, Bo (2018), 'UBI: A bad idea for the welfare state', in Philippe Van Parijs (ed.), *Basic Income and the Left: A European debate*, Berlin: Social Europe, pp. 103–9.

Rowlingson, Karen (2011), *Does Income Inequality Cause Health and Social Problems*, York: Joseph Rowntree Foundation, accessed 27 December 2018 at https://www.jrf.org.uk/report/does-income-inequality-cause-health-and-social-problems.

Rowlingson, Karen (2019), 'Why do high rates of poverty and economic inequality persist in the UK?', Social Policy Association, accessed 5 July 2019 at http://www.social-policy.org.uk/50-for-50/moral-economy/.

Royston, Sam (2017), *Broken Benefits: What's gone wrong with welfare reform*, Bristol: Policy Press.

Runciman, W.G. (1966), *Relative Deprivation and Social Justice: A study of attitudes to social inequality in twentieth-century England*, London: Routledge and Kegan Paul.

Russell, Bertie and Keir Milburn (2018), 'What can an institution do? Towards public-common partnerships and a new common-sense', *Renewal*, **26** (4), 45–55.

Ryan, Richard M. and Edward L. Deci (2000), 'Self-determination theory and the facilitation of intrinsic motivation, social development, and well-being', *American Psychologist*, **55** (1), 68–78.

Sage, Daniel and Patrick Diamond (2017), *Europe's New Social Reality: The case against Universal Basic Income*, London: Policy Network, accessed 26 April 2019 at https://policynetwork.org/publications/papers/europes-new-social-reality-the-case-against-universal-basic-income/.

Sargant, William (1976), *Battle for the Mind: A physiology of conversion and brain-washing*, London: Heinemann.

Saunders, Peter and Maneerat Pinyopusarek (2001), 'Popularity and participation: Social security reform in Australia', in Erik Schokkaert (ed.), *Ethics and Social Security Reform*, Aldershot: Ashgate, pp. 143–64.

Scanlon, T.M. (1982), 'Contractualism and utilitarianism', in Amartya Sen and Bernard Williams (eds), *Utilitarianism and Beyond*, Cambridge: Cambridge University Press, pp. 103–28.

Scheffler, Samuel (1994), *The Rejection of Consequentialism*, Oxford: Clarendon Press.

Schlenker, Barry R. and Michael F. Weigold (1992), 'Interpersonal processes involving impression regulation and management', *Annual Review of Psychology*, **43** (1), 133–68.

Schneewind, J.B. (1977), *Sidgwick's Ethics and Victorian Moral Philosophy*, Oxford: Clarendon Press.

Schofield, Philipp (2004), 'The emergence of British economic history, c.1870 to c. 1930', in Peter Lambert and Philipp Schofield (eds), *Making History: An introduction to the history and practices of a discipline*, Abingdon: Routledge, pp. 65–77.

Searle, Beverley A. (2008), *Well-being: In search of a good life*, Bristol: Policy Press.

Sedlačko, Michal (2018), 'Policy as ordering through documents', in Hal K. Colebatch and Robert Hoppe (eds), *Handbook on Policy, Process and Governing*, Cheltenham, UK and Northampton, MA, USA: Edward Elgar Publishing, pp. 32–52.

Seebrook, Jeremy (1985), *Landscapes of Poverty*, Oxford: Basil Blackwell.

Sen, Amartya (2009), *The Idea of Justice*, London: Allen Lane/Penguin.

Sherif, Muzafer (1935), 'A study of some social factors in perception', *Archives of Psychology*, no. 187, 1–60.

Sheriff, Thomas H. (2018), 'Economics is dead – Long live political economy', *The Beaver*, 20 February 2018, London: London School of Economics Students Union, p. 12.

Sherman, Barrie and Phil Jenkins (1995), *Licensed to Work*, London: Cassell.

Sherry, Patrick (1977), *Religion, Truth and Language Games,* London and Basingstoke: Macmillan.

Shone, Ronald (1981), *Applications in Intermediate Microeconomics*, Oxford: Martin Robertson.

Silla, Inmaculada, Nele De Cuyper, Francisco J. Gracia, José M. Peiró and Hans De Witte (2009), 'Job insecurity and well-being: Moderation by employability', *Journal of Happiness Studies*, **10** (6), 739–51.

Singelis, Theodore M. (1994), 'The measurement of independent and interdependent self-construals', *Personality and Social Psychology Bulletin*, **20** (5), 580–91.

Skinner, Quentin (1969), 'Meaning and understanding in the history of ideas', *History and Theory*, **8** (1), 3–53.

Sloman, Peter (2016), 'Beveridge's rival: Juliet Rhys-Williams and the campaign for basic income, 1942–55', *Contemporary British History*, **30** (2), 203–23.

Sloman, Peter (2018), 'Universal Basic Income in British politics, 1918–2018: From a "Vagabond's Wage" to a global debate', *Journal of Social Policy*, **47** (3), 625–42.

Smart, J.J.C. and Bernard Williams (1973), *Utilitarianism: For and against*, Cambridge: Cambridge University Press.

Smith, Adam (1776), *An Inquiry into the Nature and Causes of the Wealth of Nations*, book 4, 'Of systems of political economy', reprinted 2001, London: Electric Book

Company, accessed 16 November 2018 at https://ebookcentral.proquest.com/lib/londonschoolecons/reader.action?docID=3008435&query=.

Smith, Adam C. and Todd J. Zywicki (2016), 'Nudging in an evolving marketplace: How markets improve their own choice architecture', in Sherzod Abdukadirov (ed.), *Nudge Theory in Action: Behavioral design in policy and markets*, Basingstoke: Palgrave Macmillan, pp. 225–50.

Smith, Gilbert and David May (1997), 'The artificial debate between rationalist and incrementalist models of decision making', in Michael Hill (ed.), *The Policy Process: A reader*, London and New York: Prentice Hall/Harvester Wheatsheaf, pp. 163–74.

Smith, M.J. (1993a), 'Policy networks', in M.J. Smith, *Pressure, Power and Policy*, Hemel Hempstead: Harvester Wheatsheaf, pp. 56–65; also in Michael Hill (ed.) (1993), *The Policy Process: A reader*, 2nd edition, Hemel Hempstead: Prentice Hall/Harvester Wheatsheaf, pp. 76–86.

Smith, Ronald E. (1993b), *Psychology*, Minneapolis/St. Paul: West Publishing Company.

Smith-Carrier, Tracy A. and Steven Green (2017), 'Another low road to Basic Income? Mapping a pragmatic model for adopting a Basic Income in Canada', *Basic Income Studies*, **12** (2), accessed 25 April 2019 at https://doi.org/10.1515/bis-2016-0020.

Smithies, Rachel (2007), 'Making a case for flat tax credits: Income fluctuations among low-income families', *Journal of Poverty and Social Justice*, **15** (1), 3–16.

Sommer, Maximilian (2016), *A Feasible Basic Income Scheme for Germany: Effects on labour supply, poverty, and income inequality*, Cham: Springer.

Špeciánová, Jitka (2018), 'Unconditional Basic Income in the Czech Republic: What type of taxes could fund it? A theoretical tax analysis', *Basic Income Studies*, **13** (1), accessed 25 April 2019 at https://doi.org/10.1515/bis-2017-0024.

Spence, Thomas (1797), 'The rights of infants', reprinted in John Cunliffe and Guido Erreygers (eds), (2004), *The Origins of Universal Grants: An anthology of historical writings on Basic Capital and Basic Income*, Basingstoke: Palgrave Macmillan, pp. 81–91.

Spicker, Paul (2000), *The Welfare State: A general theory*, London: Sage.

Spicker, Paul (2004), 'Saving social policy', *Policy World*, **1** (1), 8–9, accessed 19 December 2018 at http://www.social-policy.org.uk/wordpress/wp-content/uploads/2012/09/PolicyWorld_Aut04.pdf.

Spicker, Paul (2005), 'Five types of complexity', *Benefits*, **13** (1), 5–9.

Spicker, Paul (2011), *How Social Security Works: An introduction to benefits in Britain*, Bristol: Policy Press.

Spicker, Paul (2014), *Social Policy: Theory and practice*, 3rd edition, Bristol: Policy Press.

Spicker, Paul (2017), 'An assessment of Basic Income', accessed 19 December 2018 at http://blog.spicker.uk/an-assessment-of-basic-income/.

Staerklé, Christian, Tina Likki and Régis Scheideggar (2012), 'A normative approach to welfare attitudes', in Stefan Svallfors (ed.), *Contested Welfare States: Welfare attitudes in Europe and beyond*, Stanford, CA: Stanford University Press, pp. 81–118.

Standing, Guy (2009), *Work after Globalization: Building occupational citizenship*, Cheltenham, UK and Northampton, MA, USA: Edward Elgar Publishing.

Standing, Guy (2011), *The Precariat: The new dangerous class*, London: Bloomsbury.

Standing, Guy (2015), 'Why Basic Income's emancipatory value exceeds its monetary value', *Basic Income Studies*, **10** (2), 193–223.

Standing, Guy (2017a), *Basic Income: And how we can make it happen*, London: Penguin Random House.

Standing, Guy (2017b), 'Why you've never heard of a charter that's as important as Magna Carta', *Open Democracy*, accessed 27 December 2018 at https://www .opendemocracy.net/uk/guy-standing/why-youve-never-heard-of-charter-thats-as -important-as-magna-carta.

Standing, Guy (2019), *Plunder of the Commons: A manifesto for sharing public wealth*, London: Penguin Random House.

Stapenhurst, Chris (2014), 'Experiments in Euromod', *Citizen's Income Newsletter*, issue 3 for 2014, pp. 11–17.

Stedman Jones, Gareth (1983), 'Rethinking Chartism', in Gareth Stedman Jones, *Languages of Class: Studies in English working class history, 1832–1982*, Cambridge: Cambridge University Press, pp. 90–178.

Steiner, Ivan D. (1972), *Group Process and Productivity*, New York: Academic Press.

Stendahl, Sara and Otto Swedrup (2017), 'The social contract as an argument in delimiting a social minimum: A critical legal reading of a booming Swedish discourse', paper presented at the seminar 'Specifying and Securing a Social Minimum', held at the International Institute for the Sociology of Law, Oñati, Spain, 29–30 June 2017.

Stenner, Paul, Marion Barnes and David Taylor (2008), 'Editorial introduction – Psychosocial welfare: Contributions to an emerging field', *Critical Social Policy*, **28** (4), 411–14.

Stephens, Lucie, Josh Ryan-Collins and David Boyle (2008), *Co-production: A manifesto for growing the core economy*, London: New Economics Foundation.

Steuart, James (1767), *An Inquiry into the Principles of Political Economy*, vol. 1, book 1, 'Of Population and Agriculture', reprinted 1998, London: Pickering and Chatto, accessed 16 November 2018 at https://www.marxists.org/reference/subject/ economics/steuart/book1.htm.

Stirling, Alfie and Sarah Arnold (2019), *Nothing Personal: Replacing the Personal Tax Allowance with a Weekly National Allowance: How we can change the tax system to be more progressive while increasing the breadth, depth and generosity of the UK's income safety net?*, London: New Economics Foundation, accessed 26 April 2019 at https://neweconomics.org/2019/03/nothing-personal.

Stirton, Lindsay and Jurgen De Wispelaere (2009), 'Promoting Citizen's Income without bashing bureaucracy? (Yes, we can)', *Citizen's Income Newsletter*, issue 2 for 2009, pp. 5–6.

Stocker, Michael (1990), *Plural and Conflicting Values*, Oxford: Clarendon Press.

Stone, Diane (1996), *Capturing the Political Imagination: Think tanks and the policy process*, London: Frank Cass.

Story, Michael (2015), *Free Market Welfare: The case for a Negative Income Tax*, London: Adam Smith Research Trust.

Stouffer, Samuel A., Edward A. Suchman, Leland C. DeVinney, Shirley A. Star and Robin M. Williams, Jr. (1949), *Studies in Social Psychology in World War II*, vol. I, *The American Soldier: Adjustment during Army life,* Princeton, NJ: Princeton University Press.

Strassheim, Holger (2018), 'Policy as a body of expertise', in Hal K. Colebatch and Robert Hoppe (eds), *Handbook on Policy, Process and Governing*, Cheltenham, UK and Northampton, MA, USA: Edward Elgar Publishing, pp. 89–108.

Svallfors, Stefan (2012a), 'Welfare states and welfare attitudes', in Stefan Svallfors (ed.), *Contested Welfare States: Welfare attitudes in Europe and beyond*, Stanford, CA: Stanford University Press, pp. 1–24.

Svallfors, Stefan (2012b), 'Welfare attitudes in context', in Stefan Svallfors (ed.), *Contested Welfare States: Welfare attitudes in Europe and beyond*, Stanford, CA: Stanford University Press, pp. 222–39.

Svendsen, Gunnar Lind Haase and Gert Tinggaard Svendsen (2016), *Trust, Social Capital and the Scandinavian Welfare State: Explaining the flight of the bumblebee*, Cheltenham, UK and Northampton, MA, USA: Edward Elgar Publishing.

Sverke, Magnus, Johnny Hellgren and Katharina Näswall (2002), 'No security: a meta-analysis and review of job insecurity and its consequences', *Journal of Occupational Health Psychology*, **7** (3), 242–64.

Swann, William B. Jr., J. Gregory Hixon and Chris De La Ronde (1992), 'Embracing the "bitter truth": Negative self-concepts and marital commitment', *Psychological Science*, **3** (2), 118–21.

Tabatabai, Hamid (2012), 'Iran: A bumpy road toward Basic Income', in Richard Caputo (ed.), *Basic Income Guarantee and Politics: International experiences and perspectives on the viability of Income Guarantee*, New York: Palgrave Macmillan, pp. 285–300.

Tang, Shua-Hua and Vernon C. Hall (1995), 'The overjustification effect: A meta-analysis', *Applied Cognitive Psychology*, **9** (5), 365–404.

Tawney, R.H. (1964), *Equality*, 5th edition, first published in 1931, London: George Allen and Unwin.

Taylor, Shelley (1999), *Health Psychology*, 4th edition, Boston, MA: McGraw-Hill.

Taylor, Steve (1982), *Durkheim and the Study of Suicide*, Basingstoke: Macmillan.

Taylor-Gooby, Peter (2009), *Reframing Social Citizenship*, Oxford: Oxford University Press.

Taylor-Gooby, Peter, Julia Gumy and Adeline Otto (2014), 'Can "New Welfare" address poverty through more and better jobs?', paper given at the 2014 Social Policy Association conference in Sheffield.

Taylor-Gooby, Peter and Benjamin Leruth (eds) (2018), *Attitudes, Aspirations and Welfare: Social policy directions in uncertain times*, Cham: Palgrave Macmillan.

Thaler, Richard H. (2015), *Misbehaving: How economics became behavioural*, London: Allen Lane.

Thaler, Richard H. and Cass R. Sunstein (2009), *Nudge: Improving decisions about health, wealth and happiness*, revised edition, London: Penguin.

Thatcher, Margaret (1987), Interview for *Woman's Own*, 31 October 1987, accessed 22 January 2019 at https://www.margaretthatcher.org/document/106689.

Thierer, Adam (2016), 'Failing better: What we learn by confronting risk and uncertainty', in Sherzod Abdukadirov (ed.), *Nudge Theory in Action: Behavioral design in policy and markets*, Basingstoke: Palgrave Macmillan, pp. 65–94.

Tiffen, Rodney (2018), 'The news media and the policy process', in Hal K. Colebatch and Robert Hoppe (eds), *Handbook on Policy, Process and Governing*, Cheltenham, UK and Northampton, MA, USA: Edward Elgar Publishing, pp. 346–59.

Titmuss, Richard (1970), *The Gift Relationship: From human blood to social policy*, London: Allen and Unwin.

Tjitske, Akkerman (1994), 'Six waves of Feminism: The language of feminism in modern history', *European Journal of Women's Studies*, **1** (2), 270–2.

Tomlinson, Daniel (2018), *Irregular Payments: Assessing the breadth and depth of month to month earnings volatility*, London: Resolution Foundation, accessed 27 December 2018 at https://www.resolutionfoundation.org/app/uploads/2018/10/Irregular-payments-RF-REPORT.pdf.

Tonkens, Evelien, Ellen Grootegoed and Jan Willem Duyvendak (2013), 'Introduction: Welfare state reform, recognition, and emotional labour', *Social Policy and Society*, **12** (3), 407–13.

Torpey, John (2017), *The Three Axial Ages*, New Brunswick: Rutgers University Press.

Torry, Malcolm (1988a), 'Mutual responsibility', *BIRG Bulletin*, no. 7, Spring 1988, 25–6.

Torry, Malcolm (1988b), *Basic Income for All: A Christian social policy*, Grove Ethical Studies no. 68, Nottingham: Grove Books.

Torry, Malcolm (1996), 'The labour market, the family, and social security reform: A dissertation for the Master of Science degree in Social Policy and Planning at the London School of Economics', unpublished dissertation.

Torry, Malcolm (2002), 'A new agenda: Complexity theory, tax and benefits', *Citizen's Income Newsletter*, issue 3 for 2002, pp. 2–3.

Torry, Malcolm (2008), 'Research note: The utility – or otherwise – of being employed for a few hours a week', *Citizen's Income Newsletter*, issue 1 for 2008, pp. 14–16.

Torry, Malcolm (2010), 'Review article: *The Spirit Level*, by Richard Wilkinson and Kate Pickett', *Citizen's Income Newsletter*, issue 1 for 2010, pp. 4–7.

Torry, Malcolm (2013), *Money for Everyone: Why we need a Citizen's Income*, Bristol: Policy Press.

Torry, Malcolm (2013: appendix for Chapter 13), 'Political ideologies and arguments for a Citizen's Income', accessed 18 December 2018 at https://citizensincome.org/wp-content/uploads/2016/01/MoneyForEveryoneAppendix_Chapter_13_political_ideologies.pdf.

Torry, Malcolm (2014), 'A Basic Income is feasible: But what do we mean by feasible?' A paper presented at the 2014 BIEN Congress in Montreal, 27–29 June 2014, accessed 4 December 2018 at https://basicincome.org/bien/pdf/montreal2014/BIEN2014_Torry.pdf.

Torry, Malcolm (2015a), 'Some options for reform of the UK's tax and benefits systems', a paper prepared for a consultation on options for reform of the benefits system organised by some of the UK's major charities in June 2015, and subsequently published as 'Alternatives to Citizen's Basic Income', London: Citizen's Basic Income Trust, January 2018, accessed 9 November 2018 at https://citizensincome.org/research-analysis/alternatives-to-citizens-basic-income/.

Torry, Malcolm (2015b), *Two Feasible Ways to Implement a Revenue Neutral Citizen's Income Scheme*, EUROMOD Working Paper EM6/15, Colchester: Institute for Social and Economic Research, accessed 14 December 2018 at https://iser.essex.ac.uk/research/publications/working-papers/euromod/em6-15.

Torry, Malcolm (2016a), *The Feasibility of Citizen's Income*, New York: Palgrave Macmillan.

Torry, Malcolm (2016b), *Citizen's Basic Income: A Christian social policy*, London: Darton, Longman and Todd.

Torry, Malcolm (2016c), *How Might we Implement a Citizen's Income*, London: Institute for Chartered Accountants of England and Wales, accessed 14 December 2018 at www.icaew.com/-/media/corporate/files/technical/sustainability/outside-insights/citizens-income-web---final.ashx?la=en.

Torry, Malcolm (2016d), 'An attempt to study the intra-household transfers generated by a Citizen's Income scheme', *Citizen's Income Newsletter*, issue 2 for 2016, pp. 8–9.

Torry, Malcolm (2016e), *Citizen's Income Schemes: An amendment, and a pilot project*, EUROMOD Working Paper EM5/16a, Colchester: Institute for Social and Economic Research, accessed 20 May 2019 at https://www.iser.essex.ac.uk/research/publications/working-papers/euromod/em5-16a.

Torry, Malcolm (2017a), '"Unconditional" and "universal": Definitions and applications', a paper for the Foundation for International Studies on Social Security conference, Sigtuna, 2017.

Torry, Malcolm (2017b), 'What's a definition? And how should we define "Basic Income"?' A paper for the Basic Income Earth Network (BIEN) Congress in Lisbon, 2017, accessed 4 June 2019 at http://basicincome.org/wp-content/uploads/2015/01/Malcolm_Torry_Whats_a_definition_And_how_should_we_define_Basic_Income.pdf.

Torry, Malcolm (2017c), 'Primary care, the basic necessity', Part I: 'Explorations in economics', and Part II: 'Explorations in ethics', in Andrew Papanikitas and John Spicer (eds), *Handbook of Primary Care Ethics*, Boca Raton, FL: CRC/Francis and Taylor, pp. 369–84.

Torry, Malcolm (2017d), *A Variety of Indicators Evaluated for Two Implementation Methods for a Citizen's Basic Income*, EUROMOD Working Paper EM12/17, Colchester: Institute for Social and Economic Research, accessed 24 November 2018 at https://www.iser.essex.ac.uk/research/publications/working-papers/euromod/em12-17.

Torry, Malcolm (2018a), *Why we Need a Citizen's Basic Income: The desirability, feasibility and implementation of an unconditional income*, Bristol: Policy Press.

Torry, Malcolm (2018b), Introduction to a debate during the London School of Economics Citizen's Basic Income Day, 20 February 2018.

Torry, Malcolm (2018c), *An Update, a Correction, and an Extension of an Evaluation of an Illustrative Citizen's Basic Income Scheme: An addendum to working paper EM12/17*, EUROMOD Working Paper EM12/17a, Colchester: Institute for Social and Economic Research, accessed 24 November 2018 at https://www.iser.essex.ac.uk/research/publications/working-papers/euromod/em12-17a.

Torry, Malcolm (2018d), 'What is an Unconditional Basic Income? A response to Rothstein', in Philippe Van Parijs, *Basic Income and the Left: A European debate*, Berlin: Social Europe, pp. 110–15.

Torry, Malcolm (2019a), *Static Microsimulation Research on Citizen's Basic Income for the UK: A personal summary and further reflections*, EUROMOD Working Paper EM13/19, Colchester: Institute to Social and Economic Research, accessed 23 September 2019 at https://www.iser.essex.ac.uk/research/publications/working-papers/euromod/em13-19.pdf.

Torry, Malcolm (ed.) (2019b), *The Palgrave International Handbook of Basic Income*, Cham: Palgrave Macmillan.

Townsend, Peter (1979), *Poverty in the UK*, Harmondsworth: Penguin.

Triandis, Harry C. (1995), *Individualism and Collectivism*, Boulder, CO: Westview Press.

Turnbull, Nick (2018), 'Policy as (mere) problem-solving', in Hal K. Colebatch and Robert Hoppe (eds), *Handbook on Policy, Process and Governing*, Cheltenham, UK and Northampton, MA, USA: Edward Elgar Publishing, pp. 53–67.

Turner, Adair (2012), Address given at the London School of Economics Department of Social Policy 100th anniversary colloquium, 17 December 2012.

Turner, Bryan S. (1999), *The Talcott Parsons Reader*, Oxford: Blackwell.

Turner, John C. (1991), *Social Influence*, Milton Keynes: Open University Press.

Twine, Fred (1994), *Citizenship and Social Rights: The interdependence of self and society*, Beverly Hills: Sage.

Twine, Fred (1996), 'What kinds of people do we wish to be?', *Citizen's Income Bulletin*, no. 22, July 1996, 16–17.

Tymoigne, Eric (2013), 'Job guarantee and its critiques', *International Journal of Political Economy*, **42** (2), 63–87.

Uhde, Zuzana (2018), 'Caring revolutionary transformation: Combined effects of a Universal Basic Income and a public model of care', *Basic Income Studies*, **13** (2), accessed 25 April 2019 at https://doi.org/10.1515/bis-2017-0019.

UK Government (2018a), 'Child Benefit if you leave the UK', accessed 29 November 2018 at https://www.gov.uk/child-benefit-abroad.

UK Government (2018b), 'Claim Child Benefit', accessed 29 November 2018 at https://www.gov.uk/child-benefit/eligibility.

UK Government (2018c), 'Apply for a National Insurance Number', accessed 29 November 2018 at https://www.gov.uk/apply-national-insurance-number.

UK Government (2018d), 'Tax when you buy shares', accessed 2 December 2018 at https://www.gov.uk/tax-buy-shares.

Ulmer, Robert (2018), 'Universal Basic Income and solidary hedonism against authoritarian naturalism', a paper given at the conference 'Basic Income and the Euro-Dividend as Sociopolitical Pillars of the EU and its Member States', at the University of Freiburg, Germany, 11 and 12 October 2018.

United Nations (2009), *Human Development Report, 2009*, New York: United Nations.

United Nations General Assembly (1949), *Universal Declaration of Human Rights*, New York: United Nations Department of Public Information.

University of Cambridge, 'The medieval university', accessed 27 September 2018 at https://www.cam.ac.uk/about-the-university/history/the-medieval-university.

University of Sheffield (2018), 'Political economy', accessed 9 January 2019 at https://www.sheffield.ac.uk/economics/undergraduate/degrees/modules/ecn305.

USBIG, www.usbig.net/whatisbig.php.

Van Avermaet, Eddy (2001), 'Social influence in small groups', in Miles Hewstone and Wolfgang Stroebe (eds), *Introduction to Social Psychology*, 3rd edition, Oxford: Blackwell, pp. 403–43.

Van der Doef, Margot and Stan Maes (1999), 'The job demand-control (-support) model and psychological well-being: A review of 20 years of empirical research', *Work and Stress*, **13** (2), 87–114.

van Gunsteren, H. (1978), 'Notes on a theory of citizenship', in P. Birnbaum, J. Lively and G. Parry (eds), *Democracy, Consensus and Social Contract*, Beverly Hills: Sage, pp. 9–35.

van Oorschot, Wim (2006), 'Making the difference in social Europe: Deservingness perceptions among citizens of European Welfare States', *Journal of European Social Policy*, **16** (1), 23–42.

van Oorschot, Wim and Bart Meuleman (2012), 'Welfare performance and welfare support', in Stefan Svallfors (ed.), *Contested Welfare States: Welfare attitudes in Europe and beyond*, Stanford, CA: Stanford University Press, pp. 25–57.

van Oorschot, Wim, Femke Roosa, Bart Meuleman and Tim Reeskens (2017), *The Social Legitimacy of Targeted Welfare: Attitudes to welfare deservingness*, Cheltenham, UK and Northampton, MA, USA: Edward Elgar Publishing.

Van Parijs, Philippe (1990), 'The second marriage of justice and efficiency', *Journal of Social Policy*, **19** (1), 1–25.

Van Parijs, Philippe (1995), *Real Freedom for All: What (if anything) can justify capitalism?*, Oxford: Clarendon Press.

Van Parijs, Philippe (1996), 'Basic Income and the two dilemmas of the welfare state', *The Political Quarterly*, **67** (1), 63–6.

Van Parijs, Philippe and Yannick Vanderborght (2017), *Basic Income: A radical proposal for a free society and a sane economy*, Cambridge, MA: Harvard University Press.

Van Reenen, John (2011), 'Wage inequality, technology and trade: 21st century evidence', *Labour Economics*, **18** (6), 730–41.

Van Trier, Walter (1995), *Every One a King: An investigation into the meaning and significance of the debate on basic incomes with special reference to three episodes from the British Inter-War experience*, Leuven: Katholieke Universiteit Leuven Faculteit Sociale Wetenschappen Departement Sociologie.

Van Trier, Walter (2002), 'Who framed social dividend', a paper presented at the first United States Basic Income Guarantee (USBIG) conference, New York, 8–10 March 2002, accessed 4 April 2019 at https://usbig.net/papers/026-VanTrier.doc.

Van Trier, Walter (2017), Private correspondence with the author.

Vanderborght, Yannick (2017), 'Épisodes de l'histoire du Revenu Universel', *La Tribune Fonda*, no. 235, 15–20.

Vollenweider, Camila (2013), 'Domestic service and gender equality: An unavoidable problem for the feminist debate on Basic Income', *Basic Income Studies*, **8** (1), 19–41.

von Below, Georg (1925), 'Über historische Periodisierungen, mit besonderem Blick auf die Grenze zwischen Mittelalter und Neuzeit', *Archiv für Politik und Geschichte*, **4**: 1–29; **22**: 170–214, quoted in Robert Harrison, Aled Jones and Peter Lambert (2004), 'Methodology: "Scientific" history and the problem of objectivity', in Peter Lambert and Philipp Schofield (eds), *Making History: An introduction to the history and practices of a discipline*, Abingdon: Routledge, pp. 26–37.

Wadsworth, Mark (2018), 'A second and distinct income tax', *Citizen's Income Newsletter*, issue 3 for 2018, pp. 7–8.

Wagner, Richard E. (2007), *Fiscal Sociology and the Theory of Public Finance: An exploratory essay*, Cheltenham, UK and Northampton, MA, USA: Edward Elgar Publishing.

Waldron, Jeremy (1986), 'John Rawls and the social minimum', *Journal of Applied Philosophy*, **3** (1), 21–33.

Walker, Alan and Tony Maltby (2012), 'Active ageing: A strategic policy solution to demographic ageing in the European Union', *International Journal of Social Welfare*, **21**, S117–S130.

Walker, Mark (2016), *Free Money for All: A Basic Income Guarantee solution for the twenty-first century*, Basingstoke: Palgrave Macmillan.

Walker, Robert, Grace Bantebya Kyomuhendo, Elaine Chase and Sohail Choudhry (2013), 'Poverty in global perspective: Is shame a common denominator?', *Journal of Social Policy*, **42** (2), 215–33.

Wallerstein, Nina (1992), 'Powerlessness, empowerment, and health: Implications for health promotion programs', *American Journal of Health Promotion*, **6** (3), 197–205.

Walter, Tony (1988), 'What are Basic Incomes?', *BIRG Bulletin*, no. 8, Autumn 1988, 3–5.

Walter, Tony (1989), *Basic Income: Freedom from poverty, freedom to work*, London: Marion Boyars.

Warwick, Ben (2017), 'The minimum core's place in social rights: Fixity vs dynamism', a paper presented at the seminar 'Specifying and Securing a Social

Minimum', held at the International Institute for the Sociology of Law, Oñati, Spain, 29–30 June 2017.

Waters, Malcolm (2001), *Globalization*, London: Routledge.

Watkins, S. (2010), 'Income and health–from a minimum wage to a citizen income?', *International Journal of Management Concepts and Philosophy*, **4** (2), 137–44.

Watts, Beth and Suzanne Fitzpatrick (2018), *Welfare Conditionality*, Abingdon: Routledge.

Weale, Albert (2013), 'The property-owning democracy versus the welfare state', *Analyse & Kritik*, **35** (1), 37–44.

Weber, Max (1963), *The Sociology of Religion,* London: Methuen.

Weber, Max (1992), *The Protestant Ethic and the Spirit of Capitalism*, London: Routledge, previously published in 1930 by Allen and Unwin.

Wehner, Burkhard (2019), *Universal Basic Income and the Reshaping of Democracy: Towards a Citizen's Stipend in a new political order*, Cham: Springer.

Weiner, Bernard (1992), *Human Motivation: Metaphors, theories, and research*, Newbury Park, CA: Sage.

Weingast, Barry R. and Donald A. Wittman (2006), 'The reach of political economy', in Donald A. Wittman and Barry R. Weingast (eds), *The Oxford Handbook of Political Economy*, Oxford: Oxford University Press, accessed 16 November 2018 at http://www.oxfordhandbooks.com/view/10.1093/oxfordhb/9780199548477.001 .0001/oxfordhb-9780199548477.

Welfare Reform Team, Oxford City Council (2016), *Evaluation of European Social Fund Pilot Project 2014–2015*, Oxford: Oxford City Council, accessed 4 June 2019 at www.oxford.gov.uk/downloads/file/2119/welfare_reform_european_social_fund _project_evaluation_report.

Welskopp, Thomas (2003), 'Social history', in Stefan Berger, Heiko Feldner and Kevin Passmore (eds), *Writing History: Theory and practice*, London: Hodder Arnold, pp. 203–22.

Westerveld, Mies and Marius Olivier (eds) (2019), *Social Security Outside the Realm of the Employment Contract: Informal work and employee-like workers*, Cheltenham, UK and Northampton, MA, USA: Edward Elgar Publishing.

White, Mark (2016), 'Overview of behavioral economics and policy', in Sherzod Abdukadirov (ed.), *Nudge Theory in Action: Behavioral design in policy and markets*, Basingstoke: Palgrave Macmillan, pp. 15–36.

White, Stuart (2003), *The Civic Minimum: On the rights and obligations of economic citizenship*, Oxford: Oxford University Press.

White, Stuart (2006), 'Reconsidering the exploitation objection to Basic Income', *Basic Income Studies*, **1** (2), 1–24.

White, Stuart (2007), *Equality*, Cambridge: Polity Press.

Whiteford, Peter (2015a), 'Tales of Robin Hood (part 1): Welfare myths and realities in the United Kingdom and Australia', *Australian Review of Public Affairs*, September 2015, accessed 11 August 2018 at http://www.australianreview.net/digest/2015/09/ whiteford3.html.

Whiteford, Peter (2015b), 'Tales of Robin Hood (part 3): The long view – social policies and the life cycle', *Australian Review of Public Affairs*, October 2015, accessed 11 August 2018 at http://www.australianreview.net/digest/2015/10/whiteford3.html.

Whiteford, Peter, Michael Mendelson and Jane Millar (2003), *Timing it Right? Tax credits and how to respond to income changes*, York: Joseph Rowntree Foundation.

Wicksell, Knut (1958), 'A new principle of just taxation', in Richard A. Musgrave and Alan T. Peacock (eds), *Classics in the Theory of Public Finance*, London: Macmillan, pp. 72–118.

Widerquist, Karl (2013), *Independence, Propertylessness, and Basic Income: A theory of freedom as the power to say no*, New York: Palgrave Macmillan.

Widerquist, Karl (2017a), 'Basic Income's third wave', *Open Democracy*, accessed 4 June 2019 at https://www.opendemocracy.net/beyondslavery/karl-widerquist/basic-income-s-third-wave.

Widerquist, Karl (2017b), 'The cost of Basic Income: Back-of-the-envelope calculations', *Basic Income Studies*, **12** (2), accessed 25 April 2019 at https://doi.org/10.1515/bis-2017-0016.

Widerquist, Karl (2018), *A Critical Analysis of Basic Income Experiments for Researchers, Policymakers, and Citizens*, Cham: Palgrave Macmillan.

Widerquist, Karl and Michael Howard (2012), *Alaska's Permanent Fund Dividend: Examining its suitability as a model*, New York: Palgrave Macmillan.

Widerquist, Karl, José A. Noguera, Yannick Vanderborght and Jurgen De Wispelaere (eds) (2013), *Basic Income: An anthology of contemporary research*, Chichester: Wiley Blackwell.

Wilkinson, Richard and Kate Pickett (2009), *The Spirit Level: Why more equal societies almost always do better*, London: Allen Lane/Penguin Books. Second edition published in 2010.

Williams, Bernard (1985), *Ethics and the Limits of Philosophy*, London: Fontana/Collins.

Williams, Richard (2016), 'Conclusion: Behavioral economics and policy interventions', in Sherzod Abdukadirov (ed.), *Nudge Theory in Action: Behavioral design in policy and markets*, Basingstoke: Palgrave Macmillan, pp. 317–29.

Wittgenstein, Ludwig (1969), *Über Gewissheit / On Certainty*, the German text with an English translation, edited by G.E.M. Anscombe and G.H. von Wright, English translation by Denis Paul and G.E.M. Anscombe, Oxford: Basil Blackwell.

Wittgenstein, Ludwig (2001), *Philosophische Untersuchungen / Philosophical Investigations*, the German text with a revised English translation, third edition, translated by G.E.M. Anscombe, Oxford: Basil Blackwell. The first edition was published in 1953. (References record the paragraph number followed by the page number.)

Woodhead, Linda, Paul Fletcher, Hiroko Kawanami and David Smith (eds) (2002), *Religions in the Modern World*, London: Routledge.

World Bank (2018), 'Financial inclusion', Washington, DC: The World Bank, accessed 20 November 2018 at https://globalfindex.worldbank.org/.

World Basic Income, www.worldbasicincome.org.uk.

World Health Organization and Calouste Gulbenkian Foundation (2014), *Social Determinants of Mental Health*, Geneva: World Health Organization.

Wrightson, Keith and David Levine (1979), *Poverty and Piety in an English Village, Terling 1525–1700*, London: Academic Press.

Wu, Xun, M. Ramesh, Michael Howlett and Scott Fritzen (2010), *The Public Policy Primer: Managing the policy process*, London and New York: Routledge.

Yamamori, Toru (2014), 'Feminist way to Unconditional Basic Income: Claimants unions and women's liberation movements in 1970s Britain', *Basic Income Studies*, **9** (1–2), 1–24.

Young, Charlie (2018), *Realising Basic Income Experiments in the UK: A typology and toolkit of Basic Income design and delivery*, London: Royal Society of Arts, accessed

26 April 2019 at https://www.thersa.org/discover/publications-and-articles/reports/realising-basic-income.

Young, Iris Marion (1989), 'Polity and group differences: A critique of the ideal of universal citizenship', *Ethics*, **99** (2), 250–74.

Yuill, Chris (2009), 'Health and the workplace: Thinking about sickness, hierarchy and workplace conditions', *International Journal of Management Concepts and Philosophy*, **3** (3), 239–56.

Zahariadis, Nikolaus (1999), 'Ambiguity, time, and multiple streams', in Paul A. Sabatier (ed.), *Theories of the Policy Process*, Boulder, CO: Westview Press, pp. 73–93.

Zelleke, Almaz (2005), 'Distributive justice and the argument for an Unconditional Basic Income', *The Journal of Socioeconomics*, **1** (34), 3–15.

Zelleke, Almaz (2008), 'Institutionalizing the universal caretaker through a Basic Income?', *Basic Income Studies*, **3** (3), 1–9.

Zimbardo, Philip G. (1972), 'Pathology of imprisonment', *Society*, **9** (6), 4–8.

Index